AF769042

SMOOTHING, FILTERING AND PREDICTION: ESTIMATING THE PAST, PRESENT AND FUTURE

Authored by **Garry A. Einicke**

Smoothing, Filtering and Prediction: Estimating the Past, Present and Future
Authored by Garry A. Einicke

Published by InTech
Janeza Trdine 9, 51000 Rijeka, Croatia

Copyright © 2012 InTech
All chapters are distributed under the Creative Commons Attribution 3.0 license, which allows users to download, copy and build upon published articles even for commercial purposes, as long as the author and publisher are properly credited, which ensures maximum dissemination and a wider impact of our publications. After this work has been published by InTech, authors have the right to republish it, in whole or part, in any publication of which they are the author, and to make other personal use of the work. Any republication, referencing or personal use of the work must explicitly identify the original source.

As for readers, this license allows users to download, copy and build upon published chapters even for commercial purposes, as long as the author and publisher are properly credited, which ensures maximum dissemination and a wider impact of our publications.

Notice
Statements and opinions expressed in the chapters are these of the individual contributors and not necessarily those of the editors or publisher. No responsibility is accepted for the accuracy of information contained in the published chapters. The publisher assumes no responsibility for any damage or injury to persons or property arising out of the use of any materials, instructions, methods or ideas contained in the book.

Publishing Process Manager Jelena Marusic

Technical Editor Teodora Smiljanic

Cover Designer InTech Design Team

I

Additional hard copies can be obtained from orders@intechopen.com

Smoothing, Filtering and Prediction: Estimating the Past, Present and Future,
Authored by Garry A. Einicke
p. cm.
ISBN 978-953-307-752-9

We are IntechOpen, the world's leading publisher of Open Access books

Built by scientists, for scientists

3,800+
Open access books available

116,000+
International authors and editors

120M+
Downloads

151
Countries delivered to

Our authors are among the
Top 1%
most cited scientists

12.2%
Contributors from top 500 universities

WEB OF SCIENCE™

Selection of our books indexed in the Book Citation Index
in Web of Science™ Core Collection (BKCI)

Interested in publishing with us?
Contact book.department@intechopen.com

Numbers displayed above are based on latest data collected.
For more information visit www.intechopen.com

For EU product safety concerns:
IN TECH d.o.o., Prolaz Marije Krucifikse Kozulić 3, 51000 Rijeka, Croatia,
info@intechopen.com or visit our website at intechopen.com.

Meet the author

Garry A. Einicke received his bachelors, masters, and doctoral degrees, all in electrical and electronic engineering, from the University of Adelaide, in 1979, 1991, and 1996, respectively. He spent 1980 to 1996 with the Defence Science and Technology Organisation, where he was a Senior Research Scientist in signal analysis discipline. He has been with the Commonwealth Scientific and Industrial Research Organisation since 1997, where he is a Principal Research Scientist and leads the signal processing and mine communications research team. Garry has received numerous science and inventor awards at the CSIRO. In his spare time, he supervises students at the University of Queensland and alternately chairs the signal processing, communications, aerospace and electronic systems chapters in the Queensland section of the IEEE.

Contents

Preface

Scientists, engineers and the like are a strange lot. Unperturbed by societal norms, they direct their energies to finding better alternatives to existing theories and concocting solutions to unsolved problems. Driven by an insatiable curiosity, they record their observations and crunch the numbers. This tome is about the science of crunching. It's about digging out something of value from the detritus that others tend to leave behind. The described approaches involve constructing models to process the available data. Smoothing entails revisiting historical records in an endeavour to understand something of the past. Filtering refers to estimating what is happening currently, whereas prediction is concerned with hazarding a guess about what might happen next.

The basics of smoothing, filtering and prediction were worked out by Norbert Wiener, Rudolf E. Kalman and Richard S. Bucy et al over half a century ago. This book describes the classical techniques together with some more recently developed embellishments for improving performance within applications. Its aims are threefold. First, to present the subject in an accessible way, so that it can serve as a practical guide for undergraduates and newcomers to the field. Second, to differentiate between techniques that satisfy performance criteria versus those relying on heuristics. Third, to draw attention to Wiener's approach for optimal non-causal filtering (or smoothing).

Optimal estimation is routinely taught at a post-graduate level while not necessarily assuming familiarity with prerequisite material or backgrounds in an engineering discipline. That is, the basics of estimation theory can be taught as a standalone subject. In the same way that a vehicle driver does not need to understand the workings of an internal combustion engine or a computer user does not need to be acquainted with its inner workings, implementing an optimal filter is hardly rocket science. Indeed, since the filter recursions are all known – its operation is no different to pushing a button on a calculator. The key to obtaining good estimator performance is developing intimacy with the application at hand, namely, exploiting any available insight, expertise and a priori knowledge to model the problem. If the measurement noise is negligible, any number of solutions may suffice. Conversely, if the observations are dominated by measurement noise, the problem may be too hard. Experienced practitioners are able recognise those intermediate sweet-spots where cost-benefits can be realised.

Systems employing optimal techniques pervade our lives. They are embedded within medical diagnosis equipment, communication networks, aircraft avionics, robotics and market forecasting – to name a few. When tasked with new problems, in which information is to be extracted from noisy measurements, one can be faced with a plethora of algorithms and techniques. Understanding the performance of candidate approaches may seem unwieldy and daunting to novices. Therefore, the philosophy here is to present the linear-quadratic-Gaussian results for smoothing, filtering and prediction with accompanying proofs about performance being attained, wherever this is appropriate. Unfortunately, this does require some maths which trades off accessibility. The treatment is little repetitive and may seem trite, but hopefully it contributes an understanding of the conditions under which solutions can value-add.

Science is an evolving process where what we think we know is continuously updated with refashioned ideas. Although evidence suggests that Babylonian astronomers were able to predict planetary motion, a bewildering variety of Earth and universe models followed. According to lore, ancient Greek philosophers such as Aristotle assumed a geocentric model of the universe and about two centuries later Aristarchus developed a heliocentric version. It is reported that Eratosthenes arrived at a good estimate of the Earth's circumference, yet there was a revival of flat earth beliefs during the middle ages. Not all ideas are welcomed - Galileo was famously incarcerated for knowing too much. Similarly, newly-appearing signal processing techniques compete with old favourites. An aspiration here is to publicise that the oft forgotten approach of Wiener, which in concert with Kalman's, leads to optimal smoothers. The ensuing results contrast with traditional solutions and may not sit well with more orthodox practitioners.

Kalman's optimal filter results were published in the early 1960s and various techniques for smoothing in a state-space framework were developed shortly thereafter. Wiener's optimal smoother solution is less well known, perhaps because it was framed in the frequency domain and described in the archaic language of the day. His work of the 1940s was borne of an analog world where filters were made exclusively of lumped circuit components. At that time, computers referred to people labouring with an abacus or an adding machine – Alan Turing's and John von Neumann's ideas had yet to be realised. In his book, Extrapolation, Interpolation and Smoothing of Stationary Time Series, Wiener wrote with little fanfare and dubbed the smoother "unrealisable". The use of the Wiener-Hopf factor allows this smoother to be expressed in a time-domain state-space setting and included alongside other techniques within the designer's toolbox.

A model-based approach is employed throughout where estimation problems are defined in terms of state-space parameters. I recall attending Michael Green's robust control course, where he referred to a distillation column control problem competition, in which a student's robust low-order solution out-performed a senior specialist's optimal high-order solution. It is hoped that this text will equip readers to do similarly, namely: make some simplifying assumptions, apply the standard solutions and back-off from optimality if uncertainties degrade performance.

Both continuous-time and discrete-time techniques are presented. Sometimes the state dynamics and observations may be modelled exactly in continuous-time. In the majority of applications, some discrete-time approximations and processing of sampled data will be required. The material is organised as a ten-lecture course.

- Chapter 1 introduces some standard continuous-time fare such as the Laplace Transform, stability, adjoints and causality. A completing-the-square approach is then used to obtain the minimum-mean-square error (or Wiener) filtering solutions.

- Chapter 2 deals with discrete-time minimum-mean-square error filtering. The treatment is somewhat brief since the developments follow analogously from the continuous-time case.

- Chapter 3 describes continuous-time minimum-variance (or Kalman-Bucy) filtering. The filter is found using the conditional mean or least-mean-square-error formula. It is shown for time-invariant problems that the Wiener and Kalman solutions are the same.

- Chapter 4 addresses discrete-time minimum-variance (or Kalman) prediction and filtering. Once again, the optimum conditional mean estimate may be found via the least-mean-square-error approach. Generalisations for missing data, deterministic inputs, correlated noises, direct feedthrough terms, output estimation and equalisation are described.

- Chapter 5 simplifies the discrete-time minimum-variance filtering results for steady-state problems. Discrete-time observability, Riccati equation solution convergence, asymptotic stability and Wiener filter equivalence are discussed.

- Chapter 6 covers the subject of continuous-time smoothing. The main fixed-lag, fixed-point and fixed-interval smoother results are derived. It is shown that the minimum-variance fixed-interval smoother attains the best performance.

- Chapter 7 is about discrete-time smoothing. It is observed that the fixed-point fixed-lag, fixed-interval smoothers outperform the Kalman filter. Once again, the minimum-variance smoother attains the best-possible performance, provided that the underlying assumptions are correct.

- Chapter 8 attends to parameter estimation. As the above-mentioned approaches all rely on knowledge of the underlying model parameters, maximum-likelihood techniques within expectation-maximisation algorithms for joint state and parameter estimation are described.

- Chapter 9 is concerned with robust techniques that accommodate uncertainties within problem specifications. An extra term within the design Riccati equations enables designers to trade-off average error and peak error performance.

- Chapter 10 rounds off the course by applying the afore-mentioned linear techniques to nonlinear estimation problems. It is demonstrated that step-wise linearisations can be used within predictors, filters and smoothers, albeit by forsaking optimal performance guarantees.

The foundations are laid in Chapters 1 – 2, which explain minimum-mean-square-error solution construction and asymptotic behaviour. In single-input-single-output cases, finding Wiener filter transfer functions may have appeal. In general, designing Kalman filters is more tractable because solving a Riccati equation is easier than pole-zero cancellation. Kalman filters are needed if the signal models are time-varying. The filtered states can be updated via a one-line recursion but the gain may require to be re-evaluated at each step in time. Extended Kalman filters are contenders if nonlinearities are present. Smoothers are advocated when better performance is desired and some calculation delays can be tolerated.

This book elaborates on ten articles published in IEEE journals and I am grateful to the anonymous reviewers who have improved my efforts over the years. The great people at the CSIRO, such as David Hainsworth and George Poropat generously make themselves available to anglicise my engineering jargon. Sometimes posing good questions is helpful, for example, Paul Malcolm once asked "is it stable?" which led down to fruitful paths. During a seminar at HSU, Udo Zoelzer provided the impulse for me to undertake this project. My sources of inspiration include interactions at the CDC meetings - thanks particularly to Dennis Bernstein whose passion for writing has motivated me along the way.

Garry Einicke
CSIRO Australia

1

Continuous-Time Minimum-Mean-Square-Error Filtering

1.1 Introduction

Optimal filtering is concerned with designing the best linear system for recovering data from noisy measurements. It is a model-based approach requiring knowledge of the signal generating system. The signal models, together with the noise statistics are factored into the design in such a way to satisfy an optimality criterion, namely, minimising the square of the error.

A prerequisite technique, the method of least-squares, has its origin in curve fitting. Amid some controversy, Kepler claimed in 1609 that the planets move around the Sun in elliptical orbits [1]. Carl Freidrich Gauss arrived at a better performing method for fitting curves to astronomical observations and predicting planetary trajectories in 1799 [1]. He formally published a least-squares approximation method in 1809 [2], which was developed independently by Adrien-Marie Legendre in 1806 [1]. This technique was famously used by Giusseppe Piazzi to discover and track the asteroid Ceres using a least-squares analysis which was easier than solving Kepler's complicated nonlinear equations of planetary motion [1]. Andrey N. Kolmogorov refined Gauss's theory of least-squares and applied it for the prediction of discrete-time stationary stochastic processes in 1939 [3]. Norbert Wiener, a faculty member at MIT, independently solved analogous continuous-time estimation problems. He worked on defence applications during the Second World War and produced a report entitled *Extrapolation, Interpolation and Smoothing of Stationary Time Series* in 1943. The report was later published as a book in 1949 [4].

Wiener derived two important results, namely, the optimum (non-causal) minimum-mean-square-error solution and the optimum causal minimum-mean-square-error solution [4] – [6]. The optimum causal solution has since become known at the Wiener filter and in the time-invariant case is equivalent to the Kalman filter that was developed subsequently. Wiener pursued practical outcomes and attributed the term "unrealisable filter" to the optimal non-causal solution because "it is not in fact realisable with a finite network of resistances, capacities, and inductances" [4]. Wiener's unrealisable filter is actually the optimum linear smoother.

The optimal Wiener filter is calculated in the frequency domain. Consequently, Section 1.2 touches on some frequency-domain concepts. In particular, the notions of spaces, state-space systems, transfer functions, canonical realisations, stability, causal systems, power spectral density and spectral factorisation are introduced. The Wiener filter is then derived by minimising the square of the error. Three cases are discussed in Section 1.3. First, the

"All men by nature desire to know." *Aristotle*

solution to general estimation problem is stated. Second, the general estimation results are specialised to output estimation. The optimal input estimation or equalisation solution is then described. An example, demonstrating the recovery of a desired signal from noisy measurements, completes the chapter.

1.2 Prerequisites

1.2.1 Signals

Consider two continuous-time, real-valued stochastic (or random) signals $v^T(t)$ = $[v_1^T(t),\ v_2^T(t),\ \ldots,\ v_n^T(t)]$, $w^T(t)$ = $[w_1^T(t),\ w_2^T(t),\ \ldots,\ w_n^T(t)]$, with $v_i(t)$, $w_i(t)$ $\in \mathbb{R}$, i = 1, … n, which are said to belong to the space $\mathbb{R}^n$, or more concisely $v(t)$, $w(t)$ $\in \mathbb{R}^n$. Let w denote the set of $w(t)$ over all time t, that is, w = $\{ w(t), t \in (-\infty,\infty) \}$.

1.2.2 Elementary Functions Defined on Signals

The inner product $\langle v, w \rangle$ of two continuous-time signals v and w is defined by

$$\langle v,w \rangle = \int_{-\infty}^{\infty} v^T w\, dt \, . \tag{1}$$

The 2-norm or Euclidean norm of a continuous-time signal w, $\|w\|_2$, is defined as $\|w\|_2$ = $\sqrt{\langle w,w \rangle}$ = $\sqrt{\int_{-\infty}^{\infty} w^T w dt}$. The square of the 2-norm, that is, $\|w\|_2^2$ = $\langle w^T w \rangle$ = $\int_{-\infty}^{\infty} w^T w\, dt$ is commonly known as energy of the signal w.

1.2.3 Spaces

The Lebesgue 2-space, defined as the set of continuous-time signals having finite 2-norm, is denoted by $\mathcal{L}_2$. Thus, $w \in \mathcal{L}_2$ means that the energy of w is bounded. The following properties hold for 2-norms.

(i) $\|v\|_2 = 0 \Rightarrow v = 0$.

(ii) $\|\alpha v\|_2 = |\alpha|\ \|v\|_2$.

(iii) $\|v + w\|_2 \le \|v\|_2 + \|w\|_2$, which is known as the triangle inequality.

(iv) $\|vw\|_2 \le \|v\|_2 \|w\|_2$.

(v) $|\langle v,w \rangle| \le \|v\|_2 \|w\|_2$, which is known as the Cauchy-Schwarz inequality.

See [8] for more detailed discussions of spaces and norms.

"Scientific discovery consists in the interpretation for our own convenience of a system of existence which has been made with no eye to our convenience at all." *Norbert Wiener*

1.2.4 Linear Systems

A linear system is defined as having an output vector which is equal to the value of a linear operator applied to an input vector. That is, the relationships between the output and input vectors are described by linear equations, which may be algebraic, differential or integral. Linear time-domain systems are denoted by upper-case script fonts. Consider two linear systems $\mathcal{G}, \mathcal{H} : \mathbb{R}^p \to \mathbb{R}^q$, that is, they operate on an input $w \in \mathbb{R}^p$ and produce outputs $\mathcal{G}w$, $\mathcal{H}w \in \mathbb{R}^q$. The following properties hold.

$$(\mathcal{G} + \mathcal{H})\, w = \mathcal{G}w + \mathcal{H}w, \tag{2}$$

$$(\mathcal{G}\mathcal{H})\, w = \mathcal{G}(\mathcal{H}w), \tag{3}$$

$$(\alpha\mathcal{G})\, w = \alpha\, (\mathcal{G}w), \tag{4}$$

where $\alpha \in \mathbb{R}$. An interpretation of (2) is that a parallel combination of $\mathcal{G}$ and $\mathcal{H}$ is equivalent to the system $\mathcal{G} + \mathcal{H}$. From (3), a series combination of $\mathcal{G}$ and $\mathcal{H}$ is equivalent to the system $\mathcal{G}\mathcal{H}$. Equation (4) states that scalar amplification of a system is equivalent to scalar amplification of a system's output.

1.2.5 Polynomial Fraction Systems

The Wiener filtering results [4] – [6] were originally developed for polynomial fraction descriptions of systems which are described below. Consider an nth-order linear, time-invariant system $\mathcal{G}$ that operates on an input $w(t) \in \mathbb{R}$ and produces an output $y(t) \in \mathbb{R}$, that is, $\mathcal{G} : \mathcal{H} : \mathbb{R} \to \mathbb{R}$. Suppose that the differential equation model for this system is

$$\begin{aligned} a_n \frac{d^n y(t)}{dt^n} + a_{n-1} \frac{d^{n-1} y(t)}{dt^{n-1}} + \dots + a_1 \frac{dy(t)}{dt} + a_0 y(t) \\ = b_m \frac{d^m w(t)}{dt^m} + b_{m-1} \frac{d^{m-1} w(t)}{dt^{n-1}} + \dots + b_1 \frac{dw(t)}{dt} + b_0 w(t), \end{aligned} \tag{5}$$

where a_0, ... a_n and b_0, ... b_m are real-valued constant coefficients, $a_n \neq 0$, with zero initial conditions. This differential equation can be written in the more compact form

$$\begin{aligned} \left(a_n \frac{d^n}{dt^n} + a_{n-1} \frac{d^{n-1}}{dt^{n-1}} + \dots + a_1 \frac{d}{dt} + a_0 \right) y(t) \\ = \left(b_m \frac{d^m}{dt^m} + b_{m-1} \frac{d^{m-1}}{dt^{n-1}} + \dots + b_1 \frac{d}{dt} + b_0 \right) w(t). \end{aligned} \tag{6}$$

1.2.6 The Laplace Transform of a Signal

The two-sided Laplace transform of a continuous-time signal $y(t) \in \mathbb{R}$ is denoted by $Y(s)$ and defined by

$$Y(s) = \int_{-\infty}^{\infty} y(t) e^{-st} dt, \tag{7}$$

"Science is a way of thinking much more than it is a body of knowledge." *Carl Edward Sagan*

where $s = \sigma + j\omega$ is the Laplace transform variable, in which $\sigma, \omega \in \mathbb{R}$ and $j = \sqrt{-1}$. Given a signal $y(t)$ with Laplace transform $Y(s)$, $y(t)$ can be calculated from $Y(s)$ by taking the inverse Laplace Transform of $Y(s)$, which is defined by

$$y(t) = \int_{\sigma - j\infty}^{\sigma + j\infty} Y(s)e^{st} ds . \tag{8}$$

Theorem 1 Parseval's Theorem [7]:

$$\int_{-\infty}^{\infty} \left|y(t)\right|^2 dt = \int_{-j\infty}^{j\infty} \left|Y(s)\right|^2 ds . \tag{9}$$

Proof. *Let* $y^H(t) = \int_{\sigma - j\infty}^{\sigma + j\infty} Y^H(s)e^{-st} ds$ *and* $Y^H(s)$ *denote the Hermitian transpose (or adjoint) of* $y(t)$ *and* $Y(s)$*, respectively. The left-hand-side of (9) may be written as*

$$\begin{aligned}
\int_{-\infty}^{\infty} \left|y(t)\right|^2 dt &= \int_{-\infty}^{\infty} y^H(t)y(t)dt \\
&= \int_{-j\infty}^{j\infty} \frac{1}{2\pi j} \int_{-\infty}^{\infty} Y^H(s)e^{-st} ds \; y(t)dt \\
&= \int_{-\infty}^{\infty} \frac{1}{2\pi j} \int_{-j\infty}^{j\infty} y(t)e^{-st} dt \; Y^H(s)ds \\
&= \int_{-j\infty}^{j\infty} Y(s)Y^H(s)ds \\
&= \int_{-j\infty}^{j\infty} \left|Y(s)\right|^2 ds .
\end{aligned}$$

□

The above theorem is attributed to Parseval whose original work [7] concerned the sums of trigonometric series. An interpretation of (9) is that the energy in the time domain equals the energy in the frequency domain.

1.2.7 Polynomial Fraction Transfer Functions

The steady-state response $y(t) = Y(s)e^{st}$ can be found by applying the complex-exponential input $w(t) = W(s)e^{st}$ to the terms of (6), which results in

$$\left(a_n s^n + a_{n-1}s^{n-1} + \ldots + a_1 s + a_0\right)Y(s)e^{st} = \left(b_m s^m + b_{m-1}s^{m-1} + \ldots + b_1 s + b_0\right)W(s)e^{st} . \tag{10}$$

Therefore,

$$\begin{aligned}
Y(s) &= \left[\frac{b_m s^m + b_{m-1}s^{m-1} + \ldots + b_1 s + b_0}{a_n s^n + a_{n-1}s^{n-1} + \ldots + a_1 s + a_0}\right] W(s) \\
&= G(s)W(s) ,
\end{aligned} \tag{11}$$

"No, no, you're not thinking; you're just being logical." *Niels Henrik David Bohr*

where

$$G(s) = \frac{b_m s^m + b_{m-1} s^{m-1} + \ldots + b_1 s + b_0}{a_n s^n + a_{n-1} s^{n-1} + \ldots + a_1 s + a_0}. \tag{12}$$

is known as the transfer function of the system. It can be seen from (6) and (12) that the polynomial transfer function coefficients correspond to the system's differential equation coefficients. Thus, knowledge of a system's differential equation is sufficient to identify its transfer function.

1.2.8 Poles and Zeros

The numerator and denominator polynomials of (12) can be factored into m and n linear factors, respectively, to give

$$G(s) = \frac{b_m (s-\beta_1)(s-\beta_2)\ldots(s-\beta_m)}{a_n (s-\alpha_1)(s-\alpha_2)\ldots(s-\alpha_n)}. \tag{13}$$

The numerator of $G(s)$ is zero when $s = \beta_i$, $i = 1 \ldots m$. These values of s are called the zeros of $G(s)$. Zeros in the left-hand-plane are called minimum-phase whereas zeros in the right-hand-plane are called non-minimum phase. The denominator of $G(s)$ is zero when $s = \alpha_i$, $i = 1 \ldots n$. These values of s are called the poles of $G(s)$.

Example 1. Consider a system described by the differential equation $\dot{y}(t) = -y(t) + w(t)$, in which $y(t)$ is the output arising from the input $w(t)$. From (6) and (12), it follows that the corresponding transfer function is given by $G(s) = (s + 1)^{-1}$, which possesses a pole at $s = -1$.

The system in Example 1 operates on a single input and produces a single output, which is known as single-input-single-output (SISO) system. Systems operating on multiple inputs and producing multiple outputs, for example, $\mathcal{G}: \mathbb{R}^p \to \mathbb{R}^q$, are known as multiple-input-multiple-output (MIMO). The corresponding transfer function matrices can be written as equation (14), where the components $G_{ij}(s)$ have the polynomial transfer function form within (12) or (13).

$$G(s) = \begin{bmatrix} G_{11}(s) & G_{12}(s) & .. & G_{1p}(s) \\ G_{21}(s) & G_{22}(s) & & \\ \vdots & & \ddots & \vdots \\ G_{q1}(s) & & .. & G_{qp}(s) \end{bmatrix}. \tag{14}$$

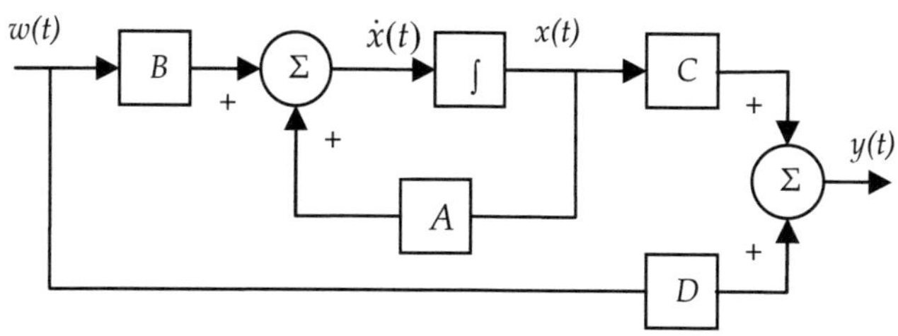

Figure 1. Continuous-time state-space system.

"Nature laughs at the difficulties of integration." *Pierre-Simon Laplace*

1.2.9 State-Space Systems

A system $\mathcal{G}: \mathbb{R}^p \to \mathbb{R}^q$ having a state-space realisation is written in the form

$$\dot{x}(t) = Ax(t) + Bw(t), \tag{15}$$

$$y(t) = Cx(t) + Dw(t), \tag{16}$$

where $A \in \mathbb{R}^{n\times n}$, $B \in \mathbb{R}^{p\times m}$, $C \in \mathbb{R}^{q\times n}$ and $D \in \mathbb{R}^{q\times q}$, in which $w \in \mathbb{R}^p$ is an input, $x \in \mathbb{R}^n$ is a state vector and $y \in \mathbb{R}^q$ is an output. A is known as the state matrix and D is known as the direct feed-through matrix. The matrices B and C are known as the input mapping and the output mapping, respectively. This system is depicted in Fig. 1.

1.2.10 Euler's Method for Numerical Integration

Differential equations of the form (15) could be implemented directly by analog circuits. Digital or software implementations require a method for numerical integration. A first-order numerical integration technique, known as Euler's method, is now derived. Suppose that $x(t)$ is infinitely differentiable and consider its Taylor series expansion in the neighbourhood of t_0

$$\begin{aligned} x(t) &= x(t_0) + \frac{(t-t_0)}{1!}\frac{dx(t_0)}{dt} + \frac{(t-t_0)^2}{2!}\frac{d^2x(t_0)}{dt^2} + \frac{(t-t_0)^3}{3!}\frac{d^3x(t_0)}{dt^3} + \cdots \\ &= x(t_0) + \frac{(t-t_0)}{1!}\dot{x}(t_0) + \frac{(t-t_0)^2}{2!}\ddot{x}(t_0) + \frac{(t-t_0)^3}{3!}\dddot{x}(t_0) + \cdots \end{aligned} \tag{17}$$

Truncating the series after the first order term yields the approximation $x(t) = x(t_0) + (t-t_0)\dot{x}(t_0)$. Defining $t_k = t_{k-1} + \delta_t$ leads to

$$\begin{aligned} x(t_1) &= x(t_0) + \delta_t \dot{x}(t_0) \\ x(t_2) &= x(t_1) + \delta_t \dot{x}(t_1) \\ &\vdots \\ x(t_{k+1}) &= x(t_k) + \delta_t \dot{x}(t_k). \end{aligned} \tag{18}$$

Thus, the continuous-time linear system (15) could be approximated in discrete-time by iterating

$$\dot{x}(t_{k+1}) = Ax(t_k) + Bw(t_k) \tag{19}$$

and (18) provided that δ_t is chosen to be suitably small. Applications of (18) – (19) appear in [9] and in the following example.

"It is important that students bring a certain ragamuffin, barefoot irreverence to their studies; they are not here to worship what is known, but to question it." *Jacob Bronowski*

Example 2. In respect of the continuous-time state evolution (15), consider $A = -1$, $B = 1$ together with the deterministic input $w(t) = \sin(t) + \cos(t)$. The states can be calculated from the known $w(t)$ using (19) and the difference equation (18). In this case, the state error is given by $e(t_k) = \sin(t_k) - x(t_k)$. In particular, root-mean-square-errors of 0.34, 0.031, 0.0025 and 0.00024, were observed for $\delta_t = 1, 0.1, 0.01$ and 0.001, respectively. This demonstrates that the first order approximation (18) can be reasonable when δ_t is sufficiently small.

1.2.11 State-Space Transfer Function Matrix

The transfer function matrix of the state-space system (15) - (16) is defined by

$$G(s) = C(sI - A)^{-1}B + D, \tag{20}$$

in which s again denotes the Laplace transform variable.

Example 3. For a state-space model with $A = -1$, $B = C = 1$ and $D = 0$, the transfer function is $G(s) = (s + 1)^{-1}$.

Example 4. For state-space parameters $A = \begin{bmatrix} -3 & -2 \\ 1 & 0 \end{bmatrix}$, $B = \begin{bmatrix} 1 \\ 0 \end{bmatrix}$, $C = \begin{bmatrix} 2 & 5 \end{bmatrix}$ and $D = 0$, the use of Cramer's rule, that is, $\begin{bmatrix} a & b \\ c & d \end{bmatrix}^{-1} = \dfrac{1}{ad - bc}\begin{bmatrix} d & -b \\ -c & a \end{bmatrix}$, yields the transfer function $G(s) = \dfrac{(2s+5)}{(s+1)(s+2)} = \dfrac{1}{(s+1)} + \dfrac{1}{(s+2)}$.

Example 5. Substituting $A = \begin{bmatrix} -1 & 0 \\ 0 & -2 \end{bmatrix}$ and $B = C = D = \begin{bmatrix} 1 & 0 \\ 0 & 1 \end{bmatrix}$ into (20) results in the transfer function matrix $G(s) = \begin{bmatrix} \dfrac{s+2}{s+1} & 0 \\ 0 & \dfrac{s+3}{s+2} \end{bmatrix}$.

1.2.12 Canonical Realisations

The mapping of a polynomial fraction transfer function (12) to a state-space representation (20) is not unique. Two standard state-space realisations of polynomial fraction transfer functions are described below. Assume that: the transfer function has been expanded into the sum of a direct feed-though term plus a strictly proper transfer function, in which the order of the numerator polynomial is less than the order of the denominator polynomial; and the strictly proper transfer function has been normalised so that $a_n = 1$. Under these assumptions, the system can be realised in the controllable canonical form which is parameterised by [10]

"Science is everything we understand well enough to explain to a computer. Art is everything else."
David Knuth

$$A = \begin{bmatrix} -a_{n-1} & -a_{n-2} & \dots & -a_1 & -a_0 \\ 1 & 0 & & \dots & 0 \\ 0 & 1 & & & \\ \vdots & & \ddots & 0 & 0 \\ 0 & 0 & \dots & 1 & 0 \end{bmatrix}, B = \begin{bmatrix} 1 \\ 0 \\ \vdots \\ 0 \\ 0 \end{bmatrix} \text{ and } C = \begin{bmatrix} b_m & b_{m-1} & \dots & b_1 & b_0 \end{bmatrix}.$$

The system can be also realised in the observable canonical form which is parameterised by

$$A = \begin{bmatrix} -a_{n-1} & 1 & 0 & \dots & 0 \\ -a_{n-2} & 0 & 1 & & 0 \\ \vdots & & & \ddots & 0 \\ -a_1 & & & 0 & 1 \\ -a_0 & 0 & \dots & 0 & 0 \end{bmatrix}, B = \begin{bmatrix} b_m \\ b_{m-1} \\ \vdots \\ b_1 \\ b_0 \end{bmatrix} \text{ and } C = \begin{bmatrix} 1 & 0 & \dots & 0 & 0 \end{bmatrix}.$$

1.2.13 Asymptotic Stability

Consider a continuous-time, linear, time-invariant n^{th}-order system $\mathcal{G}$ that operates on an input w and produces an output y. The system $\mathcal{G}$ is said to be asymptotically stable if the output remains bounded, that is, $y \in \mathcal{L}_2$, for any $w \in \mathcal{L}_2$. This is also known as bounded-input-bounded-output stability. Two equivalent conditions for $\mathcal{G}$ to be asymptotically stable are:

- The real part of the eigenvalues of the system's state matrix are in the left-hand-plane, that is, for A of (20), $\text{Re}\{\lambda_i(A)\} < 0$, $i = 1 \dots n$.
- The real part of the poles of the system's transfer function are in the left-hand-plane, that is, for α_i of (13), $\text{Re}\{\alpha_i\} < 0$, $i = 1 \dots n$.

Example 6. A state-space system having $A = -1$, $B = C = 1$ and $D = 0$ is stable, since $\lambda(A) = -1$ is in the left-hand-plane. Equivalently, the corresponding transfer function $G(s) = (s + 1)^{-1}$ has a pole at $s = -1$ which is in the left-hand-plane and so the system is stable. Conversely, the transfer function $G^T(-s) = (1 - s)^{-1}$ is unstable because it has a singularity at the pole $s = 1$ which is in the right hand side of the complex plane. $G^T(-s)$ is known as the adjoint of $G(s)$ which is discussed below.

1.2.14 Adjoint Systems

An important concept in the ensuing development of filters and smoothers is the adjoint of a system. Let $\mathcal{G} : \mathbb{R}^p \to \mathbb{R}^q$ be a linear system operating on the interval $[0, T]$. Then $\mathcal{G}^H : \mathbb{R}^q \to \mathbb{R}^p$, the adjoint of $\mathcal{G}$, is the unique linear system such that $\langle y, \mathcal{G} w\rangle = \langle \mathcal{G}^H y, w\rangle$, for all $y \in \mathbb{R}^q$ and $w \in \mathbb{R}^p$. The following derivation is a simplification of the time-varying version that appears in [11].

"Science might almost be redefined as the process of substituting unimportant questions which can be answered for important questions which cannot." *Kenneth Ewart Boulding*

Lemma 1 (State-space representation of an adjoint system): *Suppose that a continuous-time linear time-invariant system $\mathcal{G}$ is described by*

$$\dot{x}(t) = Ax(t) + Bw(t)\,, \tag{21}$$

$$y(t) = Cx(t) + Dw(t)\,, \tag{22}$$

with $x(t_0) = 0$. The adjoint $\mathcal{G}^H$ is the linear system having the realisation

$$\dot{\zeta}(t) = -A^T\zeta(t) - C^T u(t)\,, \tag{23}$$

$$z(t) = B^T\zeta(t) + D^T u(t)\,, \tag{24}$$

with $\zeta(T) = 0$.

Proof: *The system (21) – (22) can be written equivalently*

$$\begin{bmatrix} \dfrac{d}{dt}I - A & -B \\ C & D \end{bmatrix}\begin{bmatrix} x(t) \\ w(t) \end{bmatrix} = \begin{bmatrix} 0(t) \\ y(t) \end{bmatrix} \tag{25}$$

with $x(t_0) = 0$. Thus

$$\begin{aligned} \langle y, \mathcal{G} w\rangle &= \left\langle \begin{bmatrix} \zeta \\ u \end{bmatrix}, \begin{bmatrix} \dfrac{d}{dt}I - A & -B \\ C & D \end{bmatrix}\begin{bmatrix} x \\ w \end{bmatrix} \right\rangle \\ &= \int_0^T \left(\zeta^T \frac{dx}{dt} \right) dt - \int_0^T \zeta^T (Ax + Bw)\; dt + \int_0^T u^T (Cx + Dw)\; dt\,. \end{aligned} \tag{26}$$

Integrating the last term by parts gives

$$\begin{aligned} \langle y, \mathcal{G} w\rangle &= \zeta^T(T)x(T) - \int_0^T \left(\frac{d\zeta^T}{dt} \right) x\; dt - \int_0^T \zeta^T (Ax + Bw)\; dt\,. \\ &\quad + \int_0^T u^T (Cx + Dw)\; dt \\ &= \left\langle \begin{bmatrix} -\left(\dfrac{d}{dt}I - A^T\right) & C^T \\ -B^T & D^T \end{bmatrix}\begin{bmatrix} \zeta \\ u \end{bmatrix}, \begin{bmatrix} x \\ w \end{bmatrix} \right\rangle + \lambda^T(T)x(T) \\ &= \langle \mathcal{G}^H y, w \rangle, \end{aligned} \tag{27}$$

where $\mathcal{G}^H$ is given by (23) – (24). □

"If you thought that science was certain—well, that is just an error on your part." *Richard Phillips Feynman*

Thus, the adjoint of a system having the parameters $\begin{bmatrix} A & B \\ C & D \end{bmatrix}$ is a system with $\begin{bmatrix} -A^T & -C^T \\ B^T & D^T \end{bmatrix}$.

Adjoint systems have the property $(\mathcal{G}^H)^H = \mathcal{G}$. The adjoint of the transfer function matrix $G(s)$ is denoted as $G^H(s)$ and is defined by the transfer function matrix

$$G^H(s) = G^T(-s). \tag{28}$$

Example 7. Suppose that a system $\mathcal{G}$ has state-space parameters $A = -1$ and $B = C = D = 1$. From (23) – (24), an adjoint system has the state-space parameters $A = 1$, $B = D = 1$ and $C = -1$ and the corresponding transfer function is $G^H(s) = 1 - (s - 1)^{-1} = (- s + 2)(- s + 1)^{-1} = (s - 2)(s - 1)^{-1}$, which is unstable and non-minimum-phase. Alternatively, the adjoint of $G(s) = 1 + (s + 1)^{-1} = (s + 2)(s + 1)^{-1}$ can be obtained using (28), namely $G^H(s) = G^T(-s) = (- s + 2)(- s + 1)^{-1}$.

1.2.15 Causal and Noncausal Systems

A causal system is a system that depends exclusively on past and current inputs.

Example 8. The differential of $x(t)$ with respect to t is defined by $\dot{x}(t) = \lim_{dt \to 0} \frac{x(t + dt) - x(t)}{dt}$.

Consider

$$\dot{x}(t) = Ax(t) + Bw(t) \tag{29}$$

with $\mathrm{Re}\{\lambda_i(A)\} < 0$, $i = 1, \ldots, n$. The positive sign of $\dot{x}(t)$ within (29) denotes a system that proceeds forward in time. This is called a causal system because it depends only on past and current inputs.

Example 9. The negative differential of $\xi(t)$ with respect to t is defined by $-\dot{\xi}(t) = \lim_{dt \to 0} \frac{\xi(t) - \xi(t + dt)}{dt}$. Consider

$$-\dot{\zeta}(t) = A^T\zeta(t) + C^T u(t) \tag{30}$$

with $\mathrm{Re}\{\lambda_i(A)\} = \mathrm{Re}\{\lambda_i(A^T)\} < 0$, $i = 1 \ldots n$. The negative sign of $\dot{\zeta}(t)$ within (30) denotes a system that proceeds backwards in time. Since this system depends on future inputs, it is termed noncausal. Note that $\mathrm{Re}\{\lambda_i(A)\} < 0$ implies $\mathrm{Re}\{\lambda_i(-A)\} > 0$. Hence, if causal system (21) – (22) is stable, then its adjoint (23) – (24) is unstable.

1.2.16 Realising Unstable System Components

Unstable systems are termed unrealisable because their outputs are not in $\mathcal{L}_2$ that is, they are unbounded. In other words, they cannot be implemented as forward-going systems. It follows from the above discussion that an unstable system component can be realised as a stable noncausal or backwards system.

Suppose that the time domain system $\mathcal{G}$ is stable. The adjoint system $z = \mathcal{G}^H u$ can be realised by the following three-step procedure.

"We haven't the money, so we've got to think." *Baron Ernest Rutherford*

- Time-reverse the input signal $u(t)$, that is, construct $u(\tau)$, where $\tau = T - t$ is a time-to-go variable (see [12]).
- Realise the stable system $\mathcal{G}^T$

$$\dot{\zeta}(\tau) = A^T\zeta(\tau) + C^Tu(\tau), \tag{31}$$

$$z(\tau) = B^T\zeta(\tau) + D^Tu(\tau), \tag{32}$$

  with $\zeta(T) = 0$.
- Time-reverse the output signal $z(\tau)$, that is, construct $z(t)$.

The above procedure is known as noncausal filtering or smoothing; see the discrete-time case described in [13]. Thus, a combination of causal and non-causal system components can be used to implement an otherwise unrealisable system. This approach will be exploited in the realisation of smoothers within subsequent sections.

Example 10. Suppose that it is required to realise the unstable system $G(s) = G_2^H(s)G_1(s)$ over an interval [0, T], where $G_1(s) = (s+1)^{-1}$ and $G_2(s) = (s+2)^{-1}$. This system can be realised using the processes shown in Fig. 2.

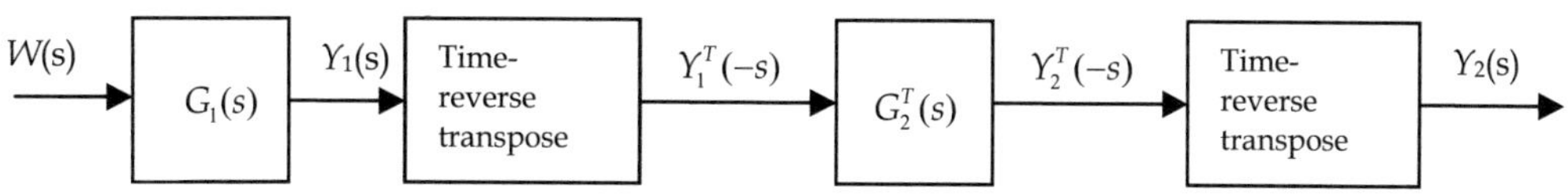

Figure 2. Realising an unstable $G(s) = G_2^H(s)G_1(s)$.

1.2.17 Power Spectral Density

The power of a voltage signal applied to a 1-ohm load is defined as the squared value of the signal and is expressed in watts. The power spectral density is expressed as power per unit bandwidth, that is, W/Hz. Consider again a linear, time-invariant system $y = \mathcal{G}w$ and its corresponding transfer function matrix $G(s)$. Assume that w is a zero-mean, stationary, white noise process with $E\{w(t)w^T(\tau)\} = Q\delta(t-\tau)$, in which δ denotes the Dirac delta function. Then $\Phi_{yy}(s)$, the power spectral density of y, is given by

$$\Phi_{yy}(s) = GQG^H(s), \tag{33}$$

which has the property $\Phi_{yy}(s) = \Phi_{yy}(-s)$.

The total energy of a signal is the integral of the power of the signal over time and is expressed in watt-seconds or joules. From Parseval's theorem (9), the average total energy of $y(t)$ is

$$\int_{-j\infty}^{j\infty} \Phi_{yy}(s)ds = \int_{-\infty}^{\infty} |y(t)|^2 dt = \|y(t)\|_2^2 = E\{y^T(t)y(t)\}, \tag{34}$$

which is equal to the area under the power spectral density curve.

"Time is what prevents everything from happening at once." *John Archibald Wheeler*

1.2.18 Spectral Factorisation

Suppose that noisy measurements

$$z(t) = y(t) + v(t) \tag{35}$$

of a linear, time-invariant system $\mathcal{G}$, described by (21) - (22), are available, where $v(t) \in \mathbb{R}^q$ is an independent, zero-mean, stationary white noise process with $E\{v(t)v^T(\tau)\} = R\delta(t-\tau)$. Let

$$\Phi_{zz}(s) = GQG^H(s) + R \tag{36}$$

denote the spectral density matrix of the measurements $z(t)$. Spectral factorisation was pioneered by Wiener (see [4] and [5]). It refers to the problem of decomposing a spectral density matrix into a product of a stable, minimum-phase matrix transfer function and its adjoint. In the case of the output power spectral density (36), a spectral factor $\Delta(s)$ satisfies $\Delta(s)\Delta^H(s) = \Phi_{zz}(s)$.

The problem of spectral factorisation within continuous-time Wiener filtering problems is studied in [14]. The roots of the transfer function polynomials need to be sorted into those within the left-hand-plane and the right-hand plane. This is an eigenvalue decomposition problem - see the survey of spectral factorisation methods detailed in [11].

Example 11. In respect of the observation spectral density (36), suppose that $G(s) = (s + 1)^{-1}$ and $Q = R = 1$, which results in $\Phi_{zz}(s) = (-s^2 + 2)(-s^2 + 1)^{-1}$. By inspection, the spectral factor $\Delta(s) = (s+\sqrt{2})(s+1)^{-1}$ is stable, minimum-phase and satisfies $\Delta(s)\Delta^H(s) = \Phi_{zz}(s)$.

1.3 Minimum-Mean-Square-Error Filtering

1.3.1 Filter Derivation

Now that some underlying frequency-domain concepts have been introduced, the Wiener filter [4] - [6] can be described. A Wiener-Hopf derivation of the Wiener filter appears in [4], [6]. This section describes a simpler completing-the-square approach (see [14], [16]). Consider a stable linear time-invariant system having a transfer function matrix $G_2(s) = C_2(sI - A)^{-1} B + D_2$. Let $Y_2(s)$, $W(s)$, $V(s)$ and $Z(s)$ denote the Laplace transforms of the system's output, measurement noise, process noise and observations, respectively, so that

$$Z(s) = Y_2(s) + V(s). \tag{37}$$

Consider also a fictitious reference system having the transfer function $G_1(s) = C_1(sI - A)^{-1}B + D_1$ as shown in Fig. 3. The problem is to design a filter transfer function $H(s)$ to calculate estimates $\hat{Y}_1(s) = H(s)Z(s)$ of $Y_1(s)$ so that the energy $\int_{-j\infty}^{j\infty} E(s)E^H(s)ds$ of the estimation error

$$E(s) = Y_1(s) - \hat{Y}_1(s) \tag{38}$$

is minimised.

"Science may be described as the art of systematic over-simplification." *Karl Raimund Popper*

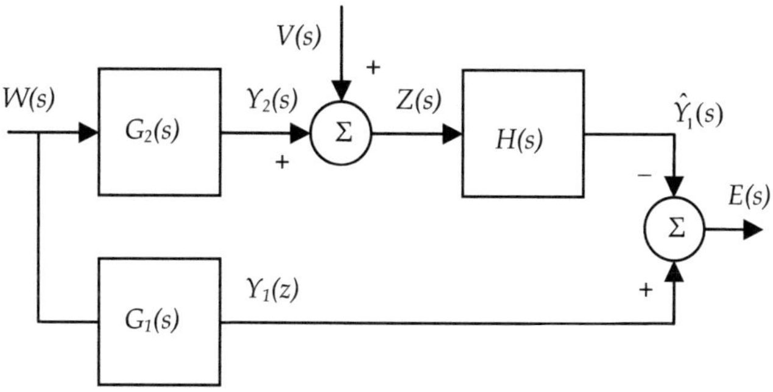

Figure 3. The s-domain general filtering problem.

It follows from Fig. 3 that $E(s)$ is generated by

$$E(s) = -\begin{bmatrix} H(s) & HG_2(s) - G_1(s) \end{bmatrix} \begin{bmatrix} V(s) \\ W(s) \end{bmatrix}. \tag{39}$$

The error power spectrum density matrix is denoted by $\Phi_{ee}(s)$ and given by the covariance of $E(s)$, that is,

$$\begin{aligned} \Phi_{ee}(s) &= E(s)E^H(s) \\ &= \begin{bmatrix} H(s) & HG_2(s) - G_1(s) \end{bmatrix} \begin{bmatrix} R & 0 \\ 0 & Q \end{bmatrix} \begin{bmatrix} H^H(s) \\ G_2^H H^H(s) - G_1^H(s) \end{bmatrix} \\ &= G_1 Q G_1^H(s) - G_1 Q G_2^H H^H(s) - HG_2 Q G_1^H(s) + H\Delta\Delta^H H^H(z), \end{aligned} \tag{40}$$

where

$$\Delta\Delta^H(s) = G_2 Q G_2^H(s) + R \tag{41}$$

is the spectral density matrix of the measurements. The quantity $\Delta(s)$ is a spectral factor, which is unique up to the product of an inner matrix. Denote $\Delta^{-H}(s) = (\Delta^H)^{-1}(s)$. Completing the square within (40) yields

$$\begin{aligned} \Phi_{ee}(s) &= G_1 Q G_1^H(s) - G_1 Q G_2^H (\Delta\Delta^H)^{-1} G_2 Q G_1^H(s) \\ &\quad + (H\Delta(s) - G_1 Q G_2^H \Delta^{-H}(s))(H\Delta(s) - G_1 Q G_2^H \Delta^{-H}(s))^H. \end{aligned} \tag{42}$$

It follows that the total energy of the error signal is given by

$$\begin{aligned} \int_{-j\infty}^{j\infty} \Phi_{ee}(s) ds &= \int_{-j\infty}^{j\infty} G_1 Q G_1^H(s) - G_1 Q G_2^H (\Delta\Delta^H)^{-1} G_2 Q G_1^H(s) ds \\ &\quad + \int_{-j\infty}^{j\infty} (H\Delta(s) - G_1 Q G_2^H \Delta^{-H}(s))(H\Delta(s) - G_1 Q G_2^H \Delta^{-H}(s))^H ds. \end{aligned} \tag{43}$$

"Science is what you know. Philosophy is what you don't know." *Earl Bertrand Arthur William Russell*

The first term on the right-hand-side of (43) is independent of $H(s)$ and represents a lower bound of $\int_{-j\infty}^{j\infty} \Phi_{ee}(s)ds$. The second term on the right-hand-side of (43) may be minimised by a judicious choice for $H(s)$.

Theorem 2: *The above linear time-invariant filtering problem with by the measurements (37) and estimation error (38) has the solution*

$$H(s) = G_1 Q G_2^H \Delta^{-H} \Delta^{-1}(s) . \tag{44}$$

which minimises $\int_{-j\infty}^{j\infty} \Phi_{ee}(s)ds$.

Proof: *The result follows by setting* $H\Delta(s) - G_1 Q G_2^H \Delta^{-H}(s) = 0$ *within (43).* □

By Parseval's theorem, the minimum mean-square-error solution (44) also minimises $\|e(t)\|_2^2$.

The solution (44) is unstable because the factor $G_2^H (\Delta^H)^{-1}(s)$ possesses right-hand-plane poles. This optimal noncausal solution is actually a smoother, which can be realised by a combination of forward and backward processes. Wiener called (44) the optimal unrealisable solution because it cannot be realised by a memory-less network of capacitors, inductors and resistors [4].

The transfer function matrix of a realisable filter is given by

$$H(s) = \left\{ G_1 Q G_2^H (\Delta^H)^{-1} \right\}_+ \Delta^{-1}(s) , \tag{45}$$

in which $\{ \}_+$ denotes the causal part. A procedure for finding the causal part of a transfer function is described below.

1.3.2 Finding the Causal Part of a Transfer Function

The causal part of transfer function can be found by carrying out the following three steps.

- If the transfer function is not strictly proper, that is, if the order of the numerator is not less than the degree of the denominator, then perform synthetic division to isolate the constant term.
- Expand out the (strictly proper) transfer function into the sum of stable and unstable partial fractions.
- The causal part is the sum of the constant term and the stable partial fractions.

Incidentally, the noncausal part is what remains, namely the sum of the unstable partial fractions.

Example 12. Consider $G(s) = (s^2 - \beta^2)(s^2 - \alpha^2)^{-1}$ with $\alpha, \beta < 0$. Since $G_2(s)$ possesses equal order numerator and denominator polynomials, synthetic division is required, which yields $G_2(s) = 1 + (\alpha^2 - \beta^2)(s^2 - \alpha^2)^{-1}$. A partial fraction expansion results in

"There is an astonishing imagination, even in the science of mathematics." *Francois-Marie Arouet de Voltaire*

$$\frac{(\alpha^2-\beta^2)}{(s^2-\alpha^2)} = \frac{0.5\alpha^{-1}(\alpha^2-\beta^2)}{(s+\alpha)} - \frac{0.5\alpha^{-1}(\alpha^2-\beta^2)}{(s-\alpha)}.$$

Thus, the causal part of $G(s)$ is $\{G(s)\}_+ = 1 - 0.5\alpha^{-1}(\alpha^2-\beta^2)(s-\alpha)^{-1}$. The noncausal part of $G(s)$ is denoted as $\{G(s)\}_-$ and is given by $\{G(s)\}_- = 0.5\alpha^{-1}(\alpha^2-\beta^2)(s-\alpha)^{-1}$. It is easily verified that $G(s) = \{G(s)\}_+ + \{G(s)\}_-$.

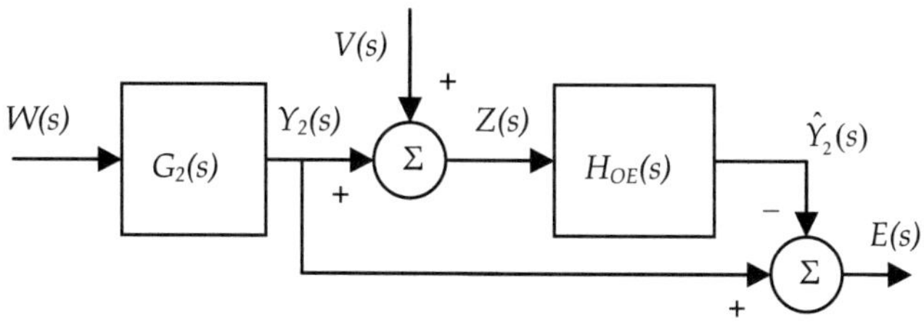

Figure 4. The s-domain output estimation problem.

1.3.3 Minimum-Mean-Square-Error Output Estimation

In output estimation, the reference system is the same as the generating system, as depicted in Fig. 4. The simplification of the optimal noncausal solution (44) of Theorem 2 for the case $G_1(s) = G_2(s)$ can be expressed as

$$\begin{aligned} H_{OE}(s) &= G_2 Q G_2^H \Delta^{-H}\Delta^{-1}(s) \\ &= G_2 Q G_2^H (\Delta\Delta^H)^{-1}(s) \\ &= (\Delta\Delta^H - R)(\Delta\Delta^H)^{-1}(s) \\ &= I - R\Delta^{-H}\Delta^{-1}(s). \end{aligned} \tag{46}$$

The optimal causal solution for output estimation is

$$\begin{aligned} H_{OE}(s) &= \left\{G_2 Q G_2^H \Delta^{-H}\right\}_+ \Delta^{-1}(s) \\ &= I - R\left\{\Delta^{-H}\right\}_+ \Delta^{-1}(s) \\ &= I - R^{1/2}\Delta^{-1}(s). \end{aligned} \tag{47}$$

When the measurement noise becomes negligibly small, the output estimator approaches a short circuit, that is,

$$\lim_{R\to 0, s\to 0} \left|H_{OE}(s)\right| = I. \tag{48}$$

"Science is the topography of ignorance." *Oliver Wendell Holmes*

The observation (48) can be verified by substituting $\Delta\Delta^H(s) = G_2QG_2^H(s)$ into (46). This observation is consistent with intuition, that is, when the measurements are perfect, filtering will be superfluous.

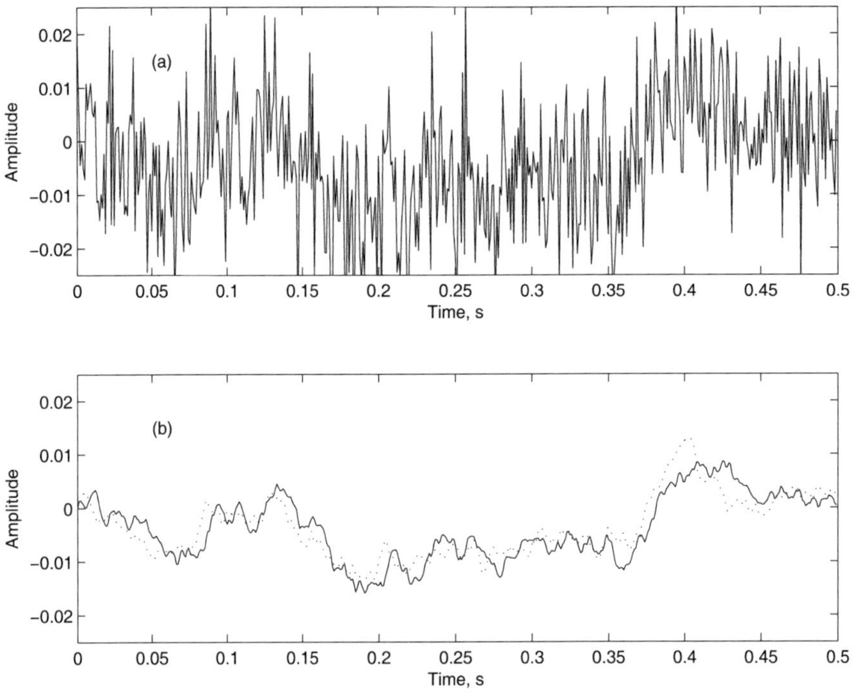

Figure 5. Sample trajectories for Example 13: (a) measurement, (b) system output (dotted line) and filtered signal (solid line).

Example 13. Consider a scalar output estimation problem, where $G_2(s) = (s-\alpha)^{-1}$, $\alpha = -1$, $Q = 1$ and $R = 0.0001$. Then $G_2QG_2^H(s) = Q(-s^2+\alpha^2)^{-1}$ and $\Delta\Delta^H(s) = -(Rs^2 + Ra^2 + Q)(-s^2+\alpha^2)^{-1}$, which leads to $\Delta(s) = R^{1/2}(s + \sqrt{\alpha^2+Q/R})(s-\alpha)^{-1}$. Therefore,
$G_2QG_2^H(\Delta^H)^{-1}(s) = \dfrac{Q}{(s-\alpha)(-s-\alpha)}\dfrac{(-s-\alpha)}{R^{1/2}(-s+\sqrt{\alpha^2+Q/R})} = \dfrac{Q}{R^{1/2}(s-\alpha)(-s+\sqrt{\alpha^2+Q/R})}$, in which a common pole and zero were cancelled. Expanding into partial fractions and taking the causal part results in

$$\{G_2QG_2^H(\Delta^H)^{-1}(s)\}_+ = \frac{\left.\dfrac{Q}{R^{1/2}(-s+\sqrt{\alpha^2+Q/R})}\right|_{s=\alpha}}{(s-\alpha)}$$

"Science is the systematic classification of experience." *George Henry Lewes*

and

$$H_{OE}(s) = \{G_2QG_2^H\Delta^{-H}\}_+\Delta^{-1}(s) = \frac{\alpha+\sqrt{\alpha^2+Q/R)}}{s+\sqrt{\alpha^2+Q/R)}}.$$

Substituting $\alpha = -1$, Q = 1 and R = 0.0001 yields $H(s)$ = $99(s+100)^{-1}$. By inspection, $\lim_{s\to 0}|H(s)| = \frac{99}{100}$, which illustrates the low measurement noise asymptote (48). Some sample trajectories from a simulation conducted with δ_t = 0.001 s are shown in Fig. 5. The input measurements are shown in Fig. 5(a). It can be seen that the filtered signal (the solid line of Fig. 5 (b)) estimates the system output (the dotted line of Fig. 5(b)).

1.3.4 Minimum-Mean-Square-Error Input Estimation

In input estimation problems, it is desired to estimate the input process $w(t)$, as depicted in Fig. 6. This is commonly known as an equalisation problem, in which it is desired to mitigate the distortion introduced by a communication channel $G_2(s)$. The simplification of the general noncausal solution (44) of Theorem 2 for the case of $G_2(s) = I$ results in

$$H_{IE}(s) = QG_2^H\Delta^{-H}\Delta^{-1}(s). \tag{49}$$

Equation (49) is known as the optimum minimum-mean-square-error noncausal equaliser [12]. Assume that: $G_2(s)$ is proper, that is, the order of the numerator is the same as the order of the denominator, and the zeros of $G_2(s)$ are in the left-hand-plane. Under these conditions, when the measurement noise becomes negligibly small, the equaliser estimates the inverse of the system model, that is,

$$\lim_{R\to 0} H_{IE}(s) = G_2^{-1}(s). \tag{50}$$

The observation (50) can be verified by substituting $\Delta\Delta^H(s)$ = $G_2QG_2^H(s)$ into (49). In other words, if the channel model is invertible and signal to noise ratio is sufficiently high, the equaliser will estimate $w(t)$. When measurement noise is present the equaliser no longer approximates the channel inverse because some filtering is also required. In the limit, when the signal to noise ratio is sufficiently low, the equaliser approaches an open circuit, namely,

$$\lim_{Q\to 0, s\to 0} |H_{IE}(s)| = 0. \tag{51}$$

The observation (51) can be verified by substituting Q = 0 into (49). Thus, when the equalisation problem is dominated by measurement noise, the estimation error is minimised by ignoring the data.

"All of the biggest technological inventions created by man - the airplane, the automobile, the computer says little about his intelligence, but speaks volumes about his laziness." *Mark Raymond Kennedy*

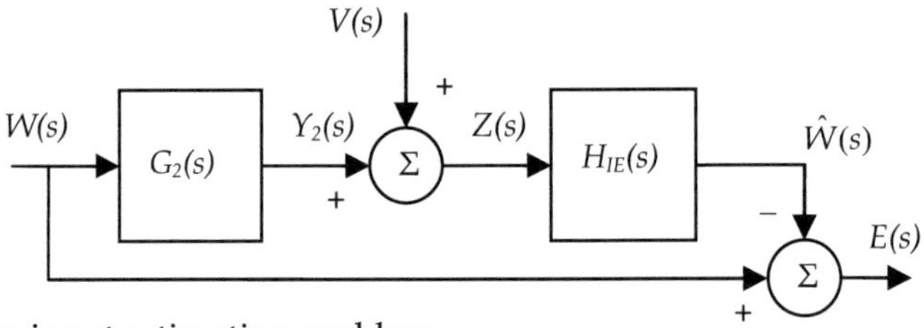

Figure 6. The s-domain input estimation problem.

1.4 Conclusion

Continuous-time, linear, time-invariant systems can be described via either a differential equation model or as a state-space model. Signal models can be written in the time-domain as

$$\left(a_n \frac{d^n}{dt^n} + a_{n-1}\frac{d^{n-1}}{dt^{n-1}} + \ldots + a_1 \frac{d}{dt} + a_0\right) y(t) = \left(b_m \frac{d^m}{dt^m} + b_{m-1}\frac{d^{m-1}}{dt^{n-1}} + \ldots + b_1 \frac{d}{dt} + b_0\right) w(t) .$$

Under the time-invariance assumption, the system transfer function matrices exist, which are written as polynomial fractions in the Laplace transform variable

$$Y(s) = \left[\frac{b_m s^m + b_{m-1} s^{m-1} + \ldots + b_1 s + b_0}{a_n s^n + a_{n-1} s^{n-1} + \ldots + a_1 s + a_0}\right] W(s) = G(s)W(s).$$

Thus, knowledge of a system's differential equation is sufficient to identify its transfer function. If the poles of a system's transfer function are all in the left-hand-plane then the system is asymptotically stable. That is, if the input to the system is bounded then the output of the system will be bounded.

The optimal solution minimises the energy of the error in the time domain. It is found in the frequency domain by minimising the mean-square-error. The main results are summarised in Table 1. The optimal noncausal solution has unstable factors. It can only be realised by a combination of forward and backward processes, which is known as smoothing. The optimal causal solution is also known as the Wiener filter.

In output estimation problems, $C_1 = C_2$, $D_1 = D_2$, that is, $G_1(s) = G_2(s)$ and when the measurement noise becomes negligible, the solution approaches a short circuit. In input estimation or equalisation, $C_1 = 0$, $D_1 = I$, that is, $G_1(s) = I$ and when the measurement noise becomes negligible, the optimal equaliser approaches the channel inverse, provided the inverse exists. Conversely, when the problem is dominated by measurement noise then the equaliser approaches an open circuit.

"Read Euler, read Euler, he is our master in everything." *Pierre-Simon Laplace*

	ASSUMPTIONS	MAIN RESULTS
Signals and systems	$E\{w(t)\} = E\{W(s)\} = E\{v(t)\} = E\{V(s)\} = 0$. $E\{w(t)w^T(t)\} = E\{W(s)W^T(s)\} = Q > 0$ and $E\{v(t)v^T(t)\} = E\{V(s)V^T(s)\} = R > 0$ are known. A, B, C_1, C_2, D_1 and D_2 are known. $G_1(s)$ and $G_2(s)$ are stable, *i.e.*, $Re\{\lambda_i(A)\} < 0$.	$G_1(s) = C_1(sI - A)^{-1}B + D_1$ $G_2(s) = C_2(sI - A)^{-1}B + D_2$
Spectral factorisation	$\Delta(s)$ and $\Delta^{-1}(s)$ are stable, *i.e.*, the poles and zeros of $\Delta(s)$ are in the left-half-plane.	$\Delta\Delta^H(s) = G_2QG_2^H(s) + R$
Non-causal solution		$H(s) = G_1QG_2^H(\Delta^H)^{-1}\Delta^{-1}(s)$
Causal solution		$H(s) = \{G_1QG_2^H(\Delta^H)^{-1}\}_+\Delta^{-1}(s)$

Table 1. Main results for the continuous-time general filtering problem.

1.5 Problems

Problem 1. Find the transfer functions and comment on stability of the systems having the following polynomial fractions.

(a) $\ddot{y} + 7\dot{y} + 12y = \ddot{w} + \dot{w} - 2w$.

(b) $\ddot{y} + 1\dot{y} - 20y = \ddot{w} + 5w + 6w$.

(c) $\ddot{y} + 11\dot{y} + 30y = \ddot{w} - 7\dot{w} + 12w$.

(d) $\ddot{y} - 13\dot{y} + 42y = \ddot{w} + 9\dot{w} + 20w$.

(e) $\ddot{y} - 15\dot{y} + 56y = \ddot{w} + 11\dot{w} + 30w$.

Problem 2. Find the transfer functions and comment on the stability for systems having the following state-space parameters.

(a) $A = \begin{bmatrix} -7 & -12 \\ 1 & 0 \end{bmatrix}$, $B = \begin{bmatrix} 1 \\ 0 \end{bmatrix}$, $C = \begin{bmatrix} -6 & -14 \end{bmatrix}$ and $D = 1$.

"The important thing in science is not so much to obtain new facts as to discover new ways of thinking about them." *William Henry Bragg*

(b) $A = \begin{bmatrix} -7 & 20 \\ 1 & 0 \end{bmatrix}$, $B = \begin{bmatrix} 1 \\ 0 \end{bmatrix}$, $C = \begin{bmatrix} -2 & 26 \end{bmatrix}$ and $D = 1$.

(c) $A = \begin{bmatrix} -11 & -30 \\ 1 & 0 \end{bmatrix}$, $B = \begin{bmatrix} 1 \\ 0 \end{bmatrix}$, $C = \begin{bmatrix} -18 & -18 \end{bmatrix}$ and $D = 1$.

(d) $A = \begin{bmatrix} 13 & -42 \\ 1 & 0 \end{bmatrix}$, $B = \begin{bmatrix} 1 \\ 0 \end{bmatrix}$, $C = \begin{bmatrix} 22 & -22 \end{bmatrix}$ and $D = 1$.

(e) $A = \begin{bmatrix} -15 & -56 \\ 1 & 0 \end{bmatrix}$, $B = \begin{bmatrix} 1 \\ 0 \end{bmatrix}$, $C = \begin{bmatrix} -4 & -26 \end{bmatrix}$ and $D = 1$.

Problem 3. Calculate the spectral factors for $\Phi_{zz}(s) = GQG^H(s) + R$ having the following models and noise statistics.

(a) $G(s) = (s+1)^{-1}$, $Q = 2$ and $R = 1$.

(b) $G(s) = (s+2)^{-1}$, $Q = 5$ and $R = 1$.

(c) $G(s) = (s+3)^{-1}$, $Q = 7$ and $R = 1$.

(d) $G(s) = (s+4)^{-1}$, $Q = 9$ and $R = 1$.

(e) $G(s) = (s+5)^{-1}$, $Q = 11$ and $R = 1$.

Problem 4. Calculate the optimal causal output estimators for Problem 3.

Problem 5. Consider the error spectral density matrix

$$\Phi_{ee}(s) = [H\Delta - G_1QG_2^H(\Delta^H)^{-1}][H\Delta - G_1QG_2^H(\Delta^H)^{-1}]^H(s)$$
$$+ [G_1QG_1^H - G_1QG_2^H(\Delta\Delta^H)^{-1}G_2QG_1^H](s) .$$

(a) Derive the optimal output estimator.

(b) Derive the optimal causal output estimator.

(c) Derive the optimal input estimator.

"Nothing shocks me. I'm a scientist." *Harrison Ford*

Problem 6 [16]. In respect of the configuration in Fig. 2, suppose that $A = \begin{bmatrix} -1 & 0 & 0 \\ 0 & -2 & 0 \\ 0 & 0 & -3 \end{bmatrix}$, $B = \begin{bmatrix} 25 \\ 25 \\ -25 \end{bmatrix}$, $C_2 = \begin{bmatrix} -1 & 2 & 1 \end{bmatrix}$, $C_1 = \begin{bmatrix} 1 & 1 & 1 \end{bmatrix}$, $D = 0$, $Q = 1$ and $R = 1$. Show that the optimal causal filter is given by $H(s) = -(16.9s^2 + 86.5s + 97.3)(s^3 + 8.64s^2 + 30.3s + 50.3)^{-1}$.

Problem 7 [18]. Suppose that $G_2QG_2^H(s) = \dfrac{-3600}{s^2(169 - s^2)}$ and $R(s) = 1$. Show that the optimal causal filter for output estimation is given by $H_{OE}(s) = (4s + 60)(s^2 + 17s + 60)^{-1}$.

1.6 Glossary

The following terms have been introduced within this section.

$\mathbb{R}$	The space of real numbers.
$\mathbb{R}^n$	The space of real-valued n-element column vectors.
t	The real-valued continuous-time variable. For example, $t \in (-\infty, \infty)$ and $t \in [0, \infty)$ denote $-\infty < t < \infty$ and $0 \le t < \infty$, respectively.
$w(t) \in \mathbb{R}^n$	A continuous-time, real-valued, *n*-element stationary stochastic input signal.
w	The set of $w(t)$ over a prescribed interval.
$\mathcal{G} : \mathbb{R}^p \to \mathbb{R}^q$	A linear system that operates on a *p*-element input signal and produces a *q*-element output signal.
$y = \mathcal{G}w$	The output of a linear system $\mathcal{G}$ that operates on an input signal w.
A, *B*, *C*, *D*	Time-invariant state space matrices of appropriate dimension. The system $\mathcal{G}$ is assumed to have the realisation $\dot{x}(t) = Ax(t) + Bw(t)$, $y(t) = Cx(t) + Dw(t)$ in which $w(t)$ is known as the process noise or input signal.
$v(t)$	A stationary stochastic measurement noise signal.
$\delta(t)$	The Dirac delta function.
Q and *R*	Time-invariant covariance matrices of stochastic signals $w(t)$ and $v(t)$, respectively.
s	The Laplace transform variable.
$Y(s)$	The Laplace transform of a continuous-time signal $y(t)$.
$G(s)$	The transfer function matrix of a system $\mathcal{G}$. For example, the transfer function matrix of the system $\dot{x}(t) = Ax(t) + Bw(t)$, $y(t) =$

"Facts are not science - as the dictionary is not literature." *Martin Henry Fischer*

	$Cx(t) + Dw(t)$ is given by $G(s) = C(sI - A)^{-1}B + D$.
$\langle v, w \rangle$	The inner product of two continuous-time signals v and w which is defined by $\langle v, w \rangle = \int_{-\infty}^{\infty} v^T w \, dt$.
$\lVert w \rVert_2$	The 2-norm of the continuous-time signal w which is defined by $\lVert w \rVert_2 = \sqrt{\langle w, w \rangle} = \sqrt{\int_{-\infty}^{\infty} w^T w dt}$.
$\mathcal{L}_2$	The set of continuous-time signals having finite 2-norm, which is known as the Lebesgue 2-space.
$\lambda_i(A)$	The i eigenvalues of A.
$\text{Re}\{ \lambda_i(A)\}$	The real part of the eigenvalues of A.
Asymptotic stability	A linear system $\mathcal{G}$ is said to be asymptotically stable if its output $y \in \mathcal{L}_2$ for any $w \in \mathcal{L}_2$. If $\text{Re}\{\lambda_i(A)\}$ are in the left-hand-plane or equivalently if the real part of transfer function's poles are in the left-hand-plane then the system is stable.
$\mathcal{G}^H$	The adjoint of $\mathcal{G}$. The adjoint of a system having the state-space parameters $\{A, B, C, D\}$ is a system parameterised by $\{- A^T, - C^T, B^T, D^T\}$.
$G^H(s)$	The adjoint (or Hermitian transpose) of the transfer function matrix $G(s)$.
$\Phi_{zz}(s)$	The spectral density matrix of the measurements z.
$\Delta(s)$	The spectral factor of $\Phi_{zz}(s)$ which satisfies $\Delta\Delta^H(s) = GQG^H(s) + R$ and $\Delta^{-H}(s) = (\Delta^H)^{-1}(s)$.
$G^{-1}(s)$	Inverse of the transfer function matrix $G(s)$.
$G^{-H}(s)$	Inverse of the adjoint transfer function matrix $G^H(s)$.
$\{G(s)\}_+$	Causal part of the transfer function matrix $G(s)$.
$H(s)$	Transfer function matrix of the minimum mean-square-error solution.
$H_{OE}(s)$	Transfer function matrix of the minimum mean-square-error solution specialised for output estimation.
$H_{IE}(s)$	Transfer function matrix of the minimum mean-square-error solution specialised for input estimation.

"Facts are stupid things." *Ronald Wilson Reagan*

1.7 References

[1] O. Neugebauer, *A history of ancient mathematical astronomy*, Springer, Berlin and New York, 1975.

[2] C. F. Gauss, *Theoria Motus Corporum Coelestium in Sectionibus Conicis Solem Ambientum*, Hamburg, 1809 (Translated: *Theory of the Motion of the Heavenly Bodies*, Dover, New York, 1963).

[3] A. N. Kolmogorov, "Sur l'interpolation et extrapolation des suites stationaires", *Comptes Rendus. de l'Academie des Sciences*, vol. 208, pp. 2043 - 2045, 1939.

[4] N. Wiener, *Extrapolation, interpolation and smoothing of stationary time series with engineering applications*, The MIT Press, Cambridge Mass.; Wiley, New York; Chapman & Hall, London, 1949.

[5] P. Masani, "Wiener's Contributions to Generalized Harmonic Analysis, Prediction Theory and Filter Theory", *Bulletin of the American Mathematical Society*, vol. 72, no. 1, pt. 2, pp. 73 - 125, 1966.

[6] T. Kailath, *Lectures on Wiener and Kalman Filtering*, Springer Verlag, Wien; New York, 1981.

[7] M.-A. Parseval Des Chênes, *Mémoires présentés à l'Institut des Sciences, Lettres et Arts, par divers savans, et lus dans ses assemblées. Sciences mathématiques et physiques (Savans étrangers)*, vol. 1, pp. 638 - 648, 1806.

[8] C. A. Desoer and M. Vidyasagar, *Feedback Systems : Input Output Properties*, Academic Press, N.Y., 1975.

[9] G. A. Einicke, "Asymptotic Optimality of the Minimum-Variance Fixed-Interval Smoother", *IEEE Transactions on Signal Processing*, vol. 55, no. 4, pp. 1543 - 1547, Apr. 2007.

[10] T. Kailath, *Linear Systems*, Prentice-Hall Inc., Englewood Cliffs, New Jersey, 1980.

[11] D. J. N. Limebeer, B. D. O. Anderson, P. Khargonekar and M. Green, "A Game Theoretic Approach to H_∞ Control for Time-varying Systems", *SIAM Journal of Control and Optimization*, vol. 30, no. 2, pp. 262 - 283, 1992.

[12] M. Green and D. J. N. Limebeer, *Linear Robust Control*, Prentice-Hall Inc, Englewood Cliffs, New Jersey, 1995.

[13] C. S. Burrus, J. H. McClellan, A. V. Oppenheim, T. W. Parks, R. W. Schafer and H. W. Schuessler, *Computer-Based Exercises for Signal Processing Using Matlab*, Prentice-Hall, Englewood Cliffs, New Jersey, 1994.

[14] U. Shaked, "A general transfer function approach to linear stationary filtering and steady state optimal control problems", *International Journal of Control*, vol. 24, no. 6, pp. 741 - 770, 1976.

[15] A. H. Sayed and T. Kailath, "A Survey of Spectral Factorization Methods", *Numerical Linear Algebra with Applications*, vol. 8, pp. 467 - 496, 2001.

[16] U. Shaked, "H_∞-Minimum Error State Estimation of Linear Stationary Processes", *IEEE Transactions on Automatic Control*, vol. 35, no. 5, pp. 554 - 558, May 1990.

[17] S. A. Kassam and H. V. Poor, "Robust Techniques for Signal Processing: A Survey", *Proceedings of the IEEE*, vol. 73, no. 3, pp. 433 - 481, Mar. 1985.

[18] A. P. Sage and J. L. Melsa, *Estimation Theory with Applications to Communications and Control*, McGraw-Hill Book Company, New York, 1971.

"All science is either physics or stamp collecting." *Baron William Thomson Kelvin*

2

Discrete-Time Minimum-Mean-Square-Error Filtering

2.1 Introduction

This chapter reviews the solutions for the discrete-time, linear stationary filtering problems that are attributed to Wiener [1] and Kolmogorov [2]. As in the continuous-time case, a model-based approach is employed. Here, a linear model is specified by the coefficients of the input and output difference equations. It is shown that the same coefficients appear in the system's (frequency domain) transfer function. In other words, frequency domain model representations can be written down without background knowledge of z-transforms.

In the 1960s and 1970s, continuous-time filters were implemented on analogue computers. This practice has been discontinued for two main reasons. First, analogue multipliers and op amp circuits exhibit poor performance whenever (temperature-sensitive) calibrations become out of date. Second, updated software releases are faster to turn around than hardware design iterations. Continuous-time filters are now routinely implemented using digital computers, provided that the signal sampling rates and data processing rates are sufficiently high. Alternatively, continuous-time model parameters may be converted into discrete-time and differential equations can be transformed into difference equations. The ensuing discrete-time filter solutions are then amenable to more economical implementation, namely, employing relatively lower processing rates.

The discrete-time Wiener filtering problem is solved in the frequency domain. Once again, it is shown that the optimum minimum-mean-square-error solution is found by completing the square. The optimum solution is noncausal, which can only be implemented by forward and backward processes. This solution is actually a smoother and the optimum filter is found by taking the causal part.

The developments rely on solving a spectral factorisation problem, which requires pole-zero cancellations. Therefore, some pertinent discrete-time concepts are introduced in Section 2.2 prior to deriving the filtering results. The discussion of the prerequisite concepts is comparatively brief since it mirrors the continuous-time material introduced previously. In Section 2.3 it is shown that the structure of the filter solutions is unchanged - only the spectral factors are calculated differently.

"If we value the pursuit of knowledge, we must be free to follow wherever that search may lead us. The free mind is not a barking dog, to be tethered on a ten foot-chain." *Adlai Ewing Stevenson Jr.*

2.2 Prerequisites

2.2.1 Spaces

Discrete-time real-valued stochastic processes are denoted as $v_k^T = [v_{1,k}^T, v_{2,k}^T, \ldots, v_{n,k}^T]$ and $w_k^T = [w_{1,k}^T, w_{2,k}^T, \ldots, w_{n,k}^T]$, where $v_{i,k}, w_{i,k} \in \mathbb{R}$, $i = 1, \ldots n$ and $k \in (-\infty, \infty)$. The v_k and w_k are said to belong to the space $\mathbb{R}^n$. In this chapter, the vector w denotes the set of w_k over all time k, that is, $w = \{w_k, k \in (-\infty,\infty)\}$. The inner product $\langle v,w \rangle$ of two discrete-time vector processes v and w is defined by

$$\langle v,w \rangle = \sum_{k=-\infty}^{\infty} v_k^T w_k . \tag{1}$$

The 2-norm or Euclidean norm of a discrete-time vector process w, $\|w\|_2$, is defined as $\|w\|_2 = \sqrt{\langle w,w \rangle} = \sqrt{\sum_{k=-\infty}^{\infty} w_k^T w_k}$. The square of the 2-norm, that is, $\|w\|_2^2 = \langle w^T w \rangle = \sum_{k=-\infty}^{\infty} w_k^T w_k$ is commonly known as energy of the signal w. The Lebesgue 2-space is denoted by ℓ_2 and is defined as the set of discrete-time processes having a finite 2-norm. Thus, $w \in \ell_2$ means that the energy of w is bounded. See [3] for more detailed discussions of spaces and norms.

2.2.2 Discrete-time Polynomial Fraction Systems

Consider a linear, time-invariant system $\mathcal{G}$ that operates on an input process $w_k \in \mathbb{R}$ and produces an output process $y_k \in \mathbb{R}$, that is, $\mathcal{G}: \mathbb{R} \rightarrow \mathbb{R}$. Suppose that the difference equation for this system is

$$a_n y_{k-n} + a_{n-1} y_{k-n+1} + \ldots + a_1 y_{k-1} + a_0 y_k = b_m w_{k-m} + b_{m-1} w_{k-m+1} + \ldots + b_1 w_{k-1} + b_0 w_k , \tag{2}$$

where $a_0, \ldots, a_n$ and $b_0, \ldots, b_n$ are real-valued constant coefficients, with $a_n \neq 0$ and zero initial conditions.

Example 1. The difference equation $y_k = 0.1x_k + 0.2\, x_{k-1} + 0.3y_{k-1}$ specifies a system in which the coefficients are $a_0 = 1$, $a_1 = -0.3$, $b_0 = 0.2$ and $b_1 = 0.3$. Note that y_k is known as the current output and y_{k-1} is known as a past output.

2.2.3 The Z-Transform of a Discrete-time Sequence

The two-sided z-transform of a discrete-time process, y_k, is denoted by $Y(z)$ and is defined by

$$Y(z) = \sum_{k=-\infty}^{\infty} y_k z^{-k} , \tag{3}$$

where $z = e^{j\omega t}$ and $j = \sqrt{-1}$. Given a process y_k with z-transform $Y(z)$, y_k can be calculated from $Y(z)$ by taking the inverse z-transform of $y(z)$,

---

"To live effectively is to live with adequate information." *Norbert Wiener*

$$y_k = \frac{1}{2\pi j}\int_{-e^{j\omega T}}^{e^{j\omega T}} Y(z)z^{k-1}dz . \quad (4)$$

Theorem 1 Parseval's Theorem:

$$\int_{-\infty}^{\infty} \left|y_k\right|^2 dk = \frac{1}{2\pi j}\int_{-e^{j\omega T}}^{e^{j\omega T}} \left|Y(z)\right|^2 dz . \quad (5)$$

That is, the energy in the time domain equals the energy in the frequency domain.

2.2.4 Polynomial Fraction Transfer Functions

In the continuous-time case, a system's differential equations lead to a transfer function in the Laplace transform variable. Here, in discrete-time, a system's difference equations lead to a transfer function in the z-transform variable. Applying the z-transform to both sides of (2) yields the difference equation

$$\begin{aligned}\left(a_n z^{-n} + a_{n-1}z^{-n+1} + \ldots + a_1 z^{-1} + a_0\right)Y(z) \\ = \left(b_m z^{-m} + b_{m-1}z^{-m+1} + \ldots + b_1 z^{-1} + b_0\right)W(z) .\end{aligned} \quad (6)$$

Therefore

$$\begin{aligned}Y(z) &= \left[\frac{b_m z^{-m} + b_{m-1}z^{-m+1} + \ldots + b_1 z^{-1} + b_0}{a_n z^{-n} + a_{n-1}z^{-n+1} + \ldots + a_1 z^{-1} + a_0}\right]W(z) \\ &= G(z)W(z) ,\end{aligned} \quad (7)$$

where

$$G(z) = \left[\frac{b_m z^{-m} + b_{m-1}z^{-m+1} + \ldots + b_1 z^{-1} + b_0}{a_n z^{-n} + a_{n-1}z^{-n+1} + \ldots + a_1 z^{-1} + a_0}\right] \quad (8)$$

is known as the transfer function of the system. It can be seen that knowledge of the system difference equation (2) is sufficient to identify its transfer function (8).

2.2.5 Poles and Zeros

The numerator and denominator polynomials of (8) can be factored into m and n linear factors, respectively, to give

$$G(z) = \frac{b_m(z-\beta_1)(z-\beta_2)\ldots(z-\beta_m)}{a_n(z-\alpha_1)(z-\alpha_2)\ldots(z-\alpha_n)} . \quad (9)$$

The numerator of $G(z)$ is zero when $z = \beta_i$, $i = 1 \ldots m$. These values of z are called the zeros of $G(z)$. Zeros inside the unit circle are called minimum-phase whereas zeros outside the unit

---

"There is no philosophy which is not founded upon knowledge of the phenomena, but to get any profit from this knowledge it is absolutely necessary to be a mathematician." *Daniel Bernoulli*

circle are called non-minimum phase. The denominator of $G(z)$ is zero when $z = \alpha_i$, $i = 1 \ldots n$. These values of z are called the poles of $G(z)$.

Example 2. Consider a system described by the difference equation $y_k + 0.3y_{k-1} + 0.04y_{k-2} = w_k + 0.5w_{k-1}$. It follows from (2) and (8) that the corresponding transfer function is given by

$$G(z) = \frac{1+0.5z^{-1}}{1+0.3z^{-1}+0.04z^{-2}} = \frac{z^2+0.5z}{z^2+0.3z+0.04} = \frac{z(z+0.5)}{(z-0.1)(z+0.4)}$$

which possesses poles at $z = 0.1, -0.4$ and zeros at $z = 0, -0.5$.

2.2.6 Polynomial Fraction Transfer Function Matrix

In the single-input-single-output case, it is assumed that $w(z)$, $G(z)$ and $y(z) \in \mathbb{R}$. In the multiple-input-multiple-output case, $G(z)$ is a transfer function matrix. For example, suppose that $w(z) \in \mathbb{R}^m$, $y(z) \in \mathbb{R}^p$, then $G(z) \in \mathbb{R}^{p\times m}$, namely

$$G(z) = \begin{bmatrix} G_{11}(z) & G_{12}(s) & .. & G_{1m}(z) \\ G_{21}(z) & G_{22}(s) & & \\ \vdots & & \ddots & \vdots \\ G_{p1}(z) & & .. & G_{pm}(z) \end{bmatrix}, \tag{10}$$

where the components $G_{ij}(z)$ have the polynomial transfer function form within (8) or (9).

2.2.7 State-Space Transfer Function Matrix

The polynomial fraction transfer function matrix (10) can be written in the state-space representation

$$G(z) = C(zI - A)^{-1}B + D, \tag{11}$$

where $A \in \mathbb{R}^{n\times n}$, $B \in \mathbb{R}^{n\times m}$, $C \in \mathbb{R}^{p\times n}$ and $D \in \mathbb{R}^{p\times p}$.

Example 3. For a state-space model with $A = -0.5$, $B = C = 1$ and $D = 0$, the transfer function is $G(z) = (z^{-1} - 0.5)^{-1}$.

Example 4. For state-space parameters $A = \begin{bmatrix} -0.33 & -0.04 \\ 1 & 0 \end{bmatrix}$, $B = \begin{bmatrix} 1 \\ 0 \end{bmatrix}$, $C = \begin{bmatrix} 0.2 & -0.04 \end{bmatrix}$ and $D = 1$, the use of Cramer's rule, that is, $\begin{bmatrix} a & b \\ c & d \end{bmatrix}^{-1} = \frac{1}{ad-bc}\begin{bmatrix} d & -b \\ -c & a \end{bmatrix}$, yields the transfer function $G(z) = \frac{z(z+0.5)}{(z-0.1)(z+0.4)}$.

"A mathematician is a blind man in a dark room looking for a black cat which isn't there." *Charles Robert Darwin*

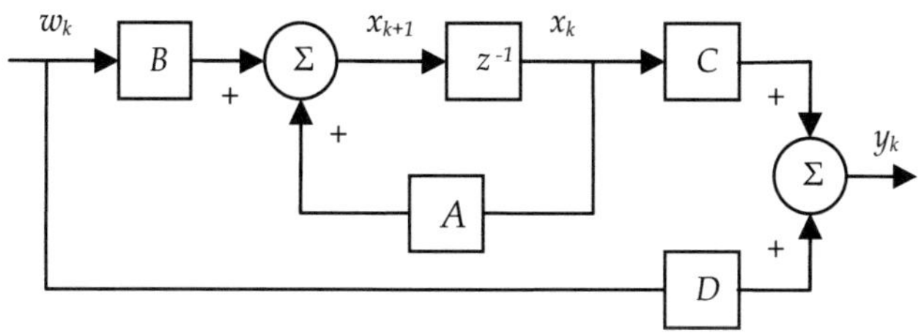

Figure 1. Discrete-time state-space system.

2.2.8 State-Space Realisation

The state-space transfer function matrix (11) can be realised as a discrete-time system $\mathcal{G} : \mathbb{R}^m \to \mathbb{R}^p$

$$x_{k+1} = Ax_k + Bw_k , \tag{12}$$

$$y_k = Cx_k + Dw_k , \tag{13}$$

where $w_k \in \mathbb{R}^m$ is an input sequence, $x_k \in \mathbb{R}^n$ is a state vector and $y_k \in \mathbb{R}^p$ is an output. This system is depicted in Fig. 1. It is assumed that w_k is a zero-mean, stationary process with $E\{w_j w_k^T\} = Q\delta_{jk}$, where $\delta_{jk} = \begin{cases} 1 & \text{if } j = k \\ 0 & \text{if } j \neq k \end{cases}$ is the Kronecker delta function. In most applications, discrete-time implementations are desired, however, the polynomial fraction transfer function or state-space transfer function parameters may be known in continuous-time. Therefore, two methods for transforming continuous-time parameters to discrete-time are set out below.

2.2.9 The Bilinear Approximation

Transfer functions in the z-plane can be mapped exactly to the s-plane by substituting $z = e^{sT_s}$, where s = jw and T_S is the sampling period. Conversely, the substitution

$$\begin{aligned} s &= \frac{1}{T_S}\log(z) \\ &= \frac{2}{T_s}\left[\frac{z-1}{z+1} + \frac{1}{3}\left(\frac{z-1}{z+1}\right)^3 + \frac{1}{5}\left(\frac{z-1}{z+1}\right)^5 + \frac{1}{7}\left(\frac{z-1}{z+1}\right)^7 + \dots\right] \end{aligned} \tag{14}$$

can be used to map s-plane transfer functions into the z-plane. The bilinear transform is a first order approximation to (14), namely,

---

"I do not like it, and I am sorry I ever had anything to do with it." *Erwin Rudolf Josef Alexander Schrödinger*

$$s \approx \frac{2}{T_S}\left[\frac{z-1}{z+1}\right]. \tag{15}$$

Example 5. Consider the continuous-time transfer function $H(s) = (s + 2)^{-1}$ with $T_S = 2$. Substituting (15) yields the discrete-time transfer function $H(z) = (3z + 1)^{-1}$. The higher order terms within the series of (14) can be included to improve the accuracy of converting a continuous-time model to discrete time.

2.2.10 Discretisation of Continuous-time Systems

The discrete-time state-space parameters, denoted here by $\{A_D, B_D, C_D, D_D, Q_D, R_D\}$, can be obtained by discretising the continuous-time system

$$\dot{x}(t) = A_C(t) + B_C w(t), \tag{16}$$

$$y(t) = C_C x(t) + D_C w(t), \tag{17}$$

$$z(t) = y(t) + v(t), \tag{18}$$

where $E\{w(t)w^T(\tau)\} = Q_C\delta(t-\tau)$ and $E\{v(t)v^T(\tau)\} = R_C\delta(t-\tau)$. Premultiplying (16) by $e^{-A_C t}$ and recognising that $\frac{d}{dt}(e^{-A_C t}x(t)) = e^{-A_C t}\dot{x}(t) - e^{-A_C t}A_C x(t)$ yields

$$\frac{d}{dt}(e^{-A_C t}x(t)) = e^{-A_C t}B_C w(t). \tag{19}$$

Integrating (19) results in

$$e^{-A_C t}x(t) - e^{-A_C t_0}x(t_0) = \int_{t_0}^{t} e^{-F\tau}B_C w(\tau)d\tau \tag{20}$$

and hence

$$\begin{aligned} x(t) &= e^{A_C(t-t_0)}x(t_0) + e^{A_C t}\int_{t_0}^{t} e^{-F\tau}B_C w(\tau)d\tau \\ &= e^{A_C(t-t_0)}x(t_0) + \int_{t_0}^{t} e^{F(t-\tau)}B_C w(\tau)d\tau \end{aligned} \tag{21}$$

is a solution to the differential equation (16). Suppose that $x(t)$ is available at integer k multiples of T_s. Assuming that $w(t)$ is constant during the sampling interval and substituting $t_0 = kT_s$, $t = (k+1)T_s$ into (21) yields

$$x((k+1)T_s) = e^{A_C T_s}x(kT_s) + \int_{kT_s}^{(k+1)T_s} e^{A_C((k+1)T_s-\tau)}B_C d\tau w(kT_s). \tag{22}$$

With the identifications $x_k = x(kT_s)$ and $w_k = w(kT_s)$ in (22), it can be seen that

---

"In the fields of observation, chance favours only the mind that is prepared." *Louis Pasteur*

$$A_D = e^{A_C T_s}, \tag{23}$$

$$B_D = \int_{kT_s}^{(k+1)T_s} e^{A_C((k+1)T_s - \tau)} B_C d\tau . \tag{24}$$

The τ within the definite integral (24) varies from kT_s to $(k+1)Ts$. For a change of variable $\lambda = (k+1)T_s - \tau$, the limits of integration become $\lambda = T_s$ and $\lambda = 0$, which results in the simplification

$$\begin{aligned} B_D &= -\int_{T_s}^{0} e^{A_C \lambda} B_C d\lambda \\ &= \int_{0}^{T_s} e^{A_C \lambda} B_C d\lambda . \end{aligned} \tag{25}$$

Denoting $E\{w_j w_k^T\} = Q_D \delta_{jk}$ and using (25) it can be shown that [4]

$$Q_D = \int_{0}^{T_s} e^{A_C \lambda} B_C Q_C B_C^T e^{A_C \lambda} d\lambda . \tag{26}$$

The exponential matrix is defined as

$$e^{A_C t} = I + A_C t + \frac{A_C^2 t^2}{2} + \cdots + \frac{A_C^N t^N}{N!}, \tag{27}$$

which leads to

$$A_D = I + A_C T_s + \frac{(A_C T_s)^2}{2!} + \frac{(A_C T_s)^3}{3!} + \frac{(A_C T_s)^4}{4!} + \cdots, \tag{28}$$

$$B_D = T_s + \frac{A_C T_s^2}{2!} + \frac{A_C^2 T_s^3}{3!} + \frac{A_C^3 T_s^4}{4!} + \cdots, \tag{29}$$

$$Q_D = B_C Q_C B_C^T T_s + \frac{(A_C B_C Q_C B_C^T + B_C Q_C B_C^T A_C^T) T_s^2}{2!} + \cdots . \tag{30}$$

It is common practice ([4] – [6]) to truncate the above series after terms linear in T_s. Some higher order terms can be retained in applications where parameter accuracy is critical. Since the limit as $N \to \infty$ of $T_s^N / N!$ is 0, the above series are valid for any value of T_s. However, the sample period needs to be sufficiently small, otherwise the above discretisations will be erroneous. According to the Nyquist-Shannon sampling theorem, the sampling rate is required to be at least twice the highest frequency component of the continuous-time signal. In respect of (17), the output map may be written as

$$y(kT_s) = C_C x(kT_s) + D_C w(kT_s) \tag{31}$$

"We are more easily persuaded, in general, by the reasons we ourselves discover than by those which are given to us by others." *Blaise Pascal*

and thus

$$C_D = C_C, \tag{32}$$

$$D_D = D_C. \tag{33}$$

Following the approach of [7], it is assumed that the continuous-time signals are integrated between samples, for example, the discretised measurement noise is $v(kT_s) = \frac{1}{T_s}\int_{kT_s}^{(k+1)T_s} v(\tau)d\tau$. Then the corresponding measurement noise covariance is

$$R_D = \frac{1}{T_s^2}\int_{kT_s}^{(k+1)T_s} R_C d\tau = \frac{1}{T_s} R_C. \tag{34}$$

In some applications, such as inertial and satellite navigation [8], the underlying dynamic equations are in continuous-time, whereas the filters are implemented in discrete-time. In this case, any underlying continuous-time equations together with (28) - (30) can be calculated within a high rate foreground task, so that the discretised state-space parameters will be sufficiently accurate. The discrete-time filter recursions can then be executed within a lower rate background task.

2.2.11 Asymptotic Stability

Consider a discrete-time, linear, time-invariant system $\mathcal{G}$ that operates on an input process w and produces an output process y. The system $\mathcal{G}$ is said to be asymptotically stable if the output remains bounded, that is, $y \in \ell_2$, for any input $w \in \ell_2$. Two equivalent conditions for $\mathcal{G}$ to be asymptotically stable are as follows.

(i) The i eigenvalues of the system's state matrix are inside the unit circle, that is, for A_i of (11), $|\lambda_i(A)| < 1$.

(ii) The i poles of the system's transfer function are inside the unit circle, that is, for α_i of (9), $|\alpha_i| < 1$.

Example 6. A state-space system having $A = -0.5$, $B = C = 1$ and $D = 0$ is stable, since $\lambda(A) = 0.5$ is in the unit circle. Equivalently, the corresponding transfer function $G(z) = (z + 0.5)^{-1}$ has a pole at $z = -0.5$ which is inside the unit circle and so the system is stable.

2.2.12 Adjoint Systems

Let $\mathcal{G} : \mathbb{R}^p \to \mathbb{R}^q$ be a linear system operating on the interval [0, T]. Then $\mathcal{G}^H : \mathbb{R}^q \to \mathbb{R}^p$, the adjoint of $\mathcal{G}$, is the unique linear system such that, for all $\alpha \in \mathbb{R}^q$ and $w \in \mathbb{R}^p$, $<\alpha, \mathcal{G} w> = <\mathcal{G}^H \alpha, w>$. The following derivation is a simplification of the time-varying version that appears in [9].

"Eighty percent of success is showing up." *(Woody) Allen Stewart Konigsberg*

Lemma 1 (State-space representation of an adjoint system): *Suppose that a discrete-time linear time-invariant system* $\mathcal{G}$ *is described by*

$$x_{k+1} = Ax_k + Bw_k, \tag{35}$$

$$y_k = Cx_k + Dw_k, \tag{36}$$

with $x_0 = 0$. *The adjoint* $\mathcal{G}^H$ *is the linear system having the realisation*

$$\zeta_{k-1} = A^T\zeta_k - C^T\alpha_k, \tag{37}$$

$$\beta_k = -B^T\zeta_k + D^T\alpha_k, \tag{38}$$

with $\zeta_T = 0$.

Proof: *The system (35) – (36) can be written equivalently*

$$\begin{bmatrix} zI - A & -B \\ C & D \end{bmatrix}\begin{bmatrix} x(t) \\ w(t) \end{bmatrix} = \begin{bmatrix} 0(t) \\ y(t) \end{bmatrix} \tag{39}$$

with $x_0 = 0$. *Thus*

$$<y, \mathcal{G}w> = \left\langle \begin{bmatrix} \zeta \\ \alpha \end{bmatrix}, \begin{bmatrix} zI - A & -B \\ C & D \end{bmatrix}\begin{bmatrix} x \\ w \end{bmatrix} \right\rangle \tag{40}$$

$$= \sum_{k=1}^{N} \zeta_k^T x_{k+1} - \sum_{k=1}^{N} \zeta_k^T (Ax_k + Bw_k) + \sum_{k=1}^{N} \alpha_k^T (Cx_k + Dw_k)$$

$$= \left\langle \begin{bmatrix} z^{-1}I - A^T & C^T \\ -B^T & D^T \end{bmatrix}\begin{bmatrix} \zeta \\ \alpha \end{bmatrix}, \begin{bmatrix} x \\ w \end{bmatrix} \right\rangle \tag{41}$$

$$= < \mathcal{G}^H \boldsymbol{\alpha}, \boldsymbol{w} >$$

where $\mathcal{G}^H$ *is given by (37) – (38).* □

Thus, the adjoint of a discrete-time system having the parameters $\begin{bmatrix} A & B \\ C & D \end{bmatrix}$ is a system with parameters $\begin{bmatrix} A^T & -C^T \\ -B^T & D^T \end{bmatrix}$. Adjoint systems have the property $(\mathcal{G}^H)^H = \mathcal{G}$. The adjoint of

"There is something fascinating about science. One gets such wholesale returns of conjecture out of such a trifling investment of fact." *Samuel Langhorne Clemens aka. Mark Twain*

the transfer function matrix $G(z)$ is denoted as $G^H(z)$ and is defined by the transfer function matrix

$$G^H(z) = G^T(z^{-1}). \tag{42}$$

Example 7. Suppose that a system $\mathcal{G}$ has the state-space parameters $A = -0.5$ and $B = C = D = 1$. From Lemma 1, an adjoint system has the state-space parameters $A = -0.5$, $B = C = -1$, $D = 1$ and the corresponding transfer function is $G^H(z) = 1 + (z^{-1} + 0.5)^{-1} = (3z + 2)(z + 2)^{-1}$, which is unstable and non-minimum-phase. Alternatively, the adjoint of $G(z) = 1 + (z + 0.5)^{-1} = (z + 1.5)(z + 0.5)^{-1}$ can be obtained using (42), namely, $G^H(z) = G^T(z{-}1) = (3z + 2)(z + 2)^{-1}$.

2.2.13 Causal Systems

A causal system is a system whose output depends exclusively on past and current inputs and outputs.

Example 8. Consider $x_{k+1} = 0.3x_k + 0.4x_{k-1} + w_k$. Since the output x_{k+1} depends only on past states x_k, x_{k-1}, and past inputs w_k, this system is causal.

Example 9. Consider $x_k = 0.3x_{k+1} + 0.4x_k + w_{k+1}$. Since the output x_k depends on future outputs x_{k+1} and future w_{k+1} inputs, this system is non-causal.

2.2.14 Realising Unstable System Components

Unstable system components are termed unrealisable because their outputs are not in ℓ_2, that is, they are unbounded. In other words, unstable systems cannot produce a useful output. However, an unstable causal component can be realised as a stable non-causal or backwards component. Consider the system $\mathcal{G}$ (35) – (36) in which the eigenvalues of A all lie outside the unit circle. In this case, a stable adjoint system $\beta = \mathcal{G}^H \alpha$ can be realised by the following three-step procedure.

(i) Time-reverse the input signal α_k, that is, construct α_τ, where $\tau = N - k$ is a time-to-go variable.

(ii) Realise the stable system $\mathcal{G}^T$

$$\zeta_{\tau+1} = A^T\zeta_\tau + C^T\alpha_\tau, \tag{43}$$

$$\beta_\tau = B^T\zeta_\tau + D^T\alpha_\tau, \tag{44}$$

with $\zeta_T = 0$.

(iii) Time-reverse the output signal β_τ, that is, construct β_k.

Thus if a system consists of a cascade of stable and unstable components, it can be realised by a combination of causal and non-causal components. This approach will be exploited in the realisation of smoothers subsequently.

"I've lost my faith in science." *Ruth Elizabeth (Bette) Davis*

Example 10. Suppose that it is desired to realise the system $G(z) = G_2^H(z)G_1(z)$, in which $G_1(z) = (z + 0.6)^{-1}$ $G_2^H(z) = z(0.9z+1)^{-1}$, that is, $G_2(z) = (z+0.9)^{-1}$. This system can be realised using the processes shown in Fig. 2.

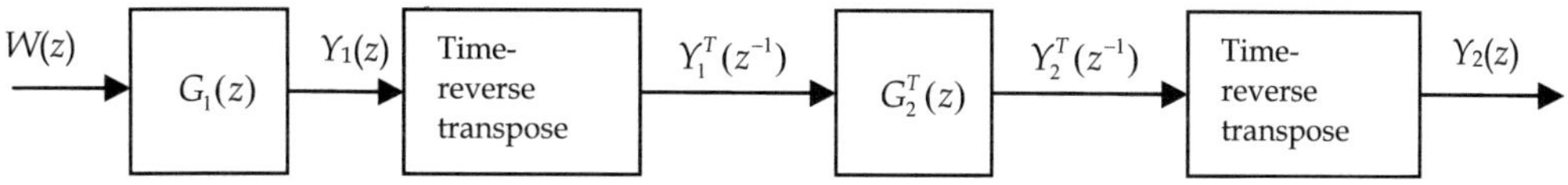

Figure 2. Realising an unstable $G(z) = G_2^H(z)G_1(z)$.

2.2.15 Power Spectral Density

Consider again a linear, time-invariant system $y = \mathcal{G} w$ and its corresponding transfer function matrix $G(z)$. Then $\Phi_{yy}(z)$, the power spectral density of y, is given by

$$\Phi_{yy}(z) = GQG^H(z), \tag{45}$$

which has the property $\Phi_{yy}(z) = \Phi_{yy}(z^{-1})$. From Parseval's Theorem (5), the average total energy of $y(t)$ is given by

$$\int_{-e^{j\omega T}}^{e^{j\omega T}} \Phi_{yy}(z)dz = \int_{-\infty}^{\infty} \left|y_k\right|^2 dk = \left\|y(t)\right\|_2^2 = E\{y^T(t)y(t)\}, \tag{46}$$

which equals the area under the power spectral density curve.

2.2.16 Spectral Factorisation

To avoid confusion with the z-transform variable, denote the noisy measurements of $y(z) = G(z)w(z)$ by

$$u(z) = y(z) + v(z), \tag{47}$$

where $v(z) \in \mathbb{R}^p$ is the z-transform of an independent, zero-mean, stationary, white measurement noise process with $E\{v_j v_k^T\} = R\delta_{jk}$. Let

$$\Phi_{uu}(z) = GQG^H(z) + R \tag{48}$$

denote the spectral density matrix of the measurements $u(t)$. A discrete-time transfer function is said to be minimum phase if its zeros lies inside the unit circle. Conversely, transfer functions having outside-unit-circle-zeros are known as non-minimum phase.

Suppose that $\Phi_{uu}(z)$ is a spectral density matrix of transfer functions possessing equal order numerator and denominator polynomials that do not have roots on the unit circle. Then the spectral factor matrix $\Delta(z)$ satisfies the following.

"Knowledge advances by steps, and not by leaps." *Baron Thomas Macaulay*

(i) $\Delta(z)\,\Delta^H(z) = \Phi_{uu}(z)$.
(ii) $\Delta(z)$ is causal, that is, the poles of $\Delta(z)$ are inside the unit circle.
(iii) $\Delta^{-1}(z)$ is causal, that is, the zeros of $\Delta(z)$ which are the poles of $\Delta^{-1}(z)$ are inside the unit circle.

The problem of spectral factorisation within discrete-time Wiener filtering problems is studied in [10]. The roots of the transfer function polynomials need to be sorted into those inside the unit circle and those outside the unit circle. Spectral factors can be found using Levinson-Durbin and Schur algorithms, Cholesky decomposition, Riccati equation solution [11] and Newton-Raphson iteration [12].

Example 11. Applying the Bilinear Transform (15) to the continuous-time low-pass plant $G(s) = (s + 1)^{-1}$ for a sample frequency of 2 Hz yields $G(z) = 0.2(z+1)(z-0.6)^{-1}$. With $Q = R = 1$, the measurement spectral density (48) is $\Phi_{uu}(z) = \frac{(1.08z-0.517)}{(z-0.6)} \times \frac{(-0.517z+1.08)}{(-0.6z-1.0)}$. By inspection, $\Delta(z) = (1.08z - 0.517)(z - 0.6)^{-1}$ has inside-unit-circle-poles and zeros that satisfy $\Delta(z)\Delta^H(z) = \Phi_{uu}(z)$.

Example 12. Consider the high-pass plant $G(z) = 4.98(z - 0.6)(z + 0.99)^{-1}$ and $Q = R = 1$. The spectral density is $\Phi_{uu}(z) = \frac{(5.39z-2.58)}{(z+0.99)} \times \frac{(-2.58z+5.39)}{(0.99z-1.0)}$. Thus the stable, minimum phase spectral factor is $\Delta(z) = (5.39z - 2.58)(z + 0.99)^{-1}$, since it has inside-unit-circle-poles and zeros.

2.2.17 Calculating Causal Parts

Suppose that a discrete-time transfer function has the form

$$G(z) = c_0 + \sum_{i=1,|a_i|<1}^{n} \frac{d_i}{z-a_i} + \sum_{j=1,|b_j|>1}^{m} \frac{e_j}{z-b_j} \tag{49}$$

$$= c_0 + G_{iucp}(z) + G_{oucp}(z),$$

where $c_0, d_i, e_j \in \mathbb{R}$, $G_{iucp}(z) = \sum_{i=1,|a_i|<1}^{n} \frac{d_i}{z-a_i}$ is the sum of partial fractions having inside-unit-circle-poles and $G_{oucp}(z) = \sum_{j=1,|b_j|>1}^{m} \frac{e_j}{z-b_j}$ is the sum of partial fractions having outside-unit-circle-poles. Assume that the roots of $G(z)$ are distinct and do not lie on the unit circle. In this case the partial fraction coefficients d_i and e_i within (49) can be calculated from the numerator and denominator polynomials of $G(z)$ via $d_i = (z-a_i)G(z)\big|_{z=a_i}$ and $e_j = (z-b_j)G(z)\big|_{z=b_j}$. Previously, in continuous-time, the convention was to define constants to be causal. This is consistent with ensuring that the non-causal part of the discrete-time

"Knowledge rests not upon truth alone, but on error also." *Carl Gustav Jung*

transfer function is zero at $z = 0$. Thus, the non-causal part of $G(z)$, denoted by $\{G(z)\}_-$, is obtained as

$$\{G(z)\}_- = G_{oucp}(z) - G_{oucp}(0) \tag{50}$$

and the causal part of $G(z)$, denoted by $\{G(z)\}_+$,is whatever remains, that is,

$$\begin{aligned}\{G(z)\}_+ &= G(z) - \{G(z)\}_- \\ &= c_0 + G_{iucp}(z) + G_{oucp}(0).\end{aligned} \tag{51}$$

Hence, the causal part of transfer function can be found by carrying out the following three steps.

(i) If the transfer function is not strictly proper, that is, if the order of the numerator not less than the degree of the denominator, perform synthetic division to extract the constant term.

(ii) Expand out the (strictly proper) transfer function into the sum of partial fractions (49).

(iii) Obtain the causal part from (51), namely, take the sum of the constant term, the partial fractions with inside-unit-circle-poles and the partial fractions with outside-unit-circle-poles evaluated at $z = 0$.

Example 13. Consider the strictly proper transfer function $G(z) = \frac{3z+3.2}{z^2+2.6z+1.2} = \frac{3z+3.2}{(z+0.6)(z+2)} = \frac{1}{z+0.6} + \frac{2}{z+2}$. It follows from (50) and (51) that $\{G(z)\}_- = \frac{2}{z+2} - 1 = \frac{-z}{z+2}$ and $\{G(z)\}_+ = \frac{1}{z+0.6} + 1 = \frac{z+1.6}{z+0.6}$, respectively. It is easily verified that $G(z) = \{G(z)\}_+ + \{G(z)\}_-$.

Example 14. Consider the proper transfer function $G(z) = \frac{2z^2+8.2z+5.6}{z^2+2.6z+1.2}$. Carrying out synthetic division results in $G(z) = 2 + \frac{1}{z+0.6} + \frac{2}{z+2}$. It follows from (50) and (51) that $\{G(z)\}_- = \frac{2}{z+2} - 1 = \frac{-z}{z+2}$ and $\{G(z)\}_+ = \frac{1}{z+0.6} + 1 + 2 = \frac{3z+2.8}{z+0.6}$, respectively.

"The beginning of knowledge is the discovery of something we do not understand." *Frank Patrick Herber*

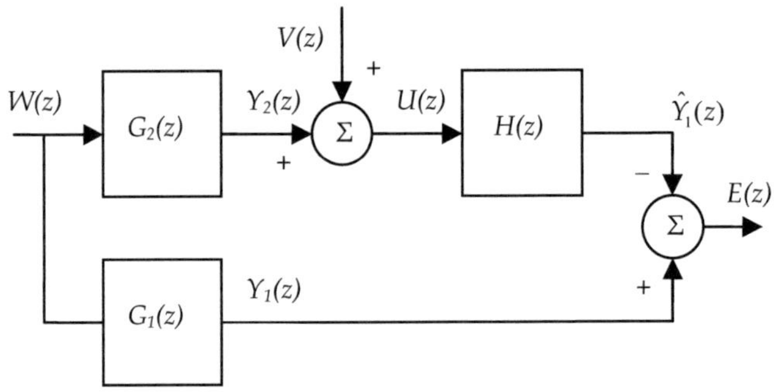

Figure 3. The general z-domain filtering problem.

2.3 Minimum-Mean-Square-Error Filtering

2.3.1 Filter Derivation

This section derives the optimal non-causal minimum-mean-square-error solution for the problem configuration of Fig. 3. The derivation is identical to the continuous-time case which is presented in Chapter 1. It is assumed that the parameters of the stable transfer function $G_2(z) = C_2(zI - A)^{-1}B + D_2$ are known. Let $Y_2(z)$, $W(z)$, $V(z)$ and $U(z)$ denote the z-transform of a system's output, process noise, measurement noise and observations, respectively. Then it follows from (47) that the z-transform of the measurements is

$$U(z) = Y_2(z) + V(z). \tag{52}$$

Consider a fictitious reference system $G_1(z) = C_1(zI - A)^{-1}B + D_1$ as shown in Fig. 3. The problem is to design a filter transfer function $H(z)$ to calculate estimates $\hat{Y}_1(z) = H(z)U(z)$ of $Y_1(z)$ so that the energy $\int_{-j\infty}^{j\infty} E(z)E^H(z)dz$ of the estimation error

$$E(z) = \hat{Y}_1(z) - Y_1(z) \tag{53}$$

is minimised. It can be seen from Fig. 3 that the estimation error is generated by the system

$$E(z) = -\begin{bmatrix} H(z) & H_2G(z) - G_1(z) \end{bmatrix} \begin{bmatrix} V(z) \\ W(z) \end{bmatrix}. \tag{54}$$

The error power spectrum density matrix is given by the covariance of $E(z)$, that is,

$$\Phi_{ee}(z) = E(z)E^H(z) \tag{55}$$

"I shall try to correct errors when shown to be errors; and I shall adopt new views so fast as they shall appear to be true views." *Abraham Lincoln*

$$=\begin{bmatrix} H(z) & HG_2(z)-G_1(z) \end{bmatrix}\begin{bmatrix} R & 0 \\ 0 & Q \end{bmatrix}\begin{bmatrix} H^H(z) \\ G_2^H H^H(z)-G_1^H(z) \end{bmatrix}$$

$$= G_1QG_1^H(z) - G_1QG_2^H H^H(z) - HG_2QG_1^H(z) + H\Delta\Delta^H H^H(z),$$

where

$$\Delta\Delta^H(z) = G_2QG_2^H(z) + R \tag{56}$$

is the spectral density matrix of the measurements. Completing the square within (55) yields

$$\begin{aligned}\Phi_{ee}(z) &= G_1QG_1^H(z) - G_1QG_2^H(\Delta\Delta^H)^{-1}G_2QG_1^H(z) \\ &\quad + (H\Delta(z) - G_1QG_2^H\Delta^{-H}(z))(H\Delta(z) - G_1QG_2^H\Delta^{-H}(z))^H,\end{aligned} \tag{57}$$

in which $\Delta^{-H}(z) = (\Delta^H)^{-1}(z)$. It follows that the total energy of the error signal can be expressed as

$$\begin{aligned}\int_{-e^{j\omega T}}^{e^{j\omega T}} \Phi_{ee}(z)dz &= \int_{-e^{j\omega T}}^{e^{j\omega T}} G_1QG_1^H(z) - G_1QG_2^H(\Delta\Delta^H)^{-1}G_2QG_1^H(z)dz \\ &\quad + \int_{-e^{j\omega T}}^{e^{j\omega T}} (H\Delta(z) - G_1QG_2^H\Delta^{-H}(z))(H\Delta(z) - G_1QG_2^H\Delta^{-H}(z))^H dz.\end{aligned} \tag{58}$$

The first term on the right-hand-side of (58) is independent of $H(z)$ and represents a lower bound of $\int_{-e^{j\omega T}}^{e^{j\omega T}} \Phi_{ee}(z)dz$. The second term on the right-hand-side of (58) may be minimised by a judicious choice for $H(z)$.

Theorem 1: *The optimal solution for the above linear time-invariant estimation problem with measurements (52) and error (53) is*

$$H(z) = G_1QG_2^H\Delta^{-H}\Delta^{-1}(z), \tag{59}$$

which minimises $\int_{-e^{j\omega T}}^{e^{j\omega T}} \Phi_{ee}(z)dz$.

Proof: *The result follows by setting* $H\Delta(z) - G_1QG_2^H\Delta^{-H}(z)$ *equal to the zero matrix within (58).* □

By Parseval's theorem, the minimum mean-square-error solution (59) also minimises $\|e(z)\|_2^2$. The solution (59) is non-causal because the factor $G_2^H(\Delta^H)^{-1}(z)$ possesses outside-unit-circle poles. This optimal non-causal solution is actually a smoother, which can be realised by a combination of forward and backward processes.

"I think anybody who doesn't think I'm smart enough to handle the job is underestimating." *George Walker Bush*

The transfer function matrix of the optimal causal solution or filter is obtained by setting the setting the causal part of $H\Delta(z) - G_1QG_2^H\Delta^{-H}(z)$ equal to the zero matrix, resulting in $\{H(z)\Delta^{-1}(z)\}_+ = \{G_1QG_2^H(\Delta^H)^{-1}\}_+$, that is $H(z)\Delta^{-1}(z) = \{G_1QG_2^H(\Delta^H)^{-1}\}_+$, which implies

$$H(z) = \left\{G_1QG_2^H(\Delta^H)^{-1}\right\}_+ \Delta^{-1}(z) . \tag{60}$$

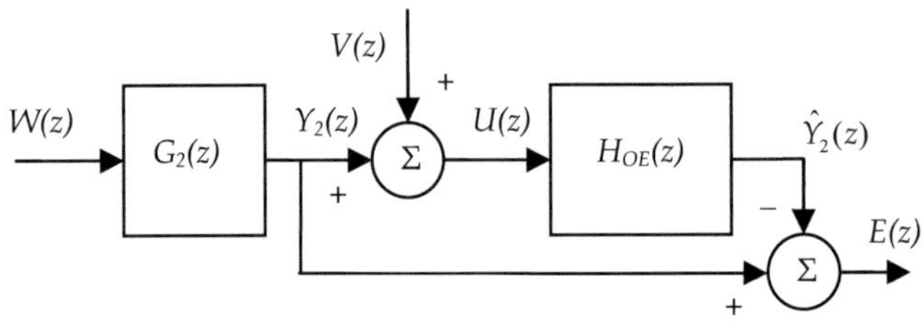

Figure 4. The z-domain output estimation problem.

2.3.2 Output Estimation

In output estimation, it is desired to estimate the output $Y_2(z)$ from the measurements $U(z)$, in which case the reference system is the same as the generating system, as shown in Fig. 4. The optimal non-causal solution (59) with $G_1(z) = G_2(z)$ becomes

$$H_{OE}(z) = G_2QG_2^H\Delta^{-H}\Delta^{-1}(z) . \tag{61}$$

Substituting $G_2QG_2^H(z) = \Delta\Delta^H(z) - R$ into (61) leads to the alternative form

$$\begin{aligned} H_{OE}(z) &= (\Delta\Delta^H - R)(\Delta\Delta^H)^{-1}(z) \\ &= I - R\Delta^{-H}\Delta^{-1}(z) . \end{aligned} \tag{62}$$

The solutions (61) and (62) are non-causal since $G^H(z)$ and $\Delta^{-H}(z)$ are non-causal. The optimal smoother or non-causal filter for output estimation is obtained by substituting $G_1(z) = G_2(z)$ into (60), namely,

$$H_{OE}(z) = \left\{G_2QG_2^H\Delta^{-H}\right\}_+ \Delta^{-1}(z) . \tag{63}$$

An alternative form arises by substituting $GQG^H(z) = \Delta\Delta^H(z) - R$ into (63), which results in

$$\begin{aligned} H_{OE}(z) &= \{\Delta(z) - R\Delta^{-H}\}_+\Delta^{-1}(z) \\ &= I - R\{\Delta^{-H}\}_+\Delta^{-1}(z) . \end{aligned} \tag{64}$$

In [10], it is recognised that $\{\Delta^H(z)\}_+ = \lim_{z\to\infty}\Delta(z)$, which is equivalent to $\{\Delta^H(z)\}_+ = \Delta^H(0)$. It follows that

---

"There is much pleasure to be gained from useless knowledge." *Bertrand Arthur William Russell*

$$H_{OE}(z) = I - R\Delta^{-H}(0)\Delta^{-1}(z)\,, \tag{65}$$

which eliminates the need for calculating causal parts.

Example 15. Consider $G_2(z) = (z + 0.2)(z + 0.5)^{-1}$ together with $R = Q = 1$. The spectral factor is $\Delta(z) = (1.43z + 0.489)(z + 0.5)^{-1}$, which leads to $G_2QG_2^H\Delta^{-H}(z) = (0.2z^2 + 1.04z + 0.2)(0.489z^2 + 1.67z + 0.716)^{-1}$ and $\{G_2QG_2^H\Delta^{-H}(z)\}_+ = (0.734z + 0.14)(z + 0.5)^{-1}$. Hence, from (63), $H_{OE}(z) = (0.513z + 0.098)(z + 0.341)^{-1}$. The same solution can be calculated using $\Delta^{-H}(0) = 0.698$ within (65).

When the measurement noise becomes negligibly small, the output estimator approaches a short circuit, that is,

$$\lim_{R \to 0, e^{j\omega T} \to 0} \left| H_{OE}(z) \right| = I\,, \tag{66}$$

The above observation can be verified by substituting $R = 0$ into (65). This asymptote is consistent with intuition, that is, when the measurements are perfect, output estimation will be superfluous.

Example 16. Substituting R = 0.001 within Example 15 yields the filter H(z) = (0.999z + 0.2)(z + 0.2)-1, which illustrates the low measurement noise asymptote (66).

2.3.3 Input Estimation

In input estimation or equalisation problems, $G_2(z)$ is known as the channel model and it is desired to estimate the input process $w(t)$, as depicted in Fig. 5. The simplification of the optimum non-causal solution (59) for the case of $G_1(z) = I$ is

$$H_{IE}(z) = QG_2^H\Delta^{-H}\Delta^{-1}(z)\,, \tag{67}$$

Assume that: the channel model $G_2(z)$ is proper, that is, the order of the numerator is the same as the order of the denominator; and that the channel model $G_2(z)$ is stable and minimum phase, that is, its poles and zeros are inside the unit circle. The causal equaliser for proper, stable, minimum-phase channels is obtained by substituting $G_1(z) = I$ into (60)

$$\begin{aligned} H_{IE}(z) &= \{QG_2^H\Delta^{-H}\}_+\Delta^{-1}(z) \\ &= QG_2^H(0)\Delta^{-H}(0)\Delta^{-1}(z)\,. \end{aligned} \tag{68}$$

Under the above assumptions, the causal equaliser may be written equivalently as

$$H_{IE}(z) = \{G_2^{-1}G_2QG_2^H\Delta^{-H}\}_+\Delta^{-1}(z) \tag{69}$$

$$= \{G_2^{-1}(\Delta\Delta^H - R)\Delta^{-H}\}_+\Delta^{-1}(z)$$

$$= G_2^{-1}(I - R\{\Delta^{-H}\}_+\Delta^{-1}(z)) \tag{70}$$

"He who knows nothing is closer to the truth than he whose mind is filled with falsehoods and errors." *Thomas Jefferson.*

$$= G_2^{-1}(I - R\Delta^{-H}(0)\Delta^{-1}(z))$$

Thus, the equaliser is equivalent to a product of the channel inverse and the output estimator. It follows that when the measurement noise becomes negligibly small, the equaliser estimates the inverse of the system model, that is,

$$\lim_{R \to 0} H_{IE}(z) = G_2^{-1}(z)\,, \tag{71}$$

The above observation follows by substituting R = 0 into (69). In other words, if the channel model is invertible and signal to noise ratio is sufficiently high, the equaliser will estimate $w(t)$. When measurement noise is present then the solution trades off channel inversion and filtering. In the high measurement noise case, the equaliser approaches an open circuit, that is,

$$\lim_{Q \to 0, e^{j\omega T} \to 0} \left| H_{IE}(z) \right| = 0\,. \tag{72}$$

The above observation can be verified by substituting $\Delta\Delta^H = R$ into (70). Thus, when the equalisation problem is dominated by measurement noise, the estimation error is minimised by ignoring the data.

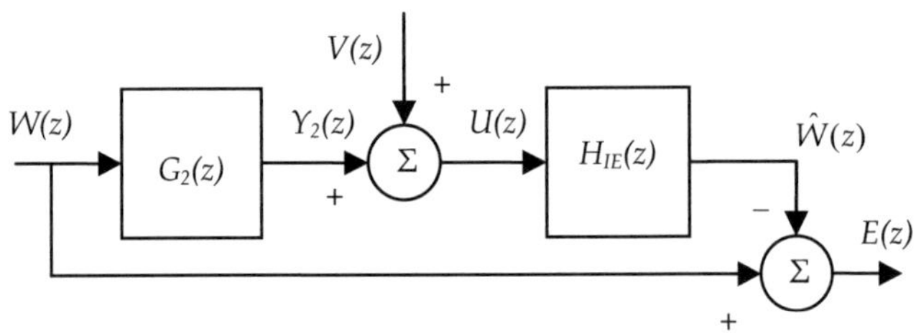

Figure 5. The z-domain input estimation problem.

Example 17. Consider the high-pass plant $G_2(s) = 100(s + 0.1)(s + 10)^{-1}$. Application of the bilinear transform for a sample frequency of 2 Hz yields $G_2(z) = (29.2857z - 27.8571)(z + 0.4286)^{-1}$. With Q = 1 and R = 0.001, the spectral factor is $\Delta(z) = (29.2861z + - 27.8568)(z + 0.4286)^{-1}$. From (67), $H_{IE}(z) = (z + 0.4286)(29.2861z - 27.8568)^{-1}$, which is high-pass and illustrates (71).

Example 18. Applying the bilinear transform for a sample frequency of 2 Hz to the low-pass plant $G_2(z) = (s + 10)(s + 0.1)^{-1}$ results in $G_2(z) = (3.4146z - 1.4634)(z - 0.9512)^{-1}$. With Q = 1 and R = 0.001, the spectral factor is $\Delta(z) = (3.4151z + 1.4629)(z - 0.9512)^{-1}$. From (67), $H_{IE}(z) = (z - 0.9512)(3.4156z + 1.4631)^{-1}$, which is low pass and is consistent with (71).

"They say that time changes things, but you actually have to change them yourself." *Andy Warhol*

	ASSUMPTIONS	MAIN RESULTS
Signals and systems	$E\{w_k\} = E\{W(z)\} = E\{v_k\} = E\{V(z)\} = 0$. $E\{w_k w_k^T\} = E\{W(z)W^T(z)\} = Q > 0$ and $E\{v_k v_k^T\} = E\{V(z)V^T(z)\} = R > 0$ are known. A, B, C_1, C_2, D_1 and D_2 are known. $G_1(z)$ and $G_2(z)$ are stable, *i.e.*, $\lvert \lambda_i(A) \rvert < 1$.	$G_1(z) = C_1(zI - A)^{-1}B + D_1$ $G_2(z) = C_2(zI - A)^{-1}B + D_2$
Spectral factorisation	$\Delta(z)$ and $\Delta^{-1}(z)$ are stable, *i.e.*, the poles and zeros of $\Delta(z)$ are inside the unit circle.	$\Delta\Delta^H(z) = G_2QG_2^H(z) + R$
Non-causal solution		$H(z) = G_1QG_2^H(\Delta^H)^{-1}\Delta^{-1}(z)$
Causal solution		$H(z) = \left\{G_1QG_2^H(\Delta^H)^{-1}\right\}_+ \Delta^{-1}(z)$

Table 1. Main results for the discrete-time general filtering problem.

2.4 Conclusion

Systems are written in the time-domain as difference equations

$$a_n y_{k-n} + a_{n-1} y_{k-n+1} + \ldots + a_1 y_{k-1} + a_0 y_k = b_m w_{k-m} + b_{m-1} w_{k-m+1} + \ldots + b_1 w_{k-1} + b_0 w_k ,$$

which can expressed as polynomial transfer functions in the z-transform variable

$$Y(z) = \left[\frac{b_m z^{-m} + b_{m-1} z^{-m+1} + \ldots + b_1 z^{-1} + b_0}{a_n z^{-n} + a_{n-1} z^{-n+1} + \ldots + a_1 z^{-1} + a_0} \right] W(z) = G(z)W(z) .$$

It can be seen that knowledge of a system's differential equation is sufficient to identify its transfer function. The optimal Wiener solution minimises the energy of the error and the mean-square-error and the main results are summarised in Table 1. The noncausal (or smoother) solution has unstable factors and can only be realised by a combination of forward and backward processes.

It is noted that $\{\Delta^H(z)\}_+ = \lim_{z\to\infty} \Delta(z) = \Delta^H(0)$, which can simplify calculating causal parts. For example, in output estimation problems where $G_1(z) = G_2(z)$, the minimum-mean-square-

---

"Time is a great teacher, but unfortunately it kills all its pupils." *Louis Hector Berlioz*

error solution is $H_{OE}(z) = I - R\Delta^{-H}(0)\Delta^{-1}(z)$. In the single-input-single-output case, when the measurement noise becomes negligible, the output estimator approaches a short circuit. Conversely, when the single-input-single-output problem is dominated by measurement noise, the output estimator approaches an open circuit.

In input estimation problems, $G_1(z) = I$. If the channel model is invertible, the optimal causal equaliser is given by $H_{IE}(z)$ $H_{IE}(z) = QG_2^H(0)\Delta^{-H}(0)\Delta^{-1}(z)$. When the measurement noise becomes negligible, that is, $\Delta^{-1}(z) \approx G_2^H(z)$, the optimal equaliser approaches the channel inverse. Conversely, when the problem is dominated by measurement noise, the equaliser approaches an open circuit.

2.5 Problems

Problem 1. Consider the error spectral density matrix

$$\Phi_{ee}(z) = [H\Delta - G_1QG_2^H(\Delta^H)^{-1}][H\Delta - G_1QG_2^H(\Delta^H)^{-1}]^H(z) + [G_1QG_1^H - G_1QG_2^H(\Delta\Delta^H)^{-1}G_2QG_1^H](z).$$

(a) Derive the optimal non-causal solution.
(b) Derive the optimal causal filter from (a).
(c) Derive the optimal non-causal output estimator.
(d) Derive the optimal causal filter from (c).
(e) Derive the optimal non-causal input estimator.
(f) Derive the optimal causal equaliser assuming that the channel inverse exists.

Problem 2. Derive the asymptotes for the following single-input-single-output estimation problems.

(a) Non-causal output estimation at $R = 0$.
(b) Non-causal output estimation at $Q = 0$.
(c) Causal output estimation at $R = 0$.
(d) Causal output estimation at $Q = 0$.
(e) Non-causal input estimation at $R = 0$.
(f) Non-causal input estimation at $Q = 0$.
(g) Causal input estimation at $R = 0$.
(h) Causal input estimation at $Q = 0$.

Problem 3. In respect of the output estimation problem with $G(z) = (z - \beta)(z - \alpha)^{-1}$, $\alpha = -0.3$, $\beta = -0.5$ and $Q=1$, verify the following.

(a) $R = 10$ yields $H(z) = (0.0948z + 0.0272)(z + 0.4798)^{-1}$.
(b) $R = 1$ yields $H(z) = (0.5059z + 0.1482)(z + 0.3953)^{-1}$.
(c) $R = 0.1$ yields $H(z) = (0.90941z + 0.2717)(z + 0.3170)^{-1}$.
(d) $R = 0.01$ yields $H(z) = (0.9901z + 0.2969)(z + 0.3018)^{-1}$.
(e) $R = 0.001$ yields $H(z) = (0.9990z + 0.2997)(z + 0.3002)^{-1}$.

"If I have ever made any valuable discoveries, it has been owing more to patient attention, that to any other talent." *Isaac Newton*

Problem 4. In respect of the input estimation problem with $G(z) = (z - \beta)(z - \alpha)^{-1}$, $\alpha = -0.9$, $\beta = -0.1$ and Q=1, verify the following.

(a) $R = 10$ yields $H(z) = (z + 0.1)(11.5988z + 1.9000)^{-1}$.
(b) $R = 1$ yields $H(z) = (z + 0.1)(2.4040z + 1.0000)^{-1}$.
(b) $R = 0.1$ yields $H(z) = (z + 0.1)(1.2468z + 0.9100)^{-1}$.
(d) $R = 0.01$ yields $H(z) = (z + 0.1)(1.0381z + 0.9010)^{-1}$.
(e) $R = 0.001$ yields $H(z) = (z + 0.1)(1.043z + 0.9001)^{-1}$.

2.6 Glossary

The following terms have been introduced within this section.

k	The integer-valued time variable. For example, $k \in (-\infty, \infty)$ and $k \in (0, \infty)$ denote $-\infty < k < \infty$ and $0 \le k < \infty$, respectively.
$w_k \in \mathbb{R}^n$	A discrete-time, real-valued, n-element stochastic input signal.
w	The set of w_k over a prescribed interval.
$\mathcal{G}: \mathbb{R}^p \to \mathbb{R}^q$	A linear system that operates on a p-element input signal and produces a q-element output signal.
$y = \mathcal{G}w$	The output of a linear system $\mathcal{G}$ that operates on an input signal w.
A, B, C, D	Time-invariant state space matrices of appropriate dimension. The system $\mathcal{G}$ is assumed to have the realisation $x_{k+1} = Ax_k + Bw_k$, $y_k = Cx_k + Dw_k$ in which w_k is known as the process noise or input signal.
v_k	A stationary stochastic measurement noise signal.
δ_{jk}	The Kronecker delta function.
Q and R	Time-invariant covariance matrices of stochastic signals w_k and v_k, respectively.
$Y(z)$	The z-transform of a continuous-time signal y_k.
$G(z)$	The transfer function matrix of the system $\mathcal{G}$. For example, the transfer function matrix of the system $x_{k+1} = Ax_k + Bw_k$, $y_k = Cx_k + Dw_k$ is given by $G(z) = C(zI - A)^{-1}B + D$.
$\langle v, w \rangle$	The inner product of two discrete-time signals v and w which is defined by $\langle v, w \rangle = \sum_{k=-\infty}^{\infty} v_k^T w_k$.
$\|w\|_2$	The 2-norm of the discrete-time signal w which is defined by $\|w\|_2$ = $\sqrt{\langle w, w \rangle}$ = $\sqrt{\sum_{k=-\infty}^{\infty} w_k^T w_k}$.
ℓ_2	The set of continuous-time signals having finite 2-norm, which is known as the Lebesgue 2-space (see [3]).

"If your result needs a statistician then you should design a better experiment." *Baron Ernest Rutherford*

Asymptotic stability	A linear discrete-time system $\mathcal{G}$ is said to be asymptotically stable if its output $y \in \ell_2$ for any $w \in \ell_2$. If the real parts of the state matrix eigenvalues are inside the unit circle or equivalently if the real part of transfer function's poles are inside the unit circle then the system is stable.
T_s	Sample period.
$\mathcal{G}^H$	The adjoint of $\mathcal{G}$. The adjoint of a system having the state-space parameters $\{A, B, C, D\}$ is a system parameterised by $\{ A^T, -C^T, -B^T, D^T\}$.
$G^H(z)$	The adjoint (or Hermitian transpose) of the transfer function matrix $G(z)$.
$\Phi_{ee}(z)$	The spectral density matrix of the measurements e.
$\Delta(z)$	The spectral factor of $\Phi_{uu}(z)$ which satisfies $\Delta\Delta^H(z) = GQG^H(z) + R$. For brevity denote $\Delta^{-H}(z) = (\Delta^H)^{-1}(z)$.
$G^{-1}(z)$	The inverse of the transfer function matrix $G(z)$.
$G^{-H}(z)$	The inverse of the adjoint transfer function matrix $G^H(z)$.
$\{G(z)\}_+$	The causal part of the transfer function matrix $G(z)$.
$H(z)$	Transfer function matrix of the minimum mean-square-error solution.
$H_{OE}(z)$	Transfer function matrix of the minimum mean-square-error solution specialised for output estimation.
$H_{IE}(z)$	Transfer function matrix of the minimum mean-square-error solution specialised for input estimation.

2.7 References

[1] N. Wiener, *Extrapolation, interpolation and smoothing of stationary time series with engineering applications*, The MIT Press, Cambridge Mass.; Wiley, New York; Chapman & Hall, London, 1949.

[2] P. Masani, "Wiener's Contributions to Generalized Harmonic Analysis, Prediction Theory and Filter Theory", *Bulletin of the American Mathematical Society*, vol. 72, no. 1, pt. 2, pp. 73 - 125, 1966.

[3] C. A. Desoer and M. Vidyasagar, *Feedback Systems : Input Output Properties*, Academic Press, N.Y., 1975.

[4] F. L. Lewis, L. Xie and D. Popa, *Optimal and Robust Estimation With an Introduction to Stochastic Control Theory*, Second Edition, CRC Press, Taylor & Francis Group, 2008.

[5] A. P. Sage and J. L. Melsa, *Estimation Theory with Applications to Communications and Control*, McGraw-Hill Book Company, New York, 1971.

[6] K. Ogata, *Discrete-time Control Systems*, Prentice-Hall, Inc., Englewood Cliffs, New Jersey, 1987.

[7] S. Shats and U. Shaked, "Discrete-Time Filtering of Noise Correlated Continuous-Time Processes: Modelling and derivation of the Sampling Period Sensitivities", *IEEE Transactions on Automatic Control*, vol. 36, no. 1, pp. 115 - 119, Jan. 1991.

"There's two possible outcomes: if the result confirms the hypothesis, then you've made a discovery. If the result is contrary to the hypothesis, then you've made a discovery." *Enrico Fermi*

[8] P. G. Savage, *Strapdown Analytics*, Strapdown Associates, Maple Plain, Minnesota, USA, vol. 1 and 2, 2000.
[9] G. A. Einicke, "Optimal and Robust Noncausal Filter Formulations", *IEEE Transactions on Signal Processing*, vol. 54, no. 3, pp. 1069 – 1077, Mar. 2006.
[10] U. Shaked, "A transfer function approach to the linear discrete stationary filtering and the steady state discrete optimal control problems", *International Journal of Control*, vol. 29, no. 2, pp 279 - 291, 1979.
[11] A. H. Sayed and T. Kailath, "A Survey of Spectral Factorization Methods", *Numerical Linear Algebra with Applications*, vol. 8, pp. 467 - 496, 2001.
[12] H. J. Orchard and A. N. Wilson, "On the Computation of a Minimum-Phase Spectral Factor", *IEEE Transactions on. Circuits and Systems I: Fundamental Theory and Applications*, vol. 50, no. 3, pp. 365 - 375, Mar. 2003.

"One of the greatest discoveries a man makes, one of his greatest surprises, is to find he can do what he was afraid he couldn't." *Henry Ford*

3

Continuous-Time Minimum-Variance Filtering

3.1 Introduction

Rudolf E. Kalman studied discrete-time linear dynamic systems for his master's thesis at MIT in 1954. He commenced work at the Research Institute for Advanced Studies (RIAS) in Baltimore during 1957 and nominated Richard S. Bucy to join him in 1958 [1]. Bucy recognised that the nonlinear ordinary differential equation studied by an Italian mathematician, Count Jacopo F. Riccati, in around 1720, now called the Riccati equation, is equivalent to the Wiener-Hopf equation for the case of finite dimensional systems [1], [2]. In November 1958, Kalman recasted the frequency domain methods developed by Norbert Wiener and Andrei N. Kolmogorov in the 1940s to state-space form [2]. Kalman noted in his 1960 paper [3] that generalising the Wiener solution to nonstationary problems was difficult, which motivated his development of the optimal discrete-time filter in a state-space framework. He described the continuous-time version with Bucy in 1961 [4] and published a generalisation in 1963 [5]. Bucy later investigated the monotonicity and stability of the underlying Riccati equation [6]. The continuous-time minimum-variance filter is now commonly attributed to both Kalman and Bucy.

Compared to the Wiener Filter, Kalman's state-space approach has the following advantages.

- It is applicable to time-varying problems.
- As noted in [7], [8], the state-space parameters can be linearisations of nonlinear models.
- The burdens of spectral factorisation and pole-zero cancelation are replaced by the easier task of solving a Riccati equation.
- It is a more intuitive model-based approach in which the estimated states correspond to those within the signal generation process.

Kalman's research at the RIAS was concerned with estimation and control for aerospace systems which was funded by the Air Force Office of Scientific Research. His explanation of why the dynamics-based Kalman filter is more important than the purely stochastic Wiener filter is that "Newton is more important than Gauss" [1]. The continuous-time Kalman filter produces state estimates $\hat{x}(t)$ from the solution of a simple differential equation

$$\dot{\hat{x}}(t) = A(t)\hat{x}(t) + K(t)\big(z(t) - C(t)\hat{x}(t)\big),$$

"What a weak, credulous, incredulous, unbelieving, superstitious, bold, frightened, what a ridiculous world ours is, as far as concerns the mind of man. How full of inconsistencies, contradictions and absurdities it is. I declare that taking the average of many minds that have recently come before me ... I should prefer the obedience, affections and instinct of a dog before it." *Michael Faraday*

in which it is tacitly assumed that the model is correct, the noises are zero-mean, white and uncorrelated. It is straightforward to include nonzero means, coloured and correlated noises. In practice, the true model can be elusive but a simple (low-order) solution may return a cost benefit.

The Kalman filter can be derived in many different ways. In an early account [3], a quadratic cost function was minimised using orthogonal projections. Other derivation methods include deriving a maximum *a posteriori* estimate, using Itô's calculus, calculus-of-variations, dynamic programming, invariant imbedding and from the Wiener-Hopf equation [6] - [17]. This chapter provides a brief derivation of the optimal filter using a conditional mean (or equivalently, a least mean square error) approach.

The developments begin by introducing a time-varying state-space model. Next, the state transition matrix is defined, which is used to derive a Lyapunov differential equation. The Kalman filter follows immediately from a conditional mean formula. Its filter gain is obtained by solving a Riccati differential equation corresponding to the estimation error system. Generalisations for problems possessing deterministic inputs, correlated process and measurement noises, and direct feedthrough terms are described subsequently. Finally, it is shown that the Kalman filter reverts to the Wiener filter when the problems are time-invariant.

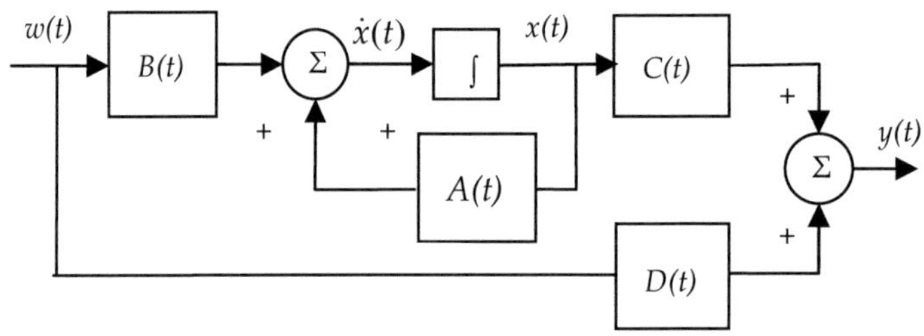

Figure 1. The continuous-time system $\mathcal{G}$ operates on the input signal $w(t) \in \mathbb{R}^m$ and produces the output signal $y(t) \in \mathbb{R}^p$.

3.2 Prerequisites

3.2.1 The Time-varying Signal Model

The focus initially is on time-varying problems over a finite time interval $t \in [0, T]$. A system $\mathcal{G}: \mathbb{R}^m \rightarrow \mathbb{R}^p$ is assumed to have the state-space representation

$$\dot{x}(t) = A(t)x(t) + B(t)w(t) , \tag{1}$$

$$y(t) = C(t)x(t) + D(t)w(t) , \tag{2}$$

where $A(t) \in \mathbb{R}^{n\times n}$, $B(t) \in \mathbb{R}^{n\times m}$, $C(t) \in \mathbb{R}^{p\times n}$, $D(t) \in \mathbb{R}^{p\times p}$ and $w(t)$ is a zero-mean white process noise with $E\{w(t)w^T(\tau)\} = Q(t)\delta(t - \tau)$, in which $\delta(t)$ is the Dirac delta function. This

"A great deal of my work is just playing with equations and seeing what they give." *Paul Arien Maurice Dirac*

system in depicted in Fig. 1. In many problems of interest, signals are band-limited, that is, the direct feedthrough matrix, $D(t)$, is zero. Therefore, the simpler case of $D(t) = 0$ is addressed first and the inclusion of a nonzero $D(t)$ is considered afterwards.

3.2.2 The State Transition Matrix

The state transition matrix is introduced below which concerns the linear differential equation (1).

Lemma 1: *The equation (1) has the solution*

$$x(t) = \Phi(t,t_0)x(t_0) + \int_{t_0}^{t} \Phi(t,s)B(s)w(s)ds \, , \tag{3}$$

where the state transition matrix, $\Phi(t,t_0)$, *satisfies*

$$\dot{\Phi}(t,t_0) = \frac{d\Phi(t,t_0)}{dt} = A(t)\Phi(t,t_0) \, , \tag{4}$$

with boundary condition

$$\Phi(t,t) = I. \tag{5}$$

Proof: *Differentiating both sides of (3) and using Leibnitz's rule, that is,* $\frac{\partial}{\partial t}\int_{\alpha(t)}^{\beta(t)} f(t,\tau)d\tau$ = $\int_{\alpha(t)}^{\beta(t)} \frac{\partial f(t,\tau)}{\partial t} d\tau - f(t,\alpha)\frac{d\alpha(t)}{dt} + f(t,\beta)\frac{d\beta(t)}{dt}$, *gives*

$$\dot{x}(t) = \dot{\Phi}(t,t_0)x(t_0) + \int_{t_0}^{t} \dot{\Phi}(t,\tau)B(\tau)w(\tau)d\tau + \Phi(t,t)B(t)w(t) \, . \tag{6}$$

Substituting (4) and (5) into the right-hand-side of (6) results in

$$\dot{x}(t) = A(t)\left(\Phi(t,t_0)x(t_0) + \int_{t_0}^{t} \Phi(t,\tau)B(\tau)w(\tau)d\tau\right) + B(t)w(t) \, . \tag{7}$$

□

3.2.3 The Lyapunov Differential Equation

The mathematical expectation, $E\{x(t)x^T(\tau)\}$ of $x(t)x^T(\tau)$, is required below, which is defined as

$$E\{x(t)x^T(\tau)\} = \int_{-\infty}^{\infty} x(t)x^T(\tau) f_{xx} x(t)x^T(\tau))dx(t) \, , \tag{8}$$

where $f_{xx}(x(t)x^T(\tau))$ is the probability density function of $x(t)x^T(\tau)$. A useful property of expectations is demonstrated in the following example.

"Life is good for only two things, discovering mathematics and teaching mathematics." *Siméon Denis Poisson*

Example 1. Suppose that $x(t)$ is a stochastic random variable and $h(t)$ is a continuous function, then

$$E\left\{\int_a^b h(t)x(t)x^T(\tau)dt\right\} = \int_a^b h(t)E\{x(t)x^T(\tau)\}dt . \tag{9}$$

To verify this, expand the left-hand-side of (9) to give

$$\begin{aligned} E\left\{\int_a^b h(t)x(t)x^T(\tau)dt\right\} &= \int_{-\infty}^{\infty}\int_a^b h(t)x(t)x^T(\tau)dt f_{xx}(x(t)x^T(\tau))dx(t) \\ &= \int_{-\infty}^{\infty}\int_a^b h(t)x(t)x^T(\tau)f_{xx}(x(t)x^T(\tau)dtdx(t) . \end{aligned} \tag{10}$$

Using Fubini's theorem, that is, $\int_c^d\int_a^b g(x,y)dxdy = \int_a^b\int_c^d g(x,y)dydx$, within (10) results in

$$\begin{aligned} E\left\{\int_a^b h(t)x(t)x^T(\tau)dt\right\} &= \int_a^b\int_{-\infty}^{\infty} h(t)x(t)x^T(\tau)f_{xx}(x(t)x^T(\tau))dx(t)dt \\ &= \int_a^b h(t)\int_{-\infty}^{\infty} x(t)x^T(\tau)f_{xx}(x(t)x^T(\tau))dx(t)dt . \end{aligned} \tag{11}$$

The result (9) follows from the definition (8) within (11).

The Dirac delta function, $\delta(t) = \begin{cases} \infty & t = 0 \\ 0 & t \neq 0 \end{cases}$, satisfies the identity $\int_{-\infty}^{\infty}\delta(t)dt = 1$. In the foregoing development, use is made of the partitioning

$$\int_{-\infty}^{0}\delta(t)dt = \int_0^{\infty}\delta(t)dt = 0.5 . \tag{12}$$

Lemma 2: *In respect of equation (1), assume that $w(t)$ is a zero-mean white process with $E\{w(t)w^T(\tau)\} = Q(t)\delta(t-\tau)$ that is uncorrelated with $x(t_0)$, namely, $E\{w(t)x^T(t_0)\} = 0$. Then the covariances $P(t,\tau) = E\{x(t)x^T(\tau)\}$ and $\dot{P}(t,\tau) = \frac{d}{dt}E\{x(t)x^T(\tau)\}$ satisfy the Lyapunov differential equation*

$$\dot{P}(t,\tau) = A(t)P(t,\tau) + P(t,\tau)A^T(\tau) + B(t)Q(t)B^T(t) . \tag{13}$$

Proof: *Using (1) within $\frac{d}{dt}E\{x(t)x^T(\tau)\} = E\{\dot{x}(t)x^T(\tau) + x(t)\dot{x}^T(\tau)\}$ yields*

$$\begin{aligned} \dot{P}(t,\tau) &= E\{A(t)x(t)x^T(\tau) + B(t)w(t)x^T(\tau)\} + E\{x(t)x^T(\tau)A^T(\tau) + x(t)w^T(\tau)B^T(\tau)\} \\ &= A(t)P(t,\tau) + P(t,\tau)A^T(\tau) + E\{B(t)w(t)x^T(\tau)\} + E\{x(t)w^T(\tau)B^T(\tau)\} . \end{aligned} \tag{14}$$

"It is a mathematical fact that the casting of this pebble from my hand alters the centre of gravity of the universe." *Thomas Carlyle*

It follows from (1) and (3) that

$$\begin{aligned} E\{B(t)w(t)x^T(\tau)\} &= B(t)E\{w(t)x^T(0)\Phi(t,0)\} + B(t)E\left\{\int_{t_0}^{t} w(t)w^T(\tau)B^T(\tau)\Phi(t,\tau)d\tau\right\} \\ &= B(t)E\{w(t)x^T(0)\Phi(t,0)\} + B(t)\int_{t_0}^{t} E\{w(t)w^T(\tau)\}B^T(\tau)\Phi(t,\tau)d\tau \,. \end{aligned} \tag{15}$$

The assumptions $E\{w(t)x^T(t_0)\} = 0$ *and* $E\{w(t)w^T(\tau)\} = Q(t)\delta(t - \tau)$ *together with (15) lead to*

$$\begin{aligned} E\{(B(t)w(t)x^T(\tau)\} &= B(t)Q(t)\int_{t_0}^{t} \delta(t-\tau)B^T(\tau)\Phi(t,\tau)d\tau \\ &= 0.5B(t)Q(t)B^T(t) \,. \end{aligned} \tag{16}$$

The above Lyapunov differential equation follows by substituting (16) into (14). □

In the case $\tau = t$, denote $P(t,t) = E\{x(t)x^T(t)\}$ and $\dot{P}(t,t) = \frac{d}{dt}E\{x(t)x^T(t)\}$. Then the corresponding Lyapunov differential equation is written as

$$\dot{P}(t) = A(t)P(t) + P(t)A^T(t) + B(t)Q(t)B^T(t) \,. \tag{17}$$

3.2.4 Conditional Expectations

The minimum-variance filter derivation that follows employs a conditional expectation formula, which is set out as follows. Consider a stochastic vector $[x^T(t)\;\; y^T(t)]^T$ having means and covariances

$$E\left\{\begin{bmatrix} x(t) \\ y(t) \end{bmatrix}\right\} = \begin{bmatrix} \bar{x} \\ \bar{y} \end{bmatrix} \tag{18}$$

and

$$E\left\{\begin{bmatrix} x(t)-\bar{x} \\ y(t)-\bar{y} \end{bmatrix}\begin{bmatrix} x^T(t)-\bar{x}^T & y^T(t)-\bar{y}^T \end{bmatrix}\right\} = \begin{bmatrix} \Sigma_{xx} & \Sigma_{xy} \\ \Sigma_{yx} & \Sigma_{yy} \end{bmatrix} . \tag{19}$$

respectively, where $\Sigma_{yx} = \Sigma_{xy}^T$. Suppose that it is desired to obtain an estimate of $x(t)$ given $y(t)$, denoted by $E\{x(t) \mid y(t)\}$, which minimises $E\{(x(t) - E\{x(t) \mid y(t)\})(x(t) - E\{x(t) \mid y(t)\})^T\}$. A standard approach (*e.g.*, see [18]) is to assume that the solution for $E\{x(t) \mid y(t)\}$ is affine to $y(t)$, namely,

$$E\{x(t) \mid y(t)\} = Ay(t) + b, \tag{20}$$

"As far as the laws of mathematics refer to reality, they are not certain; and as far as they are certain, they do not refer to reality." *Albert Einstein*

where A and b are unknowns to be found. It follows from (20) that

$$E\{(x(t)-E\{x(t)\,|\,y(t)\})(x(t)-E\{x(t)\,|\,y(t)\})^T\}$$
$$=E\{x(t)x^T(t)-x(t)y^T(t)A^T-x(t)b^T-Ay(t)x^T(t)$$
$$+Ay(t)y^T(t)A^T-Ay(t)b^T-bx^T(t)+by^T(t)A^T+bb^T\}\,. \qquad (21)$$

Substituting $E\{x(t)x^T(t)\}$ = $\overline{x}\overline{x}^T$ + Σ_{xx}, $E\{x(t)y^T(t)\}$ = $\overline{x}\overline{y}^T$ + Σ_{xy}, $E\{y(t)x^T(t)\}$ = $\overline{y}\overline{x}^T$ + Σ_{yx}, $E\{y(t)y^T(t)\}$ = $\overline{y}\overline{y}^T$ + Σ_{yy} into (21) and completing the squares yields

$$E\left\{(x(t)-E\{x(t)\,|\,y(t)\})(x(t)-E\{x(t)\,|\,y(t)\})^T\right\}$$
$$=(\overline{x}-A\overline{y}-b)(\overline{x}-A\overline{y}-b)^T+\begin{bmatrix} I & -A\end{bmatrix}\begin{bmatrix}\Sigma_{xx} & \Sigma_{xy}\\ \Sigma_{yx} & \Sigma_{yy}\end{bmatrix}\begin{bmatrix} I \\ -A^T\end{bmatrix}. \qquad (22)$$

The second term on the right-hand-side of (22) can be rearranged as

$$\begin{bmatrix} I & -A\end{bmatrix}\begin{bmatrix}\Sigma_{xx} & \Sigma_{xy}\\ \Sigma_{yx} & \Sigma_{yy}\end{bmatrix}\begin{bmatrix} I \\ -A^T\end{bmatrix}=(A-\Sigma_{xy}\Sigma_{yy}^{-1})\Sigma_{yy}(A-\Sigma_{xy}\Sigma_{yy}^{-1})^T+\Sigma_{xx}-\Sigma_{xy}\Sigma_{yy}^{-1}\Sigma_{yx}\,.$$

Thus, the choice A = $\Sigma_{xy}\Sigma_{yy}^{-1}$ and b = $\overline{x}-A\overline{y}$ minimises (22), which gives

$$E\{x(t)\,|\,y(t)\}=\overline{x}+\Sigma_{xy}\Sigma_{yy}^{-1}\left(y(t)-\overline{y}\right) \qquad (23)$$

and

$$E\left\{(x(t)-E\{x(t)\,|\,y(t)\})(x(t)-E\{x(t)\,|\,y(t)\})^T\right\}=\Sigma_{xx}+\Sigma_{xy}\Sigma_{yy}^{-1}\Sigma_{yx}\,. \qquad (24)$$

The conditional mean estimate (23) is also known as the linear least mean square estimate [18]. An important property of the conditional mean estimate is established below.

Lemma 3 (Orthogonal projections): *In respect of the conditional mean estimate (23), in which the mean and covariances are respectively defined in (18) and (19), the error vector*

$$\tilde{x}(t)=x(t)-E\{x(t)\,|\,y(t)\}\,. \qquad (25)$$

is orthogonal to y(t), that is, $E\{\tilde{x}(t)y^T(t)\}$ *= 0.*

"Statistics: The only science that enables different experts using the same figures to draw different conclusions." *Evan Esar*

Proof [8],[18]: *From (23) and (25), it can be seen that*

$$E\left\{(\tilde{x}(t)-E\{\tilde{x}(t)\})(y(t)-E\{y(t)\})^T\right\}=E\left\{\left(x(t)-\overline{x}-\Sigma_{xy}\Sigma_{yy}^{-1}(y(t)-\overline{y})\right)\left(y(t)-\overline{y}\right)^T\right\}$$

$$=\Sigma_{xy}-\Sigma_{xy}\Sigma_{yy}^{-1}\Sigma_{yy}$$

$$=0.$$

□

Sufficient background material has now been introduced for the finite-horizon filter (for time-varying systems) to be derived.

3.3 The Continuous-time Minimum-Variance Filter

3.3.1 Derivation of the Optimal Filter

Consider again the linear time-varying system $\mathcal{G}:\mathbb{R}^m \to \mathbb{R}^p$ having the state-space realisation

$$\dot{x}(t)=A(t)x(t)+B(t)w(t), \tag{26}$$

$$y(t)=C(t)x(t), \tag{27}$$

where $A(t)$, $B(t)$, $C(t)$ are of appropriate dimensions and $w(t)$ is a white process with

$$E\{w(t)\}=0,\; E\{w(t)w^T(\tau)\}=Q(t)\delta(t-\tau). \tag{28}$$

Suppose that observations

$$z(t)=y(t)+v(t) \tag{29}$$

are available, where $v(t)\in\mathbb{R}^p$ is a white measurement noise process with

$$E\{v(t)\}=0,\; E\{v(t)v^T(\tau)\}=R(t)\delta(t-\tau) \tag{30}$$

and

$$E\{w(t)v^T(\tau)\}=0. \tag{31}$$

The objective is to design a linear system $\mathcal{H}$ that operates on the measurements $z(t)$ and produces an estimate $\hat{y}(t|t) = C(t)\hat{x}(t|t)$ of $y(t) = C(t)x(t)$ given measurements at time t, so that the covariance $E\{e(t|t)e^T(t|t)\}$ is minimised, where $e(t|t) = x(t) - \hat{x}(t|t)$. This output estimation problem is depicted in Fig. 2.

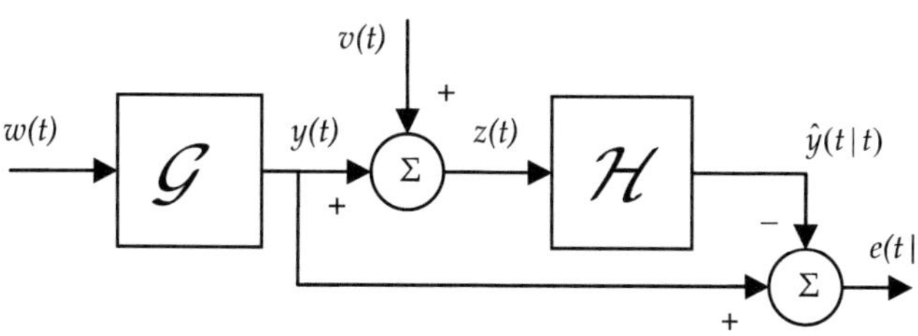

Figure 2. The continuous-time output estimation problem. The objective is to find an estimate $\hat{y}(t|t)$ of $y(t)$ which minimises $E\{(y(t)-\hat{y}(t|t))(y(t)-\hat{y}(t|t))^T\}$.

"Art has a double face, of expression and illusion, just like science has a double face: the reality of error and the phantom of truth." *René Daumal*

It is desired that $\hat{x}(t|t)$ and the estimate $\dot{\hat{x}}(t|t)$ of $\dot{x}(t)$ are unbiased, namely

$$E\{x(t) - \hat{x}(t|t)\} = 0, \tag{32}$$

$$E\{\dot{x}(t|t) - \dot{\hat{x}}(t|t)\} = 0. \tag{33}$$

If $\hat{x}(t|t)$ is a conditional mean estimate, from Lemma 3, criterion (32) will be met. Criterion (33) can be satisfied if it is additionally assumed that $E\{\dot{\hat{x}}(t|t)\} = A(t)\hat{x}(t|t)$, since this yields $E\{\dot{x}(t|t) - \dot{\hat{x}}(t|t)\} = A(t)(E\{x(t) - \hat{x}(t|t)\} = 0$. Thus, substituting $E\left\{\begin{bmatrix}\dot{\hat{x}}(t|t)\\ z(t)\end{bmatrix}\right\} = \begin{bmatrix}A(t)\hat{x}(t|t)\\ C(t)\hat{x}(t|t)\end{bmatrix}$ into (23), yields the conditional mean estimate

$$\begin{aligned}\dot{\hat{x}}(t|t) &= A(t)\hat{x}(t|t) + K(t)\big(z(t) - C(t)\hat{x}(t|t)\big)\\ &= \big(A(t) - K(t)C(t)\big)\hat{x}(t|t) + K(t)z(t),\end{aligned} \tag{34}$$

where $K(t) = E\{x(t)z^T(t)\}E\{z(t)z^T(t)\}^{-1}$. Equation (34) is known as the continuous-time Kalman filter (or the Kalman-Bucy filter) and is depicted in Fig. 3. This filter employs the state matrix $A(t)$ akin to the signal generating model $\mathcal{G}$, which Kalman and Bucy call the message process [4]. The matrix $K(t)$ is known as the filter gain, which operates on the error residual, namely the difference between the measurement $z(t)$ and the estimated output $C(t)\hat{x}(t)$. The calculation of an optimal gain is addressed in the next section.

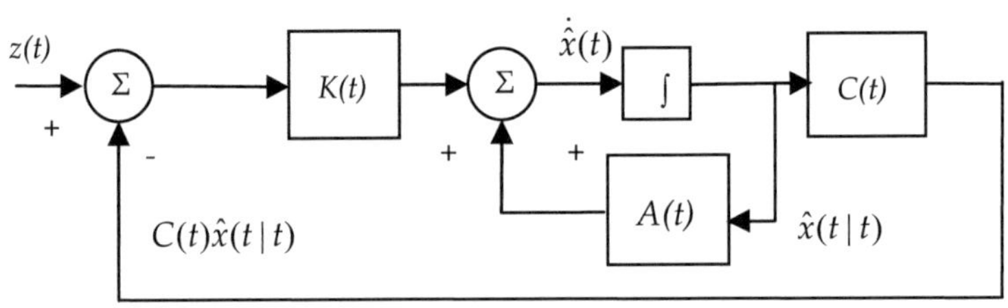

Figure 3. The continuous-time Kalman filter which is also known as the Kalman-Bucy filter. The filter calculates conditional mean estimates $\hat{x}(t|t)$ from the measurements $z(t)$.

3.3.2 The Riccati Differential Equation

Denote the state estimation error by $\tilde{x}(t|t) = x(t) - \hat{x}(t|t)$. It is shown below that the filter minimises the error covariance $E\{\tilde{x}(t|t)\tilde{x}^T(t|t)\}$ if the gain is calculated as

$$K(t) = P(t)C^T(t)R^{-1}(t), \tag{35}$$

"Somewhere, something incredible is waiting to be known." *Carl Edward Sagan*

in which $P(t) = E\{\tilde{x}(t|t)\tilde{x}^T(t|t)\}$ is the solution of the Riccati differential equation

$$\dot{P}(t) = A(t)P(t) + P(t)A^T(t) - P(t)C^T(t)R^{-1}(t)C(t)P(t) + B(t)Q(t)B^T(t). \tag{36}$$

Lemma 4: *In respect of the state estimation problem defined by (26) - (31), suppose that there exists a solution*

$$P(t) = P^T(t) \geq 0 \tag{37}$$

for the algebraic Riccati equation (36) satisfying

$$A(t) - P(t)C^T(t) \geq 0 \tag{38}$$

for all t in the interval [0,T]. Then the filter (34) having the gain (35) minimises P(t) = $E\{\tilde{x}(t|t)\tilde{x}^T(t|t)\}$.

Proof: *Subtracting (34) from (26) results in*

$$\dot{\tilde{x}}(t|t) = \big(A(t) - K(t)C(t)\big)\tilde{x}(t|t) + B(t)w(t) - K(t)v(t). \tag{39}$$

Applying Lemma 2 to the error system (39) gives

$$\dot{P}(t) = \big(A(t) - K(t)C(t)\big)P(t) + P(t)(A(t) - K(t)C(t))^T + K(t)R(t)K^T(t) + B(t)Q(t)B^T(t) \tag{40}$$

which can be rearranged as

$$\begin{aligned}\dot{P}(t) &= A(t)P(t) + P(t)A^T(t) + B(t)Q(t)B^T(t)) \\ &\quad + \big(K(t) - P(t)C^T(t)R^{-1}(t)\big)R(t)\big(K^T(t) - R^{-1}(t)C^T(t)P(t)\big) + P(t)C^T(t)R^{-1}(t)C(t)P(t).\end{aligned} \tag{41}$$

Setting $\dot{P}(t)$ equal to the zero matrix results in a stationary point at (35) which leads to (40). From the differential of (40)

$$\ddot{P}(t) = \big(A(t) - P(t)C^T(t)R^{-1}(t)C(t)\big)\dot{P}(t) + \dot{P}(t)\big(A^T(t) - P(t)C^T(t)R^{-1}(t)C(t)\big) \tag{42}$$

and it can be seen that $\ddot{P}(t) \geq 0$ provided that the assumptions (37) - (38) hold. Therefore, P(t) = $E\{\tilde{x}(t|t)\tilde{x}^T(t|t)\}$ *is minimised at (35).* □

The above development is somewhat brief and not very rigorous. Further discussions appear in [4] – [17]. It is tendered to show that the Kalman filter minimises the error covariance, provided of course that the problem assumptions are correct. In the case that it is desired to estimate an arbitrary linear combination $C_1(t)$ of states, the optimal filter is given by the system

$$\dot{\hat{x}}(t|t) = A(t)\hat{x}(t|t) + K(t)\big(z(t) - C(t)\hat{x}(t|t)\big), \tag{43}$$

$$\hat{y}_1(t) = C_1(t)\hat{x}(t). \tag{44}$$

"The worst wheel of the cart makes the most noise." *Benjamin Franklin*

This filter minimises the error covariance $C_1(t)P(t)C_1^T(t)$. The generalisation of the Kalman filter for problems possessing deterministic inputs, correlated noises, and a direct feed-through term is developed below.

3.3.3 Including Deterministic Inputs

Suppose that the signal model is described by

$$\dot{x}(t) = A(t)x(t) + B(t)w(t) + \mu(t) \tag{45}$$

$$y(t) = C(t)x(t) + \pi(t), \tag{46}$$

where $\mu(t)$ and $\pi(t)$ are deterministic (or known) inputs. In this case, the filtered state estimate can be obtained by including the deterministic inputs as follows

$$\dot{\hat{x}}(t \mid t) = A(t)\hat{x}(t \mid t) + K(t)\big(z(t) - C(t)\hat{x}(t \mid t) - \pi(t)\big) + \mu(t) \tag{47}$$

$$\hat{y}(t) = C(t)\hat{x}(t) + \pi(t). \tag{48}$$

It is easily verified that subtracting (47) from (45) yields the error system (39) and therefore, the Kalman filter's differential Riccati equation remains unchanged.

***Example* 2.** Suppose that an object is falling under the influence of a gravitational field and it is desired to estimate its position over [0, *t*] from noisy measurements. Denote the object's vertical position, velocity and acceleration by $x(t)$, $\dot{x}(t)$ and $\ddot{x}(t)$, respectively. Let g denote the gravitational constant. Then $\ddot{x}(t) = -g$ implies $\dot{x}(t) = \dot{x}(0) - gt$, so the model may be written as

$$\begin{bmatrix} \dot{x}(t) \\ \ddot{x}(t) \end{bmatrix} = A \begin{bmatrix} x(t) \\ \dot{x}(t) \end{bmatrix} + \mu(t),$$

$$z(t) = C \begin{bmatrix} x(t) \\ \dot{x}(t) \end{bmatrix} + v(t), \tag{49}$$

where $A = \begin{bmatrix} 0 & 1 \\ 0 & 0 \end{bmatrix}$ is the state matrix, $\mu(t) = \begin{bmatrix} \dot{x}(0) - gt \\ -g \end{bmatrix}$ is a deterministic input and $C = \begin{bmatrix} 1 & 0 \end{bmatrix}$ is the output mapping. Thus, the Kalman filter has the form

$$\begin{bmatrix} \dot{\hat{x}}(t \mid t) \\ \ddot{\hat{x}}(t \mid t) \end{bmatrix} = A \begin{bmatrix} \hat{x}(t \mid t) \\ \dot{\hat{x}}(t \mid t) \end{bmatrix} + K\left(z(t) - C \begin{bmatrix} \hat{x}(t \mid t) \\ \dot{\hat{x}}(t \mid t) \end{bmatrix} \right) + \mu(t), \tag{50}$$

$$\hat{y}(t \mid t) = C(t)\hat{x}(t \mid t), \tag{51}$$

where the gain K is calculated from (35) and (36), in which $BQB^T = 0$.

"These, Gentlemen, are the opinions upon which I base my facts." *Winston Leonard Spencer-Churchill*

3.3.4 Including Correlated Process and Measurement Noise

Suppose that the process and measurement noises are correlated, that is,

$$E\left\{\begin{bmatrix} w(t) \\ v(t) \end{bmatrix}\begin{bmatrix} w^T(\tau) & v^T(\tau) \end{bmatrix}\right\} = \begin{bmatrix} Q(t) & S(t) \\ S^T(t) & R(t) \end{bmatrix}\delta(t-\tau) . \tag{52}$$

The equation for calculating the optimal state estimate remains of the form (34), however, the differential Riccati equation and hence the filter gain are different. The generalisation of the optimal filter that takes into account (52) was published by Kalman in 1963 [5]. Kalman's approach was to first work out the corresponding discrete-time Riccati equation and then derive the continuous-time version.

The correlated noises can be accommodated by defining the signal model equivalently as

$$\dot{x}(t) = \bar{A}(t)x(t) + B(t)\bar{w}(t) + \mu(t) , \tag{53}$$

where

$$\bar{A}(t) = A(t) - B(t)S(t)R^{-1}(t)C(t) \tag{54}$$

is a new state matrix,

$$\bar{w}(t) = w(t) - S(t)R^{-1}(t)v(t) \tag{55}$$

is a new stochastic input that is uncorrelated with $v(t)$, and

$$\mu(t) = B(t)S(t)R^{-1}(t)y(t) \tag{56}$$

is a deterministic signal. It can easily be verified that the system (53) with the parameters (54) - (56), has the structure (26) with $E\{w(t)v^T(\tau)\} = 0$. It is convenient to define

$$\begin{aligned} \bar{Q}(t)\delta(t-\tau) &= E\{\bar{w}(t)\bar{w}^T(\tau)\} \\ &= E\{w(t)w^T(\tau)\} - E\{w(t)v^T(\tau)R^{-1}(t)S^T(t) \quad S(t)R^{-1}(t)E\{v(t)w^T(\tau)\} \\ &\quad + S(t)R^{-1}(t)E\{v(t)v^T(\tau)\}R^{-1}(t)S^T(t) \\ &= \left(Q(t) - S(t)R^{-1}(t)S^T(t)\right)\delta(t-\tau) . \end{aligned} \tag{57}$$

"I am tired of all this thing called science here. We have spent millions in that sort of thing for the last few years, and it is time it should be stopped." *Simon Cameron*

The corresponding Riccati differential equation is obtained by substituting $\bar{A}(t)$ for $A(t)$ and $\bar{Q}(t)$ for $Q(t)$ within (36), namely,

$$\dot{P}(t) = \bar{A}(t)P(t) + P(t)\bar{A}^T(t) - P(t)C^T(t)R^{-1}(t)C(t)P(t) + B(t)\bar{Q}(t)B^T(t) . \quad (58)$$

This can be rearranged to give

$$\dot{P}(t) = A(t)P(t) + P(t)A^T(t) - K(t)(t)R^{-1}(t)K^T(t) + B(t)Q(t)B^T(t) , \quad (59)$$

in which the gain is now calculated as

$$K(t) = \left(P(t)C^T(t) + B(t)S(t)\right)R^{-1}(t) . \quad (60)$$

3.3.5 Including a Direct Feedthrough Matrix

The approach of the previous section can be used to address signal models that possess a direct feedthrough matrix, namely,

$$\dot{x}(t) = A(t)x(t) + B(t)w(t) , \quad (61)$$

$$y(t) = C(t)x(t) + D(t)w(t) . \quad (62)$$

As before, the optimal state estimate is given by

$$\dot{\hat{x}}(t \mid t) = A(t)\hat{x}(t \mid t) + K(t)\left(z(t) - C(t)\hat{x}(t \mid t)\right), \quad (63)$$

where the gain is obtained by substituting $S(t) = Q(t)D^T(t)$ into (60),

$$K(t) = \left(P(t)C^T(t) + B(t)Q(t)D^T(t)\right)R^{-1}(t) , \quad (64)$$

in which $P(t)$ is the solution of the Riccati differential equation

$$\dot{P}(t) = \left(A(t) - B(t)Q(t)D^T(t)R^{-1}(t)C(t)\right)P(t)$$
$$+P(t)\left(A(t) - B(t)Q(t)D^T(t)R^{-1}(t)C(t)\right)^T + B(t)\left(Q(t) - Q(t)D(t)R^{-1}(t)D^T(t)Q(t)\right)B^T(t) .$$

Note that the above Riccati equation simplifies to

$$\dot{P}(t) = A(t)P(t) + P(t)A^T(t) - K(t)(t)R^{-1}(t)K^T(t) + B(t)Q(t)B^T(t) . \quad (65)$$

"No human investigation can be called real science if it cannot be demonstrated mathematically." *Leonardo di ser Piero da Vinci*

3.4 The Continuous-time Steady-State Minimum-Variance Filter

3.4.1 Riccati Differential Equation Monotonicity

This section sets out the simplifications for the case where the signal model is stationary (or time-invariant). In this situation the structure of the Kalman filter is unchanged but the gain is fixed and can be pre-calculated. Consider the linear time-invariant system

$$\dot{x}(t) = Ax(t) + Bw(t)\,, \tag{66}$$

$$y(t) = Cx(t)\,, \tag{67}$$

together with the observations

$$z(t) = y(t) + v(t)\,, \tag{68}$$

assuming that $\mathrm{Re}\{\lambda_i(A)\} < 0$, $E\{w(t)\} = 0$, $E\{w(t)w^T(\tau)\} = Q(t)\delta(t-\tau)$, $E\{v(t)\} = 0$, $E\{v(t)v^T(\tau)\} = R$ and $E\{w(t)v^T(\tau)\} = 0$. It follows from the approach of Section 3 that the Riccati differential equation for the corresponding Kalman filter is given by

$$\dot{P}(t) = AP(t) + P(t)A^T - P(t)C^TR^{-1}CP(t) + BQB^T\,. \tag{69}$$

It will be shown that the solution for $P(t)$ monotonically approaches a steady-state asymptote, in which case the filter gain can be calculated before running the filter. The following result is required to establish that the solutions of the above Riccati differential equation are monotonic.

Lemma 5 [11], [19], [20]: *Suppose that $X(t)$ is a solution of the Lyapunov differential equation*

$$\dot{X}(t) = AX(t) + X(t)A^T \tag{70}$$

over an interval $t \in [0, T]$. Then the existence of a solution $X(t_0) \geq 0$ implies $X(t) \geq 0$ for all $t \in [0, T]$.

Proof: *Denote the transition matrix of $\dot{x}(t) = -A(t)x(t)$ by $\Phi^T(t,\tau)$, for which $\dot{\Phi}(t,\tau) = -A^T(t)\Phi(t,\tau)$ and $\dot{\Phi}^T(t,\tau) = -\Phi^T(t,\tau)A(t)$. Let $P(t) = \Phi^T(t,\tau)X(t)\Phi(t,\tau)$, then from (70)*

$$0 = \Phi^T(t,\tau)\left(\dot{X}(t) - AX(t) - X(t)A^T\right)\Phi(t,\tau)$$

$$= \dot{\Phi}^T(t,\tau)X(t)\Phi(t,\tau) + \Phi^T(t,\tau)\dot{X}(t)\Phi(t,\tau) + \Phi^T(t,\tau)X(t)\dot{\Phi}(t,\tau)$$

$$= \dot{P}(t)\,.$$

Therefore, a solution $X(t_0) \geq 0$ of (70) implies that $X(t) \geq 0$ for all $t \in [0, T]$. □

The monotonicity of Riccati differential equations has been studied by Bucy [6], Wonham [23], Poubelle *et al* [19] and Freiling [20]. The latter's simple proof is employed below.

"Today's scientists have substituted mathematics for experiments, and they wander off through equation after equation, and eventually build a structure which has no relation to reality." *Nikola Tesla*

Lemma 6 [19], [20]: *Suppose for a* $t \geq 0$ *and a* $\delta_t > 0$ *there exist solutions* $P(t) \geq 0$ *and* $P(t + \delta_t) \geq 0$ *of the Riccati differential equations*

$$\dot{P}(t) = AP(t) + P(t)A^T - P(t)C^T R^{-1} CP(t) + BQB^T \tag{71}$$

and

$$\dot{P}(t+\delta_t) = AP(t+\delta_t) + P(t+\delta_t)A^T - P(t+\delta_t)C^T R^{-1} CP(t+\delta_t) + BQB^T , \tag{72}$$

respectively, such that $P(t) - P(t + \delta_t) \geq 0$. *Then the sequence of matrices* $P(t)$ *is monotonic nonincreasing, that is,*

$$P(t) - P(t + \delta_t) \geq 0, \text{ for all } t \geq \delta_t. \tag{73}$$

Proof: *The conditions of the Lemma are the initial step of an induction argument. For the induction step, denote* $\dot{P}(\delta_t) = \dot{P}(t) - \dot{P}(t+\delta_t)$, $P(\delta_t) = P(t) - P(t+\delta_t)$ *and* $\bar{A} = AP(t_t)C^T R^{-1} C - 0.5P(\delta_t)$. *Then*

$$\begin{aligned}\dot{P}(\delta_t) &= AP(\delta_t) + P(\delta_t)A^T - P(t+\delta_t)C^T R^{-1} CP(t+\delta_t) + P(t)C^T R^{-1} CP(t) \\ &= \bar{A}P(\delta_t) + P(\delta_t)\bar{A}^T ,\end{aligned}$$

which is of the form (70), and so the result (73) follows. □

A monotonic nondecreasing case can be established similarly - see [20].

3.4.2 Observability

The continuous-time system (66) – (67) is termed completely observable if the initial states, $x(t_0)$, can be uniquely determined from the inputs and outputs, $w(t)$ and $y(t)$, respectively, over an interval [0, T]. A simple test for observability is is given by the following lemma.

Lemma 7 [10], [21]. *Suppose that* $A \in \mathbb{R}^{n\times n}$ *and* $C \in \mathbb{R}^{p\times n}$. *The system is observable if and only if the observability matrix* $O \in \mathbb{R}^{np\times n}$ *is of rank n, where*

$$O = \begin{bmatrix} C \\ CA \\ CA^2 \\ \vdots \\ CA^{n-1} \end{bmatrix} . \tag{74}$$

"You can observe a lot by just watching." *Lawrence Peter (Yogi) Berra*

Proof: *Recall from Chapter 2 that the solution of (66) is*

$$x(t) = e^{At}x(t_0) + \int_{t_0}^{t} e^{A(t-\tau)}Bw(\tau)d\tau \; . \tag{75}$$

Since the input signal w(t) within (66) is known, it suffices to consider the unforced system $\dot{x}(t) = Ax(t)$ and $y(t) = Cx(t)$, *that is,* $Bw(t) = 0$, *which leads to*

$$y(t) = Ce^{At}x(t_0) \; . \tag{76}$$

The exponential matrix is defined as

$$\begin{aligned} e^{At} &= I + At + \frac{A^2t^2}{2} + \cdots + \frac{A^N t^N}{N!} \\ &= \sum_{k=0}^{N-1} \alpha_k(t)A^k , \end{aligned} \tag{77}$$

where $\alpha_k(t) = t^k/k!$. *Substituting (77) into (76) gives*

$$\begin{aligned} y(t) &= \sum_{k=0}^{N-1} \alpha_k(t)CA^k x(t_0) \\ &= \alpha_0(t)Cx(t_0) + \alpha_1(t)CAx(t_0) + \ldots + \alpha_{N-1}(t)CA^{N-1}x(t_0) \; . \\ &= \begin{bmatrix} \alpha_0(t) & \alpha_1(t) & \cdots & \alpha_{N-1}(t) \end{bmatrix} \begin{bmatrix} C \\ CA \\ CA^2 \\ \vdots \\ CA^{N-1} \end{bmatrix} x(t_0) \; . \end{aligned} \tag{78}$$

From the Cayley-Hamilton Theorem [22],

$$rank \left(\begin{bmatrix} C \\ CA \\ CA^2 \\ \vdots \\ CA^{N-1} \end{bmatrix} \right) = rank \left(\begin{bmatrix} C \\ CA \\ CA^2 \\ \vdots \\ CA^{n-1} \end{bmatrix} \right)$$

for all $N \geq n$. *Therefore, we can take* $N = n$ *within (78). Thus, equation (78) uniquely determines* $x(t_0)$ *if and only if O has full rank n.* □

A system that does not satisfy the above criterion is said to be unobservable. An alternate proof for the above lemma is provided in [10]. If a signal model is not observable then a Kalman filter cannot estimate all the states from the measurements.

"Who will observe the observers ?" *Arthur Stanley Eddington*

***Example** 3.* The pair $A = \begin{bmatrix} 1 & 0 \\ 0 & 1 \end{bmatrix}$, $C = \begin{bmatrix} 1 & 0 \end{bmatrix}$ is expected to be unobservable because one of the two states appears as a system output whereas the other is hidden. By inspection, the rank of the observability matrix, $\begin{bmatrix} C \\ CA \end{bmatrix} = \begin{bmatrix} 1 & 0 \\ 1 & 0 \end{bmatrix}$, is 1. Suppose instead that $C = \begin{bmatrix} 1 & 0 \\ 0 & 1 \end{bmatrix}$, namely measurements of both states are available. Since the observability matrix $\begin{bmatrix} C \\ CA \end{bmatrix} = \begin{bmatrix} 1 & 0 \\ 0 & 1 \\ 1 & 0 \\ 0 & 1 \end{bmatrix}$ is of rank 2, the pair (A, C) is observable, that is, the states can be uniquely reconstructed from the measurements.

3.4.3 The Algebraic Riccati Equation

Some pertinent facts concerning the Riccati differential equation (69) are:

- Its solutions correspond to the covariance of the state estimation error.
- From Lemma 6, if it is suitably initialised then its solutions will be monotonically nonincreasing.
- If the pair (A, C) is observable then the states can be uniquely determined from the outputs.

In view of the above, it is not surprising that if the states can be estimated uniquely, in the limit as t approaches infinity, the Riccati differential equation will have a unique steady state solution.

Lemma 8 [20], [23], [24]: *Suppose that $Re\{\lambda_i(A)\} < 0$, the pair (A, C) is observable, then the solution of the Riccati differential equation (69) satisfies*

$$\lim_{t \to \infty} P(t) = P, \tag{79}$$

where P is the solution of the algebraic Riccati equation

$$0 = AP + PA^T - PC^T R^{-1} CP + BQB^T. \tag{80}$$

A proof that the solution P is in fact unique appears in [24]. A standard way for calculating solutions to (80) arises by finding an appropriate set of Schur vectors for the Hamiltonian matrix $H = \begin{bmatrix} A & -C^T R^{-1} C \\ BQB^T & -A^T \end{bmatrix}$, see [25] and the Hamiltonian solver within *Matlab*TM.

"Stand firm in your refusal to remain conscious during algebra. In real life, I assure you, there is no such thing as algebra." *Francis Ann Lebowitz*

t	$P(t)$	$\dot{P}(t)$
1	0.9800	−2.00
10	0.8316	−1.41
100	0.4419	$-8.13*10^{-2}$
1000	0.4121	$-4.86*10^{-13}$

Table 1. Solutions of (69) for Example 4.

Example 4. Suppose that $A = -1$ and $B = C = Q = R = 1$, for which the solution of the algebraic Riccati equation (80) is $P = 0.4121$. Using Euler's integration method (see Chapter 1) with $\delta_t = 0.01$ and $P(0) = 1$, the calculated solutions of the Riccati differential equation (69) are listed in Table 1. The data in the table demonstrate that the Riccati differential equation solution converges to the algebraic Riccati equation solution and $\lim_{t \to \infty} \dot{P}(t) = 0$.

The so-called infinite-horizon (or stationary) Kalman filter is obtained by substituting time-invariant state-space parameters into (34) - (35) to give

$$\dot{\hat{x}}(t \mid t) = (A - KC)\hat{x}(t \mid t) + Kz(t), \tag{81}$$

$$\hat{y}(t \mid t) = C\hat{x}(t \mid t), \tag{82}$$

where

$$K = PC^T R^{-1}, \tag{83}$$

in which P is calculated by solving the algebraic Riccati equation (80). The output estimation filter (81) – (82) has the transfer function

$$H_{OE}(s) = C(sI - A + KC)^{-1} K. \tag{84}$$

Example 5. Suppose that a signal $y(t) \in \mathbb{R}$ is generated by the system

$$y(t) = \left(\frac{b_m \frac{d^m}{dt^m} + b_{m-1} \frac{d^{m-1}}{dt^{n-1}} + \ldots + b_1 \frac{d}{dt} + b_0}{a_n \frac{d^n}{dt^n} + a_{n-1} \frac{d^{n-1}}{dt^{n-1}} + \ldots + a_1 \frac{d}{dt} + a_0} \right) w(t).$$

This system's transfer function is

$$G(s) = \frac{b_m s^m + b_{m-1} s^{m-1} + \ldots + b_1 s + b_0}{a_n s^n + a_{n-1} s^{n-1} + \ldots + a_1 s + a_0},$$

which can be realised in the controllable canonical form [10]

"If you think dogs can't count, try putting three dog biscuits in your pocket and then giving Fido two of them." *Phil Pastoret*

$$A = \begin{bmatrix} -a_{n-1} & -a_{n-2} & \dots & -a_1 & -a_0 \\ 1 & 0 & & \dots & 0 \\ 0 & 1 & & & \vdots \\ \vdots & & \ddots & 0 & 0 \\ 0 & 0 & \dots & 1 & 0 \end{bmatrix}, B = \begin{bmatrix} 1 \\ 0 \\ \vdots \\ 0 \\ 0 \end{bmatrix} \text{ and } C = \begin{bmatrix} b_m & b_{m-1} & \dots & b_1 & b_0 \end{bmatrix}.$$

The optimal filter for estimating $y(t)$ from noisy measurements (29) is obtained by using the above state-space parameters within (81) – (83). It has the structure depicted in Figs. 3 and 4. These figures illustrate two features of interest. First, the filter's model matches that within the signal generating process. Second, designing the filter is tantamount to finding an optimal gain.

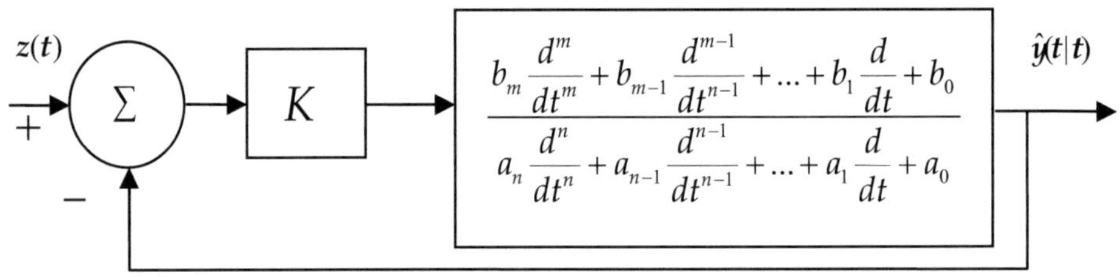

Figure 4. The optimal filter for Example 5.

3.4.4 Equivalence of the Wiener and Kalman Filters

When the model parameters and noise statistics are time-invariant, the Kalman filter reverts to the Wiener filter. The equivalence of the Wiener and Kalman filters implies that spectral factorisation is the same as solving a Riccati equation. This observation is known as the Kalman-Yakubovich-Popov Lemma (or Positive Real Lemma) [15], [26], which assumes familiarity with the following Schur complement formula.

For any matrices Φ_{11}, Φ_{12} and Φ_{22}, where Φ_{11} and Φ_{22} are symmetric, the following are equivalent.

(i) $\begin{bmatrix} \Phi_{11} & \Phi_{12} \\ \Phi_{12}^T & \Phi_{22} \end{bmatrix} \geq 0$.

(ii) $\Phi_{11} \geq 0,\ \Phi_{22} \geq \Phi_{12}^T \Phi_{11}^{-1} \Phi_{12}$.

(iii) $\Phi_{22} \geq 0,\ \Phi_{11} \geq \Phi_{12} \Phi_{22}^{-1} \Phi_{12}^T$.

"Mathematics is the queen of sciences and arithmetic is the queen of mathematics." *Carl Friedrich Gauss*

The Kalman-Yakubovich-Popov Lemma is set out below. Further details appear in [15] and a historical perspective is provided in [26]. A proof of this Lemma makes use of the identity

$$-PA^T - AP = P(-sI - A^T) + (sI - A)P. \tag{85}$$

Lemma 9 [15], [26]: *Consider the spectral density matrix*

$$\Delta\Delta^H(s) = \begin{bmatrix} C(sI - A)^{-1} & I \end{bmatrix} \begin{bmatrix} Q & 0 \\ 0 & R \end{bmatrix} \begin{bmatrix} (-sI - A^T)^{-1}C^T \\ I \end{bmatrix}. \tag{86}$$

Then the following statements are equivalent:

(i) $\Delta\Delta^H(j\omega) \ge 0$ *for all* $\omega \in (-\infty, \infty)$.

(ii) $\begin{bmatrix} BQB^T + AP + PA^T & PC^T \\ CP & R \end{bmatrix} \ge 0$.

(iii) *There exists a nonnegative solution P of the algebraic Riccati equation (80).*

Proof: *To establish equivalence between (i) and (iii), use (85) within (80) to obtain*

$$P(-sI - A^T) + (sI - A)P = BQB^T - PC^TRCP. \tag{87}$$

Premultiplying and postmultiplying (87) by $C(sI - A)^{-1}$ *and* $(-sI - A^T)^{-1}C^T$, *respectively, results in*

$$C(sI - A)^{-1}PC^T + CP(-sI - A^T)^{-1}C^T = C(sI - A)^{-1}(BQB^T - PC^TRCP)(-sI - A^T)^{-1}C^T. \tag{88}$$

Hence,

$$\begin{aligned} \Delta\Delta(s) &= GQG(s) + R \\ &= C(sI - A)^{-1}BQB^T(-sI - A^T)^{-1}C^T + R \\ &= C(sI - A)^{-1}PC^TRCP(-sI - A^T)^{-1}C^T + C(sI - A)^{-1}PC^T + CP(-sI - A^T)^{-1}C^T + R \\ &= \left(C(sI - A)^{-1}KR^{1/2} + R^{1/2}\right)\left(R^{1/2}K^T(-sI - A^T)^{-1}C^T + R^{1/2}\right) \\ &\ge 0. \end{aligned} \tag{89}$$

The Schur complement formula can be used to verify the equivalence of (ii) and (iii). □

In Chapter 1, it is shown that the transfer function matrix of the optimal Wiener solution for output estimation is given by

$$H_{OE}(s) = I - R^{1/2}\Delta^{-1}(s), \tag{90}$$

where $s = j\omega$ and

"Arithmetic is being able to count up to twenty without taking off your shoes." *Mickey Mouse*

$$\Delta\Delta^H(s) = GQG^H(s) + R\,. \tag{91}$$

is the spectral density matrix of the measurements. It follows from (91) that

$$\Delta(s) = C(sI - A)^{-1}KR^{1/2} + R^{1/2}\,. \tag{92}$$

The Wiener filter (90) requires the spectral factor inverse, $\Delta^{-1}(s)$, which can be found from (92) and using $[I + C(sI - A)^{-1}K]^{-1} = I + C(sI - A + KC)^{-1}K$ to obtain

$$\Delta^{-1}(s) = R^{-1/2} - R^{-1/2}C(sI - A + KC)^{-1}K\,. \tag{93}$$

Substituting (93) into (90) yields

$$H_{OE}(s) = C(sI - A + KC)^{-1}K\,, \tag{94}$$

which is identical to the minimum-variance output estimator (84).

***Example** 5.* Consider a scalar output estimation problem where $G(s) = (s + 1)^{-1}$, $Q = 1$, $R = 0.0001$ and the Wiener filter transfer function is

$$H(s) = 99(s + 100)^{-1}\,. \tag{95}$$

Applying the bilinear transform yields $A = -1$, $B = C = 1$, for which the solution of (80) is $P = 0.0099$. By substituting $K = PC^TR^{-1} = 99$ into (90), one obtains (95).

3.5 Conclusion

The Kalman-Bucy filter which produces state estimates $\hat{x}(t\,|\,t)$ and output estimates $\hat{y}(t\,|\,t)$ from the measurements $z(t) = y(t) + v(t)$ at time t is summarised in Table 2. This filter minimises the variances of the state estimation error, $E\{(x(t) - \hat{x}(t\,|\,t))(x(t) - \hat{x}(t\,|\,t))^T\} = P(t)$ and the output estimation error, $E\{(y(t) - \hat{y}(t\,|\,t))(y(t) - \hat{y}(t\,|\,t))^T\} = C(t)P(t)C^T(t)$.

When the model parameters and noise covariances are time-invariant, the gain is also time-invariant and can be precalculated. The time-invariant filtering results are summarised in Table 3. In this stationary case, spectral factorisation is equivalent to solving a Riccati equation and the transfer function of the output estimation filter, $H_{OE}(s) = C(sI - A + KC)^{-1}K$, is identical to that of the Wiener filter. It is not surprising that the Wiener and Kalman filters are equivalent since they are both derived by completing the square of the error covariance.

"Mathematics consists in proving the most obvious thing in the least obvious way." *George Polya*

	ASSUMPTIONS	MAIN RESULTS
Signals and system	$E\{w(t)\} = E\{v(t)\} = 0$. $E\{w(t)w^T(t)\} = Q(t)$ and $E\{v(t)v^T(t)\} = R(t)$ are known. $A(t)$, $B(t)$ and $C(t)$ are known.	$\dot{x}(t) = A(t)x(t) + B(t)w(t)$ $y(t) = C(t)x(t)$ $z(t) = y(t) + v(t)$
Filtered state and output factorisation		$\dot{\hat{x}}(t \mid t) = A(t)\hat{x}(t \mid t) + K(t)(z(t) - C(t)\hat{x}(t \mid t))$ $\hat{y}(t \mid t) = C(t)\hat{x}(t \mid t)$
Filter gain and Riccati differential equation	$Q(t) > 0$ and $R(t) > 0$.	$K(t) = P(t)C(t)R^{-1}(t)$ $\dot{P}(t) = A(t)P(t) + P(t)A^T(t)$ $-P(t)C^T(t)R^{-1}(t)C(t)P(t) + B(t)Q(t)B^T(t)$

Table 2. Main results for time-varying output estimation.

	ASSUMPTIONS	MAIN RESULTS
Signals and system	$E\{w(t)\} = E\{v(t)\} = 0$. $E\{w(t)w^T(t)\} = Q$ and $E\{v(t)v^T(t)\} = R$ are known. A, B and C are known. The pair (A, C) is observable.	$\dot{x}(t) = Ax(t) + Bw(t)$ $y(t) = Cx(t)$ $z(t) = y(t) + v(t)$
Filtered state and output factorisation		$\dot{\hat{x}}(t \mid t) = A\hat{x}(t \mid t) + K(z(t) - C\hat{x}(t \mid t))$ $\hat{y}(t \mid t) = C\hat{x}(t \mid t)$
Filter gain and algebraic Riccati equation	$Q > 0$ and $R > 0$.	$K = PCR^{-1}$ $0 = AP + PA^T - PC^TR^{-1}CP + BQB^T$

Table 3. Main results for time-invariant output estimation.

"There are two ways to do great mathematics. The first is to be smarter than everybody else. The second way is to be stupider than everybody else - but persistent." *Raoul Bott*

3.6 Problems

Problem 1. Show that $\dot{x}(t) = A(t)x(t)$ has the solution $x(t) = \Phi(t,0)x(0)$ where $\dot{\Phi}(t,0) = A(t)\Phi(t,0)$ and $\Phi(t,t) = I$. Hint: use the approach of [13] and integrate both sides of $\dot{x}(t) = A(t)x(t)$.

Problem 2. Given that:

(i) the Lyapunov differential equation for the system $\dot{x}(t) = F(t)x(t) + G(t)w(t)$ is $\frac{d}{dt}E\{x(t)x^T(t)\} = A(t)E\{x(t)x^T(t)\} + E\{x(t)x^T(t)\}F^T(t) + G(t)Q(t)G^T(t)$;

(ii) the Kalman filter for the system $\dot{x}(t) = A(t)x(t) + B(t)w(t)$, $z(t) = C(t)x(t) + v(t)$ has the structure $\dot{\hat{x}}(t|t) = A(t)\hat{x}(t|t) + K(t)(z(t) - C(t)\hat{x}(t|t))$;

write a Riccati differential equation for the evolution of the state error covariance and determine the optimal gain matrix $K(t)$.

Problem 3. Derive the Riccati differential equation for the model $\dot{x}(t) = A(t)x(t) + B(t)w(t)$, $z(t) = C(t)x(t) + v(t)$ with $E\{w(t)w^T(\tau)\} = Q(t)\delta(t-\tau)$, $E\{v(t)v^T(\tau)\} = R(t)\delta(t-\tau)$ and $E\{w(t)v^T(\tau)\} = S(t)\delta(t-\tau)$. Hint: consider $\dot{x}(t) = A(t)x(t) + B(t)w(t) + B(t)S(t)R^{-1}(t)(z(t) - C(t)x(t) - v(t))$.

Problem 4. For output estimation problems with $B = C = R = 1$, calculate the algebraic Riccati equation solution, filter gain and transfer function for the following.

(a)	$A = -1$ and $Q = 8$.	(b)	$A = -2$ and $Q = 12$.
(c)	$A = -3$ and $Q = 16$.	(d)	$A = -4$ and $Q = 20$.
(e)	$A = -5$ and $Q = 24$.	(f)	$A = -6$ and $Q = 28$.
(g)	$A = -7$ and $Q = 32$.	(h)	$A = -8$ and $Q = 36$.
(i)	$A = -9$ and $Q = 40$.	(j)	$A = -10$ and $Q = 44$.

Problem 5. Prove the Kalman-Yakubovich-Popov Lemma for the case of

$$E\left\{\begin{bmatrix} w(t) \\ v(t) \end{bmatrix}\begin{bmatrix} w^T(\tau) & v^T(\tau) \end{bmatrix}\right\} = \begin{bmatrix} Q & S \\ S^T & R \end{bmatrix}\delta(t-\tau)\text{, i.e., show}$$

$$\Delta\Delta^H(s) = \begin{bmatrix} C(sI - A)^{-1} & I \end{bmatrix}\begin{bmatrix} Q & S \\ S & R \end{bmatrix}\begin{bmatrix} (-sI - A^T)^{-1}C^T \\ I \end{bmatrix}.$$

Problem 6. Derive a state space formulation for minimum-mean-square-error equaliser using $\Delta^{-1}(s) = R^{-1/2} - R^{-1/2}C(sI - A + KC)^{-1}K$.

"Mathematics is a game played according to certain simple rules with meaningless marks on paper."
David Hilbert

3.7 Glossary

In addition to the terms listed in Section 1.6, the following have been used herein.

$\mathcal{G}: \mathbb{R}^p \rightarrow \mathbb{R}^q$	A linear system that operates on a *p*-element input signal and produces a *q*-element output signal.
$A(t)$, $B(t)$, $C(t)$, $D(t)$	Time-varying state space matrices of appropriate dimension. The system $\mathcal{G}$ is assumed to have the realisation $\dot{x}(t) = A(t)x(t) + B(t)w(t)$, $y(t) = C(t)x(t) + D(t)w(t)$.
$Q(t)$ and $R(t)$	Covariance matrices of the nonstationary stochastic signals $w(t)$and $v(t)$, respectively.
$\Phi(t,0)$	State transition matrix which satisfies $\dot{\Phi}(t,0) = \frac{d\Phi(t,0)}{dt} = A(t)\Phi(t,0)$ with the boundary condition $\Phi(t,t) = I$.
$\mathcal{G}^H$	Adjoint of $\mathcal{G}$. The adjoint of a system having the state-space parameters $\{A(t), B(t), C(t), D(t)\}$ is a system parameterised by $\{-A^T(t), -C^T(t), B^T(t), D^T(t)\}$.
$E\{.\}$, $E\{x(t)\}$	Expectation operator, expected value of $x(t)$.
$E\{x(t) \| y(t)\}$	Conditional expectation, namely the estimate of $x(t)$ given $y(t)$.
$\hat{x}(t \| t)$	Conditional mean estimate of the state $x(t)$ given data at time t.
$\tilde{x}(t \| t)$	State estimation error which is defined by $\tilde{x}(t \| t) = x(t) - \hat{x}(t \| t)$.
$K(t)$	Time-varying filter gain matrix.
$P(t)$	Time-varying error covariance, *i.e.*, $E\{\tilde{x}(t)\tilde{x}^T(t)\}$, which is the solution of a Riccati differential equation.
A, B, C, D	Time-invariant state space matrices of appropriate dimension.
Q and R	Time-invariant covariance matrices of the stationary stochastic signals $w(t)$ and $v(t)$, respectively.
O	Observability matrix.
SNR	Signal to noise ratio.
K	Time-invariant filter gain matrix.
P	Time-invariant error covariance which is the solution of an algebraic Riccati equation.
H	Hamiltonian matrix.
$G(s)$	Transfer function matrix of the signal model.
$H(s)$	Transfer function matrix of the minimum-variance solution.
$H_{OE}(s)$	Transfer function matrix of the minimum-variance solution specialised for output estimation.

"A mathematician is a device for turning coffee into theorems." *Paul Erdos*

3.8 References

[1] R. W. Bass, "Some reminiscences of control theory and system theory in the period 1955 - 1960: Introduction of Dr. Rudolf E. Kalman, *Real Time,* Spring/Summer Issue, The University of Alabama in Huntsville, 2002.
[2] M. S. Grewal and A. P. Andrews, "Applications of Kalman Filtering in Areospace 1960 to the Present", *IEEE Control Systems Magazine,* vol. 30, no. 3, pp. 69 - 78, June 2010.
[3] R. E. Kalman, "A New Approach to Linear Filtering and Prediction Problems", *Transactions of the ASME, Series D, Journal of Basic Engineering,* vol 82, pp. 35 - 45, 1960.
[4] R. E. Kalman and R. S. Bucy, "New results in linear filtering and prediction theory", *Transactions of the ASME, Series D, Journal of Basic Engineering,* vol 83, pp. 95 - 107, 1961.
[5] R. E. Kalman, "New Methods in Wiener Filtering Theory", *Proc. First Symposium on Engineering Applications of Random Function Theory and Probability,* Wiley, New York, pp. 270 - 388, 1963.
[6] R. S. Bucy, "Global Theory of the Riccati Equation", *Journal of Computer and System Sciences,* vol. 1, pp. 349 - 361, 1967.
[7] A. H. Jazwinski, *Stochastic Processes and Filtering Theory,* Academic Press, Inc., New York, 1970.
[8] A. P. Sage and J. L. Melsa, *Estimation Theory with Applications to Communications and Control,* McGraw-Hill Book Company, New York, 1971.
[9] A. Gelb, *Applied Optimal Estimation,* The Analytic Sciences Corporation, USA, 1974.
[10] T. Kailath, *Linear Systems,* Prentice-Hall, Inc., Englewood Cliffs, New Jersey, 1980.
[11] H. W. Knobloch and H. K. Kwakernaak, *Lineare Kontrolltheorie,* Springer-Verlag, Berlin, 1980.
[12] R. G. Brown and P. Y. C. Hwang, *Introduction to Random Signals and Applied Kalman Filtering,* John Wiley & Sons, Inc., USA, 1983.
[13] P. A. Ruymgaart and T. T. Soong, *Mathematics of Kalman-Bucy Filtering,* Second Edition, Springer-Verlag, Berlin, 1988.
[14] M. S. Grewal and A. P. Andrews, *Kalman Filtering, Theory and Practice,* Prentice-Hall, Inc., Englewood Cliffs, New Jersey, 1993.
[15] T. Kailath, A. H. Sayed and B. Hassibi, *Linear Estimation,* Prentice-Hall, Upper Saddle River, New Jersey, 2000.
[16] D. Simon, *Optimal State Estimation, Kalman H_∞ and Nonlinear Approaches,* John Wiley & Sons, Inc., Hoboken, New Jersey, 2006.
[17] F. L. Lewis, L. Xie and D. Popa, *Optimal and Robust Estimation With an Introduction to Stochastic Control Theory,* Second Edition, CRC Press, Taylor & Francis Group, 2008.
[18] T. Söderström, *Discrete-time Stochastic Systems: estimation and control,* Springer-Verlag London Ltd., 2002.
[19] M. - A. Poubelle, R. R. Bitmead and M. R. Gevers, "Fake Algebraic Riccati Techniques and Stability", *IEEE Transactions on Automatic Control,* vol. 33, no. 4, pp. 379 - 381, 1988.
[20] G. Freiling, V. Ionescu, H. Abou-Kandil and G. Jank, *Matrix Riccati Equations in Control and Systems Theory,* Birkhauser, Boston, 2003.
[21] K. Ogata, *Matlab for Control Engineers,* Pearson Prentice Hall, Upper Saddle River, New Jersey, 2008.

"But mathematics is the sister, as well as the servant, of the arts and is touched with the same madness and genius." *Harold Marston Morse*

[22] T. Kaczorek, "Cayley-Hamilton Theorem" in Hazewinkel, Michiel, *Encyclopedia of Mathematics*, Springer, 2001.
[23] W. M. Wonham, "On a Matrix Riccati Equation of Stochastic Control", *SIAM Journal on Control*, vol. 6, no. 4, pp. 681 - 697, 1968.
[24] M. - A. Poubelle, I. R. Petersen, M. R. Gevers and R. R. Bitmead, "A Miscellany of Results on an Equation of Count J. F. Riccati", *IEEE Transactions on Automatic Control*, vol. 31, no. 7, pp. 651 - 654, 1986.
[25] A. J. Laub, "A Schur Method for Solving Algebraic Riccati Equations", *IEEE Transactions on Automatic Control*, vol. 24, no. 6, pp. 913 - 921, 1979.
[26] S. V. Gusev and A. L. Likhtarnikov, "Kalman-Popov-Yakubovich Lemma and the S-procedure: A Historical Essay", *Automation and Remote Control*, vol. 67, no. 11, pp. 1768 - 1810, 2006.

"Mathematics are like Frenchmen: whatever you say to them they translate into their own language, and forthwith it is something entirely different." *Johann Wolfgang von Goethe*

4

Discrete-Time Minimum-Variance Prediction and Filtering

4.1 Introduction

Kalman filters are employed wherever it is desired to recover data from the noise in an optimal way, such as satellite orbit estimation, aircraft guidance, radar, communication systems, navigation, medical diagnosis and finance. Continuous-time problems that possess differential equations may be easier to describe in a state-space framework, however, the filters have higher implementation costs because an additional integration step and higher sampling rates are required. Conversely, although discrete-time state-space models may be less intuitive, the ensuing filter difference equations can be realised immediately.

The discrete-time Kalman filter calculates predicted states via the linear recursion

$$\hat{x}_{k+1/k} = A_k \hat{x}_{k-1/k} + K_k (z_k - C_k \hat{x}_{k-1/k}) ,$$

where the predictor gain, K_k, is a function of the noise statistics and the model parameters. The above formula was reported by Rudolf E. Kalman in the 1960s [1], [2]. He has since received many awards and prizes, including the National Medal of Science, which was presented to him by President Barack Obama in 2009.

The Kalman filter calculations are simple and well-established. A possibly troublesome obstacle is expressing problems at hand within a state-space framework. This chapter derives the main discrete-time results to provide familiarity with state-space techniques and filter application. The continuous-time and discrete-time minimum-square-error Wiener filters were derived using a completing-the-square approach in Chapters 1 and 2, respectively. Similarly for time-varying continuous-time signal models, the derivation of the minimum-variance Kalman filter, presented in Chapter 3, relied on a least-mean-square (or conditional-mean) formula. This formula is used again in the solution of the discrete-time prediction and filtering problems. Predictions can be used when the measurements are irregularly spaced or missing at the cost of increased mean-square-error.

This chapter develops the prediction and filtering results for the case where the problem is nonstationary or time-varying. It is routinely assumed that the process and measurement noises are zero mean and uncorrelated. Nonzero mean cases can be accommodated by including deterministic inputs within the state prediction and filter output updates. Correlated noises can be handled by adding a term within the predictor gain and the underlying Riccati equation. The same approach is employed when the signal model

---

"Man will occasionally stumble over the truth, but most of the time he will pick himself up and continue on." *Winston Leonard Spencer-Churchill*

possesses a direct-feedthrough term. A simplification of the generalised regulator problem from control theory is presented, from which the solutions of output estimation, input estimation (or equalisation), state estimation and mixed filtering problems follow immediately.

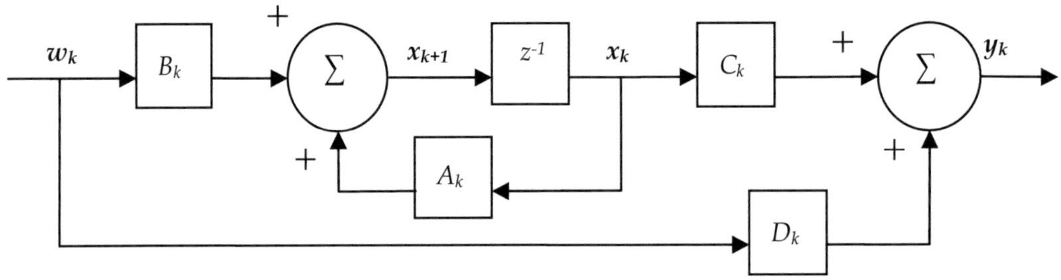

Figure 1. The discrete-time system $\mathcal{G}$ operates on the input signal $w_k \in \mathbb{R}^m$ and produces the output $y_k \in \mathbb{R}^p$.

4.2 The Time-varying Signal Model

A discrete-time time-varying system $\mathcal{G}: \mathbb{R}^m \rightarrow \mathbb{R}^p$ is assumed to have the state-space representation

$$x_{k+1} = A_k x_k + B_k w_k , \tag{1}$$

$$y_k = C_k x_k + D_k w_k , \tag{2}$$

where $A_k \in \mathbb{R}^{n \times n}$, $B_k \in \mathbb{R}^{n \times m}$, $C_k \in \mathbb{R}^{p \times n}$ and $D_k \in \mathbb{R}^{p \times p}$ over a finite interval $k \in [0, N]$. The w_k is a stochastic white process with

$$E\{w_k\} = 0,\ E\{w_j w_k^T\} = Q_k \delta_{jk} , \tag{3}$$

in which $\delta_{jk} = \begin{cases} 1 & \text{if } j = k \\ 0 & \text{if } j \neq k \end{cases}$ is the Kronecker delta function. This system is depicted in Fig. 1, in which z^{-1} is the unit delay operator. It is interesting to note that, at time k the current state

$$x_k = A_{k-1}x_{k-1} + B_{k-1}w_{k-1}, \tag{4}$$

does not involve w_k. That is, unlike continuous-time systems, here there is a one-step delay between the input and output sequences. The simpler case of $D_k = 0$, namely,

$$y_k = C_k x_k, \tag{5}$$

is again considered prior to the inclusion of a nonzero D_k.

"Rudy Kalman applied the state-space model to the filtering problem, basically the same problem discussed by Wiener. The results were astonishing. The solution was recursive, and the fact that the estimates could use only the past of the observations posed no difficulties." *Jan. C. Willems*

4.3 The State Prediction Problem

Suppose that observations of (5) are available, that is,

$$z_k = y_k + v_k, \tag{6}$$

where v_k is a white measurement noise process with

$$E\{v_k\} = 0,\ E\{v_j v_k^T\} = R_k\delta_{jk} \text{ and } E\{w_j v_k^T\} = 0. \tag{7}$$

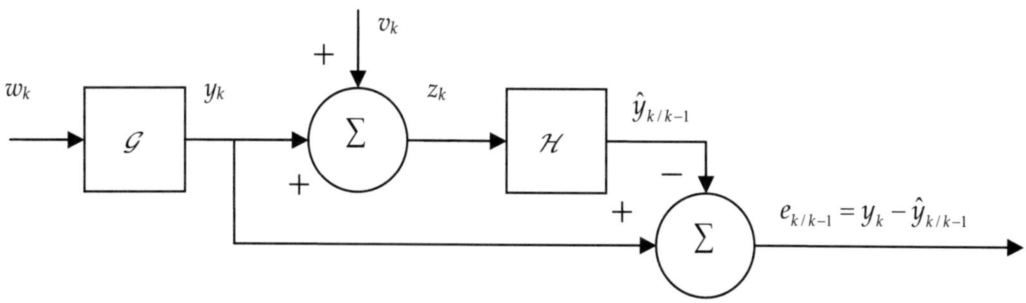

Figure 2. The state prediction problem. The objective is to design a predictor $\mathcal{H}$ which operates on the measurements and produces state estimates such that the variance of the error residual $e_{k/k-1}$ is minimised.

It is noted above for the state recursion (4), there is a one-step delay between the current state and the input process. Similarly, it is expected that there will be one-step delay between the current state estimate and the input measurement. Consequently, it is customary to denote $\hat{x}_{k/k-1}$ as the state estimate at time k, given measurements at time k – 1. The $\hat{x}_{k/k-1}$ is also known as the one-step-ahead state prediction. The objective here is to design a predictor $\mathcal{H}$ that operates on the measurements z_k and produces an estimate, $\hat{y}_{k/k-1} = C_k\hat{x}_{k/k-1}$, of $y_k = C_k y_k$, so that the covariance, $E\{e_{k/k-1}e_{k/k-1}^T\}$, of the error residual, $e_{k/k-1} = y_k - \hat{y}_{k/k-1}$, is minimised. This problem is depicted in Fig. 2

4.4 The Discrete-time Conditional Mean Estimate

The predictor derivation that follows relies on the discrete-time version of the conditional-mean or least-mean-square estimate derived in Chapter 3, which is set out as follows. Consider a stochastic vector $[\alpha_k^T \ \ \beta_k^T]^T$ having means and covariances

$$E\left\{\begin{bmatrix}\alpha_k \\ \beta_k\end{bmatrix}\right\} = \begin{bmatrix}\bar{\alpha} \\ \bar{\beta}\end{bmatrix} \tag{8}$$

"Prediction is very difficult, especially if it's about the future." *Niels Henrik David Bohr*

and

$$E\left\{\begin{bmatrix}\alpha_k \\ \beta_k\end{bmatrix}\begin{bmatrix}\alpha_k^T & \beta_k^T\end{bmatrix}\right\} = \begin{bmatrix}\Sigma_{\alpha_k\alpha_k} & \Sigma_{\alpha_k\beta_k} \\ \Sigma_{\beta_k\alpha_k} & \Sigma_{\beta_k\beta_k}\end{bmatrix}. \quad (9)$$

respectively, where $\Sigma_{\beta_k\alpha_k} = \Sigma_{\alpha_k\beta_k}^T$. An estimate of α_k given β_k, denoted by $E\{\alpha_k \mid \beta_k\}$, which minimises $E\{(\alpha_k - E\{\alpha_k \mid \beta_k\})(\alpha_k - E\{\alpha_k \mid \beta_k\})^T\}$, is given by

$$E\{\alpha_k \mid \beta_k\} = \bar{\alpha} + \Sigma_{\alpha_k\beta_k}\Sigma_{\beta_k\beta_k}^{-1}(\beta_k - \bar{\beta}). \quad (10)$$

The above formula is developed in [3] and established for Gaussian distributions in [4]. A derivation is requested in the problems. If a_k and β_k are scalars then (10) degenerates to the linear regression formula as is demonstrated below.

Example 1 (Linear regression [5]). The least-squares estimate $\hat{\alpha}_k = a\beta_k + b$ of α_k given data $a_k, \beta_k \in \mathbb{R}$ over [1, *N*], can be found by minimising the performance objective $J = \frac{1}{N}\sum_{k=1}^{N}(\alpha_k - \hat{\alpha})^2 = \frac{1}{N}\sum_{k=1}^{N}(\alpha_k - a\beta_k - b)^2$. Setting $\frac{dJ}{db} = 0$ yields $b = \bar{\alpha} - a\bar{\beta}$. Setting $\frac{dJ}{da} = 0$, substituting for *b* and using the definitions (8) – (9), results in $a = \Sigma_{\alpha_k\beta_k}\Sigma_{\beta_k\beta_k}^{-1}$.

4.5 Minimum-Variance Prediction

It follows from (1), (6), together with the assumptions $E\{w_k\} = 0$, $E\{v_k\} = 0$, that $E\{x_{k+1}\} = E\{A_k x_k\}$ and $E\{z_k\} = E\{C_k x_k\}$. It is assumed that similar results hold in the case of predicted state estimates, that is,

$$E\left\{\begin{bmatrix}\hat{x}_{k+1} \\ z_k\end{bmatrix}\right\} = \begin{bmatrix}A_k\hat{x}_{k/k-1} \\ C_k\hat{x}_{k/k-1}\end{bmatrix}. \quad (11)$$

Substituting (11) into (10) and denoting $\hat{x}_{k+1/k} = E\{\hat{x}_{k+1} \mid z_k\}$ yields the predicted state

$$\hat{x}_{k+1/k} = A_k\hat{x}_{k/k-1} + K_k(z_k - C_k\hat{x}_{k/k-1}), \quad (12)$$

where $K_k = E\{\hat{x}_{k+1}z_k^T\}E\{z_k z_k^T\}^{-1}$ is known as the predictor gain, which is designed in the next section. Thus, the optimal one-step-ahead predictor follows immediately from the least-mean-square (or conditional mean) formula. A more detailed derivation appears in [4]. The structure of the optimal predictor is shown in Fig. 3. It can be seen from the figure that $\mathcal{H}$ produces estimates $\hat{y}_{k/k-1} = C_k\hat{x}_{k/k-1}$ from the measurements z_k.

"I admired Bohr very much. We had long talks together, long talks in which Bohr did practically all the talking." *Paul Adrien Maurice Dirac*

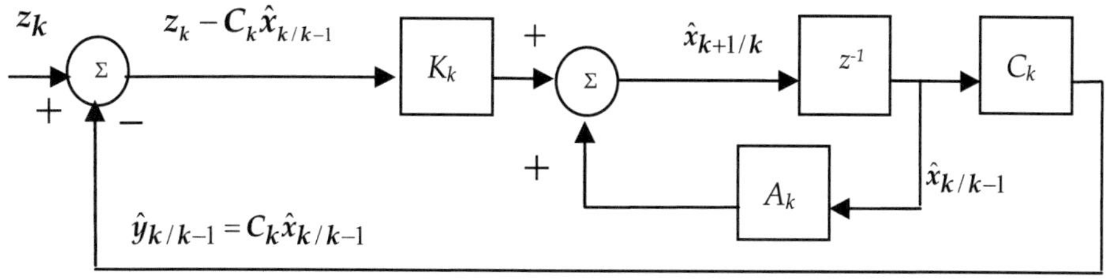

Figure 3. The optimal one-step-ahead predictor which produces estimates $\hat{x}_{k+1/k}$ of x_{k+1} given measurements z_k.

Let $\tilde{x}_{k/k-1} = x_k - \hat{x}_{k/k-1}$ denote the state prediction error. It is shown below that the expectation of the prediction error is zero, that is, the predicted state estimate is unbiased.

Lemma 1: *Suppose that* $\hat{x}_{0/0} = x_0$, *then*

$$E\{\tilde{x}_{k+1/k}\} = 0 \tag{13}$$

for all $k \in [0, N]$.

Proof: *The condition* $\hat{x}_{0/0} = x_0$ *is equivalent to* $\tilde{x}_{0/0} = 0$, *which is the initialisation step for an induction argument. Subtracting (12) from (1) gives*

$$\tilde{x}_{k+1/k} = (A_k - K_kC_k)\tilde{x}_{k/k-1} + B_kw_k - K_kv_k \tag{14}$$

and therefore

$$E\{\tilde{x}_{k+1/k}\} = (A_k - K_kC_k)E\{\tilde{x}_{k/k-1}\} + B_kE\{w_k\} - K_kE\{v_k\} . \tag{15}$$

From assumptions (3) and (7), the last two terms of the right-hand-side of (15) are zero. Thus, (13) follows by induction. □

4.6 Design of the Predictor Gain

It is shown below that the optimum predictor gain is that which minimises the prediction error covariance $E\{\tilde{x}_{k/k-1}\tilde{x}^T_{k/k-1}\}$.

Lemma 2: *In respect of the estimation problem defined by (1), (3), (5) - (7), suppose there exist solutions* $P_{k/k-1} = P^T_{k/k-1} \ge 0$ *to the Riccati difference equation*

$$P_{k+1/k} = A_kP_{k/k-1}A_k^T + B_kQ_kB_k^T - A_kP_{k/k-1}C_k^T(C_kP_{k/k-1}C_k^T + R_k)^{-1}C_kP_{k/k-1}A_k^T , \tag{16}$$

over [0, N], then the predictor gain

$$K_k = A_kP_{k/k-1}C_k^T(C_kP_{k/k-1}C_k^T + R_k)^{-1} , \tag{17}$$

within (12) minimises $P_{k/k-1} = E\{\tilde{x}_{k/k-1}\tilde{x}^T_{k/k-1}\}$.

"When it comes to the future, there are three kinds of people: those who let it happen, those who make it happen, and those who wondered what happened." *John M. Richardson Jr.*

Proof: *Constructing* $P_{k+1/k} = E\{\tilde{x}_{k+1/k}\tilde{x}_{k+1/k}^T\}$ *using (3), (7), (14),* $E\{\tilde{x}_{k/k-1}w_k^T\} = 0$ *and* $E\{\tilde{x}_{k/k-1}v_k^T\} = 0$ *yields*

$$P_{k+1/k} = (A_k - K_kC_k)P_{k/k-1}(A_k - K_kC_k)^T + B_kQ_kB_k^T + K_kR_kK_k^T, \tag{18}$$

which can be rearranged to give

$$\begin{aligned} P_{k+1/k} &= A_kP_{k/k-1}A_k^T - A_kP_{k/k-1}C_k^T(C_kP_{k/k-1}C_k^T + R_k)^{-1}C_kP_{k/k-1}A_k^T + B_kQ_kB_k^T \\ &\quad +(K_k - A_kP_{k/k-1}C_k^T(C_kP_{k/k-1}C_k^T + R_k)^{-1})(C_kP_{k/k-1}C_k^T + R_k) \\ &\quad \times(K_k - A_kP_{k/k-1}C_k^T(C_kP_{k/k-1}C_k^T + R_k)^{-1})^T, \end{aligned} \tag{19}$$

By inspection of (19), the predictor gain (17) minimises $P_{k+1/k}$. □

4.7 Minimum-Variance Filtering

It can be seen from (12) that the predicted state estimate $\hat{x}_{k/k-1}$ is calculated using the previous measurement z_{k-1} as opposed to the current data z_k. A state estimate, given the data at time k, which is known as the filtered state, can similarly be obtained using the linear least squares or conditional-mean formula. In Lemma 1 it was shown that the predicted state estimate is unbiased. Therefore, it is assumed that the expected value of the filtered state equals the expected value of the predicted state, namely,

$$E\left\{\begin{bmatrix} \hat{x}_{k/k} \\ z_k \end{bmatrix}\right\} = \begin{bmatrix} \hat{x}_{k/k-1} \\ C_k\hat{x}_{k/k-1} \end{bmatrix}. \tag{20}$$

Substituting (20) into (10) and denoting $\hat{x}_{k/k} = E\{\hat{x}_k \mid z_k\}$ yields the filtered estimate

$$\hat{x}_{k/k} = \hat{x}_{k/k-1} + L_k(z_k - C_k\hat{x}_{k/k-1}), \tag{21}$$

where $L_k = E\{\hat{x}_kz_k^T\}E\{z_kz_k^T\}^{-1}$ is known as the filter gain, which is designed subsequently. Let $\tilde{x}_{k/k} = x_k - \hat{x}_{k/k}$ denote the filtered state error. It is shown below that the expectation of the filtered error is zero, that is, the filtered state estimate is unbiased.

Lemma 3: *Suppose that* $\hat{x}_{0/0} = x_0$*, then*

$$E\{\tilde{x}_{k/k}\} = 0 \tag{22}$$

for all $k \in [0, N]$.

"To be creative you have to contribute something different from what you've done before. Your results need not be original to the world; few results truly meet that criterion. In fact, most results are built on the work of others." *Lynne C. Levesque*

Proof: *Following the approach of [6], combining (4) - (6) results in* $z_k = C_kA_{k-1}x_{k-1} + C_kB_{k-1}w_{k-1} + v_k$, *which together with (21) yields*

$$\tilde{x}_{k/k} = (I - L_kC_k)A_{k-1}\tilde{x}_{k-1/k-1} + (I - L_kC_k)B_{k-1}w_{k-1} - L_kv_k . \tag{23}$$

From (23) and the assumptions (3), (7), it follows that

$$\begin{aligned} E\{\tilde{x}_{k/k}\} &= (I - L_kC_k)A_{k-1}E\{\tilde{x}_{k-1/k-1}\} \\ &= (I - L_kC_k)A_{k-1}\cdots(I - L_1C_1)A_0E\{\tilde{x}_{0/0}\} . \end{aligned} \tag{24}$$

Hence, with the initial condition $\hat{x}_{0/0} = x_0$, $E\{\tilde{x}_{k/k}\} = 0$. □

4.8 Design of the Filter Gain

It is shown below that the optimum filter gain is that which minimises the covariance $E\{\tilde{x}_{k/k}\tilde{x}_{k/k}^T\}$, where $\tilde{x}_{k/k} = x_k - \hat{x}_{k/k}$ is the filter error.

Lemma 4: *In respect of the estimation problem defined by (1), (3), (5) - (7), suppose there exists a solution* $P_{k/k} = P_{k/k}^T \geq 0$ *to the Riccati difference equation*

$$P_{k/k} = P_{k/k-1} - P_{k/k-1}C_k^T(C_kP_{k/k-1}C_k^T + R_k)^{-1}C_kP_{k/k-1} , \tag{25}$$

over [0, N], then the filter gain

$$L_k = P_{k/k-1}C_k^T(C_kP_{k/k-1}C_k^T + R_k)^{-1} , \tag{26}$$

within (21) minimises $P_{k/k} = E\{\tilde{x}_{k/k}\tilde{x}_{k/k}^T\}$.

Proof: *Subtracting* $\hat{x}_{k/k}$ *from* x_k *yields* $\tilde{x}_{k/k} = x_k - \hat{x}_{k/k} = x_k - \hat{x}_{k/k-1} - L_k(Cx_k + v_k - C\hat{x}_{k/k-1})$, *that is,*

$$\tilde{x}_{k/k} = (I - L_kC_k)\tilde{x}_{k/k-1} - L_kv_k \tag{27}$$

and

$$P_{k/k} = (I - L_kC_k)P_{k/k-1}(I - L_kC_k)^T + L_kR_kL_k^T , \tag{28}$$

which can be rearranged as

$$\begin{aligned} P_{k/k} &= P_{k/k-1} - P_{k/k-1}C_k^T(C_kP_{k/k-1}C_k^T + R_k)^{-1}C_kP_{k/k-1} \\ &+(L_k - P_{k/k-1}C_k^T(C_kP_{k/k-1}C_k^T + R_k)^{-1})(C_kP_{k/k-1}C_k^T + R_k)(L_k - P_{k/k-1}C_k^T(C_kP_{k/k-1}C_k^T + R_k)^{-1})^T \end{aligned} \tag{29}$$

By inspection of (29), the filter gain (26) minimises $P_{k/k}$. □

Example 2 (Data Fusion). Consider a filtering problem in which there are two measurements of the same state variable (possibly from different sensors), namely $A_k, B_k, Q_k \in \mathbb{R}$, $C_k = \begin{bmatrix} 1 \\ 1 \end{bmatrix}$ and $R_k = \begin{bmatrix} R_{1,k} & 0 \\ 0 & R_{2,k} \end{bmatrix}$, with $R_{1,k}, R_{2,k} \in \mathbb{R}$. Let $P_{k/k-1}$ denote the solution of the Riccati difference equation (25). By applying Cramer's rule within (26) it can be found that the filter gain is given by

"A professor is one who can speak on any subject - for precisely fifty minutes." *Norbert Wiener*

$$L_k = \begin{bmatrix} \dfrac{R_{2,k}P_{k/k-1}}{R_{2,k}P_{k/k-1} + R_{1,k}P_{k/k-1} + R_{1,k}R_{2,k}} & \dfrac{R_{1,k}P_{k/k-1}}{R_{2,k}P_{k/k-1} + R_{1,k}P_{k/k-1} + R_{1,k}R_{2,k}} \end{bmatrix},$$

from which it follows that $\lim_{R_{1,k}\to 0 \;\; R_{2,k}\neq 0} L_k = \begin{bmatrix}1 & 0\end{bmatrix}$ and $\lim_{R_{2,k}\to 0 \;\; R_{1,k}\neq 0} L_k = \begin{bmatrix}0 & 1\end{bmatrix}$. That is, when the first measurement is noise free, the filter ignores the second measurement and *vice versa*. Thus, the Kalman filter weights the data according to the prevailing measurement qualities.

4.9 The Predictor-Corrector Form

The Kalman filter may be written in the following predictor-corrector form. The corrected (or filtered) error covariances and states are respectively given by

$$\begin{aligned} P_{k/k} &= P_{k/k-1} - P_{k/k-1}C_k^T(C_kP_{k/k-1}C_k^T + R_k)^{-1}C_kP_{k/k-1} \\ &= P_{k/k-1} - L_k(C_kP_{k/k-1}C_k^T + R_k)^{-1}L_k^T \\ &= (I - L_kC_k)P_{k/k-1}, \end{aligned} \tag{30}$$

$$\begin{aligned} \hat{x}_{k/k} &= \hat{x}_{k/k-1} + L_k(z_k - C_k\hat{x}_{k/k-1}) \\ &= (I - L_kC_k)\hat{x}_{k/k-1} + L_kz_k, \end{aligned} \tag{31}$$

where $L_k = P_{k/k-1}C_k^T(C_kP_{k/k-1}C_k^T + R_k)^{-1}$. Equation (31) is also known as the measurement update. The predicted state and error covariances are respectively given by

$$\begin{aligned} \hat{x}_{k+1/k} &= A_k\hat{x}_{k/k} \\ &= (A_k - K_kC_k)\hat{x}_{k/k-1} + K_kz_k, \end{aligned} \tag{32}$$

$$P_{k+1/k} = A_kP_{k/k}A_k^T + B_kQ_kB_k^T, \tag{33}$$

where $K_k = A_kP_{k/k-1}C_k^T(C_kP_{k/k-1}C_k^T + R_k)^{-1}$. It can be seen from (31) that the corrected estimate, $\hat{x}_{k/k}$, is obtained using measurements up to time k. This contrasts with the prediction at time k + 1 in (32), which is based on all previous measurements. The output estimate is given by

$$\begin{aligned} \hat{y}_{k/k} &= C_k\hat{x}_{k/k} \\ &= C_k\hat{x}_{k/k-1} + C_kL_k(z_k - C_k\hat{x}_{k/k-1}) \\ &= C_k(I - L_kC_k)\hat{x}_{k/k-1} + C_kL_kz_k. \end{aligned} \tag{34}$$

"Before the advent of the Kalman filter, most mathematical work was based on Norbert Wiener's ideas, but the 'Wiener filtering' had proved difficult to apply. Kalman's approach, based on the use of state space techniques and a recursive least-squares algorithm, opened up many new theoretical and practical possibilities. The impact of Kalman filtering on all areas of applied mathematics, engineering, and sciences has been tremendous." *Eduardo Daniel Sontag*

4.10 The *A* Posteriori Filter

The above predictor-corrector form is used in the construction of extended Kalman filters for nonlinear estimation problems (see Chapter 10). When state predictions are not explicitly required, the following one-line recursion for the filtered state can be employed. Substituting $\hat{x}_{k/k-1} = A_{k-1}\hat{x}_{k-1/k-1}$ into $\hat{x}_{k/k} = (I - L_kC_k)\hat{x}_{k/k-1} + L_kz_k$ yields $\hat{x}_{k/k} = (I - L_kC_k)A_{k-1}\hat{x}_{k-1/k-1} + L_kz_k$. Hence, the output estimator may be written as

$$\begin{bmatrix} \hat{x}_{k/k} \\ \hat{y}_{k/k} \end{bmatrix} = \begin{bmatrix} (I - L_kC_k)A_{k-1} & L_k \\ C_k & \end{bmatrix} \begin{bmatrix} \hat{x}_{k-1/k-1} \\ z_k \end{bmatrix}, \quad (35)$$

This form is called the *a posteriori* filter within [7], [8] and [9]. The absence of a direct feed-through matrix above reduces the complexity of the robust filter designs described in [7], [8] and [9].

4.11 The Information Form

Algebraically equivalent recursions of the Kalman filter can be obtained by propagating a so-called corrected information state

$$\underline{\hat{x}}_{k/k} = P_{k/k}^{-1}\hat{x}_{k/k}, \quad (36)$$

and a predicted information state

$$\underline{\hat{x}}_{k+1/k} = P_{k+1/k}^{-1}\hat{x}_{k+1/k}. \quad (37)$$

The expression

$$(A + BCD)^{-1} = A^{-1} - A^{-1}B(C^{-1} + DA^{-1}B)^{-1}DA^{-1}, \quad (38)$$

which is variously known as the Matrix Inversion Lemma, the Sherman-Morrison formula and Woodbury's identity, is used to derive the information filter, see [3], [4], [11], [14] and [15]. To confirm the above identity, premultiply both sides of (38) by $(A + BD^{-1}C)$ to obtain

$$\begin{aligned} I &= I + BCDA^{-1} - B(C^{-1} + DA^{-1}B)^{-1}DA^{-1} - BCDA^{-1}B(C^{-1} + DA^{-1}B)^{-1}DA^{-1} \\ &= I + BCDA^{-1} - B(I + CDA^{-1}B)^{-1}(C^{-1} + DA^{-1}B)^{-1}DA^{-1} \\ &= I + BCDA^{-1} - BC(C^{-1} + DA^{-1}B)^{-1}(C^{-1} + DA^{-1}B)^{-1}DA^{-1}, \end{aligned}$$

"I have been aware from the outset that the deep analysis of something which is now called Kalman filtering was of major importance. But even with this immodesty I did not quite anticipate all the reactions to this work." *Rudolf Emil Kalman*

from which the result follows. From the above Matrix Inversion Lemma and (30) it follows that

$$\begin{aligned} P_{k/k}^{-1} &= (P_{k/k-1} - P_{k/k-1}C_k^T(C_kP_{k/k-1}C_k^T + R_k)^{-1}C_kP_{k/k-1})^{-1} \\ &= P_{k/k-1}^{-1} + C_k^T R_k^{-1} C_k , \end{aligned} \tag{39}$$

assuming that $P_{k/k-1}^{-1}$ and R_k^{-1} exist. An expression for $P_{k+1/k}^{-1}$ can be obtained from the Matrix Inversion Lemma and (33), namely,

$$\begin{aligned} P_{k+1/k}^{-1} &= (A_kP_{k/k}A_k^T + B_kQ_kB_k^T)^{-1} \\ &= (F_k^{-1} + B_kQ_kB_k^T)^{-1} , \end{aligned} \tag{40}$$

where $F_k = (A_kP_{k/k}A_k^T)^{-1} = A_k^{-T}P_{k/k}^{-1}A_k^{-1}$, which gives

$$P_{k+1/k}^{-1} = (I - F_kB_k(B_k^TF_kB_k + Q_k^{-1})^{-1}B_k^T)F_k . \tag{41}$$

Another useful identity is

$$\begin{aligned} (A + BCD)^{-1}BC &= A^{-1}(I + BCDA^{-1})^{-1}BC \\ &= A^{-1}B(I + CDA^{-1}B)^{-1}C \\ &= A^{-1}B(C^{-1} + DA^{-1}B)^{-1} . \end{aligned} \tag{42}$$

From (42) and (39), the filter gain can be expressed as

$$\begin{aligned} L_k &= P_{k/k-1}C_k^T(C_kP_{k/k-1}C_k^T + R_k)^{-1} \\ &= (P_{k/k-1}^{-1} + C_k^TR_k^{-1}C_k)^{-1}C_k^TR_k^{-1} \\ &= P_{k/k}C_k^TR_k^{-1} . \end{aligned} \tag{43}$$

Premultiplying (39) by $P_{k/k}$ and rearranging gives

$$I - L_kC_k = P_{k/k}P_{k/k-1}^{-1} . \tag{44}$$

It follows from (31), (36) and (44) that the corrected information state is given by

$$\begin{aligned} \underline{\hat{x}}_{k/k} &= P_{k/k}^{-1}\hat{x}_{k/k} \\ &= P_{k/k}^{-1}(I - L_kC_k)\hat{x}_{k/k-1} + P_{k/k}^{-1}L_kz_k \\ &= \underline{\hat{x}}_{k/k-1} + C_k^TR_k^{-1}z_k . \end{aligned} \tag{45}$$

"Information is the oxygen of the modern age. It seeps through the walls topped by barbed wire, it wafts across the electrified borders." *Ronald Wilson Reagan*

The predicted information state follows from (37), (41) and the definition of F_k, namely,

$$\begin{aligned}\hat{\underline{x}}_{k+1/k} &= P_{k+1/k}^{-1}\hat{x}_{k+1/k} \\ &= P_{k+1/k}^{-1}A_k\hat{x}_{k/k} \\ &= (I - F_kB_k(B_k^TF_kB_k + Q_k^{-1})^{-1}B_k^T)F_kA_k\hat{x}_{k/k} \\ &= (I - F_kB_k(B_k^TF_kB_k + Q_k^{-1})^{-1}B_k^T)A_k^{-T}\hat{\underline{x}}_{k/k}.\end{aligned} \tag{46}$$

Recall from Lemma 1 and Lemma 3 that $E\{x_k - \hat{x}_{k+1/k}\}$ = 0 and $E\{x_k - \hat{x}_{k/k}\}$ = 0, provided $\hat{x}_{0/0}$ = x_0. Similarly, with $\hat{x}_{0/0}$ = $P_{0/0}^{-1}x_0$, it follows that $E\{x_k - P_{k+1/k}\hat{\underline{x}}_{k+1/k}\}$ = 0 and $E\{x_k - P_{k/k}\hat{\underline{x}}_{k/k}\}$ = 0. That is, the information states (scaled by the appropriate covariances) will be unbiased, provided that the filter is suitably initialised. The calculation cost and potential for numerical instability can influence decisions on whether to implement the predictor-corrector form (30) - (33) or the information form (39) - (46) of the Kalman filter. The filters have similar complexity, both require a $p \times p$ matrix inverse in the measurement updates (31) and (45). However, inverting the measurement covariance matrix for the information filter may be troublesome when the measurement noise is negligible.

4.12 Comparison with Recursive Least Squares

The recursive least squares (RLS) algorithm is equivalent to the Kalman filter designed with the simplifications $A_k = I$ and $B_k = 0$; see the derivations within [10], [11]. For convenience, consider a more general RLS algorithm that retains the correct A_k but relies on the simplifying assumption $B_k = 0$. Under these conditions, denote the RLS algorithm's predictor gain by

$$\underline{K}_k = A_k\underline{P}_{k/k-1}C_k^T(C_k\underline{P}_{k/k-1}C_k^T + R_k)^{-1}, \tag{47}$$

where $\underline{P}_{k/k-1}$ is obtained from the Riccati difference equation

$$\underline{P}_{k+1/k} = A_k\underline{P}_{k/k-1}A_k^T - A_k\underline{P}_{k/k-1}C_k^T(C_k\underline{P}_{k/k-1}C_k^T + R_k)^{-1}C_k\underline{P}_{k/k-1}A_k^T. \tag{48}$$

It is argued below that the cost of the above model simplification is an increase in mean-square-error.

Lemma 5: *Let* $P_{k-1/k}$ *denote the predicted error covariance within (33) for the optimal filter. Under the above conditions, the predicted error covariance,* $\overline{P}_{k/k-1}$, *exhibited by the RLS algorithm satisfies*

$$P_{k/k-1} \le \overline{P}_{k/k-1}. \tag{49}$$

"All of the books in the world contain no more information than is broadcast as video in a single large American city in a single year. Not all bits have equal value." *Carl Edward Sagan*

Proof: *From the approach of Lemma 2, the RLS algorithm's predicted error covariance is given by*

$$\overline{P}_{k+1/k} = A_k\overline{P}_{k/k-1}A_k^T - A_k\overline{P}_{k/k-1}C_k^T(C_k\overline{P}_{k/k-1}C_k^T + R_k)^{-1}C_k\overline{P}_{k/k-1}A_k^T + B_kQ_kB_k^T$$

$$+(\underline{K}_k - A_k\overline{P}_{k/k-1}C_k^T(C_k\overline{P}_{k/k-1}C_k^T + R_k)^{-1})(C_k\overline{P}_{k/k-1}C_k^T + R_k) \tag{50}$$

$$\times(\underline{K}_k - A_k\overline{P}_{k/k-1}C_k^T(C_k\overline{P}_{k/k-1}C_k^T + R_k)^{-1})^T .$$

The last term on the right-hand-side of (50) is nonzero since the above RLS algorithm relies on the erroneous assumption $B_kQ_kB_k^T = 0$. *Therefore (49) follows.* □

4.13 Repeated Predictions

When there are gaps in the data record, or the data is irregularly spaced, state predictions can be calculated an arbitrary number of steps ahead. The one-step-ahead prediction is given by (32). The two, three and *j*-step-ahead predictions, given data at time *k*, are calculated as

$$\hat{x}_{k+2/k} = A_{k+1}\hat{x}_{k+1/k} \tag{51}$$

$$\hat{x}_{k+3/k} = A_{k+2}\hat{x}_{k+2/k} \tag{52}$$

$$\vdots$$

$$\hat{x}_{k+j/k} = A_{k+j-1}\hat{x}_{k+j-1/k}, \tag{53}$$

see also [4], [12]. The corresponding predicted error covariances are given by

$$P_{k+2/k} = A_{k+1}P_{k+1/k}A_{k+1}^T + B_{k+1}Q_{k+1}B_{k+1}^T \tag{54}$$

$$P_{k+3/k} = A_{k+2}P_{k+2/k}A_{k+2}^T + B_{k+2}Q_{k+2}B_{k+2}^T \tag{55}$$

$$\vdots$$

$$P_{k+j/k} = A_{k+j-1}P_{k+j-1/k}A_{k+j-1}^T + B_{k+j-1}Q_{k+j-1}B_{k+j-1}^T . \tag{56}$$

Another way to handle missing measurements at time i is to set $C_i = 0$, which leads to the same predicted states and error covariances. However, the cost of relying on repeated predictions is an increased mean-square-error which is demonstrated below.

Lemma 6:

(i) $P_{k/k} \le P_{k/k-1}$.

(ii) *Suppose that*

$$A_kA_k^T + B_kQ_kB_k^T \ge I \tag{57}$$

for all k $\in$ *[0, N], then* $P_{k+j/k} \ge P_{k+j-1/k}$ *for all (j+k)* $\in$ *[0, N]*.

"Where a calculator on the ENIAC is equipped with 18,000 vacuum tubes and weighs 30 tones, computers in the future may have only 1,000 vacuum tubes and perhaps weigh 1.5 tons." *Popular Mechanics*, 1949

Proof:

(i) *The claim follows by inspection of (30) since* $L_{k-1}(C_{k-1}P_{k-1/k-2}C_{k-1}^T + R_{k-1})L_{k-1}^T \geq 0$. *Thus, the filter outperforms the one-step-ahead predictor.*

(ii) *For* $P_{k+j-1/k} \geq 0$, *condition (57) yields* $A_{k+j-1}P_{k+j-1/k}A_{k+j-1}^T + B_{k+j-1}Q_{k+j-1}B_{k+j-1}^T \geq P_{k+j-1/k}$ *which together with (56) results in* $P_{k+j/k} \geq P_{k+j-1/k}$. □

Example 3. Consider a filtering problem where $A = 0.9$ and $B = C = Q = R = 1$, for which $AA^T + BQB^T = 1.81 > 1$. The predicted error covariances, $P_{k+j/k}$, $j = 1 \ldots 10$, are plotted in Fig. 4. The monotonically increasing sequence of error variances shown in the figure demonstrates that degraded performance occurs during repeated predictions. Fig. 5 shows some sample trajectories of the model output (dotted line), filter output (crosses) and predictions (circles) assuming that $z_3 \ldots z_8$ are unavailable. It can be seen from the figure that the prediction error increases with time k, which illustrates Lemma 6.

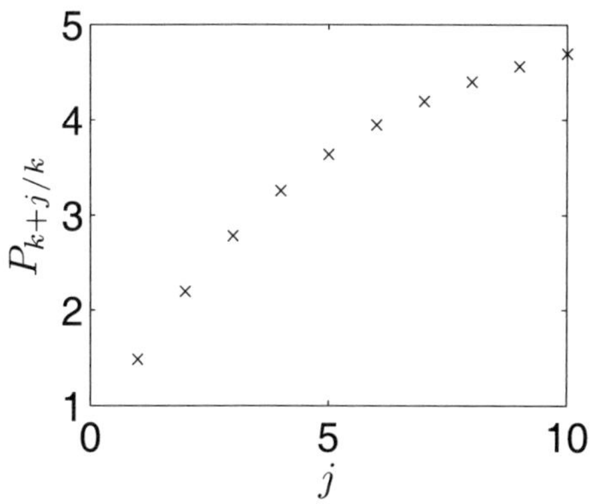

Figure 4. Predicted error variances for Example 3.

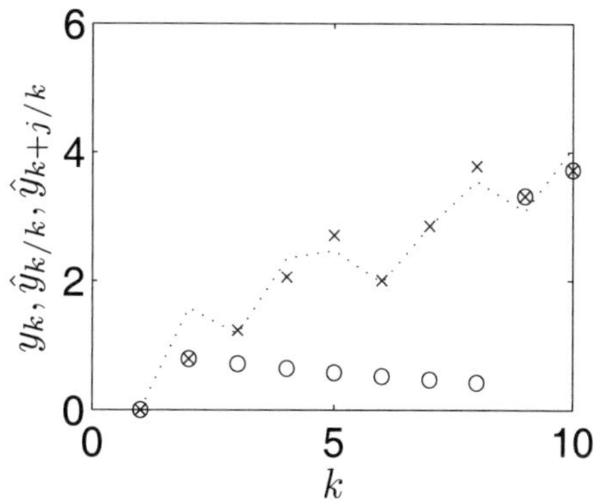

Figure 5. Sample trajectories for Example 3: y_k (dotted line), $\hat{y}_{k/k}$ (crosses) and $\hat{y}_{k+j/k}$ (circles).

4.14 Accommodating Deterministic Inputs

Suppose that the signal model is described by

$$x_{k+1} = A_k x_k + B_k w_k + \mu_k , \tag{58}$$

$$y_k = C_k x_k + \pi_k , \tag{59}$$

where μ_k and π_k are deterministic inputs (such as known non-zero means). The modifications to the Kalman recursions can be found by assuming $\hat{x}_{k+1/k} = A_k \hat{x}_{k/k} + \mu_k$ and $\hat{y}_{k/k-1} = C_k \hat{x}_{k/k-1} + \pi_k$. The filtered and predicted states are then given by

$$\hat{x}_{k/k} = \hat{x}_{k/k-1} + L_k(z_k - C_k \hat{x}_{k/k-1} - \pi_k) \tag{60}$$

"I think there is a world market for maybe five computers." *Thomas John Watson*

and

$$\hat{x}_{k+1/k} = A_k \hat{x}_{k/k} + \mu_k \tag{61}$$

$$= A_k \hat{x}_{k/k-1} + K_k (z_k - C_k \hat{x}_{k/k-1} - \pi_k) + \mu_k , \tag{62}$$

respectively. Subtracting (62) from (58) gives

$$\begin{aligned} \tilde{x}_{k+1/k} &= A_k \tilde{x}_{k/k-1} - K_k (C_k \tilde{x}_{k/k-1} + \pi_k + v_k - \pi_k) + B_k w_k + \mu_k - \mu_k \\ &= (A_k - K_k C_k) \tilde{x}_{k/k-1} + B_k w_k - K_k v_k , \end{aligned} \tag{63}$$

where $\tilde{x}_{k/k-1} = x_k - \hat{x}_{k/k-1}$. Therefore, the predicted error covariance,

$$\begin{aligned} P_{k+1/k} &= (A_k - K_k C_k) P_{k/k-1} (A_k - K_k C_k)^T + B_k Q_k B_k^T + K_k R_k K_k^T \\ &= A_k P_{k/k-1} A_k^T - K_k (C_k P_{k/k-1} C_k^T + R_k) K_k^T + B_k Q_k B_k^T , \end{aligned} \tag{64}$$

is unchanged. The filtered output is given by

$$\hat{y}_{k/k} = C_k \hat{x}_{k/k} + \pi_k . \tag{65}$$

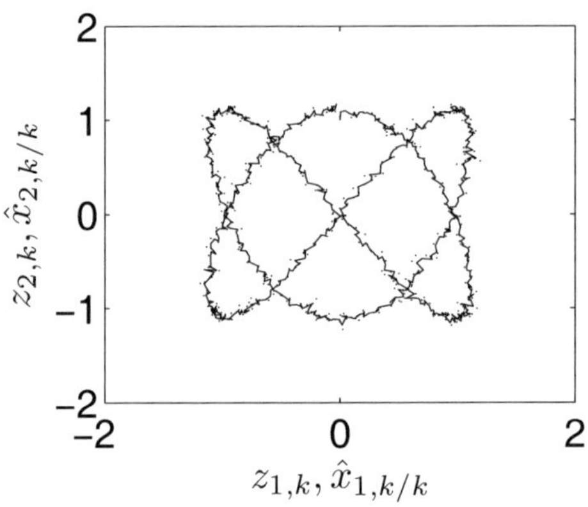

Figure 6. Measurements (dotted line) and filtered states (solid line) for Example 4.

Example 4. Consider a filtering problem where A = diag(0.1, 0.1), $B = C$ = diag(1, 1), $Q = R$ = diag(0.001, 0.001), with $\mu_k = \begin{bmatrix} \sin(2k) \\ \cos(3k) \end{bmatrix}$. The filtered states calculated from (60) are shown in Fig. 6. The resulting Lissajous figure illustrates that states having nonzero means can be modelled using deterministic inputs.

"There is no reason anyone would want a computer in their home." *Kenneth Harry Olson*

4.15 Correlated Process and Measurement Noises

Consider the case where the process and measurement noises are correlated

$$E\left\{\begin{bmatrix} w_j \\ v_j \end{bmatrix}\begin{bmatrix} w_k^T & v_k^T \end{bmatrix}\right\} = \begin{bmatrix} Q_k & S_k \\ S_k^T & R_k \end{bmatrix}\delta_{jk} . \tag{66}$$

The generalisation of the optimal filter that takes the above into account was published by Kalman in 1963 [2]. The expressions for the state prediction

$$\hat{x}_{k+1/k} = A_k\hat{x}_{k/k-1} + K_k(z_k - C_k\hat{x}_{k/k-1}) \tag{67}$$

and the state prediction error

$$\tilde{x}_{k+1/k} = (A_k - K_kC_k)\tilde{x}_{k/k-1} + B_kw_k - K_kv_k \tag{68}$$

remain the same. It follows from (68) that

$$E\{\tilde{x}_{k+1/k}\} = (A_k - K_kC_k)E\{\tilde{x}_{k/k-1}\} + \begin{bmatrix} B_k & -K_k \end{bmatrix}\begin{bmatrix} E\{w_k\} \\ E\{v_k\} \end{bmatrix} . \tag{69}$$

As before, the optimum predictor gain is that which minimises the prediction error covariance $E\{\tilde{x}_{k/k-1}\tilde{x}_{k/k-1}^T\}$.

Lemma 7: *In respect of the estimation problem defined by (1), (5), (6) with noise covariance (66), suppose there exist solutions* $P_{k/k-1} = P_{k/k-1}^T \geq 0$ *to the Riccati difference equation*

$$P_{k+1/k} = A_kP_{k/k-1}A_k^T + B_kQ_kB_k^T - (A_kP_{k/k-1}C_k^T + B_kS_k)(C_kP_{k/k-1}C_k^T + R_k)^{-1}(A_kP_{k/k-1}C_k^T + B_kS_k)^T \tag{70}$$

over [0, N], then the state prediction (67) with the gain

$$K_k = (A_kP_{k/k-1}C_k^T + B_kS_k)(C_kP_{k/k-1}C_k^T + R_k)^{-1}, \tag{71}$$

minimises $P_{k/k-1} = E\{\tilde{x}_{k/k-1}\tilde{x}_{k/k-1}^T\}$.

Proof: *It follows from (69) that*

$$\begin{aligned} E\{\tilde{x}_{k+1/k}\tilde{x}_{k+1/k}^T\} &= (A_k - K_kC_k)E\{\tilde{x}_{k/k-1}\tilde{x}_{k/k-1}^T\}(A_k - K_kC_k)^T \\ &\quad + \begin{bmatrix} B_k & -K_k \end{bmatrix}\begin{bmatrix} Q_k & S_k \\ S_k^T & R_k \end{bmatrix}\begin{bmatrix} B_k^T \\ -K_k^T \end{bmatrix} \\ &= (A_k - K_kC_k)E\{\tilde{x}_{k/k-1}\tilde{x}_{k/k-1}^T\}(A_k - K_kC_k)^T \\ &\quad + B_kQ_kB_k^T + K_kR_kK_k^T - B_kS_kK_k^T - K_kS_kB_k^T . \end{aligned} \tag{72}$$

"640K ought to be enough for anybody." *William Henry (Bill) Gates III*

Expanding (72) and denoting $P_{k/k-1} = E\{\tilde{x}_{k/k-1}\tilde{x}_{k/k-1}^T\}$ *gives*

$$P_{k+1/k} = A_k P_{k/k-1} A_k^T + B_k Q_k B_k^T - (A_k P_{k/k-1} C_k^T + B_k S_k)(C_k P_{k/k-1} C_k^T + R_k)^{-1}(A_k P_{k/k-1} C_k^T + B_k S_k)^T$$
$$+\left(K_k - (A_k P_{k/k-1} C_k^T + B_k S_k)(C_k P_{k/k-1} C_k^T + R_k)^{-1}\right)\left(C_k P_{k/k-1} C_k^T + R_k\right)$$
$$\times\left(K_k - (A_k P_{k/k-1} C_k^T + B_k S_k)(C_k P_{k/k-1} C_k^T + R_k)^{-1}\right)^T . \quad (73)$$

By inspection of (73), the predictor gain (71) minimises $P_{k+1/k}$. □

Thus, the predictor gain is calculated differently when w_k and v_k are correlated. The calculation of the filtered state and filtered error covariance are unchanged, *viz.*

$$\hat{x}_{k/k} = (I - L_k C_k)\hat{x}_{k/k-1} + L_k z_k , \quad (74)$$

$$P_{k/k} = (I - L_k C_k) P_{k/k-1} (I - L_k C_k)^T + L_k R_k L_k^T , \quad (75)$$

where

$$L_k = P_{k/k-1} C_k^T (C_k P_{k/k-1} C_k^T + R_k)^{-1} . \quad (76)$$

However, $P_{k/k-1}$ is now obtained from the Riccati difference equation (70).

4.16 Including a Direct-Feedthrough Matrix

Suppose now that the signal model possesses a direct-feedthrough matrix, D_k, namely

$$x_{k+1} = A_k x_k + B_k w_k , \quad (77)$$

$$y_k = C_k x_k + D_k w_k . \quad (78)$$

Let the observations be denoted by

$$z_k = C_k x_k + \underline{v}_k , \quad (79)$$

where $\underline{v}_k = D_k w_k + v_k$, under the assumptions (3) and (7). It follows that

$$E\left\{\begin{bmatrix} w_j \\ \underline{v}_j \end{bmatrix}\begin{bmatrix} w_k^T & \underline{v}_k^T \end{bmatrix}\right\} = \begin{bmatrix} Q_k & Q_k D_k^T \\ D_k Q_k & D_k Q_k D_k^T + R_k \end{bmatrix}\delta_{jk} . \quad (80)$$

The approach of the previous section may be used to obtain the minimum-variance predictor for the above system. Using (80) within Lemma 7 yields the predictor gain

$$K_k = (A_k P_{k/k-1} C_k^T + B_k Q_k D_k^T)\Omega_k^{-1} , \quad (81)$$

"Everything that can be invented has been invented." *Charles Holland Duell*

where

$$\Omega_k = C_k P_{k/k-1} C_k^T + D_k Q_k D_k^T + R_k \tag{82}$$

and $P_{k/k-1}$ is the solution of the Riccati difference equation

$$P_{k+1/k} = A_k P_{k/k-1} A_k^T - K_k \Omega_k K_k^T + B_k Q_k B_k^T . \tag{83}$$

The filtered states can be calculated from (74) , (82), (83) and $L_k = P_{k/k-1} C_k^T \Omega_k^{-1}$.

4.17 Solution of the General Filtering Problem

The general filtering problem is shown in Fig. 7, in which it is desired to develop a filter $\mathcal{H}$ that operates on noisy measurements of $\mathcal{G}_2$ and estimates the output of $\mathcal{G}_1$. Frequency domain solutions for time-invariant systems were developed in Chapters 1 and 2. Here, for the time-varying case, it is assumed that the system $\mathcal{G}_2$ has the state-space realisation

$$x_{k+1} = A_k x_k + B_k w_k , \tag{84}$$

$$y_{2,k} = C_{2,k} x_k + D_{2,k} w_k . \tag{85}$$

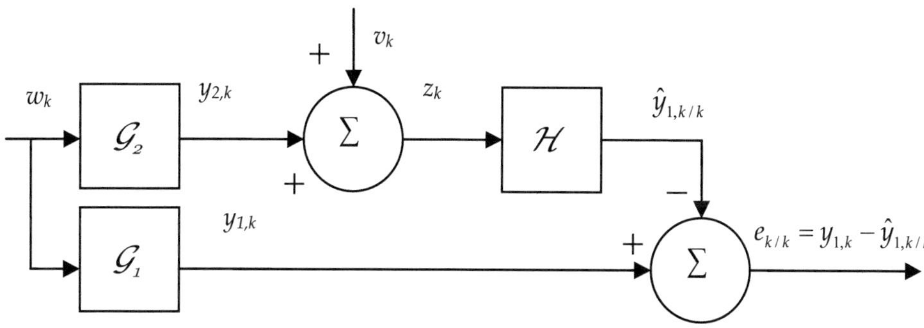

Figure 7. The general filtering problem. The objective is to estimate the output of $\mathcal{G}_1$ from noisy measurements of $\mathcal{G}_2$.

Suppose that the system $\mathcal{G}_1$ has the realisation (84) and

$$y_{1,k} = C_{1,k} x_k + D_{1,k} w_k . \tag{86}$$

The objective is to produce estimates $\hat{y}_{1,k/k}$ of $y_{1,k}$ from the measurements

$$z_k = C_{2,k} x_k + \underline{v}_k , \tag{87}$$

"He was a multimillionaire. Wanna know how he made all of his money? He designed the little diagrams that tell which way to put batteries on." *Stephen Wright*

where $\underline{v}_k = D_{2,k}w_k + v_k$, so that the variance of the estimation error,

$$e_{k/k} = y_{1,k} - \hat{y}_{1,k/k}, \tag{88}$$

is minimised. The predicted state follows immediately from the results of the previous sections, namely,

$$\begin{aligned} \hat{x}_{k+1/k} &= A_k\hat{x}_{k/k-1} + K_k(z_k - C_{2,k}\hat{x}_{k/k-1}) \\ &= (A_k - K_kC_{2,k})\hat{x}_{k/k-1} + K_kz_k \end{aligned} \tag{89}$$

where

$$K_k = (A_kP_{k/k-1}C_{2,k}^T + B_kQ_kD_{2,k}^T)\Omega_k^{-1} \tag{90}$$

and

$$\Omega_k = C_{2,k}P_{k/k-1}C_{2,k}^T + D_{2,k}Q_kD_{2,k}^T + R_k, \tag{91}$$

in which $P_{k/k-1}$ evolves from

$$P_{k+1/k} = A_kP_{k/k-1}A_k^T - K_k\Omega_kK_k^T + B_kQ_kB_k^T. \tag{92}$$

In view of the structure (89), an output estimate of the form

$$\begin{aligned} \hat{y}_{1,k/k} &= C_{1,k}\hat{x}_{k/k-1} + L_k(z_k - C_{2,k}\hat{x}_{k/k-1}) \\ &= (C_{1,k} - L_kC_{2,k})\hat{x}_{k/k-1} + L_kz_k, \end{aligned} \tag{93}$$

is sought, where L_k is a filter gain to be designed. Subtracting (93) from (86) gives

$$\begin{aligned} e_{k/k} &= y_{1,k} - \hat{y}_{1,k/k} \\ &= (C_{1,k} - L_kC_{2,k})\tilde{x}_{k/k-1} + \begin{bmatrix} D_{1,k} & -L_k \end{bmatrix}\begin{bmatrix} w_k \\ \underline{v}_k \end{bmatrix}. \end{aligned} \tag{94}$$

It is shown below that an optimum filter gain can be found by minimising the output error covariance $E\{e_{k/k}e_{k/k}^T\}$.

Lemma 8: *In respect of the estimation problem defined by (84) - (88), the output estimate* $\hat{y}_{1,k/k}$ *with the filter gain*

$$L_k = (C_{1,k}P_{k/k-1}C_{2,k}^T + D_{1,k}Q_kD_{2,k}^T)\Omega_k^{-1} \tag{95}$$

minimises $E\{e_{k/k}e_{k/k}^T\}$.

"This 'telephone' has too many shortcomings to be seriously considered as a means of communication. The device is inherently of no value to us." *Western Union* memo, 1876

Proof: *It follows from (94) that*

$$E\{e_{k/k}e_{k/k}^T\} = (C_{1,k} - L_k C_{2,k})P_{k/k-1}(C_{1,k}^T - C_{2,k}^T L_k^T)$$
$$+\begin{bmatrix} D_{1,k} & -L_k \end{bmatrix}\begin{bmatrix} Q_k & Q_k D_{2,k}^T \\ D_{2,k}Q_k^T & D_{2,k}Q_k D_{2,k}^T + R_k \end{bmatrix}\begin{bmatrix} D_{1,k}^T \\ -L_k^T \end{bmatrix} \tag{96}$$
$$= C_{1,k}P_{k/k-1}C_{1k}^T - C_{2,k}\bar{L}_k\Omega_k\bar{L}_k^T C_{2,k}^T,$$

which can be expanded to give

$$E\{e_{k/k}e_{k/k}^T\} = C_{1,k}P_{k/k-1}C_{1,k}^T + D_{2,k}Q_k D_{2,k}^T - (C_{1,k}P_{k/k-1}C2,_k^T + D_{1,k}Q_k D_{2,k}^T)\Omega_k^{-1}(C_{1,k}P_{k/k-1}C_{2,k}^T + D_{1,k}Q_k D_{2,k}^T)^T$$
$$-(C_{1,k}P_{k/k-1}C2,_k^T + D_{1,k}Q_k D_{2,k}^T)\Omega_k^{-1}(C_{1,k}P_{k/k-1}C_{2,k}^T + D_{1,k}Q_k D_{2,k}^T)^T$$
$$+(L_k - (C_{1,k}P_{k/k-1}C_{2,k}^T + D_{1,k}Q_k D_{2,k}^T)\Omega_k^{-1})\Omega_k$$
$$+(L_k - (C_{1,k}P_{k/k-1}C_{2,k}^T + D_{1,k}Q_k D_{2,k}^T)\Omega_k^{-1})^T. \tag{97}$$

By inspection of (97), the filter gain (95) minimises $E\{e_{k/k}e_{k/k}^T\}$. □

The filter gain (95) has been generalised to include arbitrary $C_{1,k}$, $D_{1,k}$, and $D_{2,k}$. For state estimation, $C_2 = I$ and $D_2 = 0$, in which case (95) reverts to the simpler form (26). The problem (84) - (88) can be written compactly in the following generalised regulator framework from control theory [13].

$$\begin{bmatrix} x_{k+1} \\ e_{k/k} \\ z_k \end{bmatrix} = \begin{bmatrix} A_k & B_{1,1,k} & 0 \\ C_{1,1,k} & D_{1,1,k} & D_{1,2,k} \\ C_{2,1,k} & D_{2,1,k} & 0 \end{bmatrix}\begin{bmatrix} x_k \\ \begin{bmatrix} v_k \\ w_k \end{bmatrix} \\ -\hat{y}_{1,k/k} \end{bmatrix}, \tag{98}$$

where $B_{1,1,k} = \begin{bmatrix} 0 & B_k \end{bmatrix}$, $C_{1,1,k} = C_{1,k}$, $C_{2,1,k} = C_{2,k}$ $D_{1,1,k} = \begin{bmatrix} 0 & D_{1,k} \end{bmatrix}$, $D_{1,2,k} = I$ and $D_{2,1,k} = \begin{bmatrix} I & D_{2,k} \end{bmatrix}$. With the above definitions, the minimum-variance solution can be written as

$$\hat{x}_{k+1/k} = A_k\hat{x}_{k/k-1} + K_k(z_k - C_{2,1,k}\hat{x}_{k/k-1}), \tag{99}$$

$$\hat{y}_{1,k/k} = C_{1,1,k}\hat{x}_{k/k-1} + L_k(z_k - C_{2,1,k}\hat{x}_{k/k-1}), \tag{100}$$

"The wireless music box has no imaginable commercial value. Who would pay for a message sent to nobody in particular?" *David Sarnoff*

where

$$K_k = \left(A_k P_{k/k-1} C_{2,1,k}^T + B_{1,1,k} \begin{bmatrix} R_k & 0 \\ 0 & Q_k \end{bmatrix} D_{2,1,k}^T \right) \left(C_{2,1,k} P_{k/k-1} C_{2,1,k}^T + D_{2,1,k} \begin{bmatrix} R_k & 0 \\ 0 & Q_k \end{bmatrix} D_{2,1,k}^T \right)^{-1}, \quad (101)$$

$$L_k = \left(C_{1,1,k} P_{k/k-1} C_{2,1,k}^T + D_{1,1,k} \begin{bmatrix} R_k & 0 \\ 0 & Q_k \end{bmatrix} D_{2,1,k}^T \right) \left(C_{2,1,k} P_{k/k-1} C_{2,1,k}^T + D_{2,1,k} \begin{bmatrix} R_k & 0 \\ 0 & Q_k \end{bmatrix} D_{2,1,k}^T \right)^{-1}, \quad (102)$$

in which $P_{k/k-1}$ is the solution of the Riccati difference equation

$$P_{k+1/k} = A_k P_{k/k-1} A_k^T - K_k (C_{2,1,k} P_{k/k-1} C_{2,1,k}^T + D_{2,1,k} \begin{bmatrix} R_k & 0 \\ 0 & Q_k \end{bmatrix} D_{2,1,k}^T) K_k^T + B_{1,1,k} \begin{bmatrix} R_k & 0 \\ 0 & Q_k \end{bmatrix} B_{1,1,k}^T. \quad (103)$$

The application of the solution (99) – (100) to output estimation, input estimation (or equalisation), state estimation and mixed filtering problems is demonstrated in the example below.

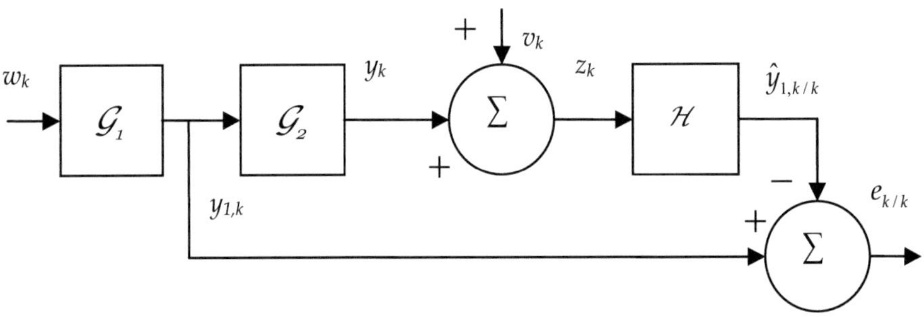

Figure 8. The mixed filtering and equalisation problem considered in Example 5. The objective is to estimate the output of the plant $\mathcal{G}_1$ which has been corrupted by the channel $\mathcal{G}_2$ and the measurement noise v_k.

Example 5.

(i) For output estimation problems, where $C_{1,k} = C_{2,k}$ and $D_{1,k} = D_{2,k}$, the predictor gain (101) and filter gain (102) are identical to the previously derived (90) and (95), respectively.

(ii) For state estimation problems, set $C_{1,k} = I$ and $D_{1,k} = 0$.

(iii) For equalisation problems, set $C_{1,k} = 0$ and $D_{1,k} = I$.

(iv) Consider a mixed filtering and equalisation problem depicted in Fig. 8, where the output of the plant $\mathcal{G}_1$ has been corrupted by the channel $\mathcal{G}_2$. Assume that $\mathcal{G}_1$ has the realisation $\begin{bmatrix} x_{1,k+1} \\ y_{1,k} \end{bmatrix} = \begin{bmatrix} A_{1,k} & B_{1,k} \\ C_{1,k} & D_{1,k} \end{bmatrix} \begin{bmatrix} x_{1,k} \\ w_k \end{bmatrix}$. Noting the realisation of

---

"Video won't be able to hold on to any market it captures after the first six months. People will soon get tired of staring at a plywood box every night." *Daryl Francis Zanuck*

the cascaded system $\mathcal{G}_1\mathcal{G}_2$ (see Problem 7), the minimum-variance solution can be found by setting $A_k = \begin{bmatrix} A_{2,k} & B_{2,k}C_{1,k} \\ 0 & A_{1,k} \end{bmatrix}$, $B_{1,1k} = \begin{bmatrix} 0 & B_{2,k}D_{1,k} \\ 0 & B_{1,k} \end{bmatrix}$, $B_{1,2,k} = \begin{bmatrix} 0 \\ 0 \end{bmatrix}$, $C_{1,1,k} = \begin{bmatrix} C_{1,k} & 0 \end{bmatrix}$, $C_{2,1,k} = \begin{bmatrix} C_{2,k} & D_{2,k}C_{1,k} \end{bmatrix}$, $D_{1,1,k} = \begin{bmatrix} 0 & D_{1,k} \end{bmatrix}$ and $D_{2,1,k} = \begin{bmatrix} I & D_{2,k}D_{1,k} \end{bmatrix}$.

4.18 Hybrid Continuous-Discrete Filtering

Often a system's dynamics evolve continuously but measurements can only be observed in discrete time increments. This problem is modelled in [20] as

$$\dot{x}(t) = A(t)x(t) + B(t)w(t), \tag{104}$$

$$z_k = C_k x_k + v_k, \tag{105}$$

where $E\{w(t)\} = 0$, $E\{w(t)w^T(\tau)\} = Q(t)\delta(t-\tau)$, $E\{v_k\} = 0$, $E\{v_j v_k^T\} = R_k\delta_{jk}$ and $x_k = x(kT_s)$, in which T_s is the sampling interval. Following the approach of [20], state estimates can be obtained from a hybrid of continuous-time and discrete-time filtering equations. The predicted states and error covariances are obtained from

$$\dot{\hat{x}}(t) = A(t)\hat{x}(t), \tag{106}$$

$$\dot{P}(t) = A(t)P(t) + P(t)A^T(t) + B(t)Q(t)B^T(t). \tag{107}$$

Define $\hat{x}_{k/k-1} = \hat{x}(t)$ and $P_{k/k-1} = P(t)$ at $t = kT_s$. The corrected states and error covariances are given by

$$\hat{x}_{k/k} = \hat{x}_{k/k-1} + L_k(z_k - C_k\hat{x}_{k/k-1}), \tag{108}$$

$$P_{k/k} = (I - L_k C_k)P_{k/k-1}, \tag{109}$$

where $L_k = P_{k/k-1}C_k^T(C_k P_{k/k-1}C_k^T + R_k)^{-1}$. The above filter is a linear system having jumps at the discrete observation times. The states evolve according to the continuous-time dynamics (106) in-between the sampling instants. This filter is applied in [20] for recovery of cardiac dynamics from medical image sequences.

4.19 Conclusion

A linear, time-varying system $\mathcal{G}_2$ is assumed to have the realisation $x_{k+1} = A_k x_k + B_k w_k$ and $y_{2,k} = C_{2,k}x_k + D_{2,k}w_k$. In the general filtering problem, it is desired to estimate the output of a second reference system $\mathcal{G}_1$ which is modelled as $y_{1,k} = C_{1,k}x_k + D_{1,k}w_k$. The Kalman filter which estimates $y_{1,k}$ from the measurements $z_k = y_{2,k} + v_k$ at time k is listed in Table 1.

"Louis Pasteur's theory of germs is ridiculous fiction." *Pierre Pachet*, Professor of Physiology at Toulouse, 1872

If the state-space parameters are known exactly then this filter minimises the predicted and corrected error covariances $E\{(x_k - \hat{x}_{k/k-1})(x_k - \hat{x}_{k/k-1})^T\}$ and $E\{(x_k - \hat{x}_{k/k})(x_k - \hat{x}_{k/k})^T\}$, respectively. When there are gaps in the data record, or the data is irregularly spaced, state predictions can be calculated an arbitrary number of steps ahead, at the cost of increased mean-square-error.

	ASSUMPTIONS	MAIN RESULTS
Signals and system	$E\{w_k\} = E\{v_k\} = 0$. $E\{w_k w_k^T\} = Q_k$ and $E\{v_k v_k^T\} = R_k$ are known. A_k, B_k, $C_{1,k}$, $C_{2,k}$, $D_{1,k}$, $D_{2,k}$ are known.	$x_{k+1} = A_k x_k + B_k w_k$ $y_{2,k} = C_{2,k} x_k + D_{2,k} w_k$ $z_k = y_{2,k} + v_k$ $y_{1,k} = C_{1,k} x_k + D_{1,k} w_k$
Filtered state and output factorisation		$\hat{x}_{k+1/k} = (A_k - K_k C_{2,k})\hat{x}_{k/k-1} + K_k z_k$ $\hat{y}_{1,k/k} = (C_{1,k} - L_k C_{2,k})\hat{x}_{k/k-1} + L_k z_k$
Predictor gain, filter gain and Riccati difference equation	$Q_k > 0$, $R_k > 0$. $C_{2,k} P_{k/k-1} C_{2,k}^T + D_{2,k} Q_k D_{2,k}^T + R_k > 0$.	$K_k = (A_k P_{k/k-1} C_{2,k}^T + B_k Q_k D_{2,k}^T)$ $\times (C_{2,k} P_{k/k-1} C_{2,k}^T + D_{2,k} Q_k D_{2,k}^T + R_k)^{-1}$ $L_k = (C_{1,k} P_{k/k-1} C_{2,k}^T + D_{1,k} Q_k D_{2,k}^T)$ $\times (C_{2,k} P_{k/k-1} C_{2,k}^T + D_{2,k} Q_k D_{2,k}^T + R_k)^{-1}$ $P_{k+1/k} = A_k P_{k/k-1} A_k^T + B_k Q_k B_k^T$ $-K_k (C_{2,k} P_{k/k-1} C_{2,k}^T + D_{2,k} Q_k D_{2,k}^T + R_k) K_k^T$

Table 1.1. Main results for the general filtering problem.

The filtering solution is specialised to output estimation with $C_{1,k} = C_{2,k}$ and $D_{1,k} = D_{2,k}$.

In the case of input estimation (or equalisation), $C_{1,k} = 0$ and $D_{1,k} = I$, which results in $\hat{w}_{k/k} = -L_k C_{2,k} \hat{x}_{k/k-1} + L_k z_k$, where the filter gain is instead calculated as $L_k = Q_k D_{2,k}^T (C_{2,k} P_{k/k-1} C_{2,k}^T + D_{2,k} Q_k D_{2,k}^T + R_k)^{-1}$.

For problems where $C_{1,k} = I$ (state estimation) and $D_{1,k} = D_{2,k} = 0$, the filtered state calculation simplifies to $\hat{x}_{k/k} = (I - L_k C_{2,k})\hat{x}_{k/k-1} + L_k z_k$, where $\hat{x}_{k/k-1} = A_k \hat{x}_{k-1/k-1}$ and $L_k =$

"Heavier-than-air flying machines are impossible." *Baron William Thomson Kelvin*

$P_{k/k-1}C_{2,k}^T(C_{2,k}P_{k/k-1}C_{2,k}^T + R_k)^{-1}$. This predictor-corrector form is used to obtain robust, hybrid and extended Kalman filters. When the predicted states are not explicitly required, the state corrections can be calculated from the one-line recursion $\hat{x}_{k/k} = (I - L_kC_{2,k})A_{k-1}\hat{x}_{k-1/k-1} + L_kz_k$.

If the simplifications $B_k = D_{2,k} = 0$ are assumed and the pair $(A_k, C_{2,k})$ is retained, the Kalman filter degenerates to the RLS algorithm. However, the cost of this model simplification is an increase in mean-square-error.

4.20 Problems

Problem 1. Suppose that $E\left\{\begin{bmatrix}\alpha_k \\ \beta_k\end{bmatrix}\right\} = \begin{bmatrix}\bar{\alpha} \\ \bar{\beta}\end{bmatrix}$ and $E\left\{\begin{bmatrix}\alpha_k \\ \beta_k\end{bmatrix}\begin{bmatrix}\alpha_k^T & \beta_k^T\end{bmatrix}\right\} = \begin{bmatrix}\Sigma_{\alpha_k\alpha_k} & \Sigma_{\alpha_k\beta_k} \\ \Sigma_{\beta_k\alpha_k} & \Sigma_{\beta_k\beta_k}\end{bmatrix}$. Show that an estimate of α_k given β_k, which minimises $E\{(\alpha_k - E\{\alpha_k \mid \beta_k\})(\alpha_k - E\{\alpha_k \mid \beta_k\})^T\}$, is given by $E\{\alpha_k \mid \beta_k\} = \bar{\alpha} + \Sigma_{\alpha_k\beta_k}\Sigma_{\beta_k\beta_k}^{-1}(\beta_k - \bar{\beta})$.

Problem 2. Derive the predicted error covariance

$P_{k+1/k} = A_kP_{k/k-1}A_k^T - A_kP_{k/k-1}C_k^T(C_kP_{k/k-1}C_k^T + R_k)^{-1}C_kP_{k/k-1}A_k^T + B_kQ_kB_k^T$ from the state prediction $\hat{x}_{k+1/k} = A_k\hat{x}_{k/k-1} + K_k(z_k - C_k\hat{x}_{k/k-1})$, the model $x_{k+1} = A_kx_k + B_kw_k$, $y_k = C_kx_k$ and the measurements $z_k = y_k + v_k$.

Problem 3. Assuming the state correction $\hat{x}_{k/k} = \hat{x}_{k/k-1} + L_k(z_k - C_k\hat{x}_{k/k-1})$, show that the corrected error covariance is given by $P_{k/k} = P_{k/k-1} - L_k(C_kP_{k/k-1}C_k^T + R_k)L_k^T$.

Problem 4 [11], [14], [17], [18], [19]. Consider the standard discrete-time filter equations

$$\hat{x}_{k/k-1} = A_k\hat{x}_{k-1/k-1},$$

$$\hat{x}_{k/k} = \hat{x}_{k/k-1} + L_k(z_k - C_k\hat{x}_{k/k-1}),$$

$$P_{k/k-1} = A_kP_{k-1/k-1}A_k^T + B_kQ_kB_k^T,$$

$$P_{k/k} = P_{k/k-1} - L_k(C_kP_{k/k-1}C_k^T + R_k)L_k^T,$$

where $L_k = P_{k/k-1}C_k^T(C_kP_{k/k-1}C_k^T + R_k)^{-1}$. Derive the continuous-time filter equations, namely

$$\dot{\hat{x}}(t_k) = A(t_k)\hat{x}(t_k) + K(t_k)\big(z(t_k) - C(t_k)\hat{x}(t_k)\big),$$

$$\dot{P}(t_k) = A(t_k)P(t_k) + P(t_k)A^T(t_k) - P(t_k)C^T(t_k)R^{-1}(t_k)C(t_k)P(t_k) + B(t_k)Q(t_k)B^T(t_k),$$

"But what is it good for?" Engineer at the Advanced Computing Systems Division of IBM, commenting on the micro chip, 1968

where $K(t_k) = P(t_k)C(t_k)R^{-1}(t_k)$. (Hint: Introduce the quantities $A_k = (I + A(t_k))\Delta t$, $B(t_k) = B_k$, $C(t_k) = C_k$, $P_{k/k}$, $Q(t_k) = Q_k/\Delta t$, $R(t_k) = R_k\Delta t$, $\hat{x}(t_k) = \hat{x}_{k/k}$, $P(t_k) = P_{k/k}$, $\dot{\hat{x}}(t_k) = \lim_{\Delta t \to 0} \frac{\hat{x}_{k/k} - \hat{x}_{k-1/k-1}}{\Delta t}$, $\dot{P}(t_k) = \lim_{\Delta t \to 0} \frac{P_{k+1/k} - P_{k/k-1}}{\Delta t}$ and $\Delta t = t_k - t_{k-1}$.)

Problem 5. Derive the two-step-ahead predicted error covariance $P_{k+2/k} = A_{k+1}P_{k+1/k}A_{k+1}^T + B_{k+1}Q_{k+1}B_{k+1}^T$.

Problem 6. Verify that the Riccati difference equation $P_{k+1/k} = A_kP_{k/k-1}A_k^T - K_k(C_kP_{k/-1}C_k^T + R_k)K_k^T + B_kQ_kB_k^T$, where $K_k = (A_kP_{k/k-1}C_k + B_kS_k)(C_kP_{k/k-1}C_k^T + R_k)^{-1}$, is equivalent to $P_{k+1/k} = (A_k - K_kC_k)P_{k/k-1}(A_k - K_kC_k)^T + K_kR_kK_k^T + B_kQ_kB_k^T - B_kS_kK_k^T - K_kS_kB_k^T$.

Problem 7 [16]. Suppose that the systems $y_{1,k} = \mathcal{G}_1 w_k$ and $y_{2,k} = \mathcal{G}_2 w_k$ have the state-space realisations

$$\begin{bmatrix} x_{1,k+1} \\ y_{1,k} \end{bmatrix} = \begin{bmatrix} A_{1,k} & B_{1,k} \\ C_{1,k} & D_{1,k} \end{bmatrix} \begin{bmatrix} x_{1,k} \\ w_k \end{bmatrix} \text{ and } \begin{bmatrix} x_{2,k+1} \\ y_{2,k} \end{bmatrix} = \begin{bmatrix} A_{2,k} & B_{2,k} \\ C_{2,k} & D_{2,k} \end{bmatrix} \begin{bmatrix} x_{2,k} \\ w_k \end{bmatrix}.$$

Show that the system $y_{3,k} = \mathcal{G}_2\mathcal{G}_1 w_k$ is given by

$$\begin{bmatrix} x_{1,k+1} \\ y_{3,k} \end{bmatrix} = \begin{bmatrix} A_{1,k} & 0 & B_{1,k} \\ B_{2,k}C_{1,k} & A_{2,k} & B_{2,k}D_{1,k} \\ D_{2,k}C_{1,k} & C_{2,k} & D_{2,k}D_{1,k} \end{bmatrix} \begin{bmatrix} x_{1,k} \\ x_{2,k} \\ w_k \end{bmatrix}.$$

4.21 Glossary

In addition to the notation listed in Section 2.6, the following nomenclature has been used herein.

$\mathcal{G}$	A system that is assumed to have the realisation $x_{k+1} = A_kx_k + B_kw_k$ and $y_k = C_kx_k + D_kw_k$ where A_k, B_k, C_k and D_k are time-varying matrices of appropriate dimension.
Q_k, R_k	Time-varying covariance matrices of stochastic signals w_k and v_k, respectively.
$\mathcal{G}^H$	Adjoint of $\mathcal{G}$. The adjoint of a system having the state-space parameters $\{A_k, B_k, C_k, D_k\}$ is a system parameterised by $\{A_k^T, -C_k^T, -B_k^T, D_k^T\}$.
$\hat{x}_{k/k}$	Filtered estimate of the state x_k given measurements at time k.
$\tilde{x}_{k/k}$	Filtered state estimation error which is defined by $\tilde{x}_{k/k} = x_k - \hat{x}_{k/k}$.
$P_{k/k}$	Corrected error covariance matrix at time k given measurements at time k.

"What sir, would you make a ship sail against the wind and currents by lighting a bonfire under her deck? I pray you excuse me. I have no time to listen to such nonsense." *Napoléon Bonaparte*

L_k	Time-varying filter gain matrix.
$\hat{x}_{k+1/k}$	Predicted estimate of the state x_{k+1} given measurements at time k.
$\tilde{x}_{k+1/k}$	Predicted state estimation error which is defined by $\tilde{x}_{k+1/k} = x_{k+1} - \hat{x}_{k+1/k}$.
$P_{k+1/k}$	Predicted error covariance matrix at time $k + 1$ given measurements at time k.
K_k	Time-varying predictor gain matrix.
RLS	Recursive Least Squares.

4.22 References

[1] R. E. Kalman, "A New Approach to Linear Filtering and Prediction Problems", *Transactions of the ASME, Series D, Journal of Basic Engineering*, vol 82, pp. 35 - 45, 1960.

[2] R. E. Kalman, "New Methods in Wiener Filtering Theory", *Proc. First Symposium on Engineering Applications of Random Function Theory and Probability*, Wiley, New York, pp. 270 - 388, 1963.

[3] T. Söderström, *Discrete-time Stochastic Systems: Estimation and Control*, Springer-Verlag London Ltd., 2002.

[4] B. D. O. Anderson and J. B. Moore, *Optimal Filtering*, Prentice-Hall Inc,Englewood Cliffs, New Jersey, 1979.

[5] G. S. Maddala, *Introduction to Econometrics*, Second Edition, Macmillan Publishing Co., New York, 1992.

[6] C. K. Chui and G. Chen, *Kalman Filtering with Real-Time Applications*, 3rd Ed., Springer-Verlag, Berlin, 1999.

[7] I. Yaesh and U. Shaked, "H_∞-Optimal Estimation - The Discrete Time Case", *Proceedings of the MTNS*, pp. 261 - 267, Jun. 1991.

[8] U. Shaked and Y. Theodor, "H_∞ Optimal Estimation: A Tutorial", *Proceedings 31st IEEE Conference on Decision and Control*, pp. 2278 - 2286, Tucson, Arizona, Dec. 1992.

[9] F. L. Lewis, L. Xie and D. Popa, *Optimal and Robust Estimation: With an Introduction to Stochastic Control Theory*, Second Edition, Series in Automation and Control Engineering, Taylor & Francis Group, LLC, 2008.

[10] T. Kailath, A. H. Sayed and B. Hassibi, *Linear Estimation*, Prentice-Hall, Inc., Upper Saddle River, New Jersey, 2000.

[11] D. Simon, *Optimal State Estimation, Kalman H_∞ and Nonlinear Approaches*, John Wiley & Sons, Inc., Hoboken, New Jersey, 2006.

[12] P. J. Brockwell and R. A. Davis, *Time Series: Theory and Methods*, Second Edition, Springer-Verlag New York, Inc., 1991.

[13] D. J. N. Limebeer, M. Green and D. Walker, "Discrete-time H_∞ Control", *Proceedings 28th IEEE Conference on Decision and Control*, Tampa, pp. 392 - 396, Dec., 1989.

[14] R. G. Brown and P. Y. C. Hwang, *Introduction to Random Signals and Applied Kalman Filtering*, Second Edition, John Wiley & Sons, Inc., New York, 1992.

"The horse is here today, but the automobile is only a novelty - a fad." President of *Michigan Savings Bank*

[15] K. Ogata, *Discrete-time Control Systems*, Prentice-Hall, Inc., Englewood Cliffs, New Jersey, 1987.
[16] M. Green and D. J. N. Limebeer, *Linear Robust Control*, Prentice-Hall Inc. Englewood Cliffs, New Jersey, 1995.
[17] A. H. Jazwinski, *Stochastic Processes and Filtering Theory*, Academic Press, Inc., New York, 1970.
[18] A. P. Sage and J. L. Melsa, *Estimation Theory with Applications to Communications and Control*, McGraw-Hill Book Company, New York, 1971.
[19] A. Gelb, *Applied Optimal Estimation*, The Analytic Sciences Corporation, USA, 197
[20] S. Tong and P. Shi, "Sampled-Data Filtering Framework for Cardiac Motion Recovery: Optimal Estimation of Continuous Dynamics From Discrete Measurements", *IEEE Transactions on Biomedical Engineering*, vol. 54, no. 10, pp. 1750 - 1761, Oct. 2007.

"Airplanes are interesting toys but of no military value." *Marechal Ferdinand Foch*

5

Discrete-Time Steady-State Minimum-Variance Prediction and Filtering

5.1 Introduction

This chapter presents the minimum-variance filtering results simplified for the case when the model parameters are time-invariant and the noise processes are stationary. The filtering objective remains the same, namely, the task is to estimate a signal in such as way to minimise the filter error covariance.

A somewhat naïve approach is to apply the standard filter recursions using the time-invariant problem parameters. Although this approach is valid, it involves recalculating the Riccati difference equation solution and filter gain at each time-step, which is computationally expensive. A lower implementation cost can be realised by recognising that the Riccati difference equation solution asymptotically approaches the solution of an algebraic Riccati equation. In this case, the algebraic Riccati equation solution and hence the filter gain can be calculated before running the filter.

The steady-state discrete-time Kalman filtering literature is vast and some of the more accessible accounts [1] – [14] are canvassed here. The filtering problem and the application of the standard time-varying filter recursions are described in Section 2. An important criterion for checking whether the states can be uniquely reconstructed from the measurements is observability. For example, sometimes states may be internal or sensor measurements might not be available, which can result in the system having hidden modes. Section 3 describes two common tests for observability, namely, checking that an observability matrix or an observability gramian are of full rank. The subject of Riccati equation monotonicity and convergence has been studied extensively by Chan [4], De Souza [5], [6], Bitmead [7], [8], Wimmer [9] and Wonham [10], which is discussed in Section 4. Chan, *et al* [4] also showed that if the underlying system is stable and observable then the minimum-variance filter is stable. Section 6 describes a discrete-time version of the Kalman-Yakubovich-Popov Lemma, which states for time-invariant systems that solving a Riccati equation is equivalent to spectral factorisation. In this case, the Wiener and Kalman filters are the same.

"Science is nothing but trained and organized common sense differing from the latter only as a veteran may differ from a raw recruit: and its methods differ from those of common sense only as far as the guardsman's cut and thrust differ from the manner in which a savage wields his club." *Thomas Henry Huxley*

5.2 Time-Invariant Filtering Problem

5.2.1 The Time-Invariant Signal Model

A discrete-time time-invariant system (or plant) $\mathcal{G}: \mathbb{R}^m \to \mathbb{R}^p$ is assumed to have the state-space representation

$$x_{k+1} = Ax_k + Bw_k, \tag{1}$$

$$y_k = Cx_k + Dw_k, \tag{2}$$

where $A \in \mathbb{R}^{n \times n}$, $B \in \mathbb{R}^{n \times m}$, $C \in \mathbb{R}^{p \times n}$, $D \in \mathbb{R}^{p \times p}$, w_k is a stationary process with $E\{w_k\} = 0$ and $E\{w_j w_k^T\} = Q\delta_{jk}$. For convenience, the simplification $D = 0$ is initially assumed within the developments. A nonzero feedthrough matrix, D, can be accommodated as described in Chapter 4. Observations z_k of the system output y_k are again modelled as

$$z_k = y_k + v_k, \tag{3}$$

where v_k is a stationary measurement noise sequence over an interval $k \in [1, N]$, with $E\{v_k\} = 0$, $E\{w_j v_k^T\} = 0$, $E\{v_j v_k^T\} = R\delta_{jk}$. An objective is to design a filter $\mathcal{H}$ that operates on the above measurements and produces an estimate, $\hat{y}_{k/k} = C_k\hat{x}_{k/k}$, of y_k so that the covariance, $E\{\tilde{y}_{k/k}\tilde{y}_{k/k}^T\}$, of the filter error, $\tilde{y}_{k/k} = y_k - \hat{y}_{k/k}$, is minimised.

5.2.2 Application of the Time-Varying Filter Recursions

A naïve but entirely valid approach to state estimation is to apply the standard minimum-variance filter recursions of Section 4 for the problem (1) - (3). The predicted and corrected state estimates are given by

$$\hat{x}_{k+1/k} = (A - K_kC_k)\hat{x}_{k/k-1} + K_kz_k, \tag{4}$$

$$\hat{x}_{k/k} = (I - L_kC_k)\hat{x}_{k/k-1} + L_kz_k, \tag{5}$$

where $L_k = P_{k/k-1}C^T(CP_{k/k-1}C + R)^{-1}$ is the filter gain, $K_k = AP_{k/k-1}C^T(CP_{k/k-1}C + R)^{-1}$ is the predictor gain, in which $P_{k/k-1} = E\{\tilde{x}_{k/k-1}\tilde{x}_{k/k-1}^T\}$ is obtained from the Riccati difference equation

$$P_{k+1} = AP_kA^T - AP_kC^T(CP_kC^T + R)^{-1}CP_kA^T + BQB^T. \tag{6}$$

As before, the above Riccati equation is iterated forward at each time k from an initial condition P_0. A necessary condition for determining whether the states within (1) can be uniquely estimated is observability which is discussed below.

"We can understand almost anything, but we can't understand how we understand." *Albert Einstein*

5.3 Observability

5.3.1 The Discrete-time Observability Matrix

Observability is a fundamental concept in system theory. If a system is unobservable then it will not be possible to recover the states uniquely from the measurements. The pair (*A*, *C*) within the discrete-time system (1) – (2) is defined to be completely observable if the initial states, x_0, can be uniquely determined from the known inputs w_k and outputs y_k over an interval $k \in [0, N]$. A test for observability is to check whether an observability matrix is of full rank. The discrete-time observability matrix, which is defined in the lemma below, is the same the continuous-time version. The proof is analogous to the presentation in Chapter 3.

Lemma 1 [1], [2]: *The discrete-time system (1) – (2) is completely observable if the observability matrix*

$$O_N = \begin{bmatrix} C \\ CA \\ CA^2 \\ \vdots \\ CA^N \end{bmatrix}, N \geq n - 1, \tag{7}$$

is of rank n .

Proof: *Since the input w_k is assumed to be known, it suffices to consider the unforced system*

$$x_{k+1} = Ax_k, \tag{8}$$

$$y_k = Cx_k . \tag{9}$$

It follows from (8) – (9) that

$$\begin{aligned} y_0 &= Cx_0 \\ y_1 &= Cx_1 = CAx_0 \\ y_2 &= Cx_2 = CA^2x_0 \\ &\vdots \\ y_N &= Cx_N = CA^Nx_0 , \end{aligned} \tag{10}$$

"What happens depends on our way of observing it or the fact that we observe it." *Werner Heisenberg*

which can be written as

$$y = \begin{bmatrix} y_0 \\ y_1 \\ y_2 \\ \vdots \\ y_N \end{bmatrix} = C \begin{bmatrix} I \\ A \\ A^2 \\ \vdots \\ A^N \end{bmatrix} x_0 . \tag{11}$$

From the Cayley-Hamilton Theorem, A^k, for $k \geq n$, can be expressed as a linear combination of A^0, A^1, ..., A^{n-1} . Thus, with $N \geq n - 1$, equation (11) uniquely determines x_0 if O_N has full rank n. □

Thus, if O_N is of full rank then its inverse exists and so x_0 can be uniquely recovered as $x_0 = O_N^{-1} y$. Observability is a property of the deterministic model equations (8) – (9). Conversely, if the observability matrix is not rank n then the system (1) – (2) is termed unobservable and the unobservable states are called unobservable modes.

5.3.2 Discrete-time Observability Gramians

Alternative tests for observability arise by checking the rank of one of the observability gramians that are described below.

Lemma 2: *The pair (A, C) is completely observable if the observability gramian*

$$W_N = O_N^T O_N = \sum_{k=0}^{N} (A^T)^k C^T C A^k , N \geq n\text{-}1 \tag{12}$$

is of full rank.

Proof: *It follows from (8) – (9) that*

$$y^T y = x_0^T \begin{bmatrix} I & A^T & (A^T)^2 & \cdots & (A^T)^N \end{bmatrix} C^T C \begin{bmatrix} I \\ A \\ A^2 \\ \vdots \\ A^N \end{bmatrix} x_0 . \tag{13}$$

From the Cayley-Hamilton Theorem, A^k, for $k \geq n$, can be expressed as a linear combination of A^0, A^1, ..., A^{n-1} . Thus, with $N = n - 1$,

$$y^T y = x_0^T O_N^T O_N x_0 = x_0^T W_N x_0 = x_0^T \left(\sum_{k=0}^{n-1} (A^T)^k C^T C A^k \right) x_0 \tag{14}$$

is unique provided that W_N is of full rank. □

"You affect the world by what you browse." *Tim Berners-Lee*

It is shown below that an equivalent observability gramian can be found from the solution of a Lyapunov equation.

Lemma 3: *Suppose that the system (8) – (9) is stable, that is,* $|\lambda_i(A)| < 1$, $i = 1$ *to* n, *then the pair (A, C) is completely observable if the nonnegative symmetric solution of the Lyapunov equation*

$$W = A^T WA + C^T C. \tag{15}$$

is of full rank.

Proof: *Pre-multiplying* $C^TC = W - A^TWA$ *by* $(A^T)^k$, *post-multiplying by* A^k *and summing from* $k = 0$ *to* N *results in*

$$\begin{aligned}\sum_{k=0}^{N}(A^T)^k C^T CA^k &= \sum_{k=0}^{N}(A^T)^k WA^k - \sum_{k=0}^{N}(A^T)^{k+1} WA^{k+1} \\ &= W_N - (A^T)^{k+1} W_N A^{k+1}.\end{aligned} \tag{16}$$

Since $\lim_{k\to\infty}(A^T)^{k+1} W_N A^{k+1} = 0$, *by inspection of (16),* $W = \lim_{k\to\infty} W_N$ *is a solution of the Lyapunov equation (15). Observability follows from Lemma 2.* □

It is noted below that observability is equivalent to asymptotic stability.

Lemma 4 [3]: *Under the conditions of Lemma 3,* $x_0 \in \ell_2$ *implies* $y \in \ell_2$.

Proof: *It follows from (16) that* $\sum_{k=0}^{N}(A^T)^k C^T CA^k \le W_N$ *and therefore*

$$\|y\|_2^2 = \sum_{k=0}^{N} y_k^T y_k = x_0^T\left(\sum_{k=0}^{N}(A^T)^k C^T CA^k\right)x_0 \le x_0^T W_N x_0,$$

from which the claim follows. □

Another criterion that is encountered in the context of filtering and smoothing is detectability. A linear time-invariant system is said to be detectable when all its modes and in particular its unobservable modes are stable. An observable system is alsodetectable.

Example 1. (i) Consider a stable second-order system with $A = \begin{bmatrix}0.1 & 0.2\\ 0 & 0.4\end{bmatrix}$ and $C = \begin{bmatrix}1 & 1\end{bmatrix}$.

The observability matrix from (7) and the observability gramian from (12) are $O_1 = \begin{bmatrix}C\\ CA\end{bmatrix} = \begin{bmatrix}1 & 1\\ 0.1 & 0.6\end{bmatrix}$ and $W_1 = O_1^T O_1 = \begin{bmatrix}1.01 & 1.06\\ 1.06 & 1.36\end{bmatrix}$, respectively. It can easily be verified that the

"It is a good morning exercise for a research scientist to discard a pet hypothesis every day before breakfast." *Konrad Zacharias Lorenz*

solution of the Lyapunov equation (15) is $W = \begin{bmatrix} 1.01 & 1.06 \\ 1.06 & 1.44 \end{bmatrix} = W_4$ to three significant figures. Since rank(O_1) = rank(W_1) = rank(W_4) = 2, the pair (A, C) is observable.

(ii) Now suppose that measurements of the first state are not available, that is, $C = \begin{bmatrix} 0 & 1 \end{bmatrix}$. Since $O_1 = \begin{bmatrix} 0 & 1 \\ 0 & 0.4 \end{bmatrix}$ and $W_1 = \begin{bmatrix} 0 & 0 \\ 0 & 1.16 \end{bmatrix}$ are of rank 1, the pair (A, C) is unobservable. This system is detectable because the unobservable mode is stable.

5.4 Riccati Equation Properties

5.4.1 Monotonicity

It will be shown below that the solution $P_{k+1/k}$ of the Riccati difference equation (6) monotonically approaches a steady-state asymptote, in which case the gain is also time-invariant and can be precalculated. Establishing monotonicity requires the following result. It is well known that the difference between the solutions of two Riccati equations also obeys a Riccati equation, see Theorem 4.3 of [4], (2.12) of [5], Lemma 3.1 of [6], (4.2) of [7], Lemma 10.1 of [8], (2.11) of [9] and (2.4) of [10].

Theorem 1: Riccati Equation Comparison Theorem [4] – [10]: *Suppose for a $t \geq 0$ and for all $k \geq 0$ the two Riccati difference equations*

$$P_{t+k} = AP_{t+k-1}A^T - AP_{t+k-1}C^T(CP_{t+k-1}C^T + R)^{-1}CP_{t+k-1}A^T + BQB^T, \tag{17}$$

$$P_{t+k+1} = AP_{t+k}A^T - AP_{t+k}C^T(CP_{t+k}C^T + R)^{-1}CP_{t+k}A^T + BQB^T, \tag{18}$$

have solutions $P_{t+k} \geq 0$ and $P_{t+k-1} \geq 0$, *respectively. Then* $\overline{P}_{t+k} = P_{t+k} - P_{t+k+1}$ *satisfies*

$$\overline{P}_{t+k+1} = \overline{A}_{t+k+1}\overline{P}_{t+k}\overline{A}_{t+k}^T - \overline{A}_{t+k+1}\overline{P}_{t+k}C^T(C\overline{P}_{t+k}C^T + \overline{R}_k)^{-1}C\overline{P}_{t+k}\overline{A}_{t+k+1}^T, \tag{19}$$

where $\overline{A}_{t+k+1} = A - AP_{t+k-1}C^T(CP_{t+k+1}C^T + \overline{R}_{t+k+1})^{-1}C_{t+k}$ *and* $\overline{R}_{t+k} = CP_{t+k}C^T + R$.

The above result can be verified by substituting $\overline{A}_{t+k+1}$ and $\overline{R}_{t+k+1}$ into (19). The above theorem is used below to establish Riccati difference equation monotonicity.

Theorem 2 [6], [9], [10], [11]: *Under the conditions of Theorem 1, suppose that the solution of the Riccati difference equation (19) has a solution $\overline{P}_{t+k} \geq 0$ for a $t \geq 0$ and $k = 0$. Then $P_{t+k} \geq P_{t+k+1}$ for all $k \geq 0$.*

"We follow abstract assumptions to see where they lead, and then decide whether the detailed differences from the real world matter." *Clinton Richard Dawkins*

Proof: *The assumption* $\overline{P}_{t+k} \geq 0$ *is the initial condition for an induction argument. For the induction step, it follows from* $C\overline{P}_{t+k}C^T(C\overline{P}_{t+k}C^T + \overline{R}_k)^{-1} \leq I$ *that* $\overline{P}_{t+k} \leq \overline{P}_{t+k}C^T(C\overline{P}_{t+k}C^T + \overline{R}_k)^{-1}C\overline{P}_{t+k}$, *which together with Theorem 1 implies* $\overline{P}_{t+k} \geq 0$. †□

The above theorem serves to establish conditions under which a Riccati difference equation solution monotonically approaches its steady state solution. This requires a Riccati equation convergence result which is presented below.

5.4.2 Convergence

When the model parameters and second-order noise statistics are constant then the predictor gain is also time-invariant andpre-calculated as

$$K = APC^T(CPC^T + R)^{-1}, \tag{20}$$

where P is the symmetric positive definite solution of the algebraic Riccati equation

$$P = APA^T - APC^T(CPC^T + R)^{-1}CPA^T + BQB^T \tag{21}$$

$$= (A - KC)P(A - KC)^T + BQB^T + KRK^T. \tag{22}$$

A real symmetric nonnegative definite solution of the Algebraic Riccati equation (21) is said to be a *strong solution* if the eigenvalues of $(A - KC)$ lie inside or on the unit circle [4], [5]. If there are no eigenvalues on the unit circle then the strong solution is termed the *stabilising solution*. The following lemma by Chan, Goodwin and Sin [4] sets out conditions for the existence of[7] solutions for the algebraic Riccati equation (21).

***Lemma 5** [4]: Provided that the pair (A, C) is detectable, then*

i) the strong solution of the algebraic Riccati equation (21) exists and is unique;

ii) if A has no modes on the unit circle then the strong solution coincides with the stabilising solution.

A detailed proof is presented in [4]. If the linear time-invariant system (1) – (2) is stable and completely observable and the solution P_k of the Riccati difference equation (6) is suitably initialised, then in the limit as k approaches infinity, P_k will asymptotically converge to the solution of the algebraic Riccati equation. This convergence property is formally restated below.

***Lemma 6** [4]: Subject to:*

i) the pair (A, C) is observable;

ii) $|\lambda_i(A)| \leq 1$, $i = 1$ *to* n;

iii) $(P_0 - P) \geq 0$;

"We know very little, and yet it is astonishing that we know so much, and still more astonishing that so little knowledge can give us so much power." *Bertrand Arthur William Russell*

then the solution of the Riccati difference equation (6) satisfies

$$\lim_{k\to\infty} P_k = P \,. \tag{23}$$

A proof appears in [4]. This important property is used in [6], which is in turn cited within [7] and [8]. Similar results are reported in [5], [13] and [14]. Convergence can occur exponentially fast which is demonstrated by the following numerical example.

Example **2.** Consider an output estimation problem where $A = 0.9$ and $B = C = Q = R = 1$. The solution to the algebraic Riccati equation (21) is $P = 1.4839$. Some calculated solutions of the Riccati difference equation (6) initialised with $P_0 = 10P$ are shown in Table 1. The data in the table demonstrate that the Riccati difference equation solution converges to the algebraic Riccati equation solution, which illustrates the Lemma.

k	P_k	$P_{k-1} - P_k$
1	1.7588	13.0801
2	1.5164	0.2425
5	1.4840	4.7955×10^{-4}
10	1.4839	1.8698×10^{-8}

Table. 1. Solutions of (21) for Example 2.

5.5 The Steady-State Minimum-Variance Filter

5.5.1 State Estimation

The formulation of the steady-state Kalman filter (which is also known as the limiting Kalman filter) follows by allowing k to approach infinity and using the result of Lemma That is, the filter employs fixed gains that are calculated using the solution of the algebraic Riccati equation (21) instead of the Riccati difference equation (6). The filtered state is calculated as

$$\begin{aligned} \hat{x}_{k/k} &= \hat{x}_{k/k-1} + L(z_k - C\hat{x}_{k/k-1}) \\ &= (I - LC)\hat{x}_{k/k-1} + Lz_k \,, \end{aligned} \tag{24}$$

where $L = PC^T(CPC^T + R)^{-1}$ is the time-invariant filter gain, in which P is the solution of the algebraic Riccati equation (21). The predicted state is given by

$$\begin{aligned} \hat{x}_{k+1/k} &= A\hat{x}_{k/k} \\ &= (A - KC)\hat{x}_{k/k-1} + Kz_k \,, \end{aligned} \tag{25}$$

where the time-invariant predictor gain, K, is calculated from (20).

"Great is the power of steady misrepresentation - but the history of science shows how, fortunately, this power does not endure long". *Charles Robert Darwin*

5.5.2 Asymptotic Stability

The asymptotic stability of the filter (24) - (25) is asserted in two ways. First, recall from Lemma 4 (ii) that if $|\lambda_i(A)| < 1$, $i = 1$ to n, and the pair (A, C) is completely observable, then $|\lambda_i(A - KC)| < 1$, $i = 1$ to n. That is, since the eigenvalues of the filter's state matrix are within the unit circle, the filter is asymptotically stable. Second, according to the Lyapunov stability theory [1], the unforced system (8) is asymptotically stable if there exists a scalar continuous function $V(x)$, satisfying the following.

(i) $V(x) > 0$ for $x \neq 0$.

(ii) $V(x_{k+1}) - V(x_k) \leq 0$ for $x_k \neq 0$.

(iii) $V(0) = 0$.

(iv) $V(x) \to \infty$ as $\|x\|_2 \to \infty$.

Consider the function $V(x_k) = x_k^T P x_k$ where P is a real positive definite symmetric matrix. Observe that $V(x_{k+1}) - V(x_k) = x_{k+1}^T P x_{k+1} - x_k^T P x_k = x_k^T (A^T P A - P) x_k \leq 0$. Therefore, the above stability requirements are satisfied if for a real symmetric positive definite Q, there exists a real symmetric positive definite P solution to the Lyapunov equation

$$APA^T - P = -Q. \tag{26}$$

By inspection, the design algebraic Riccati equation (22) is of the form (26) and so the filter is said to be stable in the sense of Lyapunov.

5.5.3 Output Estimation

For output estimation problems, the filter gain, L, is calculated differently. The output estimate is given by

$$\begin{aligned} \hat{y}_{k/k} &= C\hat{x}_{k/k} \\ &= C\hat{x}_{k/k-1} + L(z_k - C\hat{x}_{k/k-1}) \\ &= (C - LC)\hat{x}_{k/k-1} + Lz_k, \end{aligned} \tag{27}$$

where the filter gain is now obtained by $L = CPC^T(CPC^T + R)^{-1}$. The output estimation filter (24) - (25) can be written compactly as

$$\begin{bmatrix} \hat{x}_{k+1/k} \\ \hat{y}_{k/k} \end{bmatrix} = \begin{bmatrix} (A - KC) & K \\ (C - LC) & L \end{bmatrix} \begin{bmatrix} \hat{x}_{k/k-1} \\ z_k \end{bmatrix}, \tag{28}$$

from which its transfer function is

$$H_{OE}(z) = (C - LC)(zI - A + KC)^{-1}K + L. \tag{29}$$

"The scientists of today think deeply instead of clearly. One must be sane to think clearly, but one can think deeply and be quite insane." *Nikola Tesla*

5.6 Equivalence of the Wiener and Kalman Filters

As in continuous-time, solving a discrete-time algebraic Riccati equation is equivalent to spectral factorisation and the corresponding Kalman-Yakubovich-Popov Lemma (or Positive Real Lemma) is set out below. A proof of this Lemma makes use of the following identity

$$P - APA^T = (zI - A)P(z^{-1}I - A^T) + AP(z^{-1}I - A^T) + (zI - A)PA^T . \tag{30}$$

Lemma 7. *Consider the spectral density matrix*

$$\Delta\Delta^H(z) = \begin{bmatrix} C(zI - A)^{-1} & I \end{bmatrix} \begin{bmatrix} Q & 0 \\ 0 & R \end{bmatrix} \begin{bmatrix} (z^{-1}I - A^T)^{-1}C^T \\ I \end{bmatrix}. \tag{31}$$

Then the following statements are equivalent.

(i) $\Delta\Delta^H(e^{j\omega}) \ge 0$*, for all* $\omega \in (-\pi, \pi)$*.*

(ii) $\begin{bmatrix} BQB^T - P + APA^T & APC^T \\ CPA^T & CPC^T + R \end{bmatrix} \ge 0$.

(iii) There exists a nonnegative solution P of the algebraic Riccati equation (21).

Proof: *Following the approach of [12], to establish equivalence between (i) and (iii), use (21) within (30) to obtain*

$$BQB^T - APC^T(CPC^T + R)CPA^T = (zI - A)P(z^{-1}I - A^T) + AP(z^{-1}I - A^T) + (zI - A)PA^T . \tag{32}$$

Premultiplying and postmultiplying (32) by $C(zI - A)^{-1}$ *and* $(z^{-1}I - A^T)^{-1}C^T$*, respectively, results in*

$$C(zI - A)^{-1}(BQB^T - APC^T\Omega CPA^T)(z^{-1}I - A^T)C^T = CPC^T + C(zI - A)^{-1}APC^T + CPA^T(z^{-1}I - A^T)^{-1}C^T ,$$

where $\Omega = CPC^T + R$*. Hence,*

$$\begin{aligned} \Delta\Delta^H(z) &= GQG^H(z) + R \\ &= C(zI - A)^{-1}BQB^T(z^{-1}I - A^T)^{-1}C^T + R \\ &= C(zI - A)^{-1}APC^T\Omega CPA^T(z^{-1}I - A^T)^{-1}C^T + C(zI - A)^{-1}APC^T + CPA^T(z^{-1}I - A^T)^{-1}C^T + \Omega \\ &= \left(C(zI - A)^{-1}K + I\right)\Omega\left(K^T(z^{-1}I - A^T)^{-1}C^T + I\right) \qquad (33) \\ &\ge 0 . \end{aligned}$$

The Schur complement formula can be used to verify the equivalence of (ii) and (iii). □

"Any intelligent fool can make things bigger and more complex... It takes a touch of genius - and a lot of courage to move in the opposite direction." *Albert Einstein*

In Chapter 2, it is shown that the transfer function matrix of the optimal Wiener solution for output estimation is given by

$$H_{OE}(z) = I - R\{\Delta^{-H}\}_{+}\Delta^{-1}(z), \tag{34}$$

where { }+ denotes the causal part. This filter produces estimates $\hat{y}_{k/k}$ from measurements z_k. By inspection of (33) it follows that the spectral factor is

$$\Delta(z) = C(zI - A)^{-1}K\Omega^{1/2} + \Omega^{1/2}. \tag{35}$$

The Wiener output estimator (34) involves $\Delta^{-1}(z)$ which can be found using (35) and a special case of the matrix inversion lemma, namely, $[I + C(zI - A)^{-1}K]^{-1} = I - C(zI - A + KC)^{-1}K$. Thus, the spectral factor inverse is

$$\Delta^{-1}(z) = \Omega^{-1/2} - \Omega^{-1/2}C(zI - A + KC)^{-1}K. \tag{36}$$

It can be seen from (36) that $\{\Delta^{-H}\}_{+} = \Omega^{-1/2}$. Recognising that $I - R\Omega^{-1} = (CPC^T + R)(CPC^T + R)^{-1} - R(CPC^T + R)^{-1} = CPC^T(CPC^T + R)^{-1} = L$, the Wiener filter (34) can be written equivalently

$$\begin{aligned} H_{OE}(z) &= I - R\Omega^{-1}\Delta^{-1}(z) \\ &= I - R\Omega^{-1} + R\Omega^{-1}C(zI - A + KC)^{-1}K \\ &= L + (C - LC)(zI - A + KC)^{-1}K, \end{aligned} \tag{37}$$

which is identical to the transfer function matrix of the Kalman filter for output estimation (29). In Chapter 2, it is shown that the transfer function matrix of the input estimator (or equaliser) for proper, stable, minimum-phase plants is

$$H_{IE}(z) = G^{-1}(z)(I - R\{\Delta^{-H}\}_{+}\Delta^{-1}(z)). \tag{38}$$

Substituting (35) into (38) gives

$$H_{IE}(z) = G^{-1}(z)H_{OE}(z). \tag{39}$$

The above Wiener equaliser transfer function matrices require common poles and zeros to be cancelled. Although the solution (39) is not minimum-order (since some pole-zero cancellations can be made), its structure is instructive. In particular, an estimate of w_k can be obtained by operating the plant inverse on $\hat{y}_{k/k}$, provided the inverse exists. It follows immediately from $L = CPC^T(CPC^T + R)^{-1}$ that

$$\lim_{R \to 0} L = I. \tag{40}$$

By inspectionof (34) and (40), it follows that

$$\lim_{R \to 0} \sup_{\omega \in \{-\pi, \pi\}} \left| H_{OE}(e^{j\omega}) \right| = I. \tag{41}$$

Thus, under conditions of diminishing measurement noise, the output estimator will be devoid of dynamics and its maximum magnitude will approach the identity matrix.

"It is not the possession of truth, but the success which attends the seeking after it, that enriches the seeker and brings happiness to him." *Max Karl Ernst Ludwig Planck*

Therefore, for proper, stable, minimum-phase plants, the equaliser asymptotically approaches the plant inverse as the measurement noise becomes negligible, that is,

$$\lim_{R \to 0} H_{IE}(z) = G^{-1}(z) . \tag{42}$$

Time-invariant output and input estimation are demonstrated below.

```
w=sqrt(Q)*randn(N,1);                   % process noise
x=[0;0];                                % initial state
for k = 1:N
   y(k) = C*x + D*w(k);                 % plant output
   x = A*x + B*w(k);
end
v=sqrt(R)*randn(1,N);                   % measurement noise
z = y + v;                              % measurement
omega=C*P*(C') + D*Q*(D') + R;
K = (A*P*(C')+B*Q*(D'))*inv(omega);     % predictor gain
L = Q*(D')*inv(omega);                  % equaliser gain
x=[0;0];                                % initial state
for k = 1:N
   w_estimate(k) = - L*C*x + L*z(k);    % equaliser output
   x = (A - K*C)*x + K*z(k);            % predicted state
end
```

Figure 1. Fragment of *Matlab®* script for Example 3.

Example 3. Consider a time-invariant input estimation problem in which the plant is given by

$$G(z) = (z + 0.9)^2(z + 0.1)^{-2}$$

$$= (z^2 + 1.8z + 0.81)(z^2 + 0.2z + 0.01)^{-1}$$

$$= (1.6z + 0.8)(z^2 + 0.2z + 0.01)^{-1} + 1,$$

together with $Q = 1$ and $R = 0.0001$. The controllable canonical form (see Chapter 1) yields the parameters $A = \begin{bmatrix} -0.2 & -0.1 \\ 1 & 0 \end{bmatrix}$, $B = \begin{bmatrix} 1 \\ 0 \end{bmatrix}$, $C = \begin{bmatrix} 1.6 & 1.8 \end{bmatrix}$ and $D = 1$. From Chapter 4, the corresponding algebraic Riccati equation is $P = APA^T - K\Omega K^T + BQB^T$, where $K = (APC^T + BQD^T)\Omega^{-1}$ and $\Omega = CPC^T + R + DQD^T$. The minimum-variance output estimator is calculated as

"There is no result in nature without a cause; understand the cause and you will have no need of the experiment." *Leonardo di ser Piero da Vinci*

$$\begin{bmatrix} \hat{x}_{k+1/k} \\ \hat{y}_{k/k} \end{bmatrix} = \begin{bmatrix} (A - KC) & K \\ (C - LC) & L \end{bmatrix} \begin{bmatrix} \hat{x}_{k/k-1} \\ z_k \end{bmatrix},$$

where $L = (CPC^T + DQD^T)\Omega^{-1}$. The solution $P = \begin{bmatrix} 0.0026 & -0.0026 \\ -0.0026 & 0.0026 \end{bmatrix}$ for the algebraic Riccati equation was found using the Hamiltonian solver within *Matlab*®.

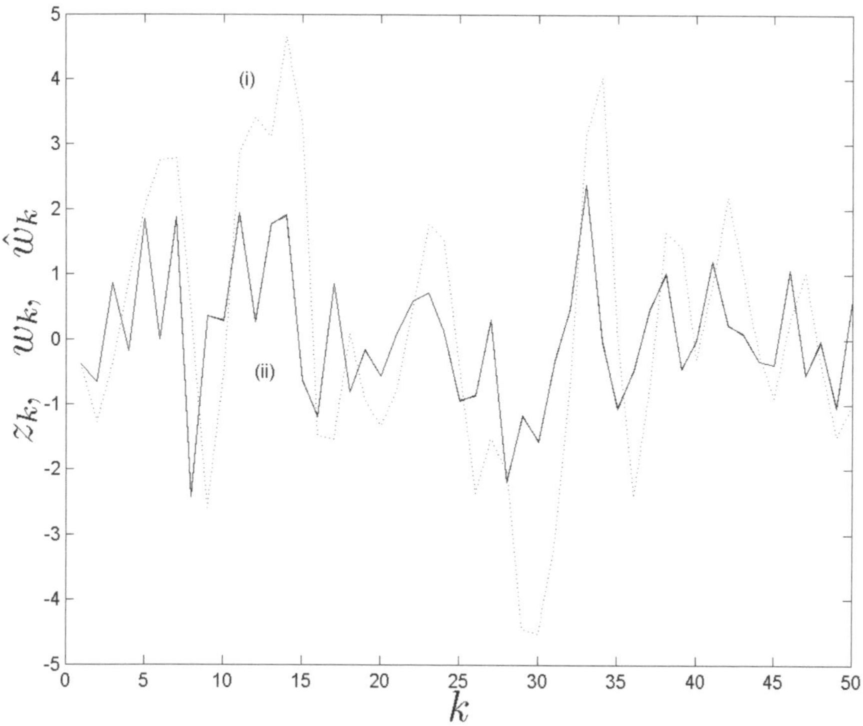

Figure 2. Sample trajectories for Example 5: (i) measurement sequence (dotted line); (ii) actual and estimated process noise sequences (superimposed solid lines).

The resulting transfer function of the output estimator is

$$H_{OE}(z) = (z + 0.9)^2(z + 0.9)^{-2},$$

which illustrates the low-measurement noise asymptote (41). The minimum-variance input estimator is calculated as

$$\begin{bmatrix} \hat{x}_{k+1/k} \\ \hat{w}_{k/k} \end{bmatrix} = \begin{bmatrix} (A - KC) & K \\ -LC & L \end{bmatrix} \begin{bmatrix} \hat{x}_{k/k-1} \\ z_k \end{bmatrix},$$

where $L = QD^T\Omega^{-1}$. The input estimator transfer function is

"Your theory is crazy, but its not crazy enough to be true." *Niels Henrik David Bohr*

$$H_{IE}(z) = (z + 0.1)^2 (z + 0.9)^{-2},$$

which corresponds to the inverse of the plant and illustrates the asymptote (42). A simulation was generated based on the fragment of *Matlab®* script shown in Fig. 1 and some sample trajectories are provided in Fig. 2. It can be seen from the figure that the actual and estimated process noise sequences are superimposed, which demonstrates that an equaliser can be successful when the plant is invertible and the measurement noise is sufficiently low. In general, when measurement noise is not insignificant, the asymptotes (41) – (42) will not apply, as the minimum-variance equaliser solution will involve a trade-off between inverting the plant and filtering the noise.

	ASSUMPTIONS	MAIN RESULTS
Signals and system	$E\{w_k\} = E\{v_k\} = 0$. $E\{w_k w_k^T\} = Q$ and $E\{v_k v_k^T\} = R$ are known. A, B and C are known.	$x_{k+1} = Ax_k + Bw_k$ $y_k = Cx_k$ $z_k = y_k + v_k$
Filtered state and output estimate		$\hat{x}_{k+1/k} = (A - KC)\hat{x}_{k/k-1} + Kz_k$ $\hat{y}_{1,k/k} = (C - LC)\hat{x}_{k/k-1} + Lz_k$
Predictor gain, filter gain and algebraic Riccati equation	$Q > 0$, $R > 0$ and $CPC^T + R_k > 0$. The pair (A, C) is observable.	$K = APC^T(CPC^T + R)^{-1}$ $L = CPC^T(CPC^T + R)^{-1}$ $P = APA^T - K(CPC^T + R)K^T + BQB^T$

Table 2. Main results for time-invariant output estimation.

5.7 Conclusion

In the linear time-invariant case, it is assumed that the signal model and observations can be described by $x_{k+1} = Ax_k + Bw_k$, $y_k = Cx_k$, and $z_k = y_k + v_k$, respectively, where the matrices A, B, C, Q and R are constant. The Kalman filter for this problem is listed in Table 2. If the pair (A, C) is completely observable, the solution of the corresponding Riccati difference equation monotonically converges to the unique solution of the algebraic Riccati equation that appears in the table.

The implementation cost is lower than for time-varying problems because the gains can be calculated before running the filter. If $|\lambda_i(A)| < 1$, $i = 1$ to n, and the pair (A, C) is completely

"Clear thinking requires courage rather than intelligence." *Thomas Stephen Szasz*

observable, then $|\lambda_i(A - KC)| < 1$, that is, the steady-state filter is asymptotically stable. The output estimator has the transfer function

$$H_{OE}(z) = C(I - LC)(zI - A + KC)^{-1}K + CL .$$

Since the task of solving an algebraic Riccati equation is equivalent to spectral factorisation, the transfer functions of the minimum-mean-square error and steady-state minimum-variance solutions are the same.

5.8 Problems

Problem 1. Calculate the observability matrices and comment on the observability of the following pairs.

(i) $A = \begin{bmatrix} 1 & 2 \\ 3 & 4 \end{bmatrix}$, $C = \begin{bmatrix} 2 & 4 \end{bmatrix}$. (ii) $A = \begin{bmatrix} 1 & -2 \\ -3 & -4 \end{bmatrix}$, $C = \begin{bmatrix} 2 & 4 \end{bmatrix}$.

Problem 2. Generalise the proof of Lemma 1 (which addresses the unforced system $x_{k+1} = Ax_k$ and $y_k = Cx_k$) for the system $x_{k+1} = Ax_k + Bw_k$ and $y_k = Cx_k + Dw_k$.

Problem 3. Consider the two Riccati difference equations

$$P_{t+k} = AP_{t+k-1}A^T - AP_{t+k-1}C^T(CP_{t+k-1}C^T + R)^{-1}CP_{t+k-1}A^T + BQB^T$$

$$P_{t+k+1} = AP_{t+k}A^T - AP_{t+k}C^T(CP_{t+k}C^T + R)^{-1}CP_{t+k}A^T + BQB^T .$$

Show that a Riccati difference equation for $\overline{P}_{t+k} = P_{t+k-1} - P_{t+k}$ is given by

$$\overline{P}_{t+k+1} = \overline{A}_k\overline{P}_{t+k}\overline{A}_k^T - \overline{A}_k\overline{P}_{t+k}C^T(C\overline{P}_{t+k}C^T + \overline{R}_k)^{-1}C\overline{P}_{t+k}\overline{A}_k^T$$

where $\overline{A}_{t+k} = A_{t+k} - A_{t+k}P_{t+k}C^T(CP_{t+k}C^T + \overline{R}_{t+k})^{-1}C_{t+k}$ and $\overline{R}_{t+k} = CP_{t+k}C^T + R$.

Problem 4. Suppose that measurements are generated by the single-input-single-output system $\underline{x}_{k+1} = ax_k + w_k$, $z_k = x_k + v_k$, where $a \in \mathbb{R}$, $E\{v_k\} = 0$, $E\{w_jw_k^T\} = (1-a^2)\delta_{jk}$, $E\{v_jv_k^T\} = \delta_{jk}$, $E\{w_jv_k^T\} = 0$.

(a) Find the predicted error variance.
(b) Find the predictor gain.

(c) Verify that the one-step-ahead minimum-variance predictor is realised by

$$\hat{x}_{k+1/k} = \frac{a}{1+\sqrt{1-a^2}}\hat{x}_{k/k-1} + \frac{a\sqrt{1-a^2}}{1+\sqrt{1-a^2}}z_k .$$

(d) Find the filter gain.
(e) Write down the realisation of the minimum-variance filter.

"Thoughts, like fleas, jump from man to man. But they don't bite everybody." *Baron Stanislaw Jerzy Lec*

Problem 5. Assuming that a system G has the realisation $x_{k+1} = A_k x_k + B_k w_k$, $y_k = C_k x_k + D_k w_k$, expand $\Delta\Delta^H(z) = GQG(z) + R$ to obtain $\Delta(z)$ and the optimal output estimation filter.

5.9 Glossary

In addition to the terms listed in Section 2.6, the notation has been used herein.

A, B, C, D	A linear time-invariant system is assumed to have the realisation $x_{k+1} = Ax_k + Bw_k$ and $y_k = Cx_k + Dw_k$ in which A, B, C, D are constant state space matrices of appropriate dimension.
Q, R	Time-invariant covariance matrices of stationary stochastic signals w_k and v_k, respectively.
O	Observability matrix.
W	Observability gramian.
P	Steady-state error covariance matrix.
K	Time-invariant predictor gain matrix.
L	Time-invariant filter gain matrix.
$\Delta(z)$	Spectral factor.
$H_{OE}(z)$	Transfer function matrix of output estimator.
$H_{IE}(z)$	Transfer function matrix of input estimator.

5.10 References

[1] K. Ogata, *Discrete-time Control Systems*, Prentice-Hall, Inc., Englewood Cliffs, New Jersey, 1987.

[2] M. Gopal, *Modern Control Systems Theory*, New Age International Limited Publishers, New Delhi, 1993.

[3] M. R. Opmeer and R. F. Curtain, "Linear Quadratic Gassian Balancing for Discrete-Time Infinite-Dimensional Linear Systems", *SIAM Journal of Control and Optimization*, vol. 43, no. 4, pp. 1196 – 1221, 2004.

[4] S. W. Chan, G. C. Goodwin and K. S. Sin, "Convergence Properties of the Riccati Difference Equation in Optimal Filtering of Nonstablizable Systems", *IEEE Transactions on Automatic Control*, vol. 29, no. 2, pp. 110 – 118, Feb. 1984.

[5] C. E. De Souza, M. R. Gevers and G. C. Goodwin, "Riccatti Equations in Optimal Filtering of Nonstabilizable Systems Having Singular State Transition Matrices", *IEEE Transactions on. Automatic Control*, vol. 31, no. 9, pp. 831 – 838, Sep. 1986.

[6] C. E. De Souza, "On Stabilizing Properties of Solutions of the Riccati Difference Equation", *IEEE Transactions on Automatic Control*, vol. 34, no. 12, pp. 1313 - 1316, Dec. 1989.

[7] R. R. Bitmead, M. Gevers and V. Wertz, *Adaptive Optimal Control. The thinking Man's GPC*, Prentice Hall, New York, 1990.

"Nothing in life is to be feared, it is only to be understood. Now is the time to understand more, so that we may fear less." *Marie Sklodowska Curie*

[8] R. R. Bitmead and Michel Gevers, "Riccati Difference and Differential Equations: Convergence, Monotonicity and Stability", In S. Bittanti, A. J. Laub and J. C. Willems (Eds.), *The Riccati Equation*, Springer Verlag, 1991.
[9] H. K. Wimmer, "Monotonicity and Maximality of Solutions of Discrete-time Algebraic Riccati Equations", *Journal of Mathematical Systems, Estimation and Control*, vol. 2, no. 2, pp. 219 - 235, 1992.
[10] H. K. Wimmer and M. Pavon, "A comparison theorem for matrix Riccati difference equations", *Systems and Control Letters*, vol. 19, pp. 233 - 239, 1992.
[11] G. A. Einicke, "Asymptotic Optimality of the Minimum Variance Fixed-Interval Smoother", *IEEE Transactions on Signal Processing*, vol. 55, no. 4, pp. 1543 - 1547, Apr. 2007.
[12] B. D. O. Anderson and J. B. Moore, *Optimal Filtering*, Prentice-Hall Inc, Englewood Cliffs, New Jersey, 1979.
[13] G. Freiling, G. Jank and H. Abou-Kandil, "Generalized Riccati Difference and Differential Equations", *Linear Algebra and its Applications*, vol. 241, pp. 291 - 303, 1996.
[14] G. Freiling and V. Ionescu, "Time-varying discrete Riccati equation: some monotonicity results", *Linear Algebra and its Applications*, vol. 286, pp. 135 - 148, 1999.

"Man is but a reed, the most feeble thing in nature, but he is a thinking reed." *Blaise Pascal*

6

Continuous-Time Smoothing

6.1 Introduction

The previously-described minimum-mean-square-error and minimum-variance filtering solutions operate on measurements up to the current time. If some processing delay can be tolerated then improved estimation performance can be realised through the use of smoothers. There are three state-space smoothing technique categories, namely, fixed-point, fixed-lag and fixed-interval smoothing. Fixed-point smoothing refers to estimating some linear combination of states at a previous instant in time. In the case of fixed-lag smoothing, a fixed time delay is assumed between the measurement and on-line estimation processes. Fixed-interval smoothing is for retrospective data analysis, where measurements recorded over an interval are used to obtain the improved estimates. Compared to filtering, smoothing has a higher implementation cost, as it has increased memory and calculation requirements.

A large number of smoothing solutions have been reported since Wiener's and Kalman's development of the optimal filtering results – see the early surveys [1] – [2]. The minimum-variance fixed-point and fixed-lag smoother solutions are well known. Two fixed-interval smoother solutions, namely the maximum-likelihood smoother developed by Rauch, Tung and Striebel [3], and the two-filter Fraser-Potter formula [4], have been in widespread use since the 1960s. However, the minimum-variance fixed-interval smoother is not well known. This smoother is simply a time-varying state-space generalisation of the optimal Wiener solution.

The main approaches for continuous-time fixed-point, fixed-lag and fixed-interval smoothing are canvassed here. It is assumed throughout that the underlying noise processes are zero mean and uncorrelated. Nonzero means and correlated processes can be handled using the approaches of Chapters 3 and 4. It is also assumed here that the noise statistics and state-space model parameters are known precisely. Note that techniques for estimating parameters and accommodating uncertainty are addressed subsequently.

Some prerequisite concepts, namely time-varying adjoint systems, backwards differential equations, Riccati equation comparison and the continuous-time maximum-likelihood method are covered in Section 6.2. Section 6.3 outlines a derivation of the fixed-point smoother by Meditch [5]. The fixed-lag smoother reported by Sage *et al* [6] and Moore [7], is the subject of Section 6.4. Section 6.5 deals with the Rauch-Tung-Striebel [3], Fraser-Potter [4] and minimum-variance fixed-interval smoother solutions [8] - [10]. As before, the approach

---

"Life has got a habit of not standing hitched. You got to ride it like you find it. You got to change with it. If a day goes by that don't change some of your old notions for new ones, that is just about like trying to milk a dead cow." *Woodrow Wilson Guthrie*

here is to accompany the developments, where appropriate, with proofs about performance being attained. Smoothing is not a panacea for all ills. If the measurement noise is negligible then smoothing (and filtering) may be superfluous. Conversely, if measurement noise obliterates the signals then data recovery may not be possible. Therefore, estimator performance is often discussed in terms of the prevailing signal-to-noise ratio.

6.2 Prerequisites

6.2.1 Time-varying Adjoint Systems

Since fixed-interval smoothers employ backward processes, it is pertinent to introduce the adjoint of a time-varying continuous-time system. Let $\mathcal{G}: \mathbb{R}^p \to \mathbb{R}^q$ denote a linear time-varying system

$$\dot{x}(t) = A(t)x(t) + B(t)w(t)\,, \tag{1}$$

$$y(t) = C(t)x(t) + D(t)w(t)\,, \tag{2}$$

operating on the interval [0, *T*]. Let w denote the set of $w(t)$ over all time t, that is, $w = \{w(t), t \in [0, T]\}$. Similarly, let $y = \mathcal{G}w$ denote $\{y(t), t \in [0, T]\}$. The adjoint of $\mathcal{G}$, denoted by $\mathcal{G}^H : \mathbb{R}^q \to \mathbb{R}^p$, is the unique linear system satisfying

$$<y, \mathcal{G}w> =< \mathcal{G}^H y, w> \tag{3}$$

for all $y \in \mathbb{R}^q$ and $w \in \mathbb{R}^p$.

Lemma 1: *The adjoint* $\mathcal{G}^H$ *of the system* $\mathcal{G}$ *described by (1) – (2), with* $x(t_0) = 0$, *having the realisation*

$$\dot{\zeta}(t) = -A^T(t)\zeta(t) - C^T(t)u(t)\,, \tag{4}$$

$$z(t) = B^T(t)\zeta(t) + D^T(t)u(t)\,, \tag{5}$$

with $\zeta(T) = 0$, *satisfies (3).*

The proof follows *mutatis mutandis* from that of Lemma 1 of Chapter 3 and is set out in [11]. The original system (1) – (2) needs to be integrated forwards in time, whereas the adjoint system (4) – (5) needs to be integrated backwards in time. Some important properties of backward systems are discussed in the next section. The simplification $D(t) = 0$ is assumed below unless stated otherwise.

6.2.2 Backwards Differential Equations

The adjoint state evolution (4) is rewritten as

$$-\dot{\zeta}(t) = A^T(t)\zeta(t) + C^T(t)u(t)\,. \tag{6}$$

"The simple faith in progress is not a conviction belonging to strength, but one belonging to acquiescence and hence to weakness." *Norbert Wiener*

The negative sign of the derivative within (6) indicates that this differential equation proceeds backwards in time. The corresponding state transition matrix is defined below.

Lemma 2: *The differential equation (6) has the solution*

$$\xi(t) = \Phi^H(t,t_0)\zeta(t_0) - \int_{t_0}^{t} \Phi^H(s,t)C^T(s)u(s)ds\,, \tag{7}$$

where the adjoint state transition matrix, $\Phi^H(t,t_0)$, satisfies

$$\dot{\Phi}^H(t,t_0) = \frac{d\Phi^H(t,t_0)}{dt} = -A^T(t)\Phi^H(t,t_0)\,, \tag{8}$$

with boundary condition

$$\Phi^H(t,t) = I. \tag{9}$$

Proof: *Following the proof of Lemma 1 of Chapter 3, by differentiating (7) and substituting (4) – (5), it is easily verified that (7) is a solution of (6).* □

The Lyapunov equation corresponding to (6) is described next because it is required in the development of backwards Riccati equations.

Lemma 3: *In respect of the backwards differential equation (6), assume that u(t) is a zero-mean white process with $E\{u(t)u^T(\tau)\} = U(t)\delta(t-\tau)$ that is uncorrelated with $\zeta(t_0)$, namely, $E\{u(t)\xi^T(t_0)\} = 0$. Then the covariances $P(t,\tau) = E\{\xi(t)\xi^T(t)\}$ and $\dot{P}(t,\tau) = \dfrac{dE\{\xi(t)\xi^T(t)\}}{dt}$ satisfy the Lyapunov differential equation*

$$-\dot{P}(t,\tau) = A(t)^T P(t,\tau) + P(t,\tau)A(t) - C^T(t)U(t)C(t)\,. \tag{10}$$

Proof: *The backwards Lyapunov differential equation (10) can be obtained by using (6) and (7) within $\dfrac{dE\{\xi(t)\xi^T(t)\}}{dt} = E\{\dot{\xi}(t)\xi^T(t) + \xi(\tau)\dot{\xi}^T(k)\}$ (see the proof of Lemma 2 in Chapter 3).* □

6.2.3 Comparison of Riccati Equations

The following Riccati Equation comparison theorem is required subsequently to compare the performance of filters and smoothers.

Theorem 1 (Riccati Equation Comparison Theorem) [12], [8]: *Let $P_1(t) \geq 0$ and $P_2(t) \geq 0$ denote solutions of the Riccati differential equations*

$$\dot{P}_1(t) = A_1(t)P_1(t) + P_1(t)A_1^T(t) - P_1(t)S_1(t)P_1(t) + B_1(t)Q_1(t)B_1^T(t) + B(t)Q(t)B^T(t) \tag{11}$$

and

"Progress always involves risk; you can't steal second base and keep your foot on first base." *Frederick James Wilcox*

$$\dot{P}_2(t) = A_2(t)P_2(t) + P_2(t)A_2^T(t) - P_2(t)S_2(t)P_2(t) + B_2(t)Q_2(t)B_2^T(t) + B(t)Q(t)B^T(t) \tag{12}$$

with $S_1(t) = C_1^T(t)R_1^{-1}(t)C_1(t)$, $S_2(t) = C_2^T(t)R_2^{-1}(t)C_2(t)$, *where* $A_1(t)$, $B_1(t)$, $C_1(t)$, $Q_1(t) \geq 0$, $R_1(t) \geq 0$, $A_2(t)$, $B_2(t)$, $C_2(t)$, $Q_2(t) \geq 0$ and $R_2(t) \geq 0$ *are of appropriate dimensions. If*

(i) $P_1(t_0) \geq P_2(t_0)$ *for a* $t_0 \geq 0$ *and*

(ii) $\begin{bmatrix} Q_1(t) & A_1(t) \\ A_1^T(t) & -S_1(t) \end{bmatrix} \geq \begin{bmatrix} Q_2(t) & A_2(t) \\ A_2^T(t) & -S_2(t) \end{bmatrix}$ *for all* $t \geq t_0$.

Then

$$P_1(t) \geq P_2(t) \tag{13}$$

for all $t \geq t_0$.

Proof: *Condition (i) of the theorem is the initial step of an induction argument. For the induction step, denote* $\dot{P}_3(t) = \dot{P}_1(t) - \dot{P}_2(t)$, $P_3(t) = P_1(t) - P_2(t)$ *and* $\bar{A}(t) = -A_1^T(t) + S_1(t)P_2(t) - 0.5S_1(t)P_3(t)$. *Then*

$$\dot{P}_3(t) = \bar{A}(t)P_3(t) + P_3(t)\bar{A}^T(t) + \begin{bmatrix} I & P_2(t) \end{bmatrix} \left(\begin{bmatrix} Q_1(t) & A_1(t) \\ A_1^t(t) & -S_1(t) \end{bmatrix} - \begin{bmatrix} Q_2(t) & A_2(t) \\ A_2^t(t) & -S_2(t) \end{bmatrix} \right) \begin{bmatrix} I \\ P_2(t) \end{bmatrix}$$

which together with condition (ii) yields

$$\dot{P}_3(t) \geq \bar{A}(t)P_3(t) + P_3(t)\bar{A}^T(t) . \tag{14}$$

Lemma 5 of Chapter 3 and (14) imply $\dot{P}_3(t) \geq 0$ *and the claim (13) follows.* □

6.2.4 The Maximum-Likelihood Method

Rauch, Tung and Streibel famously derived their fixed-interval smoother [3] using a maximum-likelihood technique which is outlined as follows. Let $x(t) \sim \mathcal{N}(\mu, R_{xx})$ denote a continuous random variable having a Gaussian (or normal) distribution within mean $E\{x(t)\} = \mu$ and covariance $E\{(x(t) - \mu)(x(t) - \mu)^T\} = R_{xx}$. The continuous-time Gaussian probability density function of $x(t) \in \mathbb{R}^n$ is defined by

$$p(x(t)) = \frac{1}{(2\pi)^{n/2} \left| R_{xx} \right|^{1/2}} \exp\left\{ -0.5(x(t) - \mu)^T R_{xx}^{-1}(x(t) - \mu) \right\} , \tag{15}$$

in which $|R_{xx}|$ denotes the determinant of R_{xx}. The probability that the continuous random variable $x(t)$ with a given probability density function $p(x(t))$ lies within an interval [a, b] is given by the likelihood function (which is also known as the cumulative distribution function)

"The price of doing the same old thing is far higher than the price of change." *William Jefferson (Bill) Clinton*

$$P(a \le x(t) \le b) = \int_a^b p(x(t))dx \,. \tag{16}$$

The Gaussian likelihood function for $x(t)$ is calculated from (15) and (16) as

$$f(x(t)) = \frac{1}{(2\pi)^{n/2} \left| R_{xx} \right|^{1/2}} \int_{-\infty}^{\infty} \exp\left\{ -0.5(x(t)-\mu)^T R_{xx}^{-1} (x(t)-\mu) \right\} dx \,. \tag{17}$$

It is often more convenient to work with the log-probability density function

$$\log\ p(x(t)) = -\log\ (2\pi)^{n/2} \left| R_{xx} \right|^{1/2} - 0.5(x(t)-\mu)^T R_{xx}^{-1} (x-\mu)dx \tag{18}$$

and the log-likelihood function

$$\log\ f(x(t)) = -\log\ (2\pi)^{n/2} \left| R_{xx} \right|^{1/2} - 0.5 \int_{-\infty}^{\infty} (x(t)-\mu)^T R_{xx}^{-1} (x-\mu)dx. \tag{19}$$

Suppose that a given record of $x(t)$ is assumed to be belong to a Gaussian distribution that is a function of an unknown quantity θ. A statistical approach for estimating the unknown θ is the method of maximum likelihood. This typically involves finding an estimate $\hat{\theta}$ that either maximises the log-probability density function

$$\hat{\theta} = \arg \max_{\theta} \ \log\ p(\theta \mid x(t)) \tag{20}$$

or maximises the log-likelihood function

$$\hat{\theta} = \arg \max_{\theta} \quad \log\ f(\theta \mid x(t)) \,. \tag{21}$$

So-called maximum likelihood estimates can be found by setting either $\frac{\partial \log\ p(\theta \mid x(t))}{\partial \theta}$ or $\frac{\partial \log\ f(\theta \mid x(t))}{\partial \theta}$ to zero and solving for the unknown θ. Continuous-time maximum likelihood estimation is illustrated by the two examples that follow.

Example 1. Consider the first-order autoregressive system

$$\dot{x}(t) = -a_0 x(t) + w(t) \,, \tag{22}$$

where $\dot{x}(t)$ = $\frac{dx(t)}{dt}$, $w(t)$ is a zero-mean Gaussian process and a_0 is unknown. It follows from (22) that $\dot{x}(t) \sim \mathcal{N}(-a_0 x(t),\ \sigma_w^2)$, namely,

$$f(\dot{x}(t)) = \frac{1}{(2\pi)^{n/2} \sigma_w} \int_0^T \exp\left\{ -0.5(\dot{x}(t) + a_0 x(t))^2 \sigma_w^{-2} \right\} dt \,. \tag{23}$$

"Faced with the choice between changing one's mind and proving that there is no need to do so, almost everyone gets busy on the proof." *John Kenneth Galbraith*

Taking the logarithm of both sides gives

$$\log\, f(\dot{x}(t)) = -\log\,(2\pi)^{n/2}\sigma_w - 0.5\sigma_w^{-2}\int_0^T (\dot{x}(t) + a_0 x(t))^2\,dt\,. \tag{24}$$

Setting $\frac{\partial \log\, f(\dot{x}(t))}{\partial a_0} = 0$ results in $\int_0^T (\dot{x}(t) + a_0 x(t))x(t)dt = 0$ and hence

$$\hat{a}_0 = -\left(\int_0^T (x^2(t)dt\right)^{-1}\int_0^T \dot{x}(t)x(t)dt\,. \tag{25}$$

***Example* 2.** Consider the third-order autoregressive system

$$\dddot{x}(t) + a_2\ddot{x}(t) + a_1\dot{x}(t) + a_0 x(t) = w(t) \tag{26}$$

where $\dddot{x}(t) = \frac{d^3x(t)}{dt^3}$ and $\ddot{x}(t) = \frac{d^2x(t)}{dt^2}$. The above system can be written in a controllable canonical form as

$$\begin{bmatrix}\dot{x}_1(t)\\ \dot{x}_2(t)\\ \dot{x}_3(t)\end{bmatrix} = \begin{bmatrix}-a_2 & -a_1 & -a_0\\ 1 & 0 & 0\\ 0 & 1 & 0\end{bmatrix}\begin{bmatrix}x_1(t)\\ x_2(t)\\ x_3(t)\end{bmatrix} + \begin{bmatrix}w(t)\\ 0\\ 0\end{bmatrix}. \tag{27}$$

Assuming $\dot{x}_1(t) \sim \mathcal{N}(-a_2 x_1(t) - a_1 x_2(t) - a_0 x_3(t),\ \sigma_w^2)$, taking logarithms, setting to zero the partial derivatives with respect to the unknown coefficients, and rearranging yields

$$\begin{bmatrix}\hat{a}_0\\ \hat{a}_1\\ \hat{a}_2\end{bmatrix} = -\begin{bmatrix}\int_0^T x_3^2 dt & \int_0^T x_2 x_3 dt & \int_0^T x_1 x_3 dt\\ \int_0^T x_2 x_3 dt & \int_0^T x_2^2 dt & \int_0^T x_2 x_1 dt\\ \int_0^T x_1 x_3 dt & \int_0^T x_2 x_1 dt & \int_0^T x_1^2 dt\end{bmatrix}^{-1}\begin{bmatrix}\int_0^T \dot{x}_1 x_3 dt\\ \int_0^T \dot{x}_1 x_2 dt\\ \int_0^T \dot{x}_1 x_1 dt\end{bmatrix}, \tag{28}$$

in which state time dependence is omitted for brevity.

6.3 Fixed-Point Smoothing

6.3.1 Problem Definition

In continuous-time fixed-point smoothing, it is desired to calculate state estimates at one particular time of interest, τ, $0 \le \tau \le t$, from measurements $z(t)$ over the interval $t \in [0, T]$. For example, suppose that a continuous measurement stream of a tennis ball's trajectory is available and it is desired to determine whether it bounced within the court boundary. In this case, a fixed-point smoother could be employed to estimate the ball position at the time of the bounce from the past and future measurements.

"When a distinguished but elderly scientist states that something is possible, he is almost certainly right. When he states that something is impossible, he is probably wrong." *Arthur Charles Clarke*

A solution for the continuous-time fixed-point smoothing problem can be developed from first principles, for example, see [5] - [6]. However, it is recognised in [13] that a simpler solution derivation follows by transforming the smoothing problem into a filtering problem that possesses an augmented state. Following the nomenclature of [14], consider an augmented state vector having two components, namely, $x^{(a)}(t) = \begin{bmatrix} x(t) \\ \xi(t) \end{bmatrix}$. The first component, $x(t) \in \mathbb{R}^n$, is the state of the system $\dot{x}(t) = A(t)x(t) + B(t)w(t)$ and $y(t) = C(t)x(t)$. The second component, $\xi(t) \in \mathbb{R}^n$, equals $x(t)$ at time $t = \tau$, that is, $\xi(t) = x(\tau)$. The corresponding signal model may be written as

$$\dot{x}^{(a)}(t) = A^{(a)}(t)x^{(a)}(t) + B^{(a)}(t)w(t) \tag{29}$$

$$z(t) = C^{(a)}(t)x^{(a)}(t) + v(t), \tag{30}$$

where $A^{(a)} = \begin{bmatrix} A(t) & 0 \\ 0 & \delta_{t\tau}A(t) \end{bmatrix}$, $B^{(a)}(t) = \begin{bmatrix} B(t) \\ \delta_{t\tau}B(t) \end{bmatrix}$ and $C^{(a)}(t) = [C(t) \quad 0]$, in which $\delta_{t\tau} = \begin{cases} 1 & \text{if } t = \tau \\ 0 & \text{if } t \neq \tau \end{cases}$ is the Kronecker delta function. Note that the simplifications $A^{(a)} = \begin{bmatrix} A(t) & 0 \\ 0 & 0 \end{bmatrix}$ and $B^{(a)}(t) = \begin{bmatrix} B(t) \\ 0 \end{bmatrix}$ arise for $t > \tau$. The smoothing objective is to produce an estimate $\hat{\xi}(t)$ of $\xi(t)$ from the measurements $z(t)$ over $t \in [0, T]$.

6.3.2 Solution Derivation

Employing the Kalman-Bucy filter recursions for the system (29) – (30) results in

$$\begin{aligned} \dot{\hat{x}}^{(a)}(t) &= A^{(a)}(t)\hat{x}^{(a)}(t) + K^{(a)}(t)\left(z(t) - C^{(a)}(t)\hat{x}(t \mid t)\right) \\ &= \left(A^{(a)}(t) - K^{(a)}(t)C^{(a)}(t)\right)x^{(a)}(t) + K^{(a)}(t)z(t), \end{aligned} \tag{31}$$

where

$$K^{(a)}(t) = P^{(a)}(t)(C^{(a)})^T(t)R^{-1}(t), \tag{32}$$

in which $P^{(a)}(t) \in \mathbb{R}^{2n \times 2n}$ is to be found. Consider the partitioning $K^{(a)}(t) = \begin{bmatrix} K(t) \\ \underline{K}(t) \end{bmatrix}$, then for $t > \tau$, (31) may be written as

$$\begin{bmatrix} \dot{\hat{x}}(t \mid t) \\ \dot{\hat{\xi}}(t) \end{bmatrix} = \begin{bmatrix} A(t) - K(t)C(t) & 0 \\ -\underline{K}(t)C(t) & 0 \end{bmatrix} \begin{bmatrix} \hat{x}(t \mid t) \\ \xi(t) \end{bmatrix} + \begin{bmatrix} K(t) \\ \underline{K}(t) \end{bmatrix} z(t). \tag{33}$$

"Don't be afraid to take a big step if one is indicated. You can't cross a chasm in two small jumps." *David Lloyd George*

Define the augmented error state as $\tilde{x}^{(a)}(t) = x^{(a)}(t) - \hat{x}^{(a)}(t)$, that is,

$$\begin{bmatrix} \tilde{x}(t\,|\,t) \\ \tilde{\xi}(t) \end{bmatrix} = \begin{bmatrix} x(t) \\ \xi(\tau) \end{bmatrix} - \begin{bmatrix} \hat{x}(t\,|\,t) \\ \hat{\xi}(t) \end{bmatrix}. \tag{34}$$

Differentiating (34) and using $z(t) = C(t)\tilde{x}(t\,|\,t) + v(t)$ gives

$$\begin{aligned} \begin{bmatrix} \dot{\tilde{x}}(t\,|\,t) \\ \dot{\tilde{\xi}}(t) \end{bmatrix} &= \begin{bmatrix} \dot{x}(t\,|\,t) \\ 0 \end{bmatrix} - \begin{bmatrix} \dot{\hat{x}}(t\,|\,t) \\ \dot{\hat{\xi}}(t) \end{bmatrix} \\ &= \begin{bmatrix} A(t) - K(t)C(t) & 0 \\ -\underline{K}(t)C(t) & 0 \end{bmatrix} \begin{bmatrix} \tilde{x}(t\,|\,t) \\ \tilde{\xi}(t) \end{bmatrix} + \begin{bmatrix} B(t) & -K(t) \\ 0 & -\underline{K}(t) \end{bmatrix} \begin{bmatrix} w(t) \\ v(t) \end{bmatrix}. \end{aligned} \tag{35}$$

Denote $P^{(a)}(t) = \begin{bmatrix} P(t) & \Sigma^T(t) \\ \Sigma(t) & \Omega(t) \end{bmatrix}$, where $P(t) = E\{[x(t) - \hat{x}(t\,|\,t)][(x(t) - \hat{x}(t\,|\,t)]^T\}$, $\Omega(t) = E\{[\xi(t) - \hat{\xi}(t)][\xi(t) - \hat{\xi}(t)]^T\}$ and $\Sigma(t) = E\{[\xi(t) - \hat{\xi}(t)][x(t) - \hat{x}(t\,|\,t)]^T\}$. Applying Lemma 2 of Chapter 3 to (35) yields the Lyapunov differential equation

$$\begin{aligned} \begin{bmatrix} \dot{P}(t) & \dot{\Sigma}^T(t) \\ \dot{\Sigma}(t) & \dot{\Omega}(t) \end{bmatrix} &= \begin{bmatrix} A(t) - K(t)C(t) & 0 \\ -\underline{K}(t)C(t) & 0 \end{bmatrix} \begin{bmatrix} P(t) & \Sigma^T(t) \\ \Sigma(t) & \Omega(t) \end{bmatrix} + \begin{bmatrix} P(t) & \Sigma^T(t) \\ \Sigma(t) & \Omega(t) \end{bmatrix} \begin{bmatrix} A^T(t) - C^T(t)K^T(t) & -C^T(t)\underline{K}^T(t) \\ 0 & 0 \end{bmatrix} \\ &+ \begin{bmatrix} B(t) & -K(t) \\ 0 & -\underline{K}(t) \end{bmatrix} \begin{bmatrix} Q(t) & 0 \\ 0 & R(t) \end{bmatrix} \begin{bmatrix} B^T(t) & 0 \\ -K^T(t) & -\underline{K}^T(t) \end{bmatrix}. \end{aligned}$$

Simplifying the above differential equation yields

$$\dot{P}(t) = A(t)P(t) + P(t)A^T(t) - P(t)C^T(t)R^{-1}(t)C(t)P(t) + B(t)Q(t)B^T(t), \tag{36}$$

$$\dot{\Sigma}(t) = \Sigma(t)\left(A^T(t) - C^T(t)K^T(t)\right), \tag{37}$$

$$\dot{\Omega}(t) = -\Sigma(t)C^T(t)R^{-1}(t)C(t)\Sigma^T(t). \tag{38}$$

Equations(37) - (38) can be initialised with

$$\Sigma(\tau) = P(\tau). \tag{39}$$

Thus, the fixed-point smoother estimate is given by

$$\hat{\xi}(t) = \Sigma(t)C^T(t)R^{-1}(t)\left(z(t) - C(t)\hat{x}(t\,|\,t)\right), \tag{40}$$

"If you don't like change, you're going to like irrelevance even less." *General Eric Shinseki*

which is initialised with $\hat{\xi}(\tau) = \hat{x}(\tau)$. Alternative derivations of (40) are presented in [5], [8], [15]. The smoother (40) and its associated error covariances (36) - (38) are also discussed in [16], [17].

6.3.3 Performance

It can be seen that the right-hand-side of the smoother error covariance (38) is non-positive and therefore $\Omega(t)$ must be monotonically decreasing. That is, the smoothed estimates improve with time. However, since the right-hand-side of (36) varies inversely with $R(t)$, the improvement reduces with decreasing signal-to-noise ratio. It is shown below the fixed-point smoother improves on the performance of the minimum-variance filter.

Lemma 4: *In respect of the fixed-point smoother (40),*

$$P(t) \ge \Omega(t) . \tag{41}$$

Proof: *The initialisation (39) accords with condition (i) of Theorem 1. Condition (ii) of the theorem is satisfied since*

$$\begin{bmatrix} Q(t) & A(t) \\ A^T(t) & -C^T(t)R^{-1}(t)C(t) \end{bmatrix} \ge \begin{bmatrix} -C^T(t)R^{-1}(t)C(t)0 & 0 \\ 0 & 0 \end{bmatrix}$$

and hence the claim (41) follows. □

6.4 Fixed-Lag Smoothing

6.4.1 Problem Definition

For continuous-time estimation problems, as usual, it assumed that the observations are modelled by $\dot{x}(t) = A(t)x(t) + B(t)w(t)$, $z(t) = C(t)x(t) + v(t)$, with $E\{w(t)w^T(\tau)\} = Q(t)\delta(t-\tau)$ and $E\{v(t)v^T(\tau)\} = R(t)\delta(t-\tau)$. In fixed-lag smoothing, it is desired to calculate state estimates at a fixed time lag behind the current measurements. That is, smoothed state estimates, $\hat{x}(t|t+\tau)$, are desired at time t, given data at time $t + \tau$, where τ is a prescribed lag. In particular, fixed-lag smoother estimates are sought which minimise $E\{[x(t) - \hat{x}(t|t+\tau)][x(t) - \hat{x}(t|t+\tau)]^T\}$. It is found in [18] that the smoother yields practically all the improvement over the minimum-variance filter when the smoothing lag equals several time constants associated with the minimum-variance filter for the problem.

6.4.2 Solution Derivation

Previously, augmented signal models together with the application of the standard Kalman filter recursions were used to obtain the smoother results. However, as noted in [19], it is difficult to derive the optimal continuous-time fixed-lag smoother in this way because an ideal delay operator cannot easily be included within an asymptotically stable state-space system. Consequently, an alternate derivation based on that in [6] is outlined in the

---

"Change is like putting lipstick on a bulldog. The bulldog's appearance hasn't improved, but now it's really angry." *Rosbeth Moss Kanter*

following. Recall that the gain of the minimum-variance filter is calculated as $K(t)$ = $P(t)C^T(t)R^{-1}(t)$, where $P(t)$ is the solution of the Riccati equation (3.36). Let $\Phi(\tau,t)$ denote the transition matrix of the filter error system $\dot{\tilde{x}}(t|t)$ = $(A(t)$ – $K(t)C(t))\tilde{x}(t|t)$ + $B(t)w(t)$ – $K(t)v(t)$, that is,

$$\dot{\Phi}(t,s) = \left(A(\tau) - K(\tau)C(\tau)\right)\Phi(t,s) \tag{42}$$

and $\Phi(s,s)$ = I. It is assumed in [6], [17], [18], [20] that a smoothed estimate $\hat{x}(t|t+\tau)$ of $x(t)$ is obtained as

$$\hat{x}(t|t+\tau) = \hat{x}(t) + P(t)\xi(t,\tau), \tag{43}$$

where

$$\xi(t,t+\tau) = \int_t^{t+\tau} \Phi^T(\tau,t)C^T(\tau)R^{-1}(\tau)\left(z(\tau) - C(\tau)\hat{x}(\tau|\tau)\right)d\tau . \tag{44}$$

The formula (43) appears in the development of fixed interval smoothers [21] - [22], in which case $\xi(t)$ is often called an adjoint variable. From the use of Leibniz' rule, that is,

$$\frac{d}{dt}\int_{a(t)}^{b(t)} f(t,s)ds = f(t,b(t))\frac{db(t)}{dt} - f(t,a(t))\frac{da(t)}{dt} + \int_{a(t)}^{b(t)} \frac{\partial}{\partial t} f(t,s)ds ,$$

it can be found that

$$\begin{aligned}\dot{\zeta}(t,t+\tau) &= \Phi^T(t+\tau)C^T(t+\tau)R^{-1}(t+\tau)\left(z(t+\tau) - C(t+\tau)\hat{x}(t+\tau)|t+\tau)\right) \\ &\quad -C^T(t)R^{-1}(t)\left(z(t) - C(t)\hat{x}(t|t)\right) - \left(A(t) - K(t)C(t)\right)^T \xi(t,t+\tau) .\end{aligned} \tag{45}$$

Differentiating (43) with respect to t gives

$$\dot{\hat{x}}(t|t+\tau) = \dot{\hat{x}}(t|t) + \dot{P}(t)\xi(t,\tau) + P(t)\dot{\xi}(t,\tau) . \tag{46}$$

Substituting $\xi(t,\tau)$ = $P^{-1}(t)\left(\hat{x}(t|t+\tau) - \hat{x}(t|t)\right)$ and expressions for $\dot{\hat{x}}(t)$, $\dot{P}(t)$, $\dot{\xi}(t,t+\tau)$ into (43) yields the fixed–lag smoother differential equation

$$\begin{aligned}\dot{\hat{x}}(t|t+\tau) &= A(t)\dot{\hat{x}}(t|t+\tau) + B(t)Q(t)B^T(t)P^{-1}(t)\left(\hat{x}(t|t+\tau) - \hat{x}(t|t)\right) \\ &\quad +P(t)\Phi^T(t+\tau,t)C^T(t+\tau)R^{-1}(t+\tau)\left(z(t+\tau) - C(t+\tau)\hat{x}(t+\tau|t+\tau)\right) .\end{aligned} \tag{47}$$

"An important scientific innovation rarely makes its way by gradually winning over and converting its opponents: What does happen is that the opponents gradually die out." *Max Karl Ernst Ludwig Planck*

6.4.3 Performance

Lemma 5 [18]:

$$P(t) - E\{[x(t) - \dot{\hat{x}}(t \mid t+\tau)][x(t) - \dot{\hat{x}}(t \mid t+\tau)]^T\} > 0. \tag{48}$$

Proof. *It is argued from the references of [18] for the fixed-lag smoothed estimate that*

$$E\{[x(t) - \dot{\hat{x}}(t \mid t+\tau)][x(t) - \dot{\hat{x}}(t \mid t+\tau)]^T\} = P(t) - P(t)\int_t^{\tau} \Phi^T(s,t)C^T(s)R^{-1}(s)C(s)\Phi(s,t)ds\; P(t) \tag{49}$$

Thus, (48) follows by inspection of (49). □

That is to say, the minimum-variance filter error covariance is greater than fixed-lag smoother error covariance. It is also argued in [18] that (48) implies the error covariance decreases monotonically with the smoother lag τ.

6.5 Fixed-Interval Smoothing

6.5.1 Problem Definition

Many data analyses occur off-line. In medical diagnosis for example, reviews of ultra-sound or CAT scan images are delayed after the time of measurement. In principle, smoothing could be employed instead of filtering for improving the quality of an image sequence.

Fixed-lag smoothers are elegant – they can provide a small performance improvement over filters at moderate increase in implementation cost. The best performance arises when the lag is sufficiently large, at the expense of increased complexity. Thus, the designer needs to trade off performance, calculation cost and delay.

Fixed-interval smoothers are a brute-force solution for estimation problems. They provide improved performance without having to fine tune a smoothing lag, at the cost of approximately twice the filter calculation complexity. Fixed interval smoothers involve two passes. Typically, a forward process operates on the measurements. Then a backward system operates on the results of the forward process.

The plants are again assumed to have state-space realisations of the form $\dot{x}(t) = A(t)x(t) + B(t)w(t)$ and $y(t) = C(t)x(t) + D(t)w(t)$. Smoothers are considered which operate on measurements $z(t) = y(t) + v(t)$ over a fixed interval $t \in [0, T]$. The performance criteria depend on the quantity being estimated, *viz.*,

- in input estimation, the objective is to calculate a $\hat{w}(t \mid T)$ that minimises $E\{[w(t) - \hat{w}(t \mid T)][w(t) - \hat{w}(t \mid T)]^T\}$;
- in state estimation, $\hat{x}(t \mid T)$ is calculated which achieves the minimum $E\{[x(t) - \hat{x}(t \mid T)][x(t) - \hat{x}(t \mid T)]^T\}$; and
- in output estimation, $\hat{y}(t \mid T)$ is produced such that $E\{[y(t) - \hat{y}(t \mid T)][y(t) - \hat{y}(t \mid T)]^T\}$ is minimised.

"If you want to truly understand something, try to change it." *Kurt Lewin*

This section focuses on three continuous-time fixed-interval smoother formulations; the maximum-likelihood smoother derived by Rauch, Tung and Streibel [3], the Fraser-Potter smoother [4] and a generalisation of Wiener's optimal unrealisable solution [8] - [10]. Some additional historical background to [3] - [4] is described within [1], [2], [17].

6.5.2 The Maximum Likelihood Smoother

6.5.2.1 Solution Derivation

Rauch, Tung and Streibel [3] employed the maximum-likelihood method to develop a discrete-time smoother for state estimation and then used a limiting argument to obtain a continuous-time version. A brief outline of this derivation is set out here. Suppose that a record of filtered estimates, $\hat{x}(\tau \mid \tau)$, is available over a fixed interval $\tau \in [0, T]$. Let $\hat{x}(\tau \mid T)$ denote smoothed state estimates at time $0 \le \tau \le T$ to be evolved backwards in time from filtered states $\hat{x}(\tau \mid \tau)$. The smoother development is based on two assumptions. First, it is assumed that $-\dot{\hat{x}}(\tau \mid T)$ is normally distributed with mean $A(\tau)\hat{x}(\tau \mid T)$ and covariance $B(\tau)Q(\tau)B^T(\tau)$, that is, $-\dot{\hat{x}}(\tau \mid T) \sim \mathcal{N}(A(\tau)\hat{x}(\tau \mid T), B(\tau)Q(\tau)B^T(\tau))$. The probability density function of $-\dot{\hat{x}}(\tau \mid T)$ is

$$p(-\dot{\hat{x}}(\tau \mid T) \mid \hat{x}(\tau \mid T)) = \frac{1}{(2\pi)^{n/2}\left|B(\tau)Q(\tau)B^T(\tau)\right|^{1/2}}$$

$$\times \exp\left\{-0.5(-\dot{\hat{x}}(\tau \mid T) - A(\tau)\hat{x}(\tau \mid T))^T (B(\tau)Q(\tau)B^T(\tau))^{-1}(-\dot{\hat{x}}(\tau \mid T) - A(\tau)\hat{x}(\tau \mid T))\right\}$$

Second, it is assumed that $\hat{x}(\tau \mid T)$ is normally distributed with mean $\hat{x}(\tau \mid \tau)$ and covariance $P(\tau)$, namely, $\hat{x}(\tau \mid T) \sim N(\hat{x}(\tau \mid \tau), P(\tau))$. The corresponding probability density function is

$$p(\hat{x}(\tau \mid T) \mid \hat{x}(\tau \mid \tau)) = \frac{1}{(2\pi)^{n/2}\left|P(\tau)\right|^{1/2}} \times \exp\left\{-0.5(\hat{x}(\tau \mid T) - \hat{x}(\tau \mid \tau))^T P^{-1}(t)(\hat{x}(\tau \mid T) - \hat{x}(\tau \mid \tau))\right\}.$$

From the approach of [3] and the further details in [6],

$$0 = \frac{\partial \log\ p(-\dot{\hat{x}}(\tau \mid T) \mid \hat{x}(\tau \mid T))p(\hat{x}(\tau \mid T) \mid \hat{x}(\tau \mid \tau))}{\partial \hat{x}(\tau \mid T)}$$

$$= \frac{\partial \log\ p(-\dot{\hat{x}}(\tau \mid T) \mid \hat{x}(\tau \mid T))}{\partial \hat{x}(\tau \mid T)} + \frac{\partial \log\ p(\hat{x}(t \mid T) \mid \hat{x}(t \mid t))}{\partial \hat{x}(t \mid T)}$$

results in

$$0 = \frac{\partial(-\dot{\hat{x}}(\tau \mid T) - A(\tau)\hat{x}(\tau \mid T))^T}{\partial \hat{x}(\tau \mid T)}(B(\tau)Q(\tau)B^T(\tau))^{-1}(-\dot{\hat{x}}(\tau \mid T) - A(\tau)\hat{x}(\tau \mid T)) + P^{-1}(\tau)(\hat{x}(t \mid T) - \hat{x}(\tau \mid \tau)).$$

"The soft-minded man always fears change. He feels security in the status quo, and he has an almost morbid fear of the new. For him, the greatest pain is the pain of a new idea." *Martin Luther King Jr.*

Hence, the solution is given by

$$-\dot{\hat{x}}(\tau \mid T) = A(\tau)\hat{x}(\tau \mid T) + G(\tau)\big(\hat{x}(\tau \mid T) - \hat{x}(\tau \mid \tau)\big), \tag{50}$$

where

$$G(\tau) = -B(\tau)Q(\tau)B^T(\tau)\frac{\partial(-\dot{\hat{x}}(\tau \mid T) - A(\tau)\hat{x}(\tau \mid T))^T}{\partial\hat{x}(\tau \mid T)}P^{-1}(\tau) \tag{51}$$

is the smoother gain. Suppose that $\hat{x}(\tau \mid T)$, $A(\tau)$, $B(\tau)$, $Q(\tau)$, $P^{-1}(\tau)$ are sampled at integer k multiples of T_s and are constant during the sampling interval. Using the Euler approximation $-\dot{\hat{x}}(kT_s \mid T) = \dfrac{\hat{x}((k-1)T_s \mid T) - \hat{x}(kT_s \mid T)}{T_s}$, the sampled gain may be written as

$$G(kT_s) = B(kT_s)T_s^{-1}Q(kT_s)B^T(kT_s)(I + AT_s)P^{-1}(kT_s)\,. \tag{52}$$

Recognising that $T_s^{-1}Q(kT_s) = Q(\tau)$, see [23], and taking the limit as $T_s \to 0$ and yields

$$G(\tau) = B(\tau)Q(\tau)B^T(\tau)P^{-1}(\tau)\,. \tag{53}$$

To summarise, the above fixed-interval smoother is realised by the following two-pass procedure.

(i) In the first pass, the (forward) Kalman-Bucy filter operates on measurements $z(\tau)$ to obtain state estimates $\hat{x}(\tau \mid \tau)$.

(ii) In the second pass, the differential equation (50) operates on the filtered state estimates $\hat{x}(\tau \mid \tau)$ to obtain smoothed state estimates $\hat{x}(\tau \mid T)$. Equation (50) is integrated backwards in time from the initial condition $\hat{x}(\tau \mid T) = \hat{x}(\tau \mid \tau)$ at $\tau = T$.

Alternative derivations of this smoother appear in [6], [20], [23], [24].

6.5.2.2 Alternative Form

For the purpose of developing an alternate form of the above smoother found in the literature, consider a fictitious forward version of (50), namely,

$$\begin{aligned}\dot{\hat{x}}(t \mid T) &= A(t)\hat{x}(t \mid T) + B(t)Q(t)B^T(t)P^{-1}(t)\big(\hat{x}(t \mid T) - \hat{x}(t \mid t)\big)\\ &= A(t)\hat{x}(t \mid T) + B(t)Q(t)B^T(t)\xi(t \mid T),\end{aligned} \tag{54}$$

where

$$\xi(t \mid T) = P^{-1}(t)(\hat{x}(t \mid T) - \hat{x}(t \mid t)) \tag{55}$$

"There is a certain relief in change, even though it be from bad to worse. As I have often found in travelling in a stagecoach that it is often a comfort to shift one's position, and be bruised in a new place." *Washington Irving*

is an auxiliary variable. An expression for the evolution of $\xi(t|T)$ is now developed. Writing (55) as

$$\hat{x}(\tau|T) = \hat{x}(t|t) + P(t)\xi(t|T) \tag{56}$$

and taking the time differential results in

$$\dot{\hat{x}}(t|T) = \dot{\hat{x}}(t|t) + \dot{P}(t)\xi(t|T) + P(t)\dot{\xi}(t|T) . \tag{57}$$

Substituting $\dot{\hat{x}}(t|t) = A(t)\hat{x}(t|t) + P(t)C^T(t)R^{-1}(z(t) - C(t)\hat{x}(t|t))$ into (57) yields

$$P(t)\dot{\xi}(t|T) = P(t)C^T(t)R^{-1}C(t) - P(t)C^T(t)R^{-1}z(t) + A(t)P(t)\xi(t) + B(t)Q(t)B^T(t) - \dot{P}(t)\xi(t). \tag{58}$$

Using $\hat{x}(t|t) = \hat{x}(t|T) - P(t)\xi(t|T)$, $-P(t)A^T(t) = A(t)P(t) - P(t)C^T(t)R^{-1}(t)C(t)P(t)\xi(t|T) + B(t)Q(t)B^T(t) - \dot{P}(t)$ within (58) and rearranging gives

$$-\dot{\xi}(t|T) = -C^T(t)R^{-1}(t)C(t)\hat{x}(t|T) + A^T(t)\xi(t) - C^T(t)R^{-1}(t)z(t) . \tag{59}$$

The filter (54) and smoother (57) may be collected together as

$$\begin{bmatrix} \dot{\hat{x}}(t|T) \\ -\dot{\xi}(t|T) \end{bmatrix} = \begin{bmatrix} A(t) & B(t)Q(t)B^T(t) \\ -C^T(t)R^{-1}(t)C(t) & A^T(t) \end{bmatrix} \begin{bmatrix} \hat{x}(t|T) \\ \xi(t|T) \end{bmatrix} + \begin{bmatrix} 0 \\ C^T(t)R^{-1}(t)z(t) \end{bmatrix} . \tag{60}$$

Equation (60) is known as the Hamiltonian form of the Rauch-Tung-Striebel smoother [17].

6.5.2.3 Performance

In order to develop an expression for the smoothed error state, consider the backwards signal model

$$-\dot{x}(\tau) = A(\tau)x(\tau) + B(\tau)w(\tau) . \tag{61}$$

Subtracting (50) from (61) results in

$$-\dot{x}(\tau) + \dot{\hat{x}}(\tau|T) = (A(\tau) + G(\tau))(x(\tau) - \hat{x}(\tau|T)) - G(\tau)(x(\tau) - \hat{x}(\tau|\tau)) + B(\tau)w(\tau) . \tag{62}$$

Let $\tilde{x}(\tau|T) = x(\tau) - \hat{x}(\tau|T)$ denote the smoothed error state and $\tilde{x}(\tau|\tau) = x(\tau) - \hat{x}(\tau|\tau)$ denote the filtered error state. Then the differential equation (62) can simply be written as

$$-\dot{\tilde{x}}(\tau|T) = (A(\tau) + G(\tau))(\tilde{x}(\tau|T) - G(\tau)\tilde{x}(\tau|\tau) + B(\tau)w(\tau) , \tag{63}$$

where $-\dot{\tilde{x}}(\tau|T) = -(\dot{\hat{x}}(\tau|T) - \dot{x}(\tau))$. Applying Lemma 3 to (63) and using $E\{\hat{x}(\tau|\tau), w^T(\tau)\} = 0$ gives

$$-\dot{\Sigma}(\tau|T) = (A(\tau) + G(\tau))\Sigma(\tau|T) + \Sigma(\tau|T)(A(\tau) + G(\tau))^T - B(\tau)Q(\tau)B^T(\tau) , \tag{64}$$

"That which comes into the world to disturb nothing deserves neither respect nor patience." *Rene Char*

where $\Sigma(\tau | T) = E\{\hat{x}(\tau | T),\ \hat{x}^T(\tau | T)\}$ is the smoother error covariance and $\dot{\Sigma}(\tau | T) = \frac{d\Sigma(\tau | T)}{d\tau}$. The smoother error covariance differential equation (64) is solved backwards in time from the initial condition

$$\Sigma(\tau | T) = P(t | t) \tag{65}$$

at $t = T$, where $P(t | t)$ is the solution of the Riccati differential equation

$$\begin{aligned}\dot{P}(t) &= (A(t) - K(t)C(t))P(t) + P(t)(A^T(t) - C^T(t)K^T(t)) + K(t)R(t)K^T(t) + B(t)Q(t)B^T(t) \\ &= A(t)P(t) + P(t)A^T(t) - K(t)R(t)K^T(t) + B(t)Q(t)B^T(t)\end{aligned} \tag{66}$$

It is shown below that this smoother outperforms the minimum-variance filter. For the purpose of comparing the solutions of forward Riccati equations, consider a fictitious forward version of (64), namely,

$$\dot{\Sigma}(t | T) = (A(t) + G(t))\Sigma(t | T) + \Sigma(t | T)(A(t) + G(t))^T - B(t)Q(t)B^T(t) \tag{67}$$

initialised with

$$\Sigma(t_0 | T) = P(t_0 | t_0) > 0 . \tag{68}$$

Lemma 6: *In respect of the fixed-interval smoother (50),*

$$P(t | t) \ge \Sigma(t | T) . \tag{69}$$

Proof: *The initialisation (68) satisfies condition (i) of Theorem 1. Condition (ii) of the theorem is met since*

$$\begin{bmatrix} B(t)Q(t)B^T(t) + K(t)R(t)K^T(t) & A(t) - K(t)C(t) \\ A^T(t) - C^T(t)K^T(t) & 0 \end{bmatrix} \ge \begin{bmatrix} -B(t)Q(t)B^T(t) & A(t) + G(t) \\ A^T(t) + G^T(t) & 0 \end{bmatrix}$$

for all $t \ge t_0$ and hence the claim (69) follows. □

6.5.3 The Fraser-Potter Smoother

The Central Limit Theorem states that the mean of a sufficiently large sample of independent identically distributed random variables will be approximately normally distributed [25]. The same is true of partial sums of random variables. The Central Limit Theorem is illustrated by the first part of the following lemma. A useful generalisation appears in the second part of the lemma.

Lemma 7: *Suppose that y_1, y_2, …, y_n are independent random variables and W_1, W_2, … W_n are independent positive definite weighting matrices. Let $\mu = E\{y\}$, $u = y_1 + y_2 + \ldots + y_n$ and*

$$v = (W_1 y_1 + W_2 y_2 + \ldots + W_n y_n)(W_1 + W_2 + \ldots W_n)^{-1}. \tag{70}$$

"Today every invention is received with a cry of triumph which soon turns into a cry of fear." *Bertolt Brecht*

(i) If $y_i \sim \mathcal{N}(\mu, R)$, $i = 1$ to n, then $u \sim \mathcal{N}(n\mu, nR)$;

(ii) If $y_i \sim \mathcal{N}(0, I)$, $i = 1$ to n, then $v \sim \mathcal{N}(0, I)$.

Proof:

(i) $E\{u\} = E\{y_1\} + E(y_2) + \ldots + E\{y_n\} = n\mu$. $E\{(u-\mu)(u-\mu)^T\} = E\{(y_1-\mu)(y_1-\mu)^T\} + E\{(y_2-\mu)(y_2-\mu)^T\} + \ldots + E\{(y_n-\mu)(y_n-\mu)^T\} = nR$.

(ii) $E\{v\} = W_1(W_1 + W_2 + \ldots + W_n)^{-1}E\{y_1\} + W_2(W_1 + W_2 + \ldots + W_n)^{-1}E(y_2) + \ldots + W_n(W_1 + W_2 + \ldots W_n)^{-1}E\{y_n\}) = 0$. $E\{vv^T\} = E\{(W_1^T + W_2^T + \ldots + W_n^T)^{-1}W_1^Ty_1^Ty_1W_1(W_1 + W_2 + \ldots W_N)^{-1}\} + E\{(W_1^T + W_2^T + \ldots + W_n^T)^{-1}W_2^Ty_2^Ty_2W_2(W_1 + W_2 + \ldots W_N)^{-1}\} + \ldots + E\{(W_1^T + W_2^T + \ldots + W_n^T)^{-1}W_n^Ty_n^Ty_nW_n(W_1 + W_2 + \ldots W_N)^{-1}\} = (W_1^T + W_2^T + \ldots + W_n^T)^{-1}(W_1^TW_1 + W_2^TW_2 + \ldots W_n^TW_n)(W_1 + W_2 + \ldots W_n)^{-1} = I$. □

Fraser and Potter reported a smoother in 1969 [4] that combined state estimates from forward and backward filters using a formula similar to (70) truncated at $n = 2$. The inverses of the forward and backward error covariances, which are indicative of the quality of the respective estimates, were used as weighting matrices. The combined filter and Fraser-Potter smoother equations are

$$\dot{\hat{x}}(t \mid t) = A(t)\hat{x}(t \mid t) + P(t \mid t)C^T(t)R^{-1}(t)(z(t) - C(t)\hat{x}(t \mid t)), \tag{71}$$

$$-\dot{\xi}(t \mid t) = A(t)\xi(t \mid t) + \Sigma(t \mid t)C^T(t)R^{-1}(t)(z(t) - C(t)\xi(t \mid t)), \tag{72}$$

$$\hat{x}(t \mid T) = (P^{-1}(t \mid t) + \Sigma^{-1}(t \mid t))^{-1}(P^{-1}(t \mid t)\hat{x}(t \mid t) + \Sigma^{-1}(t \mid t)\xi(t \mid t)), \tag{73}$$

where $P(t \mid t)$ is the solution of the forward Riccati equation $\dot{P}(t \mid t) = A(t)P(t \mid t) + P(t \mid t)A^T(t) - P(t \mid t)C^T(t)R^{-1}(t)C(t)P(t \mid t) + B(t)Q(t)B^T(t)$ and $\Sigma(t \mid t)$ is the solution of the backward Riccati equation $-\dot{\Sigma}(t \mid t) = A(t)\Sigma(t \mid t) + \Sigma(t \mid t)A^T(t) - \Sigma(t \mid t)C^T(t)R^{-1}(t)C(t)\Sigma(t \mid t) + B(t)Q(t)B^T(t)$.

It can be seen from (72) that the backward state estimates, $\zeta(t)$, are obtained by simply running a Kalman filter over the time-reversed measurements. Fraser and Potter's approach is pragmatic: when the data is noisy, a linear combination of two filtered estimates is likely to be better than one filter alone. However, this two-filter approach to smoothing is *ad hoc* and is not a minimum-mean-square-error design.

"If there is dissatisfaction with the status quo, good. If there is ferment, so much the better. If there is restlessness, I am pleased. Then let there be ideas, and hard thought, and hard work." *Hubert Horatio Humphrey.*

6.5.4 The Minimum-Variance Smoother

6.5.4.1 Problem Definition

The previously described smoothers are focussed on state estimation. A different signal estimation problem shown in Fig. 1 is considered here. Suppose that observations $z = y + v$ are available, where $y_2 = \mathcal{G}_2 w$ is the output of a linear time-varying system and v is measurement noise. A solution $\mathcal{H}$ is desired which produces estimates $\hat{y}_1$ of a second reference system $y_1 = \mathcal{G}_1 w$ in such a way to meet a performance objective. Let $e = y_1 - \hat{y}_1$ denote the output estimation error. The optimum minimum-variance filter can be obtained by finding the solution that minimises $\left\| ee^T \right\|_2$. Here, in the case of smoothing, the performance objective is to minimise $\left\| ee^H \right\|_2$.

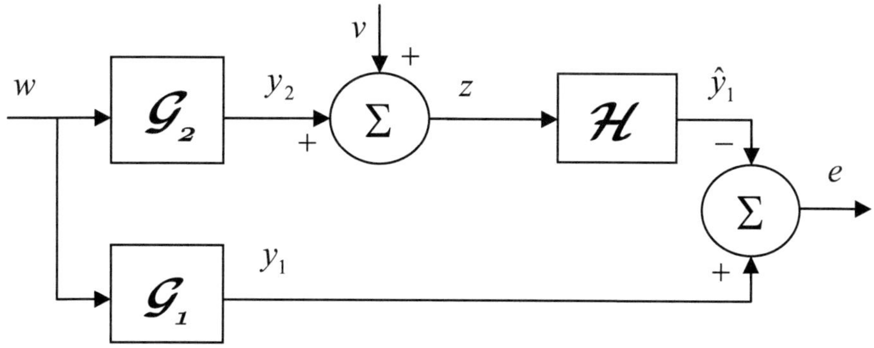

Figure 1. The general estimation problem. The objective is to produce estimates $\hat{y}_1$ of y_1 from measurements z.

6.5.4.2 Optimal Unrealisable Solutions

The minimum-variance smoother is a more recent innovation [8] - [10] and arises by generalising Wiener's optimal noncausal solution for the above time-varying problem. The solution is obtained using the same completing-the-squares technique that was previously employed in the frequency domain (see Chapters 1 and 2). It can be seen from Fig. 1 that the output estimation error is generated by $e = \mathcal{R}_{ei} i$, where

$$\mathcal{R}_{ei} = -\begin{bmatrix} \mathcal{H} & \mathcal{H}\mathcal{G}_2 - \mathcal{G}_1 \end{bmatrix} \tag{74}$$

is a linear system that operates on the inputs $i = \begin{bmatrix} v \\ w \end{bmatrix}$.

Consider the factorisation

$$\Delta\Delta^H = \mathcal{G}_2 Q \mathcal{G}_2^H + R , \tag{75}$$

"Restlessness and discontent are the first necessities of progress. Show me a thoroughly satisfied man and I will show you a failure." *Thomas Alva Edison*

in which the time-dependence of $Q(t)$ and $R(t)$ is omitted for notational brevity. Suppose that $\Delta: \mathbb{R}^p \rightarrow \mathbb{R}^p$ is causal, namely Δ and its inverse, Δ^{-1}, are bounded systems that proceed forward in time. The system Δ is known as a Wiener-Hopf factor.

Lemma 8: *Assume that the Wiener-Hopf factor inverse, Δ^{-1}, exists over $t \in [0, T]$. Then the smoother solution*

$$\begin{aligned} \mathcal{H} &= \mathcal{G}_1 Q \mathcal{G}_2^H \Delta^{-H} \Delta^{-1} \\ &= \mathcal{G}_1 Q \mathcal{G}_2^H (\Delta\Delta^H)^{-1} \\ &= \mathcal{G}_1 Q \mathcal{G}_2^H (\mathcal{G}_2 Q \mathcal{G}_2^H + R)^{-1}. \end{aligned} \tag{76}$$

minimises $\left\| ee^H \right\|_2 = \left\| \mathcal{R}_{ei} \mathcal{R}_{ei}^H \right\|_2$.

Proof: *It follows from (74) that* $\mathcal{R}_{ei}\mathcal{R}_{ei}^H = \mathcal{G}_1 Q \mathcal{G}_2^H - \mathcal{G}_1 Q \mathcal{G}_2^H \mathcal{H}^H - \mathcal{H} \mathcal{G}_2 Q \mathcal{G}_1^H + \mathcal{H}\Delta\Delta^H \mathcal{H}^H$. *Completing the square leads to* $\mathcal{R}_{ei}\mathcal{R}_{ei}^H = \mathcal{R}_{ei1}\mathcal{R}_{ei1}^H + \mathcal{R}_{ei2}\mathcal{R}_{ei2}^H$, *where*

$$\mathcal{R}_{ei2}\mathcal{R}_{ei2}^H = (\mathcal{H}\Delta - \mathcal{G}_1 Q \mathcal{G}_2^H \Delta^{-H})(\mathcal{H}\Delta - \mathcal{G}_1 Q \mathcal{G}_2^H \Delta^{-H})^H \tag{77}$$

and

$$\mathcal{R}_{ei1}\mathcal{R}_{ei1}^H = \mathcal{G}_1 Q \mathcal{G}_1^H - \mathcal{G}_1 Q \mathcal{G}_2^H (\Delta\Delta^H)^{-1} \mathcal{G}_2 Q \mathcal{G}_1^H. \tag{78}$$

By inspection of (77), the solution (76) achieves

$$\left\| \mathcal{R}_{ei2}\mathcal{R}_{ei2}^H \right\|_2 = 0. \tag{79}$$

Since $\left\| \mathcal{R}_{ei1}\mathcal{R}_{ei1}^H \right\|_2$ *excludes the estimator solution* $\mathcal{H}$, *this quantity defines the lower bound for* $\left\| \mathcal{R}_{ei}\mathcal{R}_{ei}^H \right\|_2$.

□

Example 3. Consider the output estimation case where $\mathcal{G}_1 = \mathcal{G}_2$ and

$$\mathcal{H}_{OE} = \mathcal{G}_2 Q \mathcal{G}_2^H (\mathcal{G}_2 Q \mathcal{G}_2^H + R)^{-1}, \tag{80}$$

which is of order n^4 complexity. Using $\mathcal{G}_2 Q \mathcal{G}_2^H = \Delta\Delta^H - R$ leads to the n^2-order solution

$$\mathcal{H}_{OE} = I - R(\Delta\Delta^H)^{-1}. \tag{81}$$

"Whatever has been done before will be done again. There is nothing new under the sun." *Ecclesiastes 1:9*

It is interesting to note from (81) and

$$\mathcal{R}_{ei1}\mathcal{R}_{ei1}^{H} = \mathcal{G}_2 Q \mathcal{G}_2^{H} - \mathcal{G}_2 Q \mathcal{G}_2^{H} (\mathcal{G}_2 Q \mathcal{G}_2^{H} - R)^{-1} \mathcal{G}_2 Q \mathcal{G}_2^{H} \tag{82}$$

that $\lim_{R \to 0} \mathcal{H} = I$ and $\lim_{R \to 0} \mathcal{R}_{ei}\mathcal{R}_{ei}^{H} = 0$. That is, output estimation is superfluous when measurement noise is absent. Let $\{\mathcal{R}_{ei}\mathcal{R}_{ei}^{H}\}_{+}$ = $\{\mathcal{R}_{ei1}\mathcal{R}_{ei1}^{H}\}_{+}$ + $\{\mathcal{R}_{ei2}\mathcal{R}_{ei2}^{H}\}_{+}$ denote the causal part of $\mathcal{R}_{ei}\mathcal{R}_{ei}^{H}$. It is shown below that minimum-variance filter solution can be found using the above completing-the squares technique and taking causal parts.

Lemma 9: *The filter solution*

$$\begin{aligned} \{\mathcal{H}\}_{+} &= \{\mathcal{G}_1 Q \mathcal{G}_2^{H} \Delta^{-H} \Delta^{-1}\}_{+} \\ &= \{\mathcal{G}_1 Q \mathcal{G}_2^{H} \Delta^{-H}\}_{+} \Delta^{-1} \end{aligned} \tag{83}$$

minimises $\left\| \{ee^{H}\}_{+} \right\|_2$ = $\left\| \{\mathcal{R}_{ei}\mathcal{R}_{ei}^{H}\}_{+} \right\|_2$, *provided that the inverses exist.*

Proof: *It follows from (77) that*

$$\{\mathcal{R}_{ei2}\mathcal{R}_{ei2}^{H}\}_{+} = \{(\mathcal{H}\Delta - \mathcal{G}_1 Q \mathcal{G}_2^{H} \Delta^{-H})(\mathcal{H}\Delta - \mathcal{G}_1 Q \mathcal{G}_2^{H} \Delta^{-H})^{H}\}_{+} . \tag{84}$$

By inspection of (84), the solution (83) achieves

$$\left\| \{\mathcal{R}_{ei2}\mathcal{R}_{ei2}^{H}\}_{+} \right\|_2 = 0. \tag{85}$$ □

It is worth pausing at this juncture to comment on the significance of the above results.

- The formulation (76) is an optimal solution for the time-varying smoother problem since it can be seen from (79) that it achieves the best-possible performance.
- Similarly, (83) is termed an optimal solution because it achieves the best-possible filter performance (85).
- By inspection of (79) and (85) it follows that the minimum-variance smoother outperforms the minimum-variance filter.
- In general, these optimal solutions are not very practical because of the difficulty in realising an exact Wiener-Hopf factor.

Practical smoother (and filter) solutions that make use of an approximate Wiener-Hopf factor are described below.

6.5.4.3 Optimal Realisable Solutions

Output Estimation

The Wiener-Hopf factor is modelled on the structure of the spectral factor which is described Section 3.4.4. Suppose that $R(t) > 0$ for all $t \in [0, T]$ and there exist $R^{1/2}(t) > 0$ such

---

"There is nothing more difficult to take in hand, more perilous to conduct, or more uncertain in its success, than to take the lead in the introduction of a new order of things." *Niccolo Di Bernado dei Machiavelli*

that $R(t) = R^{1/2}(t)\ R^{1/2}(t)$. An approximate Wiener-Hopf factor $\hat{\Delta}: \mathbb{R}^p \to \mathbb{R}^p$ is defined by the system

$$\begin{bmatrix} \dot{x}(t) \\ \delta(t) \end{bmatrix} = \begin{bmatrix} A(t) & K(t)R^{1/2}(t) \\ C(t) & R^{1/2}(t) \end{bmatrix} \begin{bmatrix} x(t) \\ z(t) \end{bmatrix}, \tag{86}$$

where $K(t) = P(t)C^T(t)R^{-1}(t)$ is the Kalman gain in which $P(t)$ is the solution of the Riccati differential equation

$$\dot{P}(t) = A(t)P(t) + P(t)A^T(t) - P(t)C^T(t)R^{-1}(t)C(t)P(t) + B(t)Q(t)B^T(t). \tag{87}$$

The output estimation smoother (81) can be approximated as

$$\begin{aligned} \mathcal{H}_{OE} &= I - R(\hat{\Delta}\hat{\Delta}^H)^{-1} \\ &= I - R\hat{\Delta}^{-H}\hat{\Delta}^{-1}. \end{aligned} \tag{88}$$

An approximate Wiener-Hopf factor inverse, $\hat{\Delta}^{-1}$, within (88) is obtained from (86) and the Matrix Inversion Lemma, namely,

$$\begin{bmatrix} \dot{\hat{x}}(t) \\ \alpha(t) \end{bmatrix} = \begin{bmatrix} A(t) - K(t)C(t) & K(t) \\ -R^{-1/2}(t)C(t) & R^{-1/2}(t) \end{bmatrix} \begin{bmatrix} x(t) \\ z(t) \end{bmatrix}, \tag{89}$$

where $\hat{x}(t) \in \mathbb{R}^n$ is an estimate of the state within $\hat{\Delta}^{-1}$. From Lemma 1, the adjoint of $\hat{\Delta}^{-1}$, which is denoted by $\hat{\Delta}^{-H}$, has the realisation

$$\begin{bmatrix} -\dot{\xi}(t) \\ \beta(t) \end{bmatrix} = \begin{bmatrix} A^T(t) - C^T(t)K^T(t) & -C^T(t)R^{-1/2}(t) \\ K^T(t) & R^{-1/2}(t) \end{bmatrix} \begin{bmatrix} \xi(t) \\ \alpha(t) \end{bmatrix}. \tag{90}$$

where $\xi(t) \in \mathbb{R}^p$ is an estimate of the state within $\hat{\Delta}^{-H}$. Thus, the smoother (88) is realised by (89), (90) and

$$\hat{y}(t \mid T) = z(t) - R(t)\beta(t). \tag{91}$$

Procedure 1. The above output estimator can be implemented via the following three steps.

Step 1. Operate $\hat{\Delta}^{-1}$ on the measurements $z(t)$ using (89) to obtain $\alpha(t)$.

Step 2. In lieu of the adjoint system (90), operate (89) on the time-reversed transpose of $\alpha(t)$. Then take the time-reversed transpose of the result to obtain $\beta(t)$.

Step 3. Calculate the smoothed output estimate from (91).

"If I have a thousand ideas and only one turns out to be good, I am satisfied." *Alfred Bernhard Nobel*

Example 4. Consider an estimation problem parameterised by $a = -1$, $b = \sqrt{2}$, $c = 1$, $d = 0$, $\sigma_w^2 = \sigma_v^2 = 1$, which leads to $p = k = \sqrt{3} - 1$ [26]. Smoothed output estimates may be obtained by evolving

$$\dot{\hat{x}}(t) = \sqrt{3}\hat{x}(t) + \sqrt{3}z(t)\,,\ \alpha(t) = -\hat{x}(t) + z(t)\,,$$

time-reversing the $\alpha(t)$ and evolving

$$\dot{\xi}(t) = \sqrt{3}\xi(t) + \sqrt{3}\alpha(t)\,,\ \beta(t) = -\xi(t) + \alpha(t)\,,$$

then time-reversing $\beta(t)$ and calculating

$$\hat{y}(t \mid T) = z(t) - \beta(t)\,.$$

Filtering

The causal part $\{\mathcal{H}_{OE}\}_+$ of the minimum-variance smoother (88) is given by

$$\begin{aligned}\{\mathcal{H}_{OE}\}_+ &= I - R\{\hat{\Delta}^{-H}\}_+\hat{\Delta}^{-1} \\ &= I - RR^{-1/2}\hat{\Delta}^{-1} \\ &= I - R^{1/2}\hat{\Delta}^{-1}\,.\end{aligned} \tag{92}$$

Employing (89) within (92) leads to the standard minimum-variance filter, namely,

$$\dot{\hat{x}}(t \mid t) = (A(t) - K(t)C(t))\hat{x}(t \mid t) + K(t)z(t) \tag{93}$$

$$\hat{y}(t \mid t) = C(t)\hat{x}(t \mid t)\,. \tag{94}$$

Input Estimation

As discussed in Chapters 1 and 2, input estimates can be found using $\mathcal{G}_1 = I$, and substituting $\hat{\Delta}$ for Δ within (76) yields the solution

$$\mathcal{H}_{IE} = Q\mathcal{G}_2^{-1}(\hat{\Delta}\hat{\Delta}^H)^{-1} = Q\mathcal{G}_2^{-1}\hat{\Delta}^{-H}\hat{\Delta}^{-1}\,. \tag{95}$$

As expected, the low-measurement-noise-asymptote of this equaliser is given by $\lim_{R \to 0}\mathcal{H}_{IE} = \mathcal{G}_2^{-1}$. That is, at high signal-to-noise-ratios the equaliser approaches $\mathcal{G}_2^{-1}$, provided the inverse exists.

The development of a differential equation for the smoothed input estimate, $\hat{w}(t \mid T)$, makes use of the following formula [27] for the cascade of two systems. Suppose that two linear

---

"Ten geographers who think the world is flat will tend to reinforce each others errors….Only a sailor can set them straight." *John Ralston Saul*

systems $\mathcal{G}_1$ and $\mathcal{G}_2$ have state-space parameters $\begin{bmatrix} A_1 & B_1 \\ C_1 & D_1 \end{bmatrix}$ and $\begin{bmatrix} A_2 & B_2 \\ C_2 & D_2 \end{bmatrix}$, respectively. Then $\mathcal{G}_2\mathcal{G}_1$ is parameterised by $\begin{bmatrix} A_1 & 0 & B_1 \\ B_2C_1 & A_2 & B_2D_1 \\ D_2C_1 & C_2 & D_2D_1 \end{bmatrix}$. It follows that $\hat{w}(t|T) = Q\mathcal{G}^H\hat{\Delta}^{-H}\alpha(t)$ is realised by

$$\begin{bmatrix} -\dot{\xi}(t) \\ -\dot{\gamma}(t) \\ -\hat{w}(t|T) \end{bmatrix} = \begin{bmatrix} A^T(t) - C^T(t)K^T(t) & 0 & -C^T(t)R^{-1/2}(t) \\ -C^T(t)K^T(t) & A^T(t) & C^T(t)R^{-1/2}(t) \\ Q(t)D^T(t)K^T(t) & Q(t)B^T(t) & Q(t)D^T(t)R^{-1/2}(t) \end{bmatrix} \begin{bmatrix} \xi(t) \\ \gamma(t) \\ \alpha(t) \end{bmatrix}. \tag{96}$$

in which $\gamma(t) \in \mathbb{R}^n$ is an auxiliary state.

***Procedure* 2.** Input estimates can be calculated via the following two steps.

Step 1. Operate $\hat{\Delta}^{-1}$ on the measurements $z(t)$ using (89) to obtain $\alpha(t)$.

Step 2. In lieu of (96), operate the adjoint of (96) on the time-reversed transpose of $\alpha(t)$. Then take the time-reversed transpose of the result.

State Estimation

Smoothed state estimates can be obtained by defining the reference system $\mathcal{G}_1$ within (76) as

$$\dot{\hat{x}}(t|T) = A(t)\hat{x}(t|T) + B(t)\hat{w}(t|T). \tag{97}$$

That is, a smoother for state estimation is given by (89), (96) and (97). In frequency-domain estimation problems, minimum-order solutions are found by exploiting pole-zero cancellations, see Example 1.13 of Chapter 1. Here in the time-domain, (89), (96), (97) is not a minimum-order solution and some numerical model order reduction may be required.

Suppose that $C(t)$ is of rank n and $D(t) = 0$. In this special case, an n^2-order solution for state estimation can be obtained from (91) and

$$\hat{x}(t|T) = C^{\#}(t)\hat{y}(t|T), \tag{98}$$

where

$$C^{\#}(t) = \left(C^T(t)C(t)\right)^{-1}C^T(t) \tag{99}$$

denotes the Moore-Penrose pseudoinverse.

"In questions of science, the authority of a thousand is not worth the humble reasoning of a single individual." *Galileo Galilei*

6.5.4.4 Performance

An analysis of minimum-variance smoother performance requires an identity which is described after introducing some additional notation. Let $\alpha = \mathcal{G}_0 w$ denote the output of linear time-varying system having the realisation

$$\dot{x}(t) = A(t)x(t) + w(t) \tag{100}$$

$$\alpha(t) = x(t), \tag{101}$$

where $w(t) \in \mathbb{R}^n$ and $A(t) \in \mathbb{R}^{n\times n}$. By inspection of (100) – (101), the output of the inverse system $w = \mathcal{G}_0^{-1}y$ is given by

$$w(t) = \dot{\alpha}(t) - A(t)\alpha(t). \tag{102}$$

Similarly, let $\beta = \mathcal{G}_0^{H}u$ denote the output of the adjoint system $\mathcal{G}_0^{H}$, which from Lemma 1 has the realisation

$$-\dot{\zeta}(t) = A^T(t)\zeta(t) + u(t) \tag{103}$$

$$\beta(t) = \zeta(t). \tag{104}$$

It follows that the output of the inverse system $u = \mathcal{G}_0^{-H}\beta$ is given by

$$u(t) = -\dot{\beta}(t) - A^T(t)\beta(t). \tag{105}$$

The following identity is required in the characterisation of smoother performance

$$-P(t)A^T(t) - A(t)P(t) = P(t)\mathcal{G}_0^{-H} + \mathcal{G}_0^{-1}P(t), \tag{106}$$

where $P(t)$ is an arbitrary matrix of compatible dimensions. The above equation can be verified by using (102) and (105) within (106). Using the above notation, the exact Wiener-Hopf factor satisfies

$$\Delta\Delta^H = C(t)\mathcal{G}_0 B(t)Q(t)B^T(t)\mathcal{G}_0^H C^T(t) + R(t). \tag{107}$$

It is observed below that the approximate Wiener-Hopf factor (86) approaches the exact Wiener Hopf-factor whenever the problem is locally stationary, that is, whenever $A(t)$, $B(t)$, $C(t)$, $Q(t)$ and $R(t)$ change sufficiently slowly, so that $\dot{P}(t)$ of (87) approaches the zero matrix.

Lemma 10 [8]: *In respect of the signal model (1) – (2) with $D(t) = 0$, $E\{w(t)\} = E\{v(t)\} = 0$, $E\{w(t)w^T(t)\} = Q(t)$, $E\{v(t)v^T(t)\} = R(t)$, $E\{w(t)v^T(t)\} = 0$ and the quantities defined above,*

$$\hat{\Delta}\hat{\Delta}^H = \Delta\Delta^H - C(t)\mathcal{G}_0 \dot{P}(t)\mathcal{G}_0^H C^T(t). \tag{108}$$

"Every great advance in natural knowledge has involved the absolute rejection of authority." *Thomas Henry Huxley*

Proof: *The approximate Wiener-Hopf factor may be written as* $\hat{\Delta} = C(t)\mathcal{G}_0 K(t)R^{1/2}(t) + R^{1/2}(t)$. *It is easily shown that* $\hat{\Delta}\hat{\Delta}^H = C(t)\mathcal{G}_0 (P\mathcal{G}_0^{-H} + \mathcal{G}_0^{-1}P + K(t)R(t)K^T(t))\mathcal{G}_0^H C^T(t)$ *and using (106) gives* $\hat{\Delta}\hat{\Delta}^H = C(t)\mathcal{G}_0 (B(t)Q(t)B^T(t) - \dot{P}(t)\mathcal{G}_0^H C^T(t) + R(t)$. *The result follows by comparing* $\hat{\Delta}\hat{\Delta}^H$ *and (107).* □

Consequently, the minimum-variance smoother (88) achieves the best-possible estimator performance, namely $\left\| \mathcal{R}_{ei2}\mathcal{R}_{ei2}^H \right\|_2 = 0$, whenever the problem is locally stationary.

Lemma 11 [8]: *The output estimation smoother (88) satisfies*

$$\mathcal{R}_{ei2} = R(t)[(\Delta\Delta^H)^{-1} - (\Delta\Delta^H - C(t)\mathcal{G}_0 \dot{P}(t)\mathcal{G}_0^H C^T(t))^{-1}]\Delta . \tag{109}$$

Proof: *Substituting (88) into (77) yields*

$$\mathcal{R}_{ei2} = R(t)[(\Delta\Delta^H)^{-1} - (\hat{\Delta}\hat{\Delta}^H)^{-1}]\Delta . \tag{110}$$

The result is now immediate from (108) and (110). □

Conditions for the convergence of the Riccati difference equation solution (87) and hence the asymptotic optimality of the smoother (88) are set out below.

Lemma 12 [8]: *Let* $S(t) = C^T(t)R^{-1}(t)C(t)$. *If(i) there exist solutions* $P(t) \geq P(t+\delta_t)$ *of (87) for a* $t > \delta_t > 0$*; and*

(ii)

$$\begin{bmatrix} Q(t) & A(t) \\ A^T(t) & -S(t) \end{bmatrix} \geq \begin{bmatrix} Q(t+\delta_t) & A(t+\delta_t) \\ A^T(t+\delta_t) & -S(t+\delta_t) \end{bmatrix} \tag{111}$$

for all $t > \delta_t$ *then*

$$\lim_{t\to\infty} \left\| \mathcal{R}_{ei2}\mathcal{R}_{ei2}^H \right\|_2 = 0 . \tag{112}$$

Proof: *Conditions (i) and (ii) together with Theorem 1 imply* $P(t) \geq P(t+\delta_t)$ *for all* $t > \delta_t$ *and* $\lim_{t\to\infty} \dot{P}(t) = 0$. *The claim (112) is now immediate from Lemma 11.* □

6.5.5 Performance Comparison

The following scalar time-invariant examples compare the performance of the minimum-variance filter (92), maximum-likelihood smoother (50), Fraser-Potter smoother (73) and minimum-variance smoother (88) under Gaussian and nongaussian noise conditions.

Example 5 [9]. Suppose that $A = -1$ and $B = C = Q = 1$. Simulations were conducted using $T = 100$ s, $\delta t = 1$ ms and 1000 realisations of Gaussian noise processes. The mean-square-error (MSE) exhibited by the filter and smoothers as a function of the input signal-to-noise ratio

---

"The definition of insanity is doing the same thing over and over again and expecting different results." *Albert Einstein*

(SNR) is shown in Fig. 2. As expected, it can be seen that the smoothers outperform the filter. Although the minimum-variance smoother exhibits the lowest mean-square error, the performance benefit diminishes at high signal-to-noise ratios.

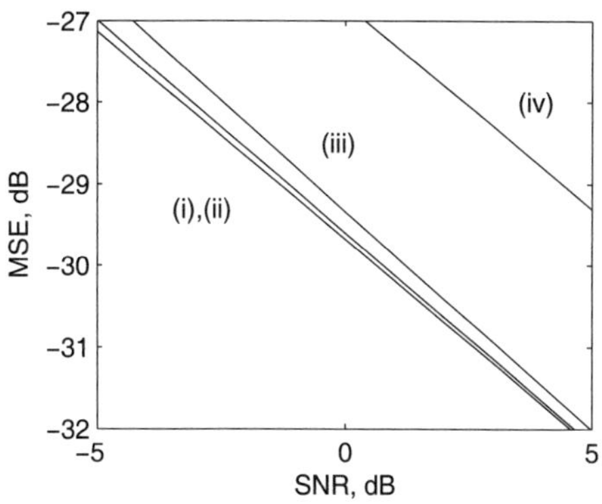

Figure 2. MSE versus SNR for Example 4: (i) minimum-variance smoother, (ii) Fraser-Potter smoother, (iii) maximum-likelihood smoother and (iv) minimum-variance filter.

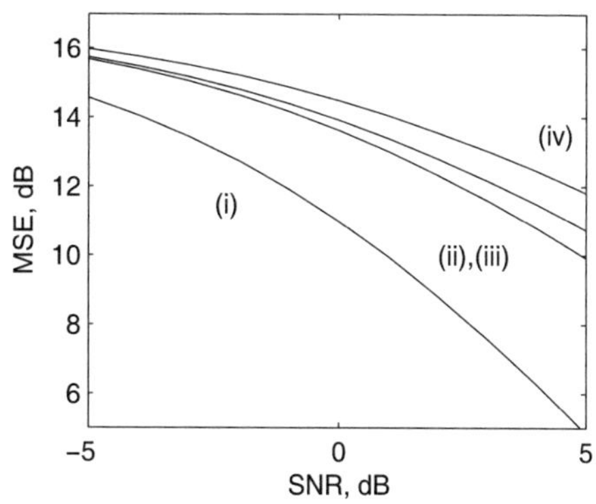

Figure 3. MSE versus SNR for Example 5: (i) minimum-variance smoother, (ii) Fraser-Potter smoother, (iii) maximum-likelihood smoother and (iv) minimum-variance filter.

Example 6 [9]. Suppose instead that the process noise is the unity-variance deterministic signal $w(t) = \sin(t)\sigma_{\sin(t)}^{-1}$, where $\sigma_{\sin(t)}^{2}$ denotes the sample variance of sin(*t*). The results of simulations employing the sinusoidal process noise and Gaussian measurement noise are shown in Fig. 3. Once again, the smoothers exhibit better performance than the filter. It can be seen that the minimum-variance smoother provides the best mean-square-error performance. The minimum-variance smoother appears to be less perturbed by nongaussian noises because it does not rely on assumptions about the underlying distributions.

6.6 Conclusion

The fixed-point smoother produces state estimates at some previous point in time, that is,

$$\hat{\xi}(t) = \Sigma(t)C^T(t)R^{-1}(t)\left(z(t) - C(t)\hat{x}(t \mid t)\right),$$

where $\Sigma(t)$ is the smoother error covariance.

In fixed-lag smoothing, state estimates are calculated at a fixed time delay τ behind the current measurements. This smoother has the form

$$\dot{\hat{x}}(t \mid t+\tau) = A(t)\hat{x}(t \mid t+\tau) + B(t)Q(t)B^T(t)P^{-1}(t)\left(\hat{x}(t \mid t+\tau) - \hat{x}(t \mid t)\right)$$

$$+P(t)\Phi^T(t+\tau,t)C^T(t+\tau)R^{-1}(t+\tau)\left(z(t+\tau) - C(t+\tau)\hat{x}(t+\tau)\right),$$

where $\Phi(t + \tau, t)$ is the transition matrix of the minimum-variance filter.

"He who rejects change is the architect of decay. The only human institution which rejects progress is the cemetery." *James Harold Wilson*

Three common fixed-interval smoothers are listed in Table 1, which are for retrospective (or off-line) data analysis. The Rauch-Tung-Streibel (RTS) smoother and Fraser-Potter (FP) smoother are minimum-order solutions. The RTS smoother differential equation evolves backward in time, in which $G(\tau) = B(\tau)Q(\tau)B^T(\tau)P^{-1}(\tau)$ is the smoothing gain. The FP smoother employs a linear combination of forward state estimates and backward state estimates obtained by running a filter over the time-reversed measurements. The optimum minimum-variance solution, in which $\bar{A}(t) = A(t) - K(t)C(t)$, where K($t$) is the predictor gain, involves a cascade of forward and adjoint predictions. It can be seen that the optimum minimum-variance smoother is the most complex and so any performance benefits need to be reconciled with the increased calculation cost.

	ASSUMPTIONS	MAIN RESULTS
Signals and system	$E\{w(t)\} = E\{v(t)\} = 0$. $E\{w(t)w^T(t)\} = Q(t) > 0$ and $E\{v(t)v^T(t)\} = R(t) > 0$ are known. $A(t)$, $B(t)$ and $C(t)$ are known.	$\dot{x}(t) = A(t)x(t) + B(t)w(t)$ $y(t) = C(t)x(t)$ $z(t) = y(t) + v(t)$
RTS smoother	Assumes that the filtered and smoothed states are normally distributed. $\hat{x}(t \mid t)$ previously calculated by Kalman filter.	$-\dot{\hat{x}}(\tau \mid T) = A(\tau)\hat{x}(\tau \mid T) + G(\tau)\big(\hat{x}(\tau \mid T) - \hat{x}(\tau \mid \tau)\big)$
FP smoother	$\hat{x}(t \mid t)$ previously calculated by Kalman filter.	$\hat{x}(t \mid T) = (P^{-1}(t \mid t) + \Sigma^{-1}(t \mid t))^{-1}$ $\times(P^{-1}(t \mid t)\hat{x}(t \mid t) + \Sigma^{-1}(t \mid t)\xi(t \mid t))$
Optimal smoother		$\begin{bmatrix} \dot{\hat{x}}(t) \\ \alpha(t) \end{bmatrix} = \begin{bmatrix} \bar{A}(t) & K(t) \\ -R^{-1/2}(t)C(t) & R^{-1/2}(t) \end{bmatrix} \begin{bmatrix} \hat{x}(t) \\ z(t) \end{bmatrix}$ $\begin{bmatrix} -\dot{\xi}(t) \\ \beta(t) \end{bmatrix} = \begin{bmatrix} \bar{A}^T(t) & -C^T(t)R^{-1/2}(t) \\ K^T(t) & R^{-1/2}(t) \end{bmatrix} \begin{bmatrix} \xi(t) \\ \alpha(t) \end{bmatrix}$ $\hat{y}(t \mid T) = z(t) - R(t)\beta(t)$

Table 1. Continuous-time fixed-interval smoothers.

The output estimation error covariance for the general estimation problem can be written as $\mathcal{R}_{ei}\mathcal{R}_{ei}^H = \mathcal{R}_{ei1}\mathcal{R}_{ei1}^H + \mathcal{R}_{ei2}\mathcal{R}_{ei2}^H$, where $\mathcal{R}_{ei1}\mathcal{R}_{ei1}^H$ specifies a lower performance bound and

"Remember a dead fish can float downstream but it takes a live one to swim upstream." *William Claude Fields*

$\mathcal{R}_{ei2}\mathcal{R}_{ei2}^H$ is a function of the estimator solution. The optimal smoother solution achieves $\left\|\{\mathcal{R}_{ei2}\mathcal{R}_{ei2}^H\}_+\right\|_2 = 0$ and provides the best mean-square-error performance, provided of course that the problem assumptions are correct. The minimum-variance smoother solution also attains best-possible performance whenever the problem is locally stationary, that is, when $A(t)$, $B(t)$, $C(t)$, $Q(t)$ and $R(t)$ change sufficiently slowly.

6.7 Problems

Problem 1. Write down augmented state-space matrices $A^{(a)}(t)$, $B^{(a)}(t)$ and $C^{(a)}(t)$ for the continuous-time fixed-point smoother problem.

(i) Substitute the above matrices into $\dot{P}^{(a)}(t) = A^{(a)}(t)P^{(a)}(t) + P^{(a)}(t)(A^{(a)})^T(t) - P^{(a)}(t)(C^{(a)})^T(t)R^{-1}(t)C^{(a)}(t)P^{(a)}(t) + B^{(a)}(t)Q(t)(B^{(a)}(t))^T$ to obtain the component Riccati differential equations.

(ii) Develop expressions for the continuous-time fixed-point smoother estimate and the smoother gain.

Problem 2. The Hamiltonian equations (60) were derived from the forward version of the maximum likelihood smoother (54). Derive the alternative form

$$\begin{bmatrix} -\dot{\hat{x}}(t \mid T) \\ \dot{\xi}(t \mid T) \end{bmatrix} = \begin{bmatrix} A(t) & B(t)Q(t)B^T(t) \\ C^T(t)R^{-1}(t)C(t) & A^T(t) \end{bmatrix} \begin{bmatrix} \hat{x}(t \mid T) \\ \xi(t \mid T) \end{bmatrix} - \begin{bmatrix} 0 \\ C^T(t)R^{-1}(t)z(t) \end{bmatrix}.$$

from the backward smoother (50). Hint: use the backward Kalman-Bucy filter and the backward Riccati equation.

Problem 3. It is shown in [6] and [17] that the intermediate variable within the Hamiltonian equations (60) is given by

$$\xi(t \mid T) = \int_t^T \Phi^T(s,t)C^T(s)R^{-1}(s)(z(s) - C(s)\hat{x}(s \mid s))ds,$$

where $\Phi^T(s,t)$ is the transition matrix of the Kalman-Bucy filter. Use the above equation to derive

$$-\dot{\xi}(t \mid T) = -C^T(t)R^{-1}(t)C(t)\hat{x}(t \mid T) + A^T(t)\xi(t) - C^T(t)R^{-1}(t)z(t).$$

Problem 4. Show that the adjoint of system having state space parameters $\begin{bmatrix} A(t) & B(t) \\ C(t) & D(t) \end{bmatrix}$ is parameterised by $\begin{bmatrix} -A^T(t) & -C^T(t) \\ B^T(t) & D^T(t) \end{bmatrix}$.

"It is not the strongest of the species that survive, nor the most intelligent, but the most responsive to change." *Charles Robert Darwin*

Problem 5. Suppose $\mathcal{G}_0$ is a system parameterised by $\begin{bmatrix} A(t) & I \\ I & 0 \end{bmatrix}$, show that $-P(t)A^T(t)$ - $A(t)P(t) = P(t)\mathcal{G}_0^{-H} + \mathcal{G}_0^{-1}P(t)$.

Problem 6. The optimum minimum-variance smoother was developed by finding the solution that minimises $\left\| \tilde{y}_2 \tilde{y}_2^H \right\|_2$. Use the same completing-the-square approach to find the optimum minimum-variance filter. (Hint: Find the solution that minimises $\left\| \tilde{y}_2 \tilde{y}_2^T \right\|_2$.)

Problem 7 [9]. Derive the output estimation minimum-variance filter by finding a solution Let $a \in \mathbb{R}$, $b = 1$, $c \in \mathbb{R}$ and $d = 0$ denote the time-invariant state-space parameters of the plant $\mathcal{G}$. Denote the error covariance, gain of the Kalman filter and gain of the maximum-likelihood smoother by p, k and g, respectively. Show that

$$H_1(s) = k(s-a+kc)^{-1},$$

$$H_2(s) = cgk(-s-a+g)^{-1}(s-a+kc)^{-1},$$

$$H_3(s) = kc(-a + kc)(s - a + kc)^{-1}(-s -a + kc)^{-1},$$

$$H_4(s) = ((-a + kc)^2 - (-a + kc - k)^2)(s - a + kc)^{-1}(-s -a + kc)^{-1}$$

are the transfer functions of the Kalman filter, maximum-likelihood smoother, the Fraser-Potter smoother and the minimum variance smoother, respectively.

Problem 8.

(i) Develop a state-space formulation of an approximate Wiener-Hopf factor for the case when the plant includes a nonzero direct feedthrough matrix (that is, $D(t) \neq 0$).

(ii) Use the matrix inversion lemma to obtain the inverse of the approximate Wiener-Hopf factor for the minimum-variance smoother.

6.8 Glossary

$p(x(t))$	Probability density function of a continuous random variable $x(t)$.
$x(t) \sim \mathcal{N}(\mu, R_{xx})$	The random variable $x(t)$ has a normal distribution with mean μ and covariance R_{xx}.
$f(x(t))$	Cumulative distribution function or likelihood function of $x(t)$.
$\hat{x}(t \mid t+\tau)$	Estimate of $x(t)$ at time t given data at fixed time lag τ.
$\hat{x}(t \mid T)$	Estimate of $x(t)$ at time t given data over a fixed interval T.
$\hat{w}(t \mid T)$	Estimate of $w(t)$ at time t given data over a fixed interval T.

"Once a new technology rolls over you, if you're not part of the steamroller, you're part of the road." *Stewart Brand*

$G(t)$	Gain of the minimum-variance smoother developed by Rauch, Tung and Striebel.
$\mathcal{R}_{ei}$	A linear system that operates on the inputs $i = \begin{bmatrix} v^T & w^T \end{bmatrix}^T$ and generates the output estimation error e.
$C^{\#}(t)$	Moore-Penrose pseudoinverse of $C(t)$.
Δ	The Wiener-Hopf factor which satisfies $\Delta\Delta^H = \mathcal{G}Q\mathcal{G}^H + R$.
$\hat{\Delta}$	Approximate Wiener-Hopf factor.
$\hat{\Delta}^H$	The adjoint of $\hat{\Delta}$.
$\hat{\Delta}^{-H}$	The inverse of $\hat{\Delta}^H$.
$\{\hat{\Delta}^{-H}\}_+$	The causal part of $\hat{\Delta}^{-H}$.

6.9 References

[1] J. S. Meditch, "A Survey of Data Smoothing for Linear and Nonlinear Dynamic Systems", *Automatica*, vol. 9, pp. 151-162, 1973

[2] T. Kailath, "A View of Three Decades of Linear Filtering Theory", *IEEE Transactions on Information Theory*, vol. 20, no. 2, pp. 146 - 181, Mar., 1974.

[3] H. E. Rauch, F. Tung and C. T. Striebel, "Maximum Likelihood Estimates of Linear Dynamic Systems", *AIAA Journal*, vol. 3, no. 8, pp. 1445 - 1450, Aug., 1965.

[4] D. C. Fraser and J. E. Potter, "The Optimum Linear Smoother as a Combination of Two Optimum Linear Filters", *IEEE Transactions on Automatic Control*, vol. AC-14, no. 4, pp. 387 - 390, Aug., 1969.

[5] J. S. Meditch, "On Optimal Fixed Point Linear Smoothing", *International Journal of Control*, vol. 6, no. 2, pp. 189 - 199, 1967.

[6] A. P. Sage and J. L. Melsa, *Estimation Theory with Applications to Communications and Control*, McGraw-Hill Book Company, New York, 1971.

[7] J. B. Moore, "Fixed-Lag Smoothing Results for Linear Dynamical Systems", *A.T.R.*, vol. 7, no. 2, pp. 16 - 21, 1973.

[8] G. A. Einicke, "Asymptotic Optimality of the Minimum-Variance Fixed-Interval Smoother", *IEEE Transactions on Signal Processing*, vol. 55, no. 4, pp. 1543 - 1547, Apr. 2007.

[9] G. A. Einicke, J. C. Ralston, C. O. Hargrave, D. C. Reid and D. W. Hainsworth, "Longwall Mining Automation, An Application of Minimum-Variance Smoothing", *IEEE Control Systems Magazine*, vol. 28, no. 6, pp. 28 - 37, Dec. 2008.

[10] G. A. Einicke, "A Solution to the Continuous-Time H-infinity Fixed-Interval Smoother Problem", *IEEE Transactions on Automatic Control*, vo. 54, no. 12, pp. 2904 - 2908, Dec. 2009.

"I don't want to be left behind. In fact, I want to be here before the action starts." *Kerry Francis Bullmore Packer*

[11] D. J. N. Limebeer, B. D. O. Anderson, P. Khargonekar and M. Green, "A Game Theoretic Approach to H_∞ Control for Time-varying Systems", *SIAM Journal on Control and Optimization*, vol. 30, no. 2, pp. 262 - 283, 1992.

[12] G. Freiling, G. Jank and H. Abou-Kandil, "Generalized Riccati Difference and Differential Equations", *Linear Algebra And Its Applications*, pp. 291 - 303, 199

[13] L. E. Zachrisson, "On Optimal Smoothing of Continuous Time Kalman Processes, *Information Sciences*, vol. 1, pp. 143 - 172, 1969.

[14] U. Shaked and Y. Theodore, "H_∞ - Optimal Estimation: A Tutorial", *Proc. 31st IEEE Conference on Decision Control*, Ucson, Arizona, pp. 2278 - 2286, Dec. 1992.

[15] J. S. Meditch, "On Optimal Linear Smoothing Theory", *Information and Control*, vol. 10, pp. 598 - 615, 1967.

[16] P. S. Maybeck, *Stochastic Models, Estimation and Control*, Vol. 2, Academic press, New York, 1982.

[17] T. Kailath, A. H. Sayed and B. Hassibi, *Linear Estimation*, Pearson Prentice Hall, New Jersey, 2000.

[18] B. D. O. Anderson, "Properties of Optimal Linear Smoothing", *IEEE Transactions on Automatic Control*, vol. 14, no. 1, pp. 114 - 115, Feb. 1969.

[19] S. Chirarattananon and B. D. O. Anderson, "Stable Fixed-Lag Smoothing of Continuous-time Processes", IEEE *Transactions on Information Theory*, vol. 20, no. 1, pp. 25 - 36, Jan. 1974.

[20] A. Gelb, *Applied Optimal Estimation*, The Analytic Sciences Corporation, USA, 1974.

[21] L. Ljung and T. Kailath, "A Unified Approach to Smoothing Formulas", *Automatica*, vol. 12, pp. 147 - 157, 197

[22] T. Kailath and P. Frost, "An Innovations Approach to Least-Squares Estimation Part II: Linear Smoothing in Additive White Noise", *IEEE Transactions on Automat. Control*, vol. 13, no. 6, pp. 655 - 660, 1968.

[23] F. L. Lewis, L. Xie and D. Popa, *Optimal and Robust Estimation With an Introduction to Stochastic Control Theory*, Second Edition, CRC Press, Taylor & Francis Group, 2008.

[24] F. A. Badawi, A. Lindquist and M. Pavon, "A Stochastic Realization Approach to the Smoothing Problem", *IEEE Transactions on Automatic Control*, vol. 24, no. 6, Dec. 1979.

[25] J. A. Rice, *Mathematical Statistics and Data Analysis* (Second Edition), Duxbury Press, Belmont, California, 1995.

[26] R. G. Brown and P. Y. C. Hwang, *Introduction to Random Signals and Applied Kalman Filtering*, Second Edition, John Wiley & Sons, Inc., New York, 1992.

[27] M. Green and D. J. N. Limebeer, *Linear Robust Control*, Prentice-Hall Inc, Englewood Cliffs, New Jersey, 1995.

"In times of profound change, the learners inherit the earth, while the learned find themselves beautifully equipped to deal with a world that no longer exists." *Al Rogers*

7

Discrete-Time Smoothing

7.1. Introduction

Observations are invariably accompanied by measurement noise and optimal filters are the usual solution of choice. Filter performances that fall short of user expectations motivate the pursuit of smoother solutions. Smoothers promise useful mean-square-error improvement at mid-range signal-to-noise ratios, provided that the assumed model parameters and noise statistics are correct.

In general, discrete-time filters and smoothers are more practical than the continuous-time counterparts. Often a designer may be able to value-add by assuming low-order discrete-time models which bear little or no resemblance to the underlying processes. Continuous-time approaches may be warranted only when application-specific performance considerations outweigh the higher overheads.

This chapter canvasses the main discrete-time fixed-point, fixed-lag and fixed interval smoothing results [1] - [9]. Fixed-point smoothers [1] calculate an improved estimate at a prescribed past instant in time. Fixed-lag smoothers [2] - [3] find application where small end-to-end delays are tolerable, for example, in press-to-talk communications or receiving public broadcasts. Fixed-interval smoothers [4] - [9] dispense with the need to fine tune the time of interest or the smoothing lags. They are suited to applications where processes are staggered such as delayed control or off-line data analysis. For example, in underground coal mining, smoothed position estimates and control signals can be calculated while a longwall shearer is momentarily stationary at each end of the face [9]. Similarly, in exploration drilling, analyses are typically carried out post-data acquisition.

The smoother descriptions are organised as follows. Section 7.2 sets out two prerequisites: time-varying adjoint systems and Riccati difference equation comparison theorems. Fixed-point, fixed-lag and fixed-interval smoothers are discussed in Sections 7.3, 7.4 and 7.5, respectively. It turns out that the structures of the discrete-time smoothers are essentially the same as those of the previously-described continuous-time versions. Differences arise in the calculation of Riccati equation solutions and the gain matrices. Consequently, the treatment

---

"An inventor is simply a person who doesn't take his education too seriously. You see, from the time a person is six years old until he graduates from college he has to take three or four examinations a year. If he flunks once, he is out. But an inventor is almost always failing. He tries and fails maybe a thousand times. If he succeeds once then he's in. These two things are diametrically opposite. We often say that the biggest job we have is to teach a newly hired employee how to fail intelligently. We have to train him to experiment over and over and to keep on trying and failing until he learns what will work." *Charles Franklin Kettering*

is somewhat condensed. It is reaffirmed that the above-mentioned smoothers outperform the Kalman filter and the minimum-variance smoother provides the best performance.

7.2. Prerequisites

7.2.1 Time-varying Adjoint Systems

Consider a linear time-varying system, $\mathcal{G}$, operating on an input, w, namely, $y = \mathcal{G} w$. Here, w denotes the set of w_k over an interval $k \in [0, N]$. It is assumed that $\mathcal{G}: \mathbb{R}^p \to \mathbb{R}^q$ has the state-space realisation

$$x_{k+1} = A_k x_k + B_k w_k, \tag{1}$$

$$y_k = C_k x_k + D_k w_k. \tag{2}$$

As before, the adjoint system, $\mathcal{G}^H$, satisfies

$$<y, \mathcal{G} w> = < \mathcal{G}^H y, w> \tag{3}$$

for all $y \in \mathbb{R}^q$ and $w \in \mathbb{R}^p$.

Lemma 1: *In respect of the system $\mathcal{G}$ described by (1) – (2), with $x_0 = 0$, the adjoint system $\mathcal{G}^H$ having the realisation*

$$\zeta_{k-1} = A_k^T \zeta_k - C_k^T u_k, \tag{4}$$

$$z_k = -B_k^T \zeta_k + D_k^T u_k, \tag{5}$$

with $\zeta_N = 0$, satisfies (3).

A proof appears in [7] and proceeds similarly to that within Lemma 1 of Chapter 2. The simplification $D_k = 0$ is assumed below unless stated otherwise.

7.2.2 Riccati Equation Comparison

The ensuing performance comparisons of filters and smoothers require methods for comparing the solutions of Riccati difference equations which are developed below. Simplified Riccati difference equations which do not involve the B_k and measurement noise covariance matrices are considered initially. A change of variables for the more general case is stated subsequently.

Suppose there exist $A_{t+k-1} \in \mathbb{R}^{n\times n}$, $\tilde{C}_{t+k-1} \in \mathbb{R}^{p\times n}$, $\tilde{Q}_{t+k-1} = \tilde{Q}_{t+k-1}^T \in \mathbb{R}^{n\times n}$ and $P_{t+k-1} = P_{t+k-1}^T \in \mathbb{R}^{n\times n}$ for a $t \geq 0$ and $k \geq 0$. Following the approach of Wimmer [10], define the Riccati operator

$$\begin{aligned}\Phi(P_{t+k-1}, A_{t+k-1}, \tilde{C}_{t+k-1}, \tilde{Q}_{t+k-1}) &= A_{t+k-1} P_{t+k-1} A_{t+k-1}^T + \tilde{Q}_{t+k-1} \\ &\quad - A_{t+k-1} P_{t+k-1} \tilde{C}_{t+k-1}^T (I + \tilde{C}_{t+k-1} P_{t+k-1} \tilde{C}_{t+k-1}^T)^{-1} \tilde{C}_{t+k-1} P_{t+k-1} A_{t+k-1}^T.\end{aligned} \tag{6}$$

"If you're not failing every now and again, it's a sign you're not doing anything very innovative." *(Woody) Allen Stewart Konigsberg*

Let $\Gamma_{t+k-1} = \begin{bmatrix} A_{t+k-1} & -\tilde{C}^T_{t+k-1}\tilde{C}_{t+k-1} \\ -\tilde{Q}_{t+k-1} & -A^T_{t+k-1} \end{bmatrix}$ denote the Hamiltonian matrix corresponding to $\Phi(P_{t+k-1}, A_{t+k-1}, \tilde{C}_{t+k-1}, \tilde{Q}_{t+k-1})$ and define $J = \begin{bmatrix} 0 & -I \\ I & 0 \end{bmatrix}$, in which I is an identity matrix of appropriate dimensions. It is known that solutions of (6) are monotonically dependent on $J\Gamma_{k+1} = \begin{bmatrix} \tilde{Q}_{t+k-1} & A^T_{t+k-1} \\ A_{t+k-1} & -\tilde{C}^T_{t+k-1}\tilde{C}_{t+k-1} \end{bmatrix}$. Consider a second Riccati operator employing the same initial solution P_{t+k-1} but different state-space parameters

$$\Phi(P_{t+k-1}, A_{t+k}, \tilde{C}_{t+k}, \tilde{Q}_{t+k}) = A_{t+k}P_{t+k-1}A^T_{t+k} + \tilde{Q}_{t+k}$$
$$- A_{t+k}P_{t+k-1}\tilde{C}^T_{t+k}(I + \tilde{C}_{t+k}P_{t+k-1}\tilde{C}^T_{t+k})^{-1}\tilde{C}_{t+k}P_{t+k-1}A^T_{t+k} . \tag{7}$$

The following theorem, which is due to Wimmer [10], compares the above two Riccati operators.

Theorem 1: [10]: *Suppose that*

$$\begin{bmatrix} \tilde{Q}_{t+k-1} & A^T_{t+k-1} \\ A_{t+k-1} & -\tilde{C}^T_{t+k-1}\tilde{C}_{t+k-1} \end{bmatrix} \geq \begin{bmatrix} \tilde{Q}_{t+k} & A^T_{t+k} \\ A_{t+k} & -\tilde{C}^T_{t+k}\tilde{C}_{t+k} \end{bmatrix}$$

for a $t \geq 0$ and for all $k \geq 0$. Then

$$\Phi(P_{t+k-1}, A_{t+k-1}, \tilde{C}_{t+k-1}, \tilde{Q}_{t+k-1}) \geq \Phi(P_{t+k-1}, A_{t+k}, \tilde{C}_{t+k}, \tilde{Q}_{t+k}) \tag{8}$$

for all $k \geq 0$.

The above result underpins the following more general Riccati difference equation comparison theorem.

Theorem 2: [11], [8]: *With the above definitions, suppose for a $t \geq 0$ and for all $k \geq 0$ that:*

(i) *there exists a* $P_t \geq P_{t+1}$ and

(ii) $\begin{bmatrix} \tilde{Q}_{t+k-1} & A^T_{t+k-1} \\ A_{t+k-1} & -\tilde{C}^T_{t+k-1}\tilde{C}_{t+k-1} \end{bmatrix} \geq \begin{bmatrix} \tilde{Q}_{t+k} & A^T_{t+k} \\ A_{t+k} & -\tilde{C}^T_{t+k}\tilde{C}_{t+k} \end{bmatrix}$.

Then $P_{t+k} \geq P_{t+k+1}$ *for all $k \geq 0$.*

Proof: *Assumption (i) is the k = 0 case for an induction argument. For the inductive step, denote* $P_{t+k} = \Phi(P_{t+k-1}, A_{t+k-1}, \tilde{C}_{t+k-1}, \tilde{Q}_{t+k-1})$ and $P_{t+k+1} = \Phi(P_{t+k}, A_{t+k}, \tilde{C}_{t+k}, \tilde{Q}_{t+k})$. Then

---

"Although personally I am quite content with existing explosives, I feel we must not stand in the path of improvement." *Winston Leonard Spencer-Churchill*

$$P_{t+k} - P_{t+k+1} = (\Phi(P_{t+k-1}, A_{t+k-1}, \tilde{C}_{t+k-1}, \tilde{Q}_{t+k-1}) - \Phi(P_{t+k-1}, A_{t+k}, \tilde{C}_{t+k}, \tilde{Q}_{t+k})) \quad (9)$$
$$+(\Phi(P_{t+k-1}, A_{t+k}, \tilde{C}_{t+k}, \tilde{Q}_{t+k}) - \Phi(P_{t+k}, A_{t+k}, \tilde{C}_{t+k}, \tilde{Q}_{t+k}))$$

The first term on the right-hand-side of (9) is non-negative by virtue of Assumption (ii) and Theorem 1. By appealing to Theorem 2 of Chapter 5, the second term on the right-hand-side of (9) is non-negative and thus $P_{t+k} - P_{t+k+1} \geq 0$. □

A change of variables [8] $\tilde{C}_k = R_k^{-1/2} C_k$ and $\tilde{Q}_k = B_k Q_k B_k^T$, allows the application of Theorem 2 to the more general forms of Riccati differential equations.

7.3 Fixed-Point Smoothing

7.3.1 Solution Derivation

The development of a discrete-time fixed-point smoother follows the continuous-time case. An innovation by Zachrisson [12] involves transforming the smoothing problem into a filtering problem that possesses an augmented state. Following the approach in [1], consider an augmented state vector $x_k^{(a)} = \begin{bmatrix} x_k \\ \xi_k \end{bmatrix}$ for the signal model

$$x_{k+1}^{(a)} = A_k^{(a)} x_k^{(a)} + B_k^{(a)} w_k , \quad (10)$$

$$z_k = C_k^{(a)} x_k^{(a)} + v_k , \quad (11)$$

where $A_k^{(a)} = \begin{bmatrix} A_k & 0 \\ 0 & I \end{bmatrix}$, $B_k^{(a)} = \begin{bmatrix} B_k \\ 0 \end{bmatrix}$ and $C_k^{(a)} = [C_k \ 0]$. It can be seen that the first component of $x_k^{(a)}$ is x_k, the state of the system $x_{k+1} = A_k x_k + B_k w_k$, $y_k = C_k x_k + v_k$. The second component, ξ_k, equals x_k at time $k = \tau$, that is, $\xi_k = x_\tau$. The objective is to calculate an estimate $\hat{\xi}_k$ of ξ_k at time $k = \tau$ from measurements z_k over $k \in [0, N]$. A solution that minimises the variance of the estimation error is obtained by employing the standard Kalman filter recursions for the signal model (10) – (11). The predicted and corrected states are respectively obtained from

$$\hat{x}_{k/k}^{(a)} = (I - L_k^{(a)} C_k^{(a)}) \hat{x}_{k/k-1}^{(a)} + L_k^{(a)} z_k , \quad (12)$$

$$\hat{x}_{k+1/k}^{(a)} = A_k^{(a)} \hat{x}_{k/k}^{(a)} \quad (13)$$

$$= (A_k^{(a)} - K_k^{(a)} C_k^{(a)}) \hat{x}_{k/k-1}^{(a)} + K_k^{(a)} z_k , \quad (14)$$

where $K_k = A_k^{(a)} L_k^{(a)}$ is the predictor gain, $L_k^{(a)} = P_{k/k-1}^{(a)} (C_k^{(a)})^T (C_k^{(a)} P_{k/k-1}^{(a)} (C_k^{a})^T + R_k)^{-1}$ is the filter gain,

---

"Never before in history has innovation offered promise of so much to so many in so short a time." *William Henry (Bill) Gates III*

$$P_{k/k}^{(a)} = P_{k/k-1}^{(a)} - P_{k/k-1}^{(a)}(C_k^{(a)})^T(L_k^{(a)})^T \tag{15}$$

is the corrected error covariance and

$$\begin{aligned} P_{k+1/k}^{(a)} &= A_k^{(a)}P_{k/k}^{(a)}(A_k^{(a)})^T + B_k^{(a)}Q_k(B_k^{(a)})^T \\ &= A_k^{(a)}P_{k/k-1}^{(a)}(A_k^{(a)})^T - A_k^{(a)}P_{k/k-1}^{(a)}(C_k^{(a)})^T(K_k^{(a)})^T + B_k^{(a)}Q_k(B_k^{(a)})^T \end{aligned} \tag{16}$$

$$= A_k^{(a)}P_{k/k-1}^{(a)}\left((A_k^{(a)})^T - (C_k^{(a)})^T(K_k^{(a)})^T\right) + B_k^{(a)}Q_k(B_k^{(a)})^T \tag{17}$$

is the predicted error covariance. The above Riccati difference equation is written in the partitioned form

$$\begin{aligned} P_{k+1/k}^{(a)} &= \begin{bmatrix} P_{k+1/k} & \Sigma_{k+1/k}^T \\ \Sigma_{k+1/k} & \Omega_{k+1/k} \end{bmatrix} \\ &= \begin{bmatrix} A_k & 0 \\ 0 & I \end{bmatrix}\begin{bmatrix} P_{k/k-1} & \Sigma_{k/k-1}^T \\ \Sigma_{k/k-1} & \Omega_{k/k-1} \end{bmatrix} \\ &\times\left(\begin{bmatrix} A_k^T & 0 \\ 0 & I \end{bmatrix} - \begin{bmatrix} C_k^T \\ 0 \end{bmatrix}\begin{bmatrix} K_k^T & \underline{K}_k^T \end{bmatrix}(C_kP_{k/k-1}C_k^T + R_k)^{-1}\right) + \begin{bmatrix} B_k \\ 0 \end{bmatrix}Q_k\begin{bmatrix} B_k^T & 0 \end{bmatrix}, \end{aligned} \tag{18}$$

in which the gains are given by

$$\begin{aligned} K_k^{(a)} &= \begin{bmatrix} K_k \\ \underline{L}_k \end{bmatrix} = \begin{bmatrix} A_k & 0 \\ 0 & I \end{bmatrix}\begin{bmatrix} P_{k/k-1} & \Sigma_{k/k-1}^T \\ \Sigma_{k/k-1} & \Pi_{k/k-1} \end{bmatrix}\begin{bmatrix} C_k^T \\ 0 \end{bmatrix}(C_kP_{k/k-1}C_k^T + R_k)^{-1} \\ &= \begin{bmatrix} A_kP_{k/k-1}C_k^T \\ \Sigma_{k/k-1}C_k^T \end{bmatrix}(C_kP_{k/k-1}C_k^T + R_k)^{-1}, \end{aligned} \tag{19}$$

see also [1]. The predicted error covariance components can be found from (18), *viz.*,

$$P_{k+1/k} = A_kP_{k/k}A_k^T + B_kQ_kB_k^T, \tag{20}$$

$$\Sigma_{k+1/k} = \Sigma_{k/k-1}(A_k^T - C_k^TK_k^T), \tag{21}$$

$$\Omega_{k+1/k} = \Omega_{k/k-1} - \Sigma_{k/k-1}C_k^T\underline{L}_k^T. \tag{22}$$

The sequences (21) - (22) can be initialised with $\Sigma_{\tau+1/\tau}$ = $P_{\tau/\tau}$ and $\Omega_{\tau+1/\tau}$ = $P_{\tau/\tau}$. The state corrections are obtained from (12), namely,

$$\hat{x}_{k/k} = \hat{x}_{k/k-1} + L_k(z_k - C_k\hat{x}_{k/k-1}), \tag{23}$$

$$\hat{\xi}_{k/k} = \hat{\xi}_{k/k-1} + \underline{L}_k(z_k - C_k\hat{x}_{k/k-1}). \tag{24}$$

Similarly, the state predictions follow from (13),

"You can't just ask customers what they want and then try to give that to them. By the time you get it built, they'll want something new." *Steven Paul Jobs*

$$\hat{x}_{k+1/k} = A_k \hat{x}_{k/k} , \tag{25}$$

$$\hat{\xi}_{k+1/k} = \hat{\xi}_{k/k} . \tag{26}$$

In summary, the fixed-point smoother estimates for $k \geq \tau$ are given by (24), which is initialised by $\hat{\xi}_{\tau/\tau} = \hat{x}_{\tau/\tau}$. The smoother gain is calculated as $\underline{L}_k = \Sigma_{k/k-1} C_k^T (C_k P_{k/k-1} C_k^T + R_k)^{-1}$, where $\Sigma_{k/k-1}$ is given by (21).

7.3.2 Performance

It follows from the above that $\Omega_{k+1/k} = \Omega_{k/k}$ and so

$$\Omega_{k+1/k+1} = \Omega_{k/k} - \Sigma_{k/k-1} C_k^T \underline{L}_k^T . \tag{27}$$

Next, it is argued that the discrete-time fixed-point smoother provides a performance improvement over the filter.

Lemma 2 [1]: *In respect of the fixed point smoother (24),*

$$P_{\tau/\tau} \geq \Omega_{k/k} . \tag{28}$$

Proof: *The recursion (22) may be written as the sum*

$$\Omega_{k+1/k+1} = \Omega_{\tau/\tau} - \sum_{i=\tau}^{k} \Sigma_{i/i-1} C_i^T (C_i P_{i/i-1} C_i^T + R)^{-1} C_i \Sigma_{i/i-1} , \tag{29}$$

where $\Omega_{\tau/\tau} = P_{\tau/\tau}$. Hence, $P_{\tau/\tau} - \Omega_{k+1/k+1} = \sum_{i=\tau}^{k} \Sigma_{i/i-1} C_i^T (C_i P_{i/i-1} C_i^T + R)^{-1} C_i \Sigma_{i/i-1} \geq 0$. □

Example 1. Consider a first-order time-invariant plant, in which $A = 0.9$, $B = 1$, $C = 0.1$ and $Q = 1$. An understanding of a fixed-point smoother's performance can be gleaned by examining the plots of the $\Sigma_{k/k}$ and $\Omega_{k/k}$ sequences shown in Fig. 1(a) and (b), respectively. The bottom lines of the figures correspond to measurement noise covariances of $R = 0.01$ and the top lines correspond to $R = 5$. It can be seen for this example, that the $\Sigma_{k/k}$ have diminishing impact after about 15 samples beyond the point of interest. From Fig. 1(b), it can be seen that smoothing appears most beneficial at mid-range measurement noise power, such as $R = 0.2$, since the plots of $\Omega_{k/k}$ become flatter for $R \geq 1$ and $R \leq 0.05$.

"There are no big problems, there are just a lot of little problems." *Henry Ford*

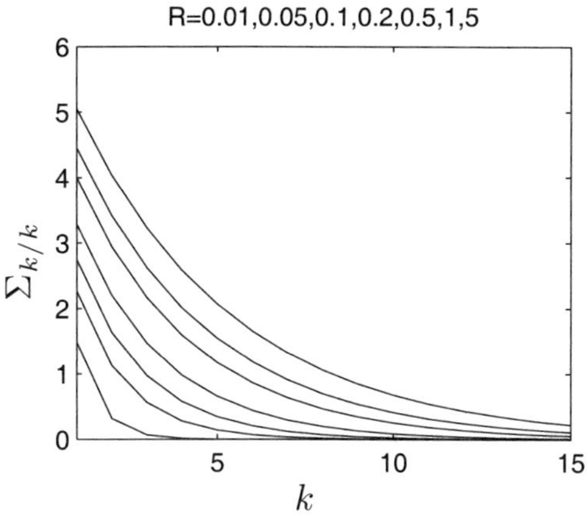

Figure 1(a). Smoother estimation variances $\Sigma_{k/k}$ versus k for Example 1.

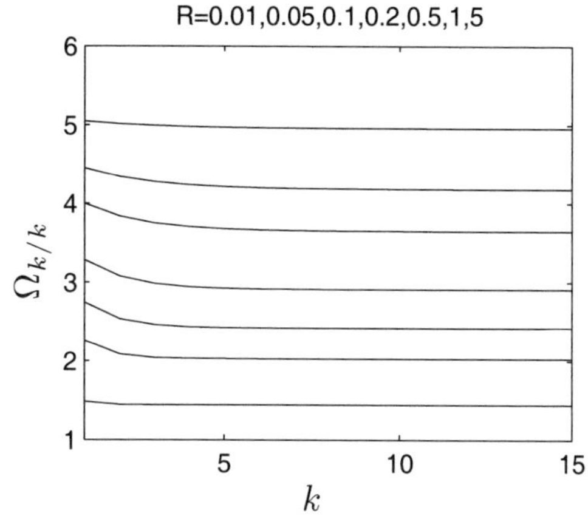

Figure 1(b). Smoother estimation variances $\Omega_{k+1/k+1}$ versus k for Example 1.

7.4 Fixed-Lag Smoothing

7.4.1 High-order Solution

Discrete-time fixed-lag smoothers calculate state estimates, $\hat{x}_{k-N/k}$, at time k given a delay of N steps. The objective is to minimise $E\{(x_{k-N} - \hat{x}_{k-N/k})(x_{k/N-1} - \hat{x}_{k-N/k})^T\}$. A common solution approach is to construct an augmented signal model that includes delayed states and then apply the standard Kalman filter recursions, see [1] - [3] and the references therein. Consider the signal model

$$\begin{bmatrix} x_{k+1} \\ x_k \\ x_{k-1} \\ \vdots \\ x_{k+1-N} \end{bmatrix} = \begin{bmatrix} A_k & 0 & \cdots & & 0 \\ I_N & & & & 0 \\ 0 & I_N & & & \vdots \\ \vdots & & \ddots & & \\ 0 & 0 & & I_N & 0 \end{bmatrix} \begin{bmatrix} x_k \\ x_{k-1} \\ x_{k-2} \\ \vdots \\ x_{k-N} \end{bmatrix} + \begin{bmatrix} B_k \\ 0 \\ 0 \\ \vdots \\ 0 \end{bmatrix} \tag{30}$$

and

$$z_k = \begin{bmatrix} C_k & 0 & 0 & \cdots & 0 \end{bmatrix} \begin{bmatrix} x_k \\ x_{k-1} \\ x_{k-2} \\ \vdots \\ x_{k-N} \end{bmatrix} + v_k . \tag{31}$$

"If the only tool you have is a hammer, you tend to see every problem as a nail." *Abraham Maslow*

By applying the Kalman filter recursions to the above signal model, the predicted states are obtained as

$$\begin{bmatrix} \hat{x}_{k+1} \\ \hat{x}_k \\ \hat{x}_{k-1} \\ \vdots \\ \hat{x}_{k+1-N} \end{bmatrix} = \begin{bmatrix} A_k & 0 & \cdots & & 0 \\ I_N & & & & 0 \\ 0 & I_N & & & \vdots \\ \vdots & & \ddots & & \\ 0 & 0 & & I_N & 0 \end{bmatrix} \begin{bmatrix} \hat{x}_k \\ \hat{x}_{k-1} \\ \hat{x}_{k-2} \\ \vdots \\ \hat{x}_{k-N} \end{bmatrix} + \begin{bmatrix} K_{0,k} \\ K_{1,k} \\ K_{2,k} \\ \vdots \\ K_{N,k} \end{bmatrix} (z_k - C_k \hat{x}_{k/k-1}), \quad (32)$$

where $K_{0,k}$, $K_{1,k}$, $K_{2,k}$, …, $K_{N,k}$ denote the submatrices of the predictor gain. Two important observations follow from the above equation. First, the desired smoothed estimates $\hat{x}_{k-1/k}$ … $\hat{x}_{k-N+1/k}$ are contained within the one-step-ahead prediction (32). Second, the fixed lag-smoother (32) inherits the stability properties of the original Kalman filter.

7.4.2 Reduced-order Solution

Equation (32) is termed a high order solution because the dimension of the above augmented state matrix is $(N+2)n \times (N+2)n$. Moore [1] - [3] simplified (32) to obtain elegant reduced order solution structures as follows. Let

$$\begin{bmatrix} P^{(0,0)}_{k+1/k} & P^{(0,1)}_{k+1/k} & \cdots & P^{(0,N)}_{k+1/k} \\ P^{(1,0)}_{k+1/k} & P^{(1,1)}_{k+1/k} & & \vdots \\ \vdots & & \ddots & \\ P^{(N,0)}_{k+1/k} & \cdots & & P^{(N,N)}_{k+1/k} \end{bmatrix}, \quad P^{(i,j)}_{k+1/k} = (P^{(j,i)}_{k+1/k})^T,$$

denote the predicted error covariance matrix. For $0 \le i \le N$, the smoothed states within (32) are given by

$$\hat{x}_{k-i/k} = \hat{x}_{k-i/k-1} + K_{i+1,k}(z_k - C_k \hat{x}_{k/k-1}), \quad (33)$$

where

$$K_{i+1,k} = P^{(i,0)}_{k+1/k} C_k^T (C_k P^{(0,0)}_{k+1/k} C_k^T + R_k)^{-1}. \quad (34)$$

Recursions for the error covariance submatrices of interest are

$$P^{(i+1,0)}_{k+1/k} = P^{(i,0)}_{k+1/k}(A_k - K_{0,k}C_k)^T, \quad (35)$$

$$P^{(i+1,i+1)}_{k+1/k} = P^{(i,i)}_{k+1/k} - P^{(i,0)}_{k+1/k} C_k K^T_{i+1,k}. \quad (36)$$

Another rearrangement of (33) − (34) to reduce the calculation cost further is described in [1].

"You have to seek the simplest implementation of a problem solution in order to know when you've reached your limit in that regard. Then it's easy to make tradeoffs, to back off a little, for performance reasons." *Stephen Gary Wozniak*

7.4.3 Performance

Two facts that stem from (36) are stated below.

Lemma 3: *In respect of the fixed-lag smoother (33) – (36), the following applies.*

(i) The error-performance improves with increasing smoothing lag.

(ii) The fixed-lag smoothers outperform the Kalman filter.

Proof:

(i) The claim follows by inspection of (34) and (36).

(ii) The observation follows by recognising that $P^{(1,1)}_{k+1/k} = E\{(x_k - \hat{x}_{k/k})(x_k - \hat{x}_{k/k})^T\}$ *within (i).* □

It can also be seen from the term $-P^{(i,0)}_{k+1/k}C_k^T(C_kP^{(0,0)}_{k+1/k}C_k^T + R_k)^{-1}C_kP^{(i,0)}_{k+1/k}$ within (36) that the benefit of smoothing diminishes as R_k becomes large.

7.5 Fixed-Interval Smoothing

7.5.1 The Maximum-Likelihood Smoother

7.5.1.1 Solution Derivation

The most commonly used fixed-interval smoother is undoubtedly the solution reported by Rauch [5] in 1963 and two years later with Tung and Striebel [6]. Although this smoother does not minimise the error variance, it has two desirable attributes. First, it is a low-complexity state estimator. Second, it can provide close to optimal performance whenever the accompanying assumptions are reasonable.

The smoother involves two passes. In the first (forward) pass, filtered state estimates, $\hat{x}_{k/k}$, are calculated from

$$\hat{x}_{k/k} = \hat{x}_{k/k-1} + L_k(z_k - C_k\hat{x}_{k/k-1}), \tag{37}$$

$$\hat{x}_{k+1/k} = A_k\hat{x}_{k/k}, \tag{38}$$

where $L_k = P_{k/k-1}C_k^T(C_kP_{k/k-1}C_k^T + R_k)^{-1}$ is the filter gain, $K_k = A_kL_k$ is the predictor gain, in which $P_{k/k} = P_{k/k-1} - P_{k/k-1}C_k^T(C_kP_{k/k-1}C_k^T + R_k)^{-1}C_kP_{k/k-1}$ and $P_{k+1/k} = A_kP_{k/k}A_k^T + B_kQ_kB_k^T$. In the second backward pass, Rauch, Tung and Striebel calculate smoothed state estimates, $\hat{x}_{k/N}$, from the beautiful one-line recursion

$$\hat{x}_{k/N} = \hat{x}_{k/k} + G_k(\hat{x}_{k+1/N} - \hat{x}_{k+1/k}), \tag{39}$$

where

$$G_k = P_{k/k}A_{k+1}^TP_{k+1/k}^{-1} \tag{40}$$

is the smoother gain. The above sequence is initialised by $\hat{x}_{k/N} = \hat{x}_{k/k}$ at $k = N$. In the first public domain appearance of (39), Rauch [5] referred to a Lockheed Missile and Space

---

"For every problem there is a solution which is simple, clean and wrong." *Henry Louis Mencken*

Company Technical Report co-authored with Tung and Striebel. Consequently, (39) is commonly known as the Rauch-Tung-Striebel smoother. This smoother was derived in [6] using the maximum-likelihood method and an outline is provided below.

The notation $x_k \sim \mathcal{N}(\mu,\ R_{xx})$ means that a discrete-time random variable x_k with mean μ and covariance R_{xx} has the normal (or Gaussian) probability density function

$$p(x_k) = \frac{1}{(2\pi)^{n/2}\left|R_{xx}\right|^{1/2}}\exp\left\{-0.5(x_k - \mu)^T R_{xx}^{-1}(x_k - \mu)\right\}. \tag{41}$$

Rauch, Tung and Striebel assumed that [6]:

$$\hat{x}_{k+1/N} \sim \mathcal{N}(A_k\hat{x}_{k/N}, B_k Q_k B_k^T). \tag{42}$$

$$\hat{x}_{k/N} \sim \mathcal{N}(\hat{x}_{k/k}, P_{k/k}). \tag{43}$$

From the approach of [6], setting the partial derivative of the logarithm of the joint density function to zero results in

$$0 = \frac{\partial(\hat{x}_{k+1/N} - A_k\hat{x}_{k/N})^T}{\partial\hat{x}_{k/N}}(B_k Q_k B_k^T)^{-1}(\hat{x}_{k+1/N} - A_k\hat{x}_{k/N})^T \frac{n!}{r!(n-r)!} + \frac{\partial(\hat{x}_{k/N} - \hat{x}_{k/N})^T}{\partial\hat{x}_{k/N}} P_{k/k}^{-1}(\hat{x}_{k/N} - \hat{x}_{k/N}).$$

Rearranging the above equation leads to

$$\hat{x}_{k/N} = (I + P_{k/k}A_k^T(B_k Q_k B_k^T)^{-1}A_k)^{-1}(\hat{x}_{k/N} + P_{k/k}A_k^T B_k Q_k B_k^T)^{-1}\hat{x}_{k/N})^T. \tag{44}$$

From the Matrix Inversion Lemma

$$(I + P_{k/k}A_k^T(B_k Q_k B_k^T)^{-1}A_k)^{-1} = I - G_k A_k. \tag{45}$$

The solution (39) is found by substituting (45) into (44). Some further details of Rauch, Tung and Striebel's derivation appear in [13].

7.5.1.2 Alternative Forms

The smoother gain (40) can be calculated in different ways. Assuming that A_k is non-singular, it follows from $P_{k+1/k} = A_k P_{k/k} A_k^T + B_k Q_k B_k^T$ that $P_{k/k}A_{k+1}^T P_{k+1/k}^{-1} = A_k^{-1}(I - B_k Q_k B_k^T P_{k+1/k}^{-1})$ and

$$G_k = A_k^{-1}(I - B_k Q_k B_k^T P_{k+1/k}^{-1}). \tag{46}$$

In applications where difficulties exist with inverting $P_{k+1/k}$, it may be preferable to calculate

$$P_{k/k-1}^{-1} = P_{k/k}^{-1} - C_k^T R_k^{-1} C_k. \tag{47}$$

It is shown in [15] that the filter (37) - (38) and the smoother (39) can be written in the following Hamiltonian form

---

"Error is the discipline through which we advance." *William Ellery Channing*

$$\begin{bmatrix} \hat{x}_{k+1/N} \\ \lambda_{k/N} \end{bmatrix} = \begin{bmatrix} A_k & B_k Q_k B_k^T \\ -C_k^T R_k^{-1} C_k & A_k^T \end{bmatrix} \begin{bmatrix} \hat{x}_{k/N} \\ \lambda_{k+1/N} \end{bmatrix} + \begin{bmatrix} 0 \\ C_k^T R_k^{-1} z_k \end{bmatrix}, \tag{48, 49}$$

where $\lambda_{k/N} \in \mathbb{R}^n$ is an auxiliary variable that proceeds backward in time k. The form (48) – (49) avoids potential numerical difficulties that may be associated with calculating $P_{k/k-1}^{-1}$.

To confirm the equivalence of (39) and (48) – (49), use the Bryson-Frazier formula [15]

$$\hat{x}_{k+1/N} = \hat{x}_{k+1/k+1} + P_{k+1/k} \lambda_{k+1/N}, \tag{50}$$

and (46) within (48) to obtain

$$\hat{x}_{k/N} = G_k \hat{x}_{k+1/k+1} + A_k^{-1} B_k Q_k B_k^T P_{k+1/k}^{-1} \hat{x}_{k+1/k}. \tag{51}$$

Employing (46) within (51) and rearranging leads to (39).

In time-invariant problems, steady state solutions for $P_{k/k}$ and $P_{k+1/k}$ can be used to precalculate the gain (40) before running the smoother. For example, the application of a time-invariant version of the Rauch-Tung-Striebel smoother for the restoration of blurred images is described in [14].

7.5.1.3 Performance

An expression for the smoother error covariance is developed below following the approach of [6], [13]. Define the smoother and filter error states as $\tilde{x}_{k/N} = x_k - \hat{x}_{k/N}$ and $\tilde{x}_{k/k} = x_k - \hat{x}_{k/k}$, respectively. It is assumed that

$$E\{\tilde{x}_{k/k} \hat{x}_{k/k}^T\} = 0, \tag{52}$$

$$E\{\tilde{x}_{k+1/N} \hat{x}_{k+1/N}^T\} = 0, \tag{53}$$

$$E\{\tilde{x}_{k+1/N} \hat{x}_{k/N}^T\} = 0. \tag{54}$$

It is straightforward to show that (52) implies

$$E\{\hat{x}_{k+1/k} \hat{x}_{k+1/k}^T\} = E\{x_{k+1} x_{k+1}^T\} - P_{k+1/k}. \tag{55}$$

Denote $\Sigma_{k/N} = E\{\hat{x}_{k+1/N} \hat{x}_{k+1/N}^T\}$. The assumption (53) implies

$$E\{\hat{x}_{k+1/N} \hat{x}_{k+1/N}^T\} = E\{x_{k+1} x_{k+1}^T\} - \Sigma_{k+1/N}. \tag{56}$$

Subtracting x_k from both sides of (39) gives

$$\tilde{x}_{k/N} - G_k \hat{x}_{k+1/N} = \tilde{x}_{k/k} - G_k A_k \hat{x}_{k/k}. \tag{57}$$

By simplifying

"Great thinkers think inductively, that is, they create solutions and then seek out the problems that the solutions might solve; most companies think deductively, that is, defining a problem and then investigating different solutions." *Joey Reiman*

$$E\{(\tilde{x}_{k/N} - G_k\hat{x}_{k+1/N})(\tilde{x}_{k/N} - G_k\hat{x}_{k+1/N})^T\} = E\{(\tilde{x}_{k/k} - G_kA_k\hat{x}_{k/k})(\tilde{x}_{k/k} - G_kA_k\hat{x}_{k/k})^T\} \quad (58)$$

and using (52), (54) - (56) yields

$$\Sigma_{k/N} = P_{k/k} - G_k(P_{k+1/k} - \Sigma_{k+1/N})G_k^T . \quad (59)$$

It can now be shown that the smoother performs better than the Kalman filter.

Lemma 4: *Suppose that the sequence (59) is initialised with*

$$\Sigma_{N+1/N} = P_{N+1/N} , \quad (60)$$

Then $\Sigma_{k/N} \le P_{k/k}$ *for* $1 \le k \le N$.

Proof: *The condition (60) implies* $\Sigma_{N/N} = P_{N/N}$, *which is the initial step for an induction argument. For the induction step, (59) is written as*

$$\Sigma_{k/N} = P_{k/k-1} - P_{k/k-1}C_k^T(C_kP_{k/k-1}C_k^T + R)C_kP_{k/k-1} - G_k(P_{k+1/k} - \Sigma_{k+1/N})G_k^T \quad (61)$$

and thus $\Sigma_{k+1/N} \le P_{k+1/k}$ *implies* $\Sigma_{k/N} \le P_{k/k-1}$ *and* $\Sigma_{k/N} \le P_{k/k}$. □

7.5.2 The Fraser-Potter Smoother

Forward and backward estimates may be merged using the data fusion formula described in Lemma 7 of Chapter 6. A variation of the Fraser-Potter discrete-time fixed-interval smoother [4] derived by Monzingo [16] is advocated below.

In the first pass, a Kalman filter produces corrected state estimates $\hat{x}_{k/k}$ and corrected error covariances $P_{k/k}$ from the measurements. In the second pass, a Kalman filter is employed to calculate predicted "backward" state estimates $\xi_{k-1/k}$ and predicted "backward" error covariances $\Sigma_{k-1/k}$ from the time-reversed measurements. The smoothed estimate is given by [16]

$$\hat{x}_{k/N} = (P_{k/k}^{-1} + \Sigma_{k/k-1}^{-1})^{-1}(P_{k/k}^{-1}\hat{x}_{k/k} + \Sigma_{k/k-1}^{-1}\xi_{k/k-1}) . \quad (62)$$

Alternatively, Kalman filters could be used to derive predicted quantities, $\hat{x}_{k/k-1}$ and $P_{k/k-1}$, from the measurements, and backward corrected quantities $\xi_{k/k}$ and $\Sigma_{k/k}$. Smoothed estimates may then be obtained from the linear combination

$$\hat{x}_{k/N} = (P_{k/k-1}^{-1} + \Sigma_{k/k}^{-1})^{-1}(P_{k/k-1}^{-1}\hat{x}_{k/k-1} + \Sigma_{k/k}^{-1}\xi_{k/k}) . \quad (63)$$

It is observed that the fixed-point smoother (24), the fixed-lag smoother (32), maximum-likelihood smoother (39), the smoothed estimates (62) − (63) and the minimum-variance smoother (which is described subsequently) all use each measurement z_k once.

Note that Fraser and Potter's original smoother solution [4] and Monzingo's variation [16] are *ad hoc* and no claims are made about attaining a prescribed level of performance.

"No great discovery was ever made without a bold guess." *Isaac Newton*

7.5.3 Minimum-Variance Smoothers

7.5.3.1 Optimal Unrealisable Solutions

Consider again the estimation problem depicted in Fig. 1 of Chapter 6, where w and v are now discrete-time inputs. As in continuous-time, it is desired to construct a solution $\mathcal{H}$ is that produces output estimates $\hat{y}_1$ of a reference system $y_1 = \mathcal{G}_1 w$ from observations $z = y_2 + v$, where $y_2 = \mathcal{G}_2 w$. The objective is to minimise the energy of the output estimation error $e = y_1 - \hat{y}_1$.

The following discussion is perfunctory since it is a regathering of the results from Chapter 6. Recall that the output estimation error is generated by $e = \mathcal{R}_{ei} i$, where $\mathcal{R}_{ei} = -\begin{bmatrix} \mathcal{H} & \mathcal{H}\mathcal{G}_2 - \mathcal{G}_1 \end{bmatrix}$ and $i = \begin{bmatrix} v \\ w \end{bmatrix}$. It has been shown previously that $\mathcal{R}_{ei}\mathcal{R}_{ei}^H = \mathcal{R}_{ei1}\mathcal{R}_{ei1}^H + \mathcal{R}_{ei2}\mathcal{R}_{ei2}^H$ where

$$\mathcal{R}_{ei2} = \mathcal{H}\Delta - \mathcal{G}_1 Q \mathcal{G}_2^H \Delta^{-H}, \tag{64}$$

in which $\Delta : \mathbb{R}^p \to \mathbb{R}^p$, is known as the Wiener-Hopf factor, which satisfies $\Delta\Delta^H = \mathcal{G}Q\mathcal{G}^H + R$. From Lemma 8 of Chapter 6, the smoother solution $\mathcal{H} = \mathcal{G}_2 Q \mathcal{G}_2^H (\Delta\Delta^H)^{-1}$ achieves the best-possible performance, namely, it minimises $\left\| ee^H \right\|_2 = \left\| \mathcal{R}_{ei}\mathcal{R}_{ei}^H \right\|_2$. For example, in output estimation problems $\mathcal{G}_1 = \mathcal{G}_2$ and the optimal smoother simplifies to $\mathcal{H}_{OE} = I - R(\Delta\Delta^H)^{-1}$. From Lemma 9 of Chapter 6, the (causal) filter solution $\mathcal{H}_{OE} = \{\mathcal{G}_2 Q \mathcal{G}_2^H \Delta^{-H}\Delta^{-1}\}_+ = \{\mathcal{G}_2 Q \mathcal{G}_2^H \Delta^{-H}\}_+ \Delta^{-1}$ achieves the best-possible filter performance, that is, it minimises $\left\| \{\tilde{y}_2 \tilde{y}_2^H\}_+ \right\|_2 = \left\| \{\mathcal{R}_{ei}\mathcal{R}_{ei}^H\}_+ \right\|_2$. The optimal smoother outperforms the optimal filter since $\left\| \{\mathcal{R}_{ei}\mathcal{R}_{ei}^H\}_+ \right\|_2 \geq \left\| \mathcal{R}_{ei}\mathcal{R}_{ei}^H \right\|_2$. The above solutions are termed unrealisable because of the difficulty in obtaining Δ when $\mathcal{G}_1$ and $\mathcal{G}_2$ are time-varying systems. Realisable solutions that use an approximate Wiener-Hopf factor in place of Δ are presented below.

7.5.3.2 Non-causal Output Estimation

Suppose that the time-varying linear system $\mathcal{G}_2$ has the realisation (1) - (2). An approximate Wiener-Hopf factor $\hat{\Delta} : \mathbb{R}^p \to \mathbb{R}^p$ is introduced in [7], [13] and defined by

$$\begin{bmatrix} x_{k+1} \\ \delta_k \end{bmatrix} = \begin{bmatrix} A_k & K_k \Omega_k^{1/2} \\ C_k & \Omega_k^{1/2} \end{bmatrix} \begin{bmatrix} x_k \\ z_k \end{bmatrix}, \tag{65}$$

"Life is pretty simple. You do stuff. Most fails. Some works. You do more of what works. If it works big, others quickly copy it. Then you do something else. The trick is the doing something else." *Leonardo da Vinci*

where $K_k = (A_k P_{k/k-1} C_k^T + B_k Q_k D_k^T)\Omega_k^{-1}$ is the predictor gain, $\Omega_k = C_k P_{k/k-1} C_k^T + D_k Q_k D_k^T + R_k$ and $P_{k/k-1}$ evolves from the Riccati difference equation $P_{k+1/k} = A_k P_{k/k-1} A_k^T - (A_k P_{k/k-1} C_k^T + B_k Q_k D_k^T)(C_k P_{k/k-1} C_k^T + D_k Q_k D_k^T + R_k)^{-1}(C_k P_{k/k-1} A_k^T + D_k Q_k B_k^T) + B_k Q_k B_k^T$. The inverse of the system (65), denoted by $\hat{\Delta}^{-1}$, is obtained using the Matrix Inversion Lemma

$$\begin{bmatrix} \hat{x}_{k+1/k} \\ \alpha_k \end{bmatrix} = \begin{bmatrix} A_k - K_k C_k & K_k \\ -\Omega_k^{-1/2} C_k & -\Omega_k^{-1/2} C_k \end{bmatrix} \begin{bmatrix} \hat{x}_{k/k-1} \\ z_k \end{bmatrix}. \tag{66}$$

The optimal output estimation smoother can be approximated as

$$\begin{aligned} \mathcal{H}_{OE} &= I - R(\hat{\Delta}\hat{\Delta}^H)^{-1} \\ &= I - R\hat{\Delta}^{-H}\hat{\Delta}^{-1}. \end{aligned} \tag{67}$$

A state-space realisation of (67) is given by (66),

$$\begin{bmatrix} \xi_{k-1} \\ \beta_k \end{bmatrix} = \begin{bmatrix} A_k^T - C_k^T K_k^T & C_k^T \Omega_k^{-1/2} \\ -K_k^T & \Omega_k^{-1/2} \end{bmatrix} \begin{bmatrix} \xi_k \\ \alpha_k \end{bmatrix}, \quad \xi_N = 0 \tag{68}$$

and

$$\hat{y}_{k/N} = z_k - R_k \beta_k . \tag{69}$$

Note that Lemma 1 is used to obtain the realisation (68) of $\hat{\Delta}^{-H} = (\hat{\Delta}^H)^{-1}$ from (66). A block diagram of this smoother is provided in Fig. 2. The states $\hat{x}_{k/k-1}$ within (66) are immediately recognisable as belonging to the one-step-ahead predictor. Thus, the optimum realisable solution involves a cascade of familiar building blocks, namely, a Kalman predictor and its adjoint.

Procedure 1. The above output estimation smoother can be implemented via the following three-step procedure.

Step 1. Operate $\hat{\Delta}^{-1}$ on z_k using (66) to obtain α_k.

Step 2. In lieu of the adjoint system (68), operate (66) on the time-reversed transpose of α_k. Then take the time-reversed transpose of the result to obtain β_k.

Step 3. Calculate the smoothed output estimate from (69).

It is shown below that $\hat{y}_{k/N}$ is an unbiased estimate of y_k.

"When I am working on a problem, I never think about beauty but when I have finished, if the solution is not beautiful, I know it is wrong." *Richard Buckminster Fuller*

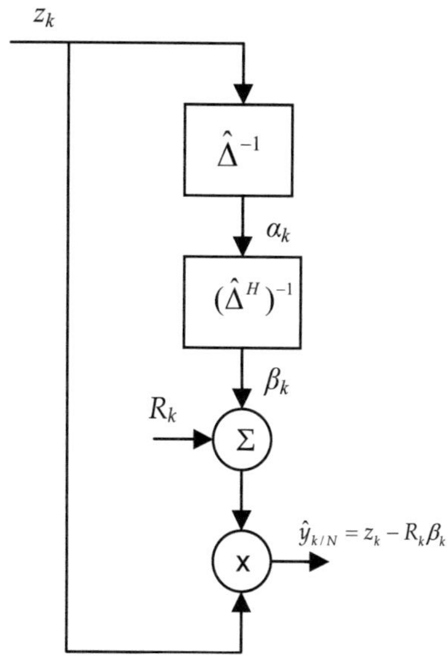

Figure 2. Block diagram of the output estimation smoother

Lemma 5 $E\{\hat{y}_{k/N}\} = E\{y_k\}$.

Proof: *Denote the one-step-head prediction error by* $\tilde{x}_{k/k-1} = x_k - \hat{x}_{k/k-1}$. *The output of (66) may be written as* $\alpha_k = \Omega_k^{-1/2}C_k\tilde{x}_{k/k-1} + \Omega_k^{-1/2}v_k$ *and therefore*

$$E\{\alpha_k\} = \Omega_k^{-1/2}C_kE\{\tilde{x}_{k/k-1}\} + \Omega_k^{-1/2}E\{v_k\}. \tag{70}$$

The first term on the right-hand-side of (70) is zero since it pertains to the prediction error of the Kalman filter. The second term is zero since it is assumed that $E\{v_k\} = 0$. *Thus* $E\{\alpha_k\} = 0$. *Since the recursion (68) is initialized with* $\zeta_N = 0$, *it follows that* $E\{\zeta_k\} = 0$, *which implies* $E\{\zeta_k\} = -K_kE\{\zeta_k\} + \Omega_k^{-1/2}E\{\alpha_k\} = 0$. *Thus, from (69),* $E\{\hat{y}_{k/N}\} = E\{z_k\} = E\{y_k\}$, *since it is assumed that* $E\{v_k\} = 0$. □

7.5.3.3 Causal Output Estimation

The minimum-variance (Kalman) filter is obtained by taking the causal part of the optimum minimum-variance smoother (67)

$$\{\mathcal{H}_{OE}\}_+ = I - R_k\{\hat{\Delta}^{-H}\}_+\hat{\Delta}^{-1} \tag{71}$$

"The practical success of an idea, irrespective of its inherent merit, is dependent on the attitude of the contemporaries. If timely it is quickly adopted; if not, it is apt to fare like a sprout lured out of the ground by warm sunshine, only to be injured and retarded in its growth by the succeeding frost." *Nicola Tesla*

$$= I - R_k \Omega_k^{-1/2} \hat{\Delta}^{-1} .$$

To confirm this linkage between the smoother and filter, denote L_k = $(C_k P_{k/k-1} C_k^T + D_k Q_k D_k^T)\Omega_k^{-1}$ and use (71) to obtain

$$\begin{aligned}\hat{y}_{k/k} &= z_k - R_k \Omega_k^{-1/2} \alpha_k \\ &= R_k \Omega_k^{-1} C_k x_k + (I - R_k \Omega_k^{-1/2}) z_k \\ &= (C_k - L_k C_k) x_k + L_k z_k ,\end{aligned} \tag{72}$$

which is identical to (34) of Chapter 4.

7.5.3.4 Input Estimation

As discussed in Chapter 6, the optimal realisable smoother for input estimation is

$$\mathcal{H}_{IE} = Q \mathcal{G}_2^H \hat{\Delta}^{-H} \hat{\Delta}^{-1} . \tag{73}$$

The development of a state-space realisation for $\hat{w}_{k/N}$ = $Q \mathcal{G}_2^H \hat{\Delta}^{-H} \alpha_k$ makes use of the formula for the cascade of two systems described in Chapter 6. The smoothed input estimate is realised by

$$\begin{bmatrix} \xi_{k-1} \\ \gamma_{k-1} \\ \hat{w}_{k-1/N} \end{bmatrix} = \begin{bmatrix} A_k^T - C_k^T K_k & 0 & C_k^T \Omega_k^{-1/2} \\ C_k^T K_k^T & A_k^T & -C_k^T \Omega_k^{-1/2} \\ -Q_k D_k^T K_k^T & -Q_k B_k^T & Q_k D_k^T \Omega_k^{-1/2} \end{bmatrix} \begin{bmatrix} \xi_k \\ \gamma_k \\ \alpha_k \end{bmatrix} , \tag{74}$$

in which $\gamma_k \in \mathbb{R}^n$ is an auxiliary state.

***Procedure* 2.** The above input estimator can be implemented via the following three steps.

Step 1. Operate $\hat{\Delta}^{-1}$ on the measurements z_k using (66) to obtain α_k.

Step 2. Operate the adjoint of (74) on the time-reversed transpose of α_k. Then take the time-reversed transpose of the result.

7.5.3.5 State Estimation

Smoothed state estimates can be obtained by defining the reference system $\mathcal{G}_1$ = I which yields

$$\begin{aligned}\hat{x}_{k+1/N} &= A_k \hat{x}_{k/N} + B_k \hat{w}_{k/N} \\ &= A_k \hat{x}_{k/N} + B_k Q \mathcal{G}_2^H \hat{\Delta}^{-H} \alpha_k .\end{aligned} \tag{75}$$

"Doubt is the father of invention." *Galileo Galilei*

Thus, the minimum-variance smoother for state estimation is given by (66) and (74) – (75). As remarked in Chapter 6, some numerical model order reduction may be required. In the special case of C_k being of rank n and $D_k = 0$, state estimates can be calculated from (69) and

$$\hat{x}_{k/N} = C_k^{\#}\hat{y}_{k/N} . \tag{76}$$

where $C_k^{\#} = (C_k^T C_k)^{-1} C_k^T$ is the Moore-Penrose pseudo-inverse.

7.5.3.6 Performance

The characterisation of smoother performance requires the following additional notation. Let $\gamma = \mathcal{G}_0 w$ denote the output of the linear time-varying system having the realisation

$$x_{k+1} = A_k x_k + w_k , \tag{77}$$

$$\gamma_k = x_k , \tag{78}$$

where $A_k \in \mathbb{R}^{n \times n}$. By inspection of (77) – (78), the output of the inverse system $w = \mathcal{G}_0^{-1} y$ is given by

$$w_k = \gamma_{k+1} - A_k \gamma_k . \tag{79}$$

Similarly, let $\varepsilon = \mathcal{G}_0^H u$ denote the output of the adjoint system $\mathcal{G}_0^H$, which from Lemma 1 has the realisation

$$\zeta_{k-1} = A_k^T \zeta_k - u_k , \tag{80}$$

$$\varepsilon_k = -\zeta_k . \tag{81}$$

It follows that the output of the inverse system $u = \mathcal{G}_0^{-H} \varepsilon$ is given by

$$u_k = \varepsilon_{k-1} - A_k^T \varepsilon_k . \tag{82}$$

The exact Wiener-Hopf factor may now be written as

$$\Delta\Delta^H = C_k \mathcal{G}_0 B_k Q_k B_k^T \mathcal{G}_0^H C_k^T + R_k . \tag{83}$$

The subsequent lemma, which relates the exact and approximate Wiener-Hopf factors, requires the identity

$$P_k - A_k P_k A_k^T = A_k P_k \mathcal{G}_0^{-H} + \mathcal{G}_0^{-1} P_k A_k^T + \mathcal{G}_0^{-1} P_k \mathcal{G}_0^{-H} , \tag{84}$$

in which P_k is an arbitrary matrix of appropriate dimensions. A verification of (84) is requested in the problems.

"The theory of our modern technique shows that nothing is as practical as the theory." *Julius Robert Oppenheimer*

Lemma 6 [7]: In respect of the signal model (1) – (2) with $D_k = 0$, $E\{w_k\} = E\{v_k\} = 0$, $E\{w_j w_k^T\} = Q_k \delta_{jk}$, $E\{v_j v_k^T\} = R_k \delta_{jk}$, $E\{w_k v_k^T\} = 0$ and the quantities defined above,

$$\hat{\Delta}\hat{\Delta}^H = \Delta\Delta^H + C_k \mathcal{G}_0 (P_{k/k-1} - P_{k+1/k}) \mathcal{G}_0^H C_k^T . \tag{85}$$

Proof: *The approximate Wiener-Hopf factor may be written as* $\hat{\Delta} = C_k \mathcal{G}_0 K_k \Omega_k^{1/2} + \Omega_k^{1/2}$. *Using* $P_{k/k-1} - A_k P_{k/k-1} A_k^T = - A_k P_{k/k-1} C_k^T (C_k P_{k/k-1} C_k^T + R_k)^{-1} C_k P_{k/k-1} A_k^T + B_k Q_k B_k^T + P_{k/k-1} - P_{k+1/k}$ *within (84) and simplifying leads to (85).* □

It can be seen from (85) that the approximate Wiener-Hopf factor approaches the exact Wiener-Hopf factor whenever the estimation problem is locally stationary, that is, when the model and noise parameters vary sufficiently slowly so that $P_{k/k-1} \approx P_{k+1/k}$. Under these conditions, the smoother (69) achieves the best-possible performance, as is shown below.

Lemma 7 [7]: *The smoother (67) satisfies*

$$\mathcal{R}_{ei2} = R_k [(\Delta\Delta^H)^{-1} - (\Delta\Delta^H - C_k \mathcal{G}_0 (P_{k/k-1} - P_{k+1/k}) \mathcal{G}_0^H C_k^T)^{-1}]\Delta , \tag{86}$$

Proof: *Substituting (67) into (64) yields*

$$\mathcal{R}_{ei2} = R_k [(\Delta\Delta^H)^{-1} - (\hat{\Delta}\hat{\Delta}^H)^{-1}]\Delta . \tag{87}$$

The result (86) is now immediate from (85) and (87). □

Some conditions under which $P_{k+1/k}$ asymptotically approaches $P_{k/k-1}$ and the smoother (67) attaining optimal performance are set out below.

Lemma 8 [8]: *Suppose*

(i) *for a $t > 0$ that there exist solutions $P_t \ge P_{t+1} \ge 0$ of the Riccati difference equation*

(ii) $P_{k+1/k} = A_k P_{k/k-1} A_k^T - A_k P_{k/k-1} C_k^T (C_k P_{k/k-1} C_k^T + R_k)^{-1} C_k P_{k/k-1} A_k^T + B_k Q_k B_k^T$ *; and*

(iii) $\begin{bmatrix} B_{t+k-1} Q_{t+k-1} B_{t+k-1}^T & A_{t+k-1}^T \\ A_{t+k-1} & -C_{t+k-1}^T R_{t+k-1}^{-1} C_{t+k-1} \end{bmatrix} \ge \begin{bmatrix} B_{t+k} Q_{t+k} B_{t+k}^T & A_{t+k}^T \\ A_{t+k} & -C_{t+k}^T R_{t+k}^{-1} C_{t+k} \end{bmatrix}$ *for all $k \ge 0$.*

Then the smoother (67) achieves

$$\lim_{t \to \infty} \left\| \mathcal{R}_{ei2} \mathcal{R}_{ei2}^H \right\|_2 = 0 . \tag{88}$$

Proof: *Conditions i) and ii) together with Theorem 1 imply* $P_{k/k-1} \ge P_{k+1/k}$ *for all $k \ge 0$ and* $P_{k/k-1} = 0$. *The claim (88) is now immediate from Theorem 2.* □

An example that illustrates the performance benefit of the minimum-variance smoother (67) is described below.

"Whoever, in the pursuit of science, seeks after immediate practical utility may rest assured that he seeks in vain." *Hermann Ludwig Ferdinand von Helmholtz*

Example 2 [9]. The nominal drift rate of high quality inertial navigation systems is around one nautical mile per hour, which corresponds to position errors of about 617 m over a twenty minute period. Thus, inertial navigation systems alone cannot be used to control underground mining equipment. An approach which has been found to be successful in underground mines is called dead reckoning, where the Euler angles, θ_k, φ_k and ϕ_k, reported by an inertial navigation system are combined with external odometer measurements, d_k. The dead reckoning position estimates in the x-y-z plane are calculated as

$$\begin{bmatrix} x_{k+1} \\ y_{k+1} \\ z_{k+1} \end{bmatrix} = \begin{bmatrix} x_k \\ y_k \\ z_k \end{bmatrix} + (d_k - d_{k-1}) \begin{bmatrix} \sin(\theta_k) \\ \sin(\varphi_k) \\ \sin(\phi_k) \end{bmatrix}. \tag{89}$$

A filter or a smoother may then be employed to improve the noisy position estimates calculated from (89). Euler angles were generated using $\begin{bmatrix} \theta_{k+1} \\ \varphi_{k+1} \\ \phi_{k+1} \end{bmatrix} = A \begin{bmatrix} \theta_k \\ \varphi_k \\ \phi_k \end{bmatrix} + \begin{bmatrix} w_k^{(1)} \\ w_k^{(2)} \\ w_k^{(3)} \end{bmatrix}$, with $A = \begin{bmatrix} 0.95 & 0 & 0 \\ 0 & 0.95 & 0 \\ 0 & 0 & 0.95 \end{bmatrix}$ and $w_k^{(i)} \sim \mathcal{N}(0, 0.01)$, $i = 1\ldots3$. Simulations were conducted with 1000 realisations of Gaussian measurement noise added to position estimates calculated from (89). The mean-square error exhibited by the minimum-variance filter and smoother operating on the noisy dead reckoning estimates are shown in Fig. 3. It can be seen that filtering the noisy dead reckoning positions can provide a significant mean-square-error improvement. The figure also demonstrates that the smoother can offer a few dB of further improvement at mid-range signal-to-noise ratios.

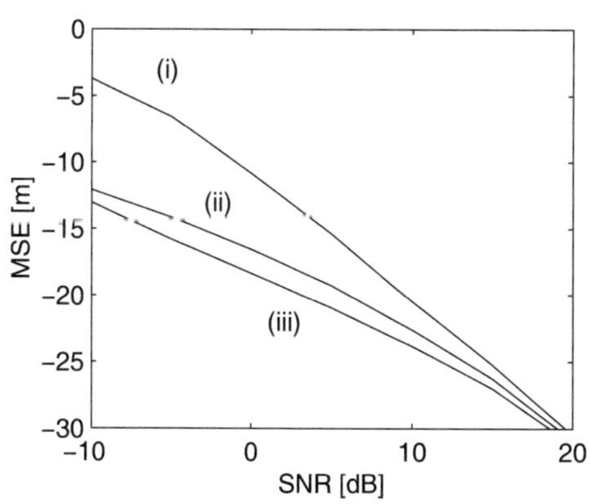

Figure 3. Mean-square-error of the position estimate versus input signal to noise ratio for Example 2: (i) noisy dead reckoning data, (ii) Kalman filter, and (iii) minimum-variance smoother (69).

"I do not think that the wireless waves that I have discovered will have any practical application." *Heinrich Rudolf Hertz*

7.6 Performance Comparison

It has been demonstrated by the previous examples that the optimal fixed-interval smoother provides a performance improvement over the maximum-likelihood smoother. The remaining example of this section compares the behaviour of the fixed-lag and the optimum fixed-interval smoother.

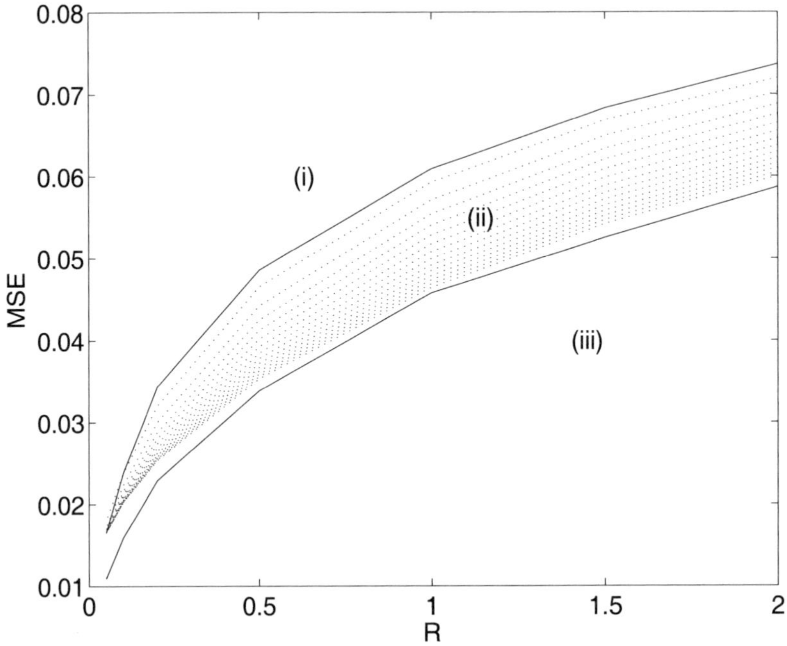

Figure 4. Mean-square-error versus measurement noise covariance for Example 3: (i) Kalman filter, (ii) fixed-lag smoothers, and (iii) optimal minimum-variance smoother (67).

Example 3. Simulations were conducted for a first-order output estimation problem, in which $A = 0.95$, $B = 1$, $C = 0.1$, $Q = 1$, $R = \{0.01, 0.02, 0.5, 1, 1.5, 2\}$ and $N = 20{,}000$. The mean-square-errors exhibited by the Kalman filter and the optimum fixed-interval smoother (69) are indicated by the top and bottom solid lines of Fig. 4, respectively. Fourteen fixed-lag smoother output error covariances, $CP_{k+1/k}^{(i+1,i+1)}C^T$, $i = 2 \ldots 15$, were calculated from (35) – (36) and are indicated by the dotted lines of Fig. 4. The figure illustrates that the fixed-lag smoother mean-square errors are bounded above and below by those of the Kalman filter and optimal fixed-interval smoother, respectively. Thus, an option for asymptotically attaining optimal performance is to employ Moore's reduced-order fixed-lag solution [1] – [3] with a sufficiently long lag.

"You see, wire telegraph is a kind of a very, very long cat. You pull his tail in New York and his head is meowing in Los Angeles. Do you understand this? And radio operates exactly the same way: you send signals here, they receive them there. The only difference is that there is no cat." *Albert Einstein*

	ASSUMPTIONS	MAIN RESULTS
Signals and system	$E\{w_k\} = E\{v_k\} = 0$. $E\{w_k w_k^T\} = Q_k > 0$ and $E\{v_k v_k^T\} = R_k > 0$ are known. A_k, B_k, $C_{1,k}$ and $C_{2,k}$ are known.	$x_{k+1} = A_k x_k + B_k w_k$ $y_{2,k} = C_{2,k} x_k$ $z_k = y_{2,k} + v_k$ $y_{1,k} = C_{1,k} x_k$
RTS smoother	Assumes that the filtered and smoothed states are normally distributed. $\hat{x}_{k+1/k}$ previously calculated by Kalman filter.	$\hat{x}_{k/N} = \hat{x}_{k/k} + G_k(\hat{x}_{k+1/N} - \hat{x}_{k+1/k})$ $\hat{y}_{1,k/N} = C_{1,k}\hat{x}_{k/N}$
FP smoother	$\hat{x}_{k/k}$ and $\xi_{k/k-1}$ previously calculated by forward and backward Kalman filters.	$\hat{x}_{k/N} = (P_{k/k}^{-1} + \Sigma_{k/k-1}^{-1})^{-1}(P_{k/k}^{-1}\hat{x}_{k/k} + \Sigma_{k/k-1}^{-1}\xi_{k/k-1})$ $\hat{y}_{1,k/N} = C_{1,k}\hat{x}_{k/N}$
Optimal minimum-variance smoother		$\begin{bmatrix} x_{k+1/k} \\ \alpha_k \end{bmatrix} = \begin{bmatrix} A_k - K_k C_{2,k} & K_k \\ -\Omega_k^{-1/2} C_{2,k} & \Omega_k^{-1/2} \end{bmatrix} \begin{bmatrix} x_{k/k-1} \\ z_k \end{bmatrix}$ $\begin{bmatrix} \xi_{k-1} \\ \beta_k \end{bmatrix} = \begin{bmatrix} A_k^T - C_{2,k}^T K_k^T & C_{2,k}^T \Omega_k^{-1/2} \\ -K_k^T & \Omega_k^{-1/2} \end{bmatrix} \begin{bmatrix} \xi_k \\ \alpha_k \end{bmatrix}$ $\hat{y}_{2,k/N} = z_k - R_k \beta_k$ $\hat{w}_{k/N} = Q\mathcal{G}_2^H \hat{\Delta}^{-H}\alpha_k$ $\hat{x}_{k+1/N} = A_k \hat{x}_{k/N} + B_k \hat{w}_{k/N}$ $\hat{y}_{1,k/N} = C_{1,k}\hat{x}_{k/N}$

Table 1. Main results for discrete-time fixed-interval smoothing.

7.7 Conclusion

Solutions to the fixed-point and fixed-lag smoothing problems can be found by applying the standard Kalman filter recursions to augmented systems. Where possible, it is shown that the smoother error covariances are less than the filter error covariance, namely, the fixed-point and fixed-lag smoothers provide a performance improvement over the filter.

Table 1 summarises three common fixed-interval smoothers that operate on measurements $z_k = y_{2,k} + v_k$ of a system $\mathcal{G}_2$ realised by $x_{k+1} = A_k x_k + B_k w_k$ and $y_{2,k} = C_{2,k} x_k$. Monzingo modified the Fraser-Potter smoother solution so that each measurement is only used once. Rauch, Tung and Striebel employed the maximum-likelihood method to derive their fixed-interval

"To invent, you need a good imagination and a pile of junk." *Thomas Alva Edison*

smoother in which $G_k = P_{k/k}A_{k+1}^{T}P_{k+1/k}^{-1}$ is a gain matrix. Although this is not a minimum-mean-square-error solution, it outperforms the Kalman filter and can provide close to optimal performance whenever the underlying assumptions are reasonable.

The minimum-variance smoothers are state-space generalisations of the optimal noncausal Wiener solutions. They make use of the inverse of the approximate Wiener-Hopf factor $\hat{\Delta}^{-1}$ and its adjoint $\hat{\Delta}^{-H}$. These smoothers achieve the best-possible performance, however, they are not minimum-order solutions. Consequently, any performance benefits need to be reconciled against the increased complexity.

7.8 Problems

Problem 1.

(i) Simplify the fixed-lag smoother

$$\begin{bmatrix} \hat{x}_{k+1/k} \\ \hat{x}_{k/k} \\ \hat{x}_{k-1/k} \\ \vdots \\ \hat{x}_{k-N+1/k} \end{bmatrix} = \begin{bmatrix} A_k & 0 & \cdots & & 0 \\ I_n & 0 & & & 0 \\ 0 & I_n & & & \vdots \\ \vdots & \vdots & \ddots & & \\ 0 & 0 & & I_n & 0 \end{bmatrix} \begin{bmatrix} \hat{x}_{k/k-1} \\ \hat{x}_{k-1/k-1} \\ \hat{x}_{k-2/k-1} \\ \vdots \\ \hat{x}_{k-N/k-1} \end{bmatrix} + \begin{bmatrix} K_{0,k} \\ K_{1,k} \\ K_{2,k} \\ \vdots \\ K_{N,k} \end{bmatrix} (z_k - C_k\hat{x}_{k/k-1})$$

to obtain an expression for the components of the smoothed state.

(ii) Derive expressions for the two predicted error covariance submatrices of interest.

Problem 2.

(i) With the quantities defined in Section 4 and the assumptions $\hat{x}_{k+1/N} \sim \mathcal{N}(A_k\hat{x}_{k/N}, B_kQ_kB_k^T)$, $\hat{x}_{k/N} \sim \mathcal{N}(\hat{x}_{k/k}, P_{k/k})$, use the maximum-likelihood method to derive

$$\hat{x}_{k/N} = (I + P_{k/k}A_k^T(B_kQ_kB_k^T)^{-1}A_k)^{-1}(\hat{x}_{k/N} + P_{k/k}A_k^TB_kQ_kB_k^T)^{-1}\hat{x}_{k/N})^T .$$

(i) Use the Matrix Inversion Lemma to obtain Rauch, Tung and Striebel's smoother

$$\hat{x}_{k/N} = \hat{x}_{k/k} + G_k(\hat{x}_{k+1/N} - \hat{x}_{k+1/k}) .$$

(ii) Employ the additional assumptions $E\{\tilde{x}_{k/k}\hat{x}_{k/k}^T\} = 0$, $E\{\tilde{x}_{k+1/N}\hat{x}_{k+1/N}^T\}$ and $E\{\tilde{x}_{k+1/N}\hat{x}_{k/N}^T\}$ to show that $E\{\hat{x}_{k+1/k}\hat{x}_{k+1/k}^T\} = E\{x_{k+1}x_{k+1}^T\} - P_{k+1/k}$, $E\{\hat{x}_{k+1/N}\hat{x}_{k+1/N}^T\} = E\{x_{k+1}x_{k+1}^T\} - \Sigma_{k+1/N}$ and $\Sigma_{k/N} = P_{k/k} - G_k(P_{k+1/k} - \Sigma_{k+1/N})G_k^T$.

"My invention, (the motion picture camera), can be exploited for a certain time as a scientific curiosity, but apart from that it has no commercial value whatsoever." *August Marie Louis Nicolas Lumiere*

(iii) Use $G_k = A_k^{-1}(I - B_kQ_kB_k^TP_{k+1/k}^{-1})$ and $\hat{x}_{k+1/N} = \hat{x}_{k+1/k+1} + P_{k+1/k}\lambda_{k+1/N}$ to confirm that the smoothed estimate within

$$\begin{bmatrix} \hat{x}_{k+1/N} \\ \lambda_{k/N} \end{bmatrix} = \begin{bmatrix} A_k & B_kQ_kB_k^T \\ -C_k^TR_k^{-1}C_k & A_k^T \end{bmatrix} \begin{bmatrix} \hat{x}_{k+1/N} \\ \lambda_{k+1/N} \end{bmatrix} + \begin{bmatrix} 0 \\ C_k^TR_k^{-1}z_k \end{bmatrix}$$

is equivalent to Rauch, Tung and Striebel's maximum-likelihood solution.

Problem 3. Let $a = \mathcal{G}_0 w$ denote the output of linear time-varying system having the realisation $x_{k+1} = A_kx_k + w_k$, $y_k = x_k$. Verify that $P_k - A_kP_kA_k^T = A_kP_k\mathcal{G}_0^{-H} + \mathcal{G}_0^{-1}P_kA_k^T + \mathcal{G}_0^{-1}P_k\mathcal{G}_0^{-H}$.

Problem 4. For the model (1) – (2). assume that $D_k = 0$, $E\{w_k\} = E\{v_k\} = 0$, $E\{w_kw_k^T\} = Q_k\delta_{jk}$, $E\{v_jv_k^T\} = R_k\delta_{jk}$ and $E\{w_kv_k^T\} = 0$. Use the result of Problem 3 to show that $\hat{\Delta}\hat{\Delta}^H = \Delta\Delta^H - C_k\mathcal{G}_0(P_{k/k-1} - P_{k+1/k})\mathcal{G}_0^HC_k^T$.

Problem 5. Under the assumptions of Problem 4, obtain an expression relating $\hat{\Delta}\hat{\Delta}^H$ and $\Delta\Delta^H$ for the case where $D_k \neq 0$.

Problem 6. From $\mathcal{R}_{ei} = -[\mathcal{H} \;\; \mathcal{H}\mathcal{G}_2 - \mathcal{G}_1]$, $\mathcal{R}_{ei}\mathcal{R}_{ei}^H = \mathcal{R}_{ei1}\mathcal{R}_{ei1}^H + \mathcal{R}_{ei2}\mathcal{R}_{ei2}^H$ and $\mathcal{R}_{ei2} = \mathcal{H}\Delta - \mathcal{G}_1Q\mathcal{G}_2^H\Delta^{-H}$, obtain the optimal realisable smoother solutions for output estimation, input estimation and state estimation problems.

7.9 Glossary

$p(x_k)$	Probability density function of a discrete random variable x_k.
$x_k \sim \mathcal{N}(\mu, R_{xx})$	The random variable x_k has a normal distribution with mean μ and covariance R_{xx}.
$\Omega_{k/k}$	Error covariance of the fixed-point smoother.
$P_{k+1/k}^{(i,i)}$	Error covariance of the fixed-lag smoother.
$\hat{w}_{k/N}$, $\hat{x}_{k/N}$, $\hat{y}_{k/N}$	Estimates of w_k, x_k and y_k at time k, given data z_k over an interval $k \in [0, N]$.
G_k	Gain of the smoother developed by Rauch, Tung and Striebel.
α_k	Output of $\hat{\Delta}^{-1}$, the inverse of the approximate Wiener-Hopf factor.
β_k	Output of $\hat{\Delta}^{-H}$, the adjoint of the inverse of the approximate Wiener-Hopf factor.
$C_k^{\#}$	Moore-Penrose pseudoinverse of C_k.

"The cinema is little more than a fad. It's canned drama. What audiences really want to see is flesh and blood on the stage." *Charles Spencer (Charlie) Chaplin*

$\mathcal{R}_{ei}$ A system (or map) that operates on the problem inputs $i = \begin{bmatrix} v \\ w \end{bmatrix}$ to produce an estimation error e. It is convenient to make use of the factorisation $\mathcal{R}_{ei}\mathcal{R}_{ei}^H = \mathcal{R}_{ei1}\mathcal{R}_{ei1}^H + \mathcal{R}_{ei2}\mathcal{R}_{ei2}^H$, where $\mathcal{R}_{ei2}\mathcal{R}_{ei2}^H$ includes the filter/smoother solution and $\mathcal{R}_{ei1}\mathcal{R}_{ei1}^H$ is a lower performance bound.

7.10 References

[1] B. D. O. Anderson and J. B. Moore, *Optimal Filtering*, Prentice-Hall Inc, Englewood Cliffs, New Jersey, 1979.

[2] J. B. Moore, "Fixed-Lag Smoothing Results for Linear Dynamical Systems", *A.T.R.*, vol. 7, no. 2, pp. 16 – 21, 1973.

[3] J. B. Moore, "Discrete-Time Fixed-Lag Smoothing Algorithms", *Automatica*, vol. 9, pp. 163 – 173, 1973.

[4] D. C. Fraser and J. E. Potter, "The Optimum Linear Smoother as a Combination of Two Optimum Linear Filters", *IEEE Transactions on Automatic Control*, vol. AC-14, no. 4, pp. 387 – 390, Aug., 1969.

[5] H. E. Rauch, "Solutions to the Linear Smoothing Problem", *IEEE Transactions on Automatic Control*, vol. 8, no. 4, pp. 371 – 372, Oct.1963.

[6] H. E. Rauch, F. Tung and C. T. Striebel, "Maximum Likelihood Estimates of Linear Dynamic Systems", *AIAA Journal*, vol. 3, no. 8, pp. 1445 – 1450, Aug., 1965.

[7] G. A. Einicke, "Optimal and Robust Noncausal Filter Formulations", *IEEE Transactions on Signal Process.*, vol. 54, no. 3, pp. 1069 - 1077, Mar. 2006.

[8] G. A. Einicke, "Asymptotic Optimality of the Minimum Variance Fixed-Interval Smoother", *IEEE Transactions on Signal Process.*, vol. 55, no. 4, pp. 1543 – 1547, Apr. 200

[9] G. A. Einicke, J. C. Ralston, C. O. Hargrave, D. C. Reid and D. W. Hainsworth, "Longwall Mining Automation, An Application of Minimum-Variance Smoothing", *IEEE Control Systems Magazine*, vol. 28, no. 6, pp. 28 – 37, Dec. 2008.

[10] H. K. Wimmer, "Monotonicity and Maximality of Solutions of Discrete-Time Algebraic Riccati Equations", *Journal of Mathematics, Systems, Estimation and Control*, vol. 2, no. 2, pp. 219 – 235, 1992

[11] H. K. Wimmer and M. Pavon, "A comparison theorem for matrix Riccati difference equations", *Systems & Control Letters*, vol. 19, pp. 233 – 239, 1992.

[12] L. E. Zachrisson, "On Optimal Smoothing of Continuous Time Kalman Processes, *Information Sciences*, vol. 1, pp. 143 – 172, 1969.

[13] A. P. Sage and J. L. Melsa, *Estimation Theory with Applications to Communications and Control*, McGraw-Hill Book Company, New York, 1971.

[14] A. Asif, "Fast Rauch-Tung-Striebel Smoother-Base Image Restoration for Noncausal Images", *IEEE Signal Processing Letters*, vol. 11, no. 3, pp. 371 – 374, Mar. 2004.

[15] T. Kailath, A. H. Sayed and B. Hassibi, *Linear Estimation*, Prentice-Hall, Inc., Upper Saddle River, New Jersey, 2000.

[16] R. A. Monzingo, "Discrete Optimal Linear Smoothing for Systems with Uncertain Observations", *IEEE Transactions on Information Theory*, vol. 21, no. 3, pp. 271 – 275, May 1975.

"Who the hell wants to hear actors talk?" *Harry Morris Warner*

8

Parameter Estimation

8.1 Introduction

Predictors, filters and smoothers have previously been described for state recovery under the assumption that the parameters of the generating models are correct. More often than not, the problem parameters are unknown and need to be identified. This section describes some standard statistical techniques for parameter estimation. Paradoxically, the discussed parameter estimation methods rely on having complete state information available. Although this is akin to a chicken-and-egg argument (state availability obviates the need for filters along with their attendant requirements for identified models), the task is not insurmountable.

The role of solution designers is to provide a cost benefit. That is, their objectives are to deliver improved performance at an acceptable cost. Inevitably, this requires simplifications so that the problems become sufficiently tractable and amenable to feasible solution. For example, suppose that speech emanating from a radio is too noisy and barely intelligible. In principle, high-order models could be proposed to equalise the communication channel, demodulate the baseband signal and recover the phonemes. Typically, low-order solutions tend to offer better performance because of the difficulty in identifying large numbers of parameters under low-SNR conditions. Consider also the problem of monitoring the output of a gas sensor and triggering alarms when environmental conditions become hazardous. Complex models could be constructed to take into account diurnal pressure variations, local weather influences and transients due to passing vehicles. It often turns out that low-order solutions exhibit lower false alarm rates because there are fewer assumptions susceptible to error.

Thus, the absence of complete information need not inhibit solution development. Simple schemes may suffice, such as conducting trials with candidate parameter values and assessing the consequent error performance.

In maximum-likelihood estimation [1] - [5], unknown parameters θ_1, θ_2, …, θ_M, are identified given states, x_k, by maximising a log-likelihood function, $\log f(\theta_1, \theta_2, \ldots, \theta_M \mid x_k)$. For example, the subject of noise variance estimation was studied by Mehra in [6], where maximum-likelihood estimates (MLEs) were updated using the Newton-Raphson method. Rife and Boorstyn obtained Cramér-Rao bounds for some MLEs, which "indicate the best estimation that can be made with the available data" [7]. Nayak *et al* used the pseudo-

---

"The sciences do not try to explain, they hardly even try to interpret, they mainly make models. By a model is meant a mathematical construct which, with the addition of certain verbal interpretations, describes observed phenomena. The justification of such a mathematical construct is solely and precisely that it is expected to work" *John Von Neuman*

inverse to estimate unknown parameters in [8]. Belangér subsequently employed a least-squares approach to estimate the process noise and measurement noise variances [9]. A recursive technique for least-squares parameter estimation was developed by Strejc [10]. Dempster, Laird and Rubin [11] proved the convergence of a general purpose technique for solving joint state and parameter estimation problems, which they called the expectation-maximization (EM) algorithm. They addressed problems where complete (state) information is not available to calculate the log-likelihood and instead maximised the expectation of $\log f(\theta_1, \theta_2, ..., \theta_M \mid z_k)$, given incomplete measurements, z_k. That is, by virtue of Jensen's inequality the unknowns are found by using an objective function (also called an approximate log-likelihood function), $E\{\log f(\theta_1, \theta_2, ..., \theta_M \mid z_k)\}$, as a surrogate for $\log f(\theta_1, \theta_2, ..., \theta_M \mid x_k)$.

The system identification literature is vast and some mature techniques have evolved. It is acknowledged that subspace identification methods have been developed for general problems where a system's stochastic inputs, deterministic inputs and outputs are available. The subspace algorithms [12] - [14] consist of two steps. First, the order of the system is identified from stacked vectors of the inputs and outputs. Then the unknown parameters are determined from an extended observability matrix.

Continuous-time maximum-likelihood estimation has been mentioned previously. Here, the attention is focussed on the specific problem of joint state and parameter estimation exclusively from discrete measurements of a system's outputs. The developments proceed as follows. Section 8.2 reviews the maximum-likelihood estimation method for obtaining unknown parameters. The same estimates can be found using the method of least squares, which was pioneered by Gauss for fitting astronomical observations. Well known (filtering) EM algorithms for variance and state matrix estimation are described in Section 8.3. Improved parameter estimation accuracy can be obtained via smoothing EM algorithms, which are introduced in Section 8.4.

The filtering and smoothing EM algorithms discussed herein require caution. When perfect state information is available, the corresponding likelihood functions are exact. However, the use of imperfect state estimates leads to approximate likelihood functions, approximate Cramér-Rao bounds and biased MLEs. When the SNR is sufficiently high and the states are recovered exactly, the bias terms within the state matrix elements and process noise variances diminish to zero. Consequently, process noise variance and state matrix estimation is recommended only when the measurement noise is negligible. Conversely, measurement noise variance estimation is advocated when the SNR is sufficiently low.

"A hen is only an egg's way of making another egg." *Samuel Butler*

8.2 Maximum-Likelihood Estimation

8.2.1 General Method

Let $p(\theta\,|\,x_k)$ denote the probability density function of an unknown parameter θ, given samples of a discrete random variable x_k. An estimate, $\hat{\theta}$, can be obtained by finding the argument θ that maximises the probability density function, that is,

$$\hat{\theta} = \arg\max_{\theta} = p(\theta\,|\,x_k)\,. \tag{1}$$

A solution can be found by setting $\frac{\partial p(\theta\,|\,x_k)}{\partial \theta}$ = 0 and solving for the unknown θ. Since the logarithm function is monotonic, a solution may be found equivalently by maximising

$$\hat{\theta} = \arg\max_{\theta} = \log p(\theta\,|\,x_k) \tag{2}$$

and setting $\frac{\partial \log p(\theta\,|\,x_k)}{\partial \theta}$ = 0. For exponential families of distributions, the use of (2) considerably simplifies the equations to be solved.

Suppose that N mutually independent samples of x_k are available, then the joint density function of all the observations is the product of the densities

$$\begin{aligned} f(\theta\,|\,x_k) &= p(\theta\,|\,x_1)p(\theta\,|\,x_2)\cdots p(\theta\,|\,x_N) \\ &= \prod_{k=1}^{K} p(\theta\,|\,x_k)\,, \end{aligned} \tag{3}$$

which serves as a likelihood function. The MLE of θ may be found maximising the log-likelihood

$$\begin{aligned} \hat{\theta} &= \arg\max_{\theta}\ \log f(\theta\,|\,x_k) \\ &= \arg\max_{\theta}\ \sum_{k=1}^{N} p(\theta\,|\,x_k) \end{aligned} \tag{4}$$

by solving for a θ that satisfies $\frac{\partial \log f(\theta\,|\,x_k)}{\partial \theta} = \frac{\partial \log \sum_{k=1}^{N} p(\theta\,|\,x_k)}{\partial \theta}$ = 0. The above maximum-likelihood approach is applicable to a wide range of distributions. For example, the task of estimating the intensity of a Poisson distribution from measurements is demonstrated below.

"Therefore I would not have it unknown to Your Holiness, the only thing which induced me to look for another way of reckoning the movements of the heavenly bodies was that I knew that mathematicians by no means agree in their investigation thereof." *Nicolaus Copernicus*"

Example 1. Suppose that N observations of integer x_k have a Poisson distribution $f(x_k) = \frac{e^{-\mu}\mu^{x_k}}{x_k!}$, where the intensity, μ, is unknown. The corresponding log-likelihood function is

$$\log f(\mu \mid x_k) = \log\left(\frac{e^{-\mu}\mu^{x_1}}{x_1!}\frac{e^{-\mu}\mu^{x_2}}{x_2!}\frac{e^{-\mu}\mu^{x_3}}{x_3!}\cdots\frac{e^{-\mu}\mu^{x_N}}{x_N!}\right)$$

$$= \log\left(\frac{1}{x_1!x_2!\cdots x_N!}\mu^{x_1+x_2+\ldots+x_N}e^{-N\mu}\right) \tag{5}$$

$$= -\log(x_1!x_2!\cdots x_N!) + \log(\mu^{x_1+x_2+\ldots+x_N}) - N\mu .$$

Taking $\frac{\partial \log f(\mu \mid x_k)}{\partial \mu} = \frac{1}{\mu}\sum_{k=1}^{N} x_k - N = 0$ yields

$$\hat{\mu} = \frac{1}{N}\sum_{k=1}^{N} x_k . \tag{6}$$

Since $\frac{\partial^2 \log f(\mu \mid x_k)}{\partial \mu^2} = -\frac{1}{\mu^2}\sum_{k=1}^{N} x_k$ is negative for all μ and $x_k \geq 0$, the stationary point (6) occurs at a maximum of (5). That is to say, $\hat{\mu}$ is indeed a maximum-likelihood estimate.

8.2.2 State Matrix Estimation

From the Central Limit Theorem, which was mentioned in Chapter 6, the mean of a sufficiently large sample of independent identically distributed random variables will asymptotically approach a normal distribution. Consequently, in many maximum-likelihood estimation applications it is assumed that random variables are normally distributed. Recall that the normal (or Gaussian) probability density function of a discrete random variable x_k with mean μ and covariance R_{xx} is

$$p(x_k) = \frac{1}{(2\pi)^{N/2}\left|R_{xx}\right|^{1/2}}\exp\left\{-\frac{1}{2}(x_k-\mu)^T R_{xx}^{-1}(x_k-\mu)\right\}, \tag{7}$$

in which $\left|R_{xx}\right|$ denotes the determinant of R_{xx}. A likelihood function for a sample of N independently identically distributed random variables is

$$f(x_k) = \prod_{k=1}^{N} p(x_k) = \frac{1}{(2\pi)^{N/2}\left|R_{xx}\right|^{N/2}}\sum_{k=1}^{N}\exp\left\{-\frac{1}{2}(x_k-\mu)^T R_{xx}^{-1}(x_k-\mu)\right\}. \tag{8}$$

In general, it is more convenient to work with the log-likelihood function

---

"How wonderful that we have met with a paradox. Now we have some hope of making progress." *Niels Henrik David Bohr*

$$\log f(x_k) = -\log\ (2\pi)^{N/2} \left|R_{xx}\right|^{N/2} - \frac{1}{2}\sum_{k=1}^{N}(x_k - \mu)^T R_{xx}^{-1}(x_k - \mu)\,. \tag{9}$$

An example of estimating a model coefficient using the Gaussian log-likelihood approach is set out below.

***Example* 2.** Consider an autoregressive order-one process $x_{k+1} = a_0 x_k + w_k$ in which it is desired to estimate $a_0 \in \mathbb{R}$ from samples of x_k. It follows from $x_{k+1} \sim \mathcal{N}(a_0 x_k,\ \sigma_w^2)$ that

$$\log f(a_0 \mid x_{k+1}) = -\log\ (2\pi)^{N/2}\sigma_w^N - \frac{1}{2}\sum_{k=1}^{N}\sigma_w^{-2}(x_{k+1} - a_0 x_k)^2\,.$$

Setting $\dfrac{\partial \log\ f(a_0 \mid x_{k+1})}{\partial a_0}$ equal to zero gives $\sum_{k=1}^{N} x_{k+1}x_k = a_0\sum_{k=1}^{N} x_k^2$ which results in the MLE

$$\hat{a}_0 = \frac{\sum_{k=1}^{N} x_{k+1}x_k}{\sum_{k=1}^{N} x_k^2}\,.$$

Often within filtering and smoothing applications there are multiple parameters to be identified. Denote the unknown parameters by $\theta_1, \theta_2, \ldots, \theta_M$, then the MLEs may be found by solving the M equations

$$\frac{\partial \log f(\theta_1, \theta_2, \cdots \theta_M \mid x_k)}{\partial \theta_1} = 0$$

$$\frac{\partial \log f(\theta_1, \theta_2, \cdots \theta_M \mid x_k)}{\partial \theta_2} = 0$$

$$\vdots$$

$$\frac{\partial \log f(\theta_1, \theta_2, \cdots \theta_M \mid x_k)}{\partial \theta_M} = 0.$$

An vector parameter estimation example is outlined below.

***Example* 3.** Consider the third-order autoregressive model

$$x_{k+3} + a_2 x_{k+2} + a_1 x_{k+1} + a_0 x_k = w_k \tag{10}$$

which can be written in the state-space form

"If we all worked on the assumption that what is accepted as true is really true, there would be little hope of advance." *Orville Wright*

$$\begin{bmatrix} x_{1,k+1} \\ x_{2,k+1} \\ x_{3,k+1} \end{bmatrix} = \begin{bmatrix} -a_2 & -a_1 & -a_0 \\ 1 & 0 & 0 \\ 0 & 1 & 0 \end{bmatrix} \begin{bmatrix} x_{1,k} \\ x_{2,k} \\ x_{3,k} \end{bmatrix} + \begin{bmatrix} w_k \\ 0 \\ 0 \end{bmatrix}. \tag{11}$$

Assuming $x_{1,k+1} \sim \mathcal{N}(-a_2 x_{1,k} - a_1 x_{2,k} - a_0 x_{3,k}, \sigma_w^2)$ and setting to zero the partial derivatives of the corresponding log-likelihood function with respect to a_0, a_1 and a_2 yields

$$-\begin{bmatrix} \sum_{k=1}^{N} x_{3,k}^2 & \sum_{k=1}^{N} x_{2,k}x_{3,k} & \sum_{k=1}^{N} x_{1,k}x_{3,k} \\ \sum_{k=1}^{N} x_{2,k}x_{3,k} & \sum_{k=1}^{N} x_{2,k}^2 & \sum_{k=1}^{N} x_{2,k}x_{1,k} \\ \sum_{k=1}^{N} x_{1,k}x_{3,k} & \sum_{k=1}^{N} x_{2,k}x_{1,k} & \sum_{k=1}^{N} x_{1,k}^2 \end{bmatrix} \begin{bmatrix} a_0 \\ a_1 \\ a_2 \end{bmatrix} = \begin{bmatrix} \sum_{k=1}^{N} x_{1,k+1}x_{3,k} \\ \sum_{k=1}^{N} x_{1,k+1}x_{2,k} \\ \sum_{k=1}^{N} x_{1,k+1}x_{1,k} \end{bmatrix}. \tag{12}$$

Hence, the MLEs are given by

$$\begin{bmatrix} \hat{a}_0 \\ \hat{a}_1 \\ \hat{a}_2 \end{bmatrix} = -\begin{bmatrix} \sum_{k=1}^{N} x_{3,k}^2 & \sum_{k=1}^{N} x_{2,k}x_{3,k} & \sum_{k=1}^{N} x_{1,k}x_{3,k} \\ \sum_{k=1}^{N} x_{2,k}x_{3,k} & \sum_{k=1}^{N} x_{2,k}^2 & \sum_{k=1}^{N} x_{2,k}x_{1,k} \\ \sum_{k=1}^{N} x_{1,k}x_{3,k} & \sum_{k=1}^{N} x_{2,k}x_{1,k} & \sum_{k=1}^{N} x_{1,k}^2 \end{bmatrix}^{-1} \begin{bmatrix} \sum_{k=1}^{N} x_{1,k+1}x_{3,k} \\ \sum_{k=1}^{N} x_{1,k+1}x_{2,k} \\ \sum_{k=1}^{N} x_{1,k+1}x_{1,k} \end{bmatrix}. \tag{13}$$

8.2.3 Variance Estimation

MLEs can be similarly calculated for unknown variances, as is demonstrated by the following example.

Example 4. Consider a random variable generated by $x_k = \mu + w_k$ where $\mu \in \mathbb{R}$ is fixed and $w_k \in \mathbb{R}$ is assumed to be a zero-mean Gaussian white input sequence. Since $x_k \sim \mathcal{N}(\mu, \sigma_w^2)$, it follows that

$$\log f(\sigma_w^2 \mid x_k) = -\frac{N}{2}\log 2\pi - \frac{N}{2}\log \sigma_w^2 - \frac{1}{2}\sigma_w^{-2}\sum_{k=1}^{N}(x_k - \mu)^2$$

and

$$\frac{\partial \log f(\sigma_w^2 \mid x_k)}{\partial \sigma_w^2} = -\frac{N}{2}(\sigma_w^2)^{-1} + \frac{1}{2}(\sigma_w^2)^{-2}\sum_{k=1}^{N}(x_k - \mu)^2 .$$

From the solution of $\frac{\partial \log f(\sigma_w^2 \mid x_k)}{\partial \sigma_w^2} = 0$, the MLE is

"In science one tries to tell people, in such a way as to be understood by everyone, something that no-one knew before. But in poetry, it's the exact opposite." *Paul Adrien Maurice Dirac*

$$\hat{\sigma}_w^2 = \frac{1}{N}\sum_{k=1}^{N}(x_k - \mu)^2 \text{, without replacement.} \quad (14)$$

If the random samples are taken from a population without replacement, the samples are not independent, the covariance between two different samples is nonzero and the MLE (14) is biased. If the sampling is done with replacement then the sample values are independent and the following correction applies

$$\hat{\sigma}_w^2 = \frac{1}{N-1}\sum_{k=1}^{N}(x_k - \mu)^2 \text{, with replacement.} \quad (15)$$

The corrected denominator within the above sample variance is only noticeable for small sample sizes, as the difference between (14) and (15) is negligible for large N. The MLE (15) is unbiased, that is, its expected value equals the variance of the population. To confirm this property, observe that

$$\begin{aligned} E\{\sigma_w^2\} &= E\left\{\frac{1}{N-1}\sum_{k=1}^{N}(x_k - \mu)^2\right\} \\ &= E\left\{\frac{1}{N-1}\sum_{k=1}^{N}x_k^2 - 2\mu x_k + \mu^2\right\} \\ &= \frac{N}{N-1}(E\{x_k^2\} - E\{\mu^2\}). \end{aligned} \quad (16)$$

Using $E\{x_k^2\} = \sigma_w^2 + \bar{x}^2$, $E\{E\{x_k^2\}\} = E\{\sigma_w^2\} + E\{\mu\}^2$, $E\{E\{x_k^2\}\} = E\{\mu^2\} = \mu^2$ and $E\{\sigma_w^2\} = \sigma_w^2/N$ within (16) yields $E\{\sigma_w^2\} = \sigma_w^2$ as required. Unless stated otherwise, it is assumed herein that the sample size is sufficiently large so that $N^{-1} \approx (N - 1)^{-1}$ and (15) may be approximated by (14). A caution about modelling error contributing bias is mentioned below.

Example 5. Suppose that the states considered in Example 4 are actually generated by $x_k = \mu + w_k + s_k$, where s_k is an independent input that accounts for the presence of modelling error. In this case, the assumption $x_k \sim \mathcal{N}(\mu, \sigma_w^2 + \sigma_s^2)$ leads to $\hat{\sigma}_w^2 + \hat{\sigma}_s^2 = \frac{1}{N}\sum_{k=1}^{N}(x_k - \mu)^2$, in which case (14) is no longer an unbiased estimate of σ_w^2.

8.2.4 Cramér-Rao Lower Bound

The Cramér-Rao Lower Bound (CRLB) establishes a limit of precision that can be achieved for any unbiased estimate of a parameter θ. It actually defines a lower bound for the variance $\sigma_{\hat{\theta}}^2$ of $\hat{\theta}$. As is pointed out in [1], since $\hat{\theta}$ is assumed to be unbiased, the variance $\sigma_{\hat{\theta}}^2$ equals the parameter error variance. Determining lower bounds for parameter error

"Everyone hears only what he understands." *Johann Wolfgang von Goethe*

variances is useful for model selection. Another way of selecting models involves comparing residual error variances [23]. A lucid introduction to Gaussian CRLBs is presented in [2]. An extensive survey that refers to the pioneering contributions of Fisher, Cramér and Rao appears in [4].

The bounds on the parameter variances are found from the inverse of the so-called Fisher information. A formal definition of the CRLB for scalar parameters is as follows.

Theorem 1 (Cramér-Rao Lower Bound) [2] - [5]: Assume that $f(\theta | x_k)$ satisfies the following regularity conditions:

(i) $\dfrac{\partial \log f(\theta | x_k)}{\partial \theta}$ *and* $\dfrac{\partial^2 \log f(\theta | x_k)}{\partial \theta^2}$ *exist for all* θ, *and*

(ii) $E\left\{\dfrac{\partial \log f(\theta | x_k)}{\partial \theta}\right\} = 0$, *for all* θ.

Define the Fisher information by

$$F(\theta) = -E\left\{\frac{\partial^2 \log f(\theta | x_k)}{\partial \theta^2}\right\}, \tag{17}$$

where the derivative is evaluated at the actual value of θ. *Then the variance* $\sigma^2_{\hat{\theta}}$ *of an unbiased estimate* $\hat{\theta}$ *satisfies*

$$\sigma^2_{\hat{\theta}} \ge F^{-1}(\theta) . \tag{18}$$

Proofs for the above theorem appear in [2] – [5].

Example 6. Suppose that samples of $x_k = \mu + w_k$ are available, where w_k is a zero-mean Gaussian white input sequence and $\mu \in \mathbb{R}$ is unknown. Since $w_k \sim \mathcal{N}(0, \sigma^2_w)$,

$$\log f(\mu | x_k) = -\frac{N}{2}\log 2\pi - \frac{N}{2}\log \sigma^2_w - \frac{1}{2}\sigma^{-2}_w \sum_{k=1}^{N}(x_k - \mu)^2$$

and

$$\frac{\partial \log f(\mu | x_k)}{\partial \mu} = \sigma^{-2}_w \sum_{k=1}^{N}(x_k - \mu) .$$

Setting $\dfrac{\partial \log f(\mu | x_k)}{\partial \mu} = 0$ yields the MLE

$$\hat{\mu} = \frac{1}{N}\sum_{k=1}^{N} x_k , \tag{19}$$

"Wall street people learn nothing and forget everything." *Benjamin Graham*

which is unbiased because $E\{\hat{\mu}\} = E\left\{\frac{1}{N}\sum_{k=1}^{N} x_k\right\} = E\left\{\frac{1}{N}\sum_{k=1}^{N} \mu\right\} = \mu$. From Theorem 1, the Fisher information is

$$F(\mu) = E\left\{-\frac{\partial^2 \log f(\mu \mid x_k)}{\partial \mu^2}\right\} = E\{N\sigma_w^{-2}\} = N\sigma_w^{-2}$$

and therefore

$$\sigma_{\hat{\mu}}^2 \geq \sigma_w^2 / N. \tag{20}$$

The above inequality suggests that a minimum of one sample is sufficient to bound the variance of the MLE (19). It is also apparent from (20) that the error variance of $\hat{\mu}$ decreases withincreasing sample size.

The CRLB is extended for estimating a vector of parameters $\theta_1, \theta_2, \ldots, \theta_M$ by defining the $M \times M$ Fisher information matrix

$$\begin{bmatrix} \hat{x}_{k+1/k}^{(u)} \\ \hat{x}_{k/k}^{(u)} \end{bmatrix} = \begin{bmatrix} (A - K_k^{(u)}C) & K_k^{(u)} \\ (I - L_k^{(u)}C) & L_k^{(u)} \end{bmatrix} \begin{bmatrix} \hat{x}_{k/k-1}^{(u)} \\ z_k \end{bmatrix}, \tag{21}$$

for $i, j = 1 \ldots M$. The parameter error variances are then bounded by the diagonal elements of Fisher information matrix inverse

$$\sigma_{\hat{\theta}_i}^2 \geq F_{ii}^{-1}(\theta). \tag{22}$$

Formal vector CRLB theorems and accompanying proofs are detailed in [2] – [5].

Example 7. Consider the problem of estimating both μ and σ_w^2 from N samples of $x_k = \mu + w_k$, with $w_k \sim \mathcal{N}(0, \sigma_w^2)$. Recall from Example 6 that

$$\log f(\mu, \sigma_w^2 \mid x_k) = -\frac{N}{2}\log 2\pi - \frac{N}{2}\log \sigma_w^2 - \frac{1}{2}\sigma_w^{-2}\sum_{k=1}^{N}(x_k - \mu)^2.$$

Therefore, $\frac{\partial \log f(\mu, \sigma_w^2 \mid x_k)}{\partial \mu} = \sigma_w^{-2}\sum_{k=1}^{N}(x_k - \mu)$ and $\frac{\partial^2 \log f(\mu, \sigma_w^2 \mid x_k)}{\partial \mu^2} = -N\sigma_w^{-2}$. In Example 4 it is found that $\frac{\partial \log f(\mu, \sigma_w^2 \mid x_k)}{\partial \sigma_w^2} = -\frac{N}{2}(\sigma_w^2)^{-1} + \frac{1}{2}(\sigma_w^2)^{-2}\sum_{k=1}^{N}(x_k - \mu)^2$, which implies

$$\frac{\partial^2 \log f(\mu, \sigma_w^2 \mid x_k)}{\partial (\sigma_w^2)^2} = \frac{N}{2}(\sigma_w^2)^{-2} - (\sigma_w^2)^{-3}\sum_{k=1}^{N}(x_k - \mu)^2$$

"Laying in bed this morning contemplating how amazing it would be if somehow Oscar Wilde and Mae West could twitter from the grave." *@DitaVonTeese*

$$= \frac{N}{2}(\sigma_w^2)^{-2} - N(\sigma_w^2)^{-2}$$

$$= -\frac{N}{2}\sigma_w^{-4},$$

$$\frac{\partial^2 \log f(\mu,\sigma_w^2 \mid x_k)}{\partial\mu\partial\sigma_w^2} = -(\sigma_w^2)^{-2}\sum_{k=1}^{N}(x_k - \mu) \text{ and } E\left\{\frac{\partial^2 \log f(\mu,\sigma_w^2 \mid x_k)}{\partial\mu\partial\sigma_w^2}\right\} = 0.$$

The Fisher information matrix and its inverse are then obtained from (21) as

$$F(u,\sigma_w^2) = \begin{bmatrix} N\sigma_w^{-2} & 0 \\ 0 & 0.5N\sigma_w^{-4} \end{bmatrix},\ F^{-1}(u,\sigma_w^2) = \begin{bmatrix} \sigma_w^2 / N & 0 \\ 0 & 2\sigma_w^4 / N \end{bmatrix}.$$

It is found from (22) that the lower bounds for the MLE variances are $\sigma_{\hat{\mu}}^2 \geq \sigma_w^2 / N$ and $\sigma_{\hat{\sigma}_w^2}^2 \geq 2\sigma_w^4 / N$. The impact of modelling error on parameter estimation accuracy is examined below.

Example 8. Consider the problem of estimating σ_w^2 given samples of states which are generated by $x_k = \mu + w_k + s_k$, where s_k is an independent sequence that accounts for the presence of modelling error. From the assumption $x_k \sim \mathcal{N}(\mu,\ \sigma_w^2 + \sigma_s^2)$, the associated log likelihood function is

$$\frac{\partial \log f(\sigma_w^2 \mid x_k)}{\partial \sigma_w^2} = -\frac{N}{2}(\sigma_w^2 + \sigma_s^2)^{-1} + \frac{1}{2}(\sigma_w^2 + \sigma_s^2)^{-2}\sum_{k=1}^{N}(x_k - \mu)^2,$$

which leads to $\frac{\partial^2 \log f(\sigma_w^2 \mid x_k)}{\partial(\sigma_w^2)^2} = -\frac{N}{2}(\sigma_w^2 + \sigma_s^2)^{-2}$, that is, $\sigma_{\hat{\sigma}_w^2}^2 \geq 2(\sigma_w^2 + \sigma_s^2)^2 / N$. Thus, parameter estimation accuracy degrades as the variance of the modelling error increases. If σ_s^2 is available *a priori* then setting $\frac{\partial \log f(\sigma_w^2 \mid x_k)}{\partial \sigma_w^2} = 0$ leads to the improved estimate

$$\hat{\sigma}_w^2 = -\sigma_s^2 + \frac{1}{N}\sum_{k=1}^{K}(x_k - \mu)^2.$$

"There are only two kinds of people who are really fascinating; people who know absolutely everything, and people who know absolutely nothing." *Oscar Fingal O'Flahertie Wills Wilde*

8.3 Filtering EM Algorithms

8.3.1 Background

The EM algorithm [3], [7], [11], [15] - [17], [19] - [22] is a general purpose technique for solving joint state and parameter estimation problems. In maximum-likelihood estimation, it is desired to estimate parameters $\theta_1, \theta_2, \ldots, \theta_M$, given states by maximising the log-likelihood $\log f(\theta_1, \theta_2, \ldots, \theta_M \mid x_k)$. When complete state information is not available to calculate the log-likelihood, the expectation of $\log f(\theta_1, \theta_2, \ldots, \theta_M \mid x_k)$, given incomplete measurements, z_k, is maximised instead. This basic technique was in use prior to Dempster, Laird and Rubin naming it the EM algorithm 1977 [11]. They published a general formulation of the algorithm, which consists of iterating an expectation step and a maximization step. Their expectation step involves least squares calculations on the incomplete observations using the current parameter iterations to estimate the underlying states. In the maximization step, the unknown parameters are re-estimated by maximising a joint log likelihood function using state estimates from the previous expectation step. This sequence is repeated for either a finite number of iterations or until the estimates and the log likelihood function are stable. Dempster, Laird and Rubin [11] also established parameter map conditions for the convergence of the algorithm, namely that the incomplete data log likelihood function is monotonically nonincreasing.

Wu [16] subsequently noted an equivalence between the conditions for a map to be closed and the continuity of a function. In particular, if the likelihood function satisfies certain modality, continuity and differentiability conditions, the parameter sequence converges to some stationary value. A detailed analysis of Wu's convergence results appears in [3]. Shumway and Stoffer [15] introduced a framework that is employed herein, namely, the use of a Kalman filter within the expectation step to recover the states. Feder and Weinstein [17] showed how a multiparameter estimation problem can be decoupled into separate maximum likelihood estimations within an EM algorithm. Some results on the convergence of EM algorithms for variance and state matrix estimation [19] - [20] are included within the developments below.

8.3.2 Measurement Noise Variance Estimation

8.3.2.1 EM Algorithm

The problem of estimating parameters from incomplete information has been previously studied in [11] - [16]. It is noted in [11] that the likelihood functions for variance estimation do not exist in explicit closed form. This precludes straightforward calculation of the Hessians required in [3] to assert convergence. Therefore, an alternative analysis is presented here to establish the monotonicity of variance iterations.

The expectation step described below employs the approach introduced in [15] and involves the use of a Kalman filter to obtain state estimates. The maximization step requires the calculation of decoupled MLEs similarly to [17]. Measurements of a linear time-invariant system are modelled by

---

"I'm no model lady. A model is just an imitation of the real thing." *Mary (Mae) Jane West*

$$x_{k+1} = Ax_k + Bw_k, \tag{23}$$

$$y_k = Cx_k + Dw_k, \tag{24}$$

$$z_k = y_k + v_k, \tag{25}$$

where $A \in \mathbb{R}^{n\times n}$, $B \in \mathbb{R}^{n\times m}$, $C \in \mathbb{R}^{p\times n}$, $D \in \mathbb{R}^{p\times m}$ and w_k, v_k are stationary processes with $E\{w_k\} = 0$, $E\{w_j w_k^T\} = Q\delta_{jk}$, $E\{v_k\} = E\{w_j v_k^T\} = 0$ and $E\{v_j v_k^T\} = R\delta_{jk}$. To simplify the presentation, it is initially assumed that the direct feed-through matrix, D, is zero. A nonzero D will be considered later.

Suppose that it is desired to estimate $R = \text{diag}(\sigma_{1,v}^2, \sigma_{2,v}^2, \ldots, \sigma_{p,v}^2)$ given N samples of z_k and y_k. Let $z_{i,k}$, $y_{i,k}$ and $v_{i,k}$ denote the ith element of the vectors z_k, y_k and v_k, respectively. Then (25) may be written in terms of its i components, $z_{i,k} = y_{i,k} + v_{i,k}$, that is,

$$v_{i,k} = z_{i,k} - y_{i,k}. \tag{26}$$

From the assumption $v_{i,k} \sim \mathcal{N}(0, \sigma_{i,v}^2)$, an MLE for the unknown $\sigma_{i,v}^2$ is obtained from the sample variance formula

$$\hat{\sigma}_{i,v}^2 = \frac{1}{N}\sum_{k=1}^{N}(z_{i,k} - y_{i,k})^2. \tag{27}$$

An EM algorithm for updating the measurement noise variance estimates is described as follows. Assume that there exists an estimate $\hat{R}^{(u)} = \text{diag}((\hat{\sigma}_{1,v}^{(u)})^2, (\hat{\sigma}_{2,v}^{(u)})^2, \ldots, (\hat{\sigma}_{p,v}^{(u)})^2)$ of R at iteration u. A Kalman filter designed with $\hat{R}^{(u)}$ may then be employed to produce corrected output estimates $\hat{y}_{k/k}^{(u)}$. The filter's design Riccati equation is given by

$$P_{k+1/k}^{(u)} = (A - K_k^{(u)}C)P_{k/k-1}^{(u)}(A - K_k^{(u)}C)^T + K_k^{(u)}\hat{R}^{(u)}(K_k^{(u)})^T + BQB^T, \tag{28}$$

where $K_k^{(u)} = AP_{k/k-1}^{(u)}C^T(CP_{k/k-1}^{(u)}C^T + \hat{R}^{(u)})^{-1}$ is the predictor gain. The output estimates are calculated from

$$\begin{bmatrix} \hat{x}_{k+1/k}^{(u)} \\ \hat{x}_{k/k}^{(u)} \end{bmatrix} = \begin{bmatrix} (A - K_k^{(u)}C) & K_k^{(u)} \\ (I - L_k^{(u)}C) & L_k^{(u)} \end{bmatrix} \begin{bmatrix} \hat{x}_{k+1/k}^{(u)} \\ z_k \end{bmatrix}, \tag{29}$$

$$\hat{y}_{k/k}^{(u)} = C\hat{x}_{k/k}^{(u)}, \tag{30}$$

where $L_k^{(u)} = P_{k/k-1}^{(u)}C^T(CP_{k/k-1}^{(u)}C^T + \hat{R}^{(u)})^{-1}$ is the filter gain.

Procedure 1 [19]. Assume that an initial estimate $\hat{R}^{(1)}$ of R is available. Subsequent estimates, $\hat{R}^{(u)}$, $u > 1$, are calculated by repeating the following two-step procedure.

"There are known knowns. These are things we know that we know. There are known unknowns. That is to say, there are things that we know we don't know. But there are also unknown unknowns. There are things we don't know we don't know." *Donald Henry Rumsfeld*

Step 1. Operate the Kalman filter (29) – (30) designed with $\hat{R}^{(u)}$ to obtain corrected output estimates $\hat{y}^{(u)}_{k/k}$.

Step 2. For i = 1, ..., p, use $\hat{y}^{(u)}_{k/k}$ instead of y_k within (27) to obtain $\hat{R}^{(u+1)}$ = diag($(\hat{\sigma}^{(u+1)}_{1,v})^2$, $(\hat{\sigma}^{(u+1)}_{2,v})^2$, ..., $(\hat{\sigma}^{(u+1)}_{p,v})^2$).

8.3.2.2 Properties

The above EM algorithm involves a repetition of two steps: the states are deduced using the current variance estimates and then the variances are re-identified from the latest states. Consequently, a two-part argument is employed to establish the monotonicity of the variance sequence. For the expectation step, it is shown that monotonically non-increasing variance iterates lead to monotonically non-increasing error covariances. Then for the maximisation step, it is argued that monotonic error covariances result in a monotonic measurement noise variance sequence. The design Riccati difference equation (28) can be written as

$$P^{(u)}_{k+1/k} = (A - K^{(u)}_k C)P^{(u)}_{k/k-1}(A - K^{(u)}_k C)^T + K^{(u)}_k R(K^{(u)}_k)^T + Q + S^{(u)}_k, \qquad (31)$$

where $S^{(u)}_k = K^{(u)}_k(\hat{R}^{(u)} - R)(K^{(u)}_k)^T$ accounts for the presence of parameter error. Subtracting x_k from $\hat{x}^{(u)}_{k/k}$ yields

$$\tilde{x}^{(u)}_{k/k} = (I - L^{(u)}_k C)\tilde{x}^{(u)}_{k/k-1} - L^{(u)}_k v_k, \qquad (32)$$

where $\tilde{x}^{(u)}_{k/k}$ = x_k − $\hat{x}^{(u)}_{k/k}$ and $\tilde{x}^{(u)}_{k/k-1}$ = x_k − $\hat{x}^{(u)}_{k/k-1}$ are the corrected and predicted state errors, respectively. The observed corrected error covariance is defined as $\Sigma^{(u)}_{k/k}$ = $E\{\tilde{x}^{(u)}_{k/k}(\tilde{x}^{(u)}_{k/k})^T\}$ and obtained from

$$\begin{aligned}\Sigma^{(u)}_{k/k} &= (I - L^{(u)}_k C)\Sigma^{(u)}_{k/k-1}(I - L^{(u)}_k C)^T + L^{(u)}_k R(L^{(u)}_k)^T \\ &= \Sigma^{(u)}_{k/k-1} - \Sigma^{(u)}_{k/k-1}C^T(C\Sigma^{(u)}_{k/k-1}C^T + R)^{-1}C\Sigma^{(u)}_{k/k-1},\end{aligned} \qquad (33)$$

where $\Sigma^{(u)}_{k/k-1}$ = $E\{\tilde{x}^{(u)}_{k/k-1}(\tilde{x}^{(u)}_{k/k-1})^T\}$. The observed predicted state error satisfies

$$\tilde{x}^{(u)}_{k+1/k} = A\tilde{x}^{(u)}_{k/k} + Bw_k. \qquad (34)$$

Hence, the observed predicted error covariance obeys the recursion

$$\Sigma^{(u)}_{k+1/k} = A\Sigma^{(u)}_{k/k}A^T + BQB^T. \qquad (35)$$

Some observations concerning the above error covariances are described below. These results are used subsequently to establish the monotonicity of the above EM algorithm.

"I want minimum information given with maximum politeness." *Jacqueline (Jackie) Lee Bouvier Kennedy Onassis*

***Lemma 1 [19]:** In respect of Procedure 1 for estimating R, suppose the following:*

(i) *the data z_k has been generated by (23) – (25) in which A, B, C, Q are known, $|\lambda_i(A)| < 1$, i = 1, …, n, and the pair (A, C) is observable;*

(ii) *there exist $P_{1/0}^{(2)} \le P_{1/0}^{(1)}$ and $R \le \hat{R}^{(2)} \le \hat{R}^{(1)}$ (or $P_{1/0}^{(1)} \le P_{1/0}^{(2)}$ and $\hat{R}^{(1)} \le \hat{R}^{(2)} \le R$).*

Then:

(i) $\Sigma_{k+1/k}^{(u)} \le P_{k+1/k}^{(u)}$;

(ii) $\Sigma_{k/k}^{(u)} \le P_{k/k}^{(u)}$;

(iii) $R \le \hat{R}^{(u+1)} \le \hat{R}^{(u)}$ *implies* $P_{k+1/k}^{(u+1)} \le P_{k+1/k}^{(u)}$ (*or* $\hat{R}^{(u)} \le \hat{R}^{(u+1)} \le R$ *implies* $P_{k+1/k}^{(u)} \le P_{k+1/k}^{(u+1)}$)

for all $u \ge 1$.

Proof:

(i) *Condition (i) ensures that the problem is well-posed. Condition (ii) stipulates that $S_k^{(1)} \ge 0$, which is the initialisation step for an induction argument. For the inductive step, subtracting (33) from (31) yields $P_{k+1/k}^{(u)} - \Sigma_{k+1/k}^{(u)} = (A - K_k^{(u)}C)(P_{k/k-1}^{(u)} - \Sigma_{k/k-1}^{(u)})(A - K_k^{(u)}C)^T + S_k^{(u)}$ and thus $\Sigma_{k/k-1}^{(u)} \le P_{k/k-1}^{(u)}$ implies $\Sigma_{k+1/k}^{(u)} \le P_{k+1/k}^{(u)}$.*

(ii) *The result is immediate by considering A = I within the proof for (i).*

(iii) *The condition $\hat{R}^{(u+1)} \le \hat{R}^{(u)}$ ensures that $\begin{bmatrix} Q & A^T \\ A & -C^T(\hat{R}^{(m+1)})^{-1}C \end{bmatrix} \le \begin{bmatrix} Q & A^T \\ A & -C^T(\hat{R}^{(m)})^{-1}C \end{bmatrix}$, which together with $P_{1/0}^{(u+1)} \le P_{1/0}^{(u)}$ within Theorem 2 of Chapter 7 results in $P_{k+1/k}^{(u+1)} \le P_{k+1/k}^{(u)}$.* □

Thus the sequences of observed prediction and correction error covariances are bounded above by the design prediction and correction error covariances. Next, it is shown that the observed error covariances are monotonically non-increasing (or non-decreasing).

***Lemma 2 [19]:** Under the conditions of Lemma 1:*

i) $\Sigma_{k+1/k}^{(u+1)} \le \Sigma_{k+1/k}^{(u)}$ (*or* $\Sigma_{k+1/k}^{(u)} \le \Sigma_{k+1/k}^{(u+1)}$) *and*

ii) $\Sigma_{k/k}^{(u+1)} \le \Sigma_{k/k}^{(u)}$ (*or* $\Sigma_{k/k}^{(u)} \le \Sigma_{k/k}^{(u+1)}$).

***Proof:** To establish that the solution of (33) is monotonic non-increasing, from Theorem 2 of Chapter 7, it is required to show that*

$$\begin{bmatrix} Q + K_k^{(u+1)}R(K_k^{(u+1)})^T & (A - K_k^{(u+1)}C)^T \\ A - K_k^{(u+1)}C & 0 \end{bmatrix} \le \begin{bmatrix} Q + K_k^{(u)}R(K_k^{(u)})^T & (A - K_k^{(u)}C)^T \\ A - K_k^{(u)}C & 0 \end{bmatrix}.$$

"Technology is so much fun but we can drown in our technology. The fog of information can drive out knowledge." *Daniel Joseph Boostin*

Since A, Q and R are time-invariant, it suffices to show that

$$\begin{bmatrix} L_k^{(u+1)}(L_k^{(u+1)})^T & (I - L_k^{(u+1)}C)^T \\ I - L_k^{(u+1)}C & 0 \end{bmatrix} \le \begin{bmatrix} L_k^{(u)}(L_k^{(u)})^T & (I - L_k^{(u)}C)^T \\ I - L_k^{(u)}C & 0 \end{bmatrix}. \tag{36}$$

Note for an X and Y satisfying $I \ge Y \ge X \ge 0$ that $YY^T - XX^T \ge (I - X)(I - X)^T - (I - Y)(I - Y)^T$. Therefore, $\hat{R}^{(u+1)} \le \hat{R}^{(u)}$ and $P_{k+1/k}^{(u+1)} \le P_{k+1/k}^{(u)}$ (from Lemma 1) imply $L^{(u+1)}C \le L^{(u)}C \le I$ and thus (36) follows. □

It is established below that monotonic non-increasing error covariances result in a monotonic non-increasing measurement noise variance sequence.

Lemma 3 [19]: *In respect of Procedure 1 for estimating R, suppose the following:*

(i) the data z_k has been generated by (23) – (25) in which A, B, C, Q are known, $|\lambda_i(A)| < 1$, i = 1, …, n and the pair (A, C) is observable;

(ii) there exist $\hat{R}^{(1)} \ge R \ge 0$ and $P_{1/0}^{(u+1)} \le P_{1/0}^{(u)}$ (or $P_{1/0}^{(u)} \le P_{1/0}^{(u+1)}$) for all u > 1.

Then $\hat{R}^{(u+1)} \le \hat{R}^{(u)}$ (or $\hat{R}^{(u)} \le \hat{R}^{(u+1)}$) for all u > 1.

Proof: *Let C_i denote the ith row of C. The approximate MLE within Procedure 1 is written as*

$$(\hat{\sigma}_{i,v}^{(u+1)})^2 = \frac{1}{N}\sum_{k=1}^{N}(z_{i,k} - C_i\hat{x}_{k/k}^{(u)})^2 \tag{37}$$

$$= \frac{1}{N}\sum_{k=1}^{N}(C_i\tilde{x}_{k/k}^{(u)} + v_{i,k})^2 \tag{38}$$

$$= C_i\Sigma_{k/k}^{(u)}C_i^T + \sigma_{i,v}^2 \tag{39}$$

and thus $\hat{R}^{(u+1)} = C\Sigma_{k/k}^{(u)}C^T + R$. Since $\hat{R}^{(u+1)}$ is affine to $\Sigma_{k/k}^{(u)}$, which from Lemma 2 is monotonically non-increasing, it follows that $\hat{R}^{(u+1)} \le \hat{R}^{(u)}$. □

If the estimation problem is dominated by measurement noise, the measurement noise MLEs converge to the actual values.

Lemma 4 [19]: *Under the conditions of Lemma 3,*

$$\lim_{Q \to 0, R^{-1} \to 0, u \to \infty} \hat{R}^{(u+1)} = R. \tag{40}$$

"Getting information off the internet is like taking a drink from a fire hydrant." *Mitchell David Kapor*

Proof: *By inspection of* $L_k^{(u)} = P_{k/k-1}^{(u)} C^T (C P_{k/k-1}^{(u)} C^T + R^{(u)})^{-1}$, *it follows that* $\lim_{Q \to 0, R^{-1} \to 0, u \to \infty} L_k^{(u)} = 0$. *Therefore,* $\lim_{Q \to 0, R^{-1} \to 0, u \to \infty} \hat{x}_{k/k}^{(u)} = 0$ *and* $\lim_{Q \to 0, R^{-1} \to 0} z_k = v_k$, *which implies (40), since the MLE (37) is unbiased for large N.* □

Example 9. In respect of the problem (23) – (25), assume $A = 0.9$, $B = C = 1$ and $\sigma_w^2 = 0.1$ are known. Suppose that $\sigma_v^2 = 10$ but is unknown. Samples z_k and $\hat{x}_{k/k}^{(u)}$ were generated from $N = 20{,}000$ realisations of zero-mean Gaussian w_k and v_k. The sequence of MLEs obtained using Procedure 1, initialised with $(\hat{\sigma}_v^{(1)})^2 = 14$ and 12 are indicated by traces (i) and (ii) of Fig. 1, respectively. The variance sequences are monotonically decreasing, which is consistent with Lemma 3. The figure shows that the MLEs converge (to a local maximum of the approximate log-likelihood function), and are reasonably close to the actual value of $\sigma_v^2 = 10$. This illustrates the high measurement noise observation described by Lemma 4. An alternative to the EM algorithm involves calculating MLEs using the Newton-Raphson method [5], [6]. The calculated Newton-Raphson measurement noise variance iterates, initialised with $(\hat{\sigma}_v^{(1)})^2 = 14$ and 12 are indicated by traces (iii) and (iv) of Fig. 1, respectively. It can be seen that the Newton-Raphson estimates converge to those of the EM algorithm, albeit at a slower rate.

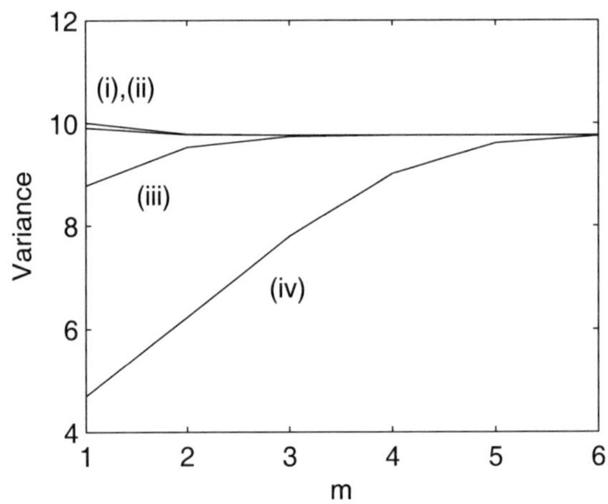

Figure 1. Variance MLEs (27) versus iteration number for Example 9: (i) EM algorithm with $(\hat{\sigma}_v^{(1)})^2 = 14$, (ii) EM algorithm with $(\hat{\sigma}_v^{(1)})^2 = 12$, (iii) Newton-Raphson with $(\hat{\sigma}_v^{(1)})^2 = 14$ and (iv) Newton-Raphson with $(\hat{\sigma}_v^{(1)})^2 = 12$.

"The Internet is the world's largest library. It's just that all the books are on the floor." *John Allen Paulos*

8.3.3 Process Noise Variance Estimation

8.3.3.1 EM Algorithm

In respect of the model (23), suppose that it is desired to estimate Q given N samples of x_{k+1}. The vector states within (23) can be written in terms of its i components, $x_{i,k+1} = A_i x_k + w_{i,k}$, that is

$$w_{i,k} = A_i x_k - x_{i,k+1}, \tag{41}$$

where $w_{i,k} = B_i w_k$, A_i and B_i refer the ith row of A and B, respectively. Assume that $w_{i,k} \sim \mathcal{N}(0, \sigma_{i,w}^2)$, where $\sigma_{i,w}^2 \in \mathbb{R}$ is to be estimated. An MLE for the scalar $\sigma_{i,w}^2 = B_i Q B_i^T$ can be calculated from the sample variance formula

$$\sigma_{i,w}^2 = \frac{1}{N}\sum_{k=1}^{N} w_{i,k} w_{i,k}^T \tag{42}$$

$$= \frac{1}{N}\sum_{k=1}^{N} (x_{i,k+1} - A_i x_k)(x_{i,k+1} - A_i x_k)^T \tag{43}$$

$$= \frac{1}{N}\sum_{k=1}^{N} B_i w_k w_k^T B_i^T \tag{44}$$

$$= B_i\left(\frac{1}{N}\sum_{k=1}^{N} w_k w_k^T\right) B_i^T . \tag{45}$$

Substituting $w_k = Ax_k - x_{k+1}$ into (45) and noting that $\sigma_{i,w}^2 = B_i Q B_i^T$ yields

$$\hat{Q} = \frac{1}{N}\sum_{k=1}^{N} (Ax_k - x_{k+1})(Ax_k - x_{k+1})^T , \tag{46}$$

which can be updated as follows.

Procedure 2 [19]. Assume that an initial estimate $\hat{Q}^{(1)}$ of Q is available. Subsequent estimates can be found by repeating the following two-step algorithm.

Step 1. Operate the filter recursions (29) designed with $\hat{Q}^{(u)}$ on the measurements (25) over $k \in [1, N]$ to obtain corrected state estimates $\hat{x}_{k/k}^{(u)}$ and $\hat{x}_{k+1/k+1}^{(u)}$.

Step 2. For $i = 1, \ldots, n$, use $\hat{x}_{k/k}^{(u)}$ and $\hat{x}_{k+1/k+1}^{(u)}$ instead of x_k and x_{k+1} within (46) to obtain $\hat{Q}^{(u+1)} = \text{diag}((\hat{\sigma}_{1,w}^{(u+1)})^2, (\hat{\sigma}_{2,w}^{(u+1)})^2, \ldots, (\hat{\sigma}_{n,w}^{(u+1)})^2)$.

"Information on the Internet is subject to the same rules and regulations as conversations at a bar." *George David Lundberg*

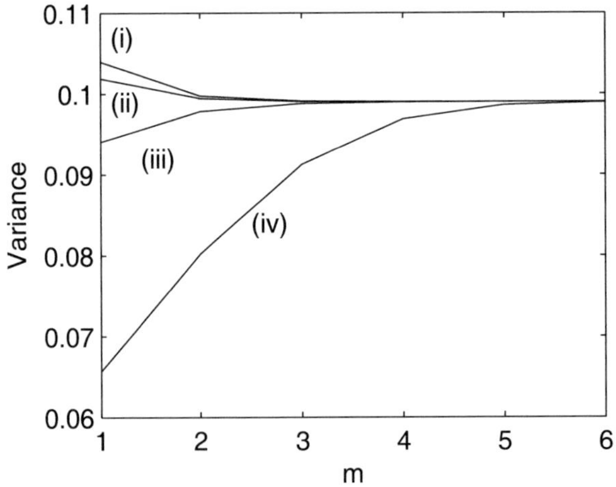

Figure 2. Variance MLEs (46) versus iteration number for Example 10: (i) EM algorithm with $(\hat{\sigma}_w^{(1)})^2$ = 0.14, (ii) EM algorithm with $(\hat{\sigma}_w^{(1)})^2$ = 0.12, (iii) Newton-Raphson with $(\hat{\sigma}_w^{(1)})^2$ = 0.14 and (iv) Newton-Raphson with $(\hat{\sigma}_w^{(1)})^2$ = 0.12.

8.3.3.2 Properties

Similarly to Lemma 1, it can be shown that a monotonically non-increasing (or non-decreasing) sequence of process noise variance estimates results in a monotonically non-increasing (or non-decreasing) sequence of design and observed error covariances, see [19]. The converse case is stated below, namely, the sequence of variance iterates is monotonically non-increasing, provided the estimates and error covariances are initialized appropriately. The accompanying proof makes use of

$$\begin{aligned} \hat{x}_{k+1/k+1}^{(u)} - A\hat{x}_{k/k}^{(u)} &= \hat{x}_{k+1/k}^{(u)} + L_{k+1}^{(u)}(z_{k+1} - C\hat{x}_{k+1/k}^{(u)}) - A\hat{x}_{k/k}^{(u)} \\ &= A\hat{x}_{k/k}^{(u)} + L_{i,k+1}(z_{k+1} - C\hat{x}_{k+1/k}^{(u)}) - A\hat{x}_{k/k}^{(u)} \\ &= L_k^{(u)}(C\tilde{x}_{k+1/k}^{(u)} + v_{k+1}) . \end{aligned} \tag{47}$$

The components of (47) are written as

$$\hat{x}_{i,k+1/k+1}^{(u)} - a_i\hat{x}_{k/k}^{(u)} = L_{i,k+1}^{(u)}(C\tilde{x}_{k+1/k}^{(u)} + v_{k+1}) , \tag{48}$$

where $L_{i,k+1}^{(u)}$ is the ith row of $L_{k+1}^{(u)}$.

"I must confess that I've never trusted the Web. I've always seen it as a coward's tool. Where does it live? How do you hold it personally responsible? Can you put a distributed network of fibre-optic cable on notice? And is it male or female? In other words, can I challenge it to a fight?" *Stephen Tyrone Colbert*

Lemma 5 [19]: *In respect of Procedure 2 for estimating Q, suppose the following:*

(i) the data z_k has been generated by (23) – (25) in which A, B, C, R are known, $|\lambda_i(A)| < 1$, i = 1, ..., n and the pair (A, C) is observable;

(ii) there exist $\hat{Q}^{(1)} \ge Q \ge 0$ and $P_{1/0}^{(u+1)} \le P_{1/0}^{(u)}$ (or $P_{1/0}^{(u)} \le P_{1/0}^{(u+1)}$) for all u > 1.

Then $\hat{Q}^{(u+1)} \le \hat{Q}^{(u)}$ (or $\hat{Q}^{(u)} \le \hat{Q}^{(u+1)}$) for all u > 1.

***Proof**: Using (47)within (46) gives*

$$(\hat{\sigma}_{i,w}^{(u)})^2 = \frac{1}{N} L_{i,k+1}^{(u)} \left(\sum_{k=1}^{N} C\tilde{x}_{k+1/k} + v_{k+1} \right)^2 (L_{i,k+1}^{(u)})^T$$
$$= L_{i,k+1}^{(u)} (C\Sigma_{k+1/k}^{(u)} C^T + R)(L_{i,k+1}^{(u)})^T \tag{49}$$

and thus $\hat{Q}^{(u+1)} = L_{k+1}^{(u)}(C\Sigma_{k+1/k}^{(u)}C^T + R)(L_{k+1}^{(u)})^T$. Since $\hat{Q}^{(u+1)}$ varies with $L_{k+1}^{(u)}(L_{j,k+1}^{(u)})^T$ and $\Sigma_{k+1/k}^{(u)}$, which from Lemma 2 are monotonically non-increasing, it follows that $\hat{Q}^{(u+1)} \le \hat{Q}^{(u)}$. □

It is observed that the approximate MLEs asymptotically approach the actual values when the SNR is sufficiently high.

Lemma 6 [19]: *Under the conditions of Lemma 5,*

$$\lim_{Q^{-1}\to 0, R\to 0, u\to\infty} \hat{Q}^{(u+1)} = Q\,. \tag{50}$$

Proof: *It is straight forward to show that $\lim_{Q^{-1}\to 0, R\to 0} L_{i,k}C = I$ and therefore $\lim_{Q^{-1}\to 0, R\to 0, u\to\infty} \hat{x}_{k/k}^{(u)} = x_k$, which implies (50), since the MLE (46) is unbiased for large N.* □

Example 10. For the model described in Example 8, suppose that $\sigma_v^2 = 0.01$ is known, and $(\hat{\sigma}_w^{(1)})^2 = 0.1$ but is unknown. Procedure 2 and the Newton-Raphson method [5], [6] were used to jointly estimate the states and the unknown variance. Some example variance iterations, initialised with $(\hat{\sigma}_w^{(1)})^2 = 0.14$ and 0.12, are shown in Fig. 2. The EM algorithm estimates are seen to be monotonically decreasing, which is in agreement with Lemma 5. At the final iteration, the approximate MLEs do not quite reach the actual value of $(\hat{\sigma}_w^{(1)})^2 = 0.1$, because the presence of measurement noise results in imperfect state reconstruction and introduces a small bias (see Example 5). The figure also shows that MLEs calculated via the Newton-Raphson method converge at a slower rate.

"Four years ago nobody but nuclear physicists had ever heard of the Internet. Today even my cat, Socks, has his own web page. I'm amazed at that. I meet kids all the time, been talking to my cat on the Internet." *William Jefferson (Bill) Clinton*

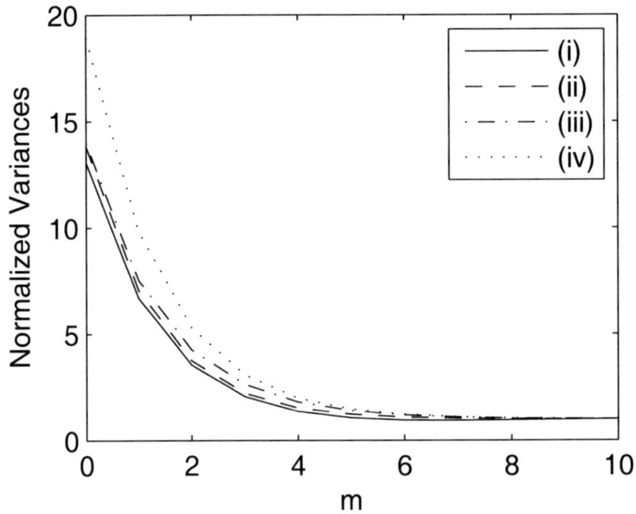

Figure 3. (i) $\hat{\sigma}^2_{1,w}$, (ii) $\hat{\sigma}^2_{2,w}$, (iii) $\hat{\sigma}^2_{3,w}$ and (iv) $\hat{\sigma}^2_{4,w}$, normalised by their steady state values, versus EM iteration number for Example 11.

Example 11. Consider the problem of calculating the initial alignment of an inertial navigation system. Alignment is the process of estimating the Earth rotation rate and rotating the attitude direction cosine matrix, so that it transforms the body-frame sensor signals to a locally-level frame, wherein certain components of accelerations and velocities approach zero when the platform is stationary. This can be achieved by a Kalman filter that uses the model (23), where $x_k \in \mathbb{R}^4$ comprises the errors in earth rotation rate, tilt, velocity and position vectors respectively, and $w_k \in \mathbb{R}^4$ is a deterministic signal which is a nonlinear function of the states (see [24]). The state matrix is calculated as $A = I + \Phi T_s + \frac{1}{2!}(\Phi T_s)^2 + \frac{1}{3!}(\Phi T_s)^3$, where T_s is the sampling interval, $\Phi = \begin{bmatrix} 0 & 0 & 0 & 0 \\ 1 & 0 & 0 & 0 \\ 0 & g & 0 & 0 \\ 0 & 0 & 1 & 0 \end{bmatrix}$ is a continuous-time state matrix and g is the universal gravitational constant. The output mapping within (24) is $C = \begin{bmatrix} 0 & 0 & 0 & 1 \end{bmatrix}$. Raw three-axis accelerometer and gyro data was recorded from a stationary Litton LN270 Inertial Navigation System at a 500 Hz data rate. In order to generate a compact plot, the initial variance estimates were selected to be 10 times the steady state values.

"On the Internet, nobody knows you're a dog." *Peter Steiner*

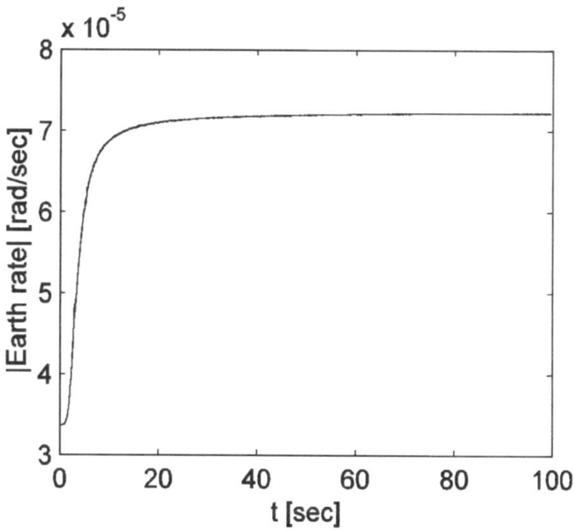

Figure 4. Estimated magnitude of Earth rotation rate for Example 11.

The estimated variances after 10 EM iterations are shown in Fig. 3. The figure demonstrates that approximate MLEs (46) approach steady state values from above, which is consistent with Lemma 5. The estimated Earth rotation rate magnitude versus time is shown in Fig. 4. At 100 seconds, the estimated magnitude of the Earth rate is 72.53 micro-radians per second, that is, one revolution every 24.06 hours. This estimated Earth rate is about 0.5% in error compared with the mean sidereal day of 23.93 hours [25]. Since the estimated Earth rate is in reasonable agreement, it is suggested that the MLEs for the unknown variances are satisfactory (see [19] for further details).

8.3.4 State Matrix Estimation

8.3.4.1 EM Algorithm

The components of the states within (23) are now written as

$$x_{i,k+1} = \sum_{j=1}^{n} a_{i,j} x_{i,k} + w_{i,k}, \tag{51}$$

where $a_{i,j}$ denotes the element in row i and column j of A. Consider the problem of estimating $a_{i,j}$ from samples of $x_{i,k}$. The assumption $x_{i,k+1} \sim \mathcal{N}(\sum_{j=1}^{n} a_{i,j} x_{i,k},\ \sigma_{i,w}^2)$, leads to the log-likelihood

$$\log f(a_{i,j}) \mid x_{j,k+1}) = -\frac{N}{2}\log 2\pi - \frac{N}{2}\log \sigma_{i,w}^2 - \frac{1}{2}\sigma_{j,w}^{-2} \sum_{k=1}^{N} \left(x_{i,k+1} - \sum_{j=1}^{n} a_{i,j} x_{i,k} \right)^2 . \tag{52}$$

"It's important for us to explain to our nation that life is important. It's not only the life of babies, but it's life of children living in, you know, the dark dungeons of the internet." *George Walker Bush*

By setting $\frac{\partial \log f(a_{i,j}) | x_{j,k+1})}{\partial a_{i,j}}$ = 0, an MLE for $a_{i,j}$ is obtained as [20]

$$\hat{a}_{i,j} = \frac{\sum_{k=1}^{N}\left(x_{i,k+1} - \sum_{j=1, j\neq i}^{n} a_{i,j}x_{i,k}\right) x_{j,k}}{\sum_{k=1}^{N} x_{j,k}^2} . \tag{53}$$

Incidentally, the above estimate can also be found using the least-squares method [2], [10] and minimising the cost function $\sum_{k=1}^{N}\left(x_{i,k+1} - \sum_{j=1}^{n} a_{i,j}x_{i,k}\right)^2$. The expectation of $\hat{a}_{i,j}$ is [20]

$$E\{\hat{a}_{i,j}\} = E\left\{ \frac{\sum_{k=1}^{N}\left(\sum_{j=1}^{n} a_{i,j}x_{i,k} + w_{i,k} - \sum_{j=1, j\neq i}^{n} a_{i,j}x_{i,k}\right) x_{j,k}}{\sum_{k=1}^{N} x_{j,k}^2} \right\}$$

$$= a_{i,j} + E\left\{ \frac{\sum_{k=1}^{N} w_{i,k}x_{j,k}}{\sum_{k=1}^{N} x_{j,k}^2} \right\}$$

$$= a_{i,j} ,$$

Since $w_{i,k}$ and $x_{i,k}$ are independent. Hence, the MLE (53) is unbiased.

Suppose that an estimate $\hat{A}^{(u)} = \{a_{i,j}^{(u)}\}$ of A is available at an iteration u. The predicted state estimates within (29) can be calculated from

$$\hat{x}_{k+1/k}^{(u)} = (\hat{A}^{(u)} - K_k^{(u)}C)\hat{x}_{k+1/k}^{(u)} + K_k^{(u)}z_k , \tag{54}$$

where $K_k^{(u)} = \hat{A}^{(u)}P_{k/k-1}^{(u)}C^T(CP_{k/k-1}^{(u)}C^T + R)^{-1}$, in which $P_{k/k-1}^{(u)}$ is obtained from the design Riccati equation

$$P_{k+1/k}^{(u)} = (\hat{A}^{(u)} - K_k^{(u)}C)P_{k/k-1}^{(u)}(\hat{A}^{(u)} - K_k^{(u)}C)^T + K_k^{(u)}R(K_k^{(u)})^T + Q . \tag{55}$$

An approximate MLE for $a_{i,j}$ is obtained by replacing x_k by $\hat{x}_{k/k}^{(u)}$ within (53) which results in

$$\hat{a}_{i,j}^{(u+1)} = \frac{\sum_{k=1}^{N}\left(\hat{x}_{i,k+1/k+1}^{(u)} - \sum_{j=1, j\neq i}^{n} \hat{a}_{i,j}^{(u)}\hat{x}_{i,k/k}^{(u)}\right) \hat{x}_{j,k/k}^{(u)}}{\sum_{k=1}^{N} (\hat{x}_{j,k/k}^{(u)})^2} . \tag{56}$$

"The internet is like a gold-rush; the only people making money are those who sell the pans." *Will Hobbs*

An iterative procedure for re-estimating an unknown state matrix is proposed below.

Procedure 3 [20]. Assume that there exists an initial estimate $\hat{A}^{(1)}$ satisfying $|\lambda_i(\hat{A}^{(1)})| < 1$, i = 1, …, n. Subsequent estimates are calculated using the following two-step EM algorithm.

Step 1. Operate the Kalman filter (29) using (54) on the measurements z_k over $k \in [1, N]$ to obtain corrected state estimates $\hat{x}^{(u)}_{k/k}$ and $\hat{x}^{(u)}_{k+1/k+1}$.

Step 2. Copy $\hat{A}^{(u)}$ to $\hat{A}^{(u+1)}$. Use $\hat{x}^{(u)}_{k/k}$ within (56) to obtain candidate estimates $\hat{a}^{(u+1)}_{i,j}$, i, j = 1, …, n. Include $\hat{a}^{(u+1)}_{i,j}$ within $\hat{A}^{(u+1)}$ if $|\lambda_i(\hat{A}^{(u+1)})| < 1$, i = 1, …, n.

The condition $|\lambda_i(\hat{A}^{(u+1)})| < 1$ within Step 2 ensures that the estimated system is asymptotically stable.

8.3.4.2 Properties

The design Riccati difference equation (55) can be written as

$$P^{(u)}_{k+1/k} = (A - K^{(u)}_k C)P^{(u)}_{k/k-1}(A - K^{(u)}_k C)^T + K^{(u)}_k R(K^{(u)}_k)^T + Q + S^{(u)}_k, \tag{57}$$

where

$$S^{(u)}_k = (\hat{A}^{(u)} - K^{(u)}_k C)P^{(u)}_{k/k-1}(\hat{A}^{(u)} - K^{(u)}_k C)^T - (A - K^{(u)}_k C)P^{(u)}_{k/k-1}(A - K^{(u)}_k C)^T \tag{58}$$

accounts for the presence of modelling error. In the following, the notation of Lemma 1 is employed to argue that a monotonically non-increasing state matrix estimate sequence results in monotonically non-increasing error covariance sequences.

Lemma 7 [20]. *In respect of Procedure 3 for estimating A, suppose the following:*

(i) the data z_k has been generated by (23) – (25) in which B, C, Q, R are known;

(ii) $|\lambda_i(\hat{A}^{(1)})| < 1$, i = 1, …, n, the pair (A, C) is observable;

(iii) there exist $\hat{A}^{(1)} \geq A$ and $P^{(u+1)}_{1/0} \leq P^{(u)}_{1/0}$ (or $P^{(u)}_{1/0} \leq P^{(u+1)}_{1/0}$) for all u > 1.

Then:

(i) $\Sigma^{(u)}_{k+1/k} \leq P^{(u)}_{k+1/k}$ (or $P^{(u)}_{k+1/k} \leq \Sigma^{(u)}_{k+1/k}$);

(ii) $\Sigma^{(u)}_{k/k} \leq P^{(u)}_{k/k}$ (or $P^{(u)}_{k/k} \leq \Sigma^{(u)}_{k/k}$);

(iii) $\hat{A}^{(u+1)} \leq \hat{A}^{(u)}$ which implies $P^{(u+1)}_{k+1/k} \leq P^{(u)}_{k+1/k}$ ($\hat{A}^{(u)} \leq \hat{A}^{(u+1)}$ which implies $P^{(u)}_{k+1/k} \leq P^{(u+1)}_{k+1/k}$)

for all u ≥ 1.

"It may not always be profitable at first for businesses to be online, but it is certainly going to be unprofitable not to be online." *Ester Dyson*

The proof follows *mutatis mutandis* from that of Lemma 1. A heuristic argument is outlined below which suggests that non-increasing error variances lead to a non-increasing state matrix estimate sequence. Suppose that there exists a residual error $s_k^{(u)} \in \mathbb{R}^n$ at iteration u such that

$$\hat{x}_{k+1/k+1}^{(u)} = \hat{A}^{(u)}\hat{x}_{k/k}^{(u)} + s_k^{(u)} . \tag{59}$$

The components of (59) are denoted by

$$\hat{x}_{i,k+1/k+1}^{(u)} = \sum_{j=1}^{n} a_{i,j}^{(u)}\hat{x}_{i,k/k}^{(u)} + s_{i,k}^{(u)} , \tag{60}$$

where $s_{i,k}^{(u)}$ is the ith element of $s_k^{(u)}$. It follows from (60) and (48) that

$$s_k^{(u)} = L_k^{(u)}(C\tilde{x}_{k+1/k}^{(u)} + v_{k+1}) \tag{61}$$

and

$$s_{i,k}^{(u)} = L_{i,k}^{(u)}(C\tilde{x}_{k+1/k}^{(u)} + v_{k+1}) . \tag{62}$$

Using (61) and (63) within (57) yields

$$\begin{aligned} \hat{a}_{i,j}^{(u+1)} &= \hat{a}_{i,j}^{(u)} + \left(\sum_{k=1}^{N} s_{i,k}^{(u)}\hat{x}_{j,k/k}^{(u)} \right)\left(\sum_{k=1}^{N} (\hat{x}_{j,k/k}^{(u)})^2 \right)^{-1} \\ &= \hat{a}_{i,j}^{(u)} + L_{i,k}^{(u)}C\left(\sum_{k=1}^{N} (\tilde{x}_{k+1/k}^{(u)} + C^{\#}v_{k+1})\hat{x}_{j,k/k}^{(u)} \right)\left(\sum_{k=1}^{N} (\hat{x}_{j,k/k}^{(u)})^2 \right)^{-1} , \end{aligned} \tag{63}$$

where $C^{\#}$ denotes the Moore-Penrose pseudo-inverse of C. It is shown in Lemma 2 under prescribed conditions that $L^{(u+1)}C \le L^{(u)}C \le I$. Since the non-increasing sequence $L^{(u)}C$ is a factor of the second term on the right-hand-side of (63), the sequence $\hat{a}_{i,j}^{(u+1)}$ is expected to be non-increasing.

Lemma 8 [20]: *Under the conditions of Lemma 7, suppose that C is full rank, then*

$$\lim_{Q^{-1}\to 0, R\to 0, u\to\infty} \hat{A}^{(u+1)} = A . \tag{64}$$

Proof: *It is straight forward to show that* $\lim_{Q^{-1}\to 0, R\to 0, u\to\infty} L_{i,k}C = I$ *and therefore* $\lim_{Q^{-1}\to 0, R\to 0, u\to\infty} \hat{x}_{k/k}^{(u)} = x_k$, *which implies (64) since the MLE (53) is unbiased.* □

"New scientific ideas never spring from a communal body, however organized, but rather from the head of an individually inspired researcher who struggles with his problems in lonely thought and unites all his thought on one single point which is his whole world for the moment." *Max Karl Ernst Ludwig Planck*

An illustration is presented below.

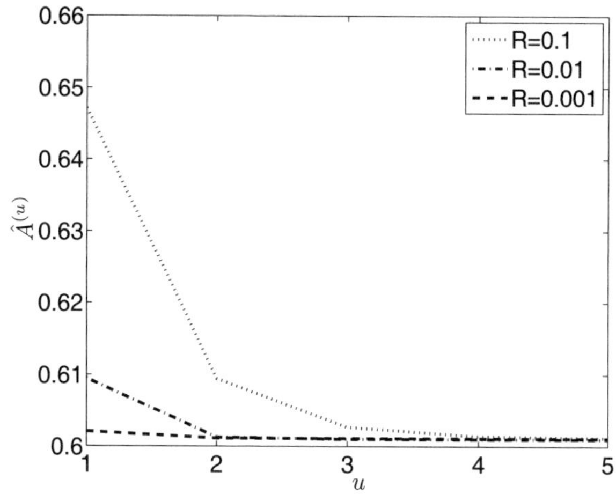

Figure 5. Sequence of $\hat{A}^{(u)}$ versus iteration number for Example 12.

Example 12. In respect of the model (23) – (25), suppose that $B = C = 1$, $\sigma_w^2 = 0.2$ are known and $A = 0.6$ is unknown. Simulations were conducted with 100 realizations of Gaussian process noise and measurement noise of length N = 500,000 for R = 0.1, 0.01 and 0.001. The EM algorithms were initialised with $\hat{A}^{(1)} = 0.9999$. It was observed that the resulting estimate sequences were all monotonically decreasing, however, this becomes imperceptible at R = 0.001, due to the limited resolution of the plot. The mean estimates are shown in Fig. 5. As expected from Lemma 8, $\hat{A}^{(u)}$ asymptotically approaches the true value of A = 0.6 when the measurement noise becomes negligible.

8.4 Smoothing EM Algorithms

8.4.1 Process Noise Variance Estimation

8.4.1.1 EM Algorithm

In the previous EM algorithms, the expectation step involved calculating filtered estimates. Similar EM procedures are outlined in [26] and here where smoothed estimates are used at iteration u within the expectation step. The likelihood functions described in Sections 8.2.2 and 8.2.3 are exact, provided that the underlying assumptions are correct and actual random variables are available. Under these conditions, the ensuing parameter estimates maximise the likelihood functions and their limit of precision is specified by the associated CRLBs. However, the use of filtered or smoothed quantities leads to approximate likelihood functions, MLEs and CRLBs. It turns out that the approximate MLEs approach the true parameter values under prescribed SNR conditions. It will be shown that the use of

---

"The best way to prepare is to write programs, and to study great programs that other people have written. In my case, I went to the garbage cans at the Computer Science Center and I fished out listings of their operating system." *William Henry (Bill) Gates III*

smoothed (as opposed to filtered) quantities results in smaller approximate CRLBs, which suggests improved parameter estimation accuracy.

Suppose that the system $\mathcal{G}$ having the realisation (23) – (24) is non-minimum phase and D is of full rank. Under these conditions $\mathcal{G}^{-1}$ exists and the minimum-variance smoother (described in Chapter 7) may be employed to produce input estimates. Assume that an estimate $\hat{Q}^{(u)} = \text{diag}((\hat{\sigma}_{1,w}^{(u)})^2, (\hat{\sigma}_{2,w}^{(u)})^2, \ldots, (\hat{\sigma}_{n,w}^{(u)})^2)$ of Q is are available at iteration u. The smoothed input estimates, $\hat{w}_{k/N}^{(u)}$, are calculated from

$$\begin{bmatrix} x_{k+1/k}^{(u)} \\ \alpha_k^{(u)} \end{bmatrix} = \begin{bmatrix} A_k - K_k^{(u)} C_k & K_k^{(u)} \\ -(\Omega_k^{(u)})^{-1/2} C_k & (\Omega_k^{(u)})^{-1/2} \end{bmatrix} \begin{bmatrix} x_{k/k-1}^{(u)} \\ z_k \end{bmatrix}, \tag{65}$$

$$\begin{bmatrix} \xi_{k-1}^{(u)} \\ \gamma_{k-1}^{(u)} \\ \hat{w}_{k-1/N}^{(u)} \end{bmatrix} = \begin{bmatrix} A_k^T - C_k^T (K_k^{(u)})^T & 0 & C_k^T (\Omega_k^{(u)})^{-1/2} \\ C_k^T (K_k^{(u)})^T & A_k^T & -C_k^T (\Omega_k^{(u)})^{-1/2} \\ -\hat{Q}_k^{(u)} D_k^T (K_k^{(u)})^T & -\hat{Q}_k^{(u)} B_k^T & \hat{Q}_k^{(u)} D_k^T (\Omega_k^{(u)})^{-1/2} \end{bmatrix} \begin{bmatrix} \xi_k^{(u)} \\ \gamma_k^{(u)} \\ \alpha_k^{(u)} \end{bmatrix}, \tag{66}$$

where $K_k^{(u)} = (A_k P_{k/k-1}^{(u)} C_k^T + B_k \hat{Q}_k^{(u)} D_k^T)(\Omega_k^{(u)})^{-1}$, $\Omega_k^{(u)} = C_k P_{k/k-1}^{(u)} C_k^T + D_k \hat{Q}_k^{(u)} D_k^T + R_k$ and $P_{k/k-1}^{(u)}$ evolves from the Riccati difference equation $P_{k+1/k}^{(u)} = A_k P_{k/k-1}^{(u)} A_k^T - (A_k P_{k/k-1}^{(u)} C_k^T + B_k \hat{Q}_k^{(u)} D_k^T)(C_k P_{k/k-1}^{(u)} C_k^T + D_k \hat{Q}_k^{(u)} D_k^T + R_k)^{-1}(C_k P_{k/k-1}^{(u)} A_k^T + D_k Q_k^{(u)} B_k^T) + B_k \hat{Q}_k^{(u)} B_k^T$. A smoothing EM algorithm for iteratively re-estimating $\hat{Q}^{(u)}$ is described below.

***Procedure* 4.** Suppose that an initial estimate $\hat{Q}^{(1)} = \text{diag}((\hat{\sigma}_{1,w}^{(1)})^2, (\hat{\sigma}_{2,w}^{(1)})^2, \ldots, (\hat{\sigma}_{n,w}^{(1)})^2)$ is available. Then subsequent estimates $\hat{Q}^{(u)}$, $u > 1$, are calculated by repeating the following two steps.

Step 1. Use $\hat{Q}^{(u)} = \text{diag}((\hat{\sigma}_{1,w}^{(u)})^2, (\hat{\sigma}_{2,w}^{(u)})^2, \ldots, (\hat{\sigma}_{n,w}^{(u)})^2))$ within (65) – (66) to calculate smoothed input estimates $\hat{w}_{k/N}^{(u)}$.

Step 2. Calculate the elements of $\hat{Q}^{(u+1)} = \text{diag}((\hat{\sigma}_{1,w}^{(u+1)})^2, (\hat{\sigma}_{2,w}^{(u+1)})^2, \ldots, (\hat{\sigma}_{n,w}^{(u+1)})^2)$ using $\hat{w}_{k/N}^{(u)}$ from Step 1 instead of w_k within the MLE formula (46).

8.4.1.2 Properties

In the following it is shown that the variance estimates arising from the above procedure result in monotonic error covariances. The additional term within the design Riccati difference equation (57) that accounts for the presence of parameter error is now given by $S_k^{(u)} = B(\hat{Q}^{(u)} - Q)B^T$. Let $\hat{\Delta}^{(u)}$ denote an approximate spectral factor arising in the design of a

---

"Don't worry about people stealing your ideas. If your ideas are any good, you'll have to ram them down people's throats." *Howard Hathaway Aiken*

smoother using $P_{k/k-1}^{(u)}$ and $K_k^{(u)}$. Employing the notation and approach of Chapter 7, it is straightforward to show that

$$\hat{\Delta}^{(u)}(\hat{\Delta}^{(u)})^H = \Delta\Delta^H + C_k \mathcal{G}_0 (P_{k/k-1}^{(u)} - P_{k+1/k}^{(u)} + S^{(u)}) \mathcal{G}_0^H C_k^T . \quad (67)$$

Define the stacked vectors $v = [v_1^T, \ldots, v_K^T]^T$, $w = [w_1^T, \ldots, w_N^T]^T$, $\hat{w}^{(u)} = [(\hat{w}_{1/N}^{(u)})^T, \ldots, (\hat{w}_{N/N}^{(u)})^T]^T$ and $\tilde{w}^{(u)} = w - \hat{w}^{(u)} = [(\tilde{w}_{1/N}^{(u)})^T, \ldots, (\tilde{w}_{N/N}^{(u)})^T]^T$. The input estimation error is generated by $\tilde{w}^{(u)} = \mathcal{R}^{(u)} \begin{bmatrix} v \\ w \end{bmatrix}$, where $\mathcal{R}_{ei}^{(u)}(\mathcal{R}_{ei}^{(u)})^H = \mathcal{R}_{ei1}^{(u)}(\mathcal{R}_{ei1}^{(u)})^H + \mathcal{R}_{ei2}^{(u)}(\mathcal{R}_{ei2}^{(u)})^H$, in which

$$\mathcal{R}_{ei2}^{(u)} = Q\mathcal{G}^H \left((\hat{\Delta}^{(u)}(\hat{\Delta}^{(u)})^H)^{-1} - (\Delta\Delta^H)^{-1} \right) \Delta , \quad (68)$$

and $\mathcal{R}_{ei1}^{(u)}(\mathcal{R}_{ei1}^{(u)})^H = Q\mathcal{G}_2^H - Q\mathcal{G}^H(\Delta\Delta^H)^{-1}\mathcal{G}Q$. It is shown in the lemma below that the sequence $\left\| \tilde{w}^{(u)}(\tilde{w}^{(u)})^T \right\|_2 = \left\| \mathcal{R}_{ei}^{(u)}(\mathcal{R}_{ei}^{(u)})^H \right\|_2$ is monotonically non-increasing or monotonically non-decreasing, depending on the initial conditions.

Lemma 9: *In respect of Procedure 4 for estimating Q, suppose the following:*

(i) the system (23) – (24) is non-minimum phase, in which A, B, C, D, R are known, $|\lambda_i(\hat{A}^{(1)})| < 1$, i = 1, …, n, the pair (A, C) is observable and D is of full rank;

(ii) the solutions $P_{1/0}^{(1)}$, $P_{1/0}^{(2)}$ of (57) for $\hat{Q}^{(2)} \geq \hat{Q}^{(1)}$ satisfy $P_{1/0}^{(2)} \leq P_{1/0}^{(1)}$ (or the solutions $P_{1/0}^{(1)}$, $P_{1/0}^{(2)}$ of (57) for $\hat{Q}^{(1)} \geq \hat{Q}^{(2)}$ satisfy $P_{1/0}^{(1)} \leq P_{1/0}^{(2)}$).

Then:

(i) $P_{k+1/k}^{(u)} \leq P_{k/k-1}^{(u)}$ *(or $P_{k/k-1}^{(u)} \leq P_{k+1/k}^{(u)}$) for all k, $u \geq 1$;*

(ii) $P_{k+1/k}^{(u+1)} \leq P_{k+1/k}^{(u)}$ *and* $P_{k/k-1}^{(u+1)} \leq P_{k/k-1}^{(u)}$ *(or $P_{k+1/k}^{(u)} \leq P_{k+1/k}^{(u+1)}$ and $P_{k/k-1}^{(u)} \leq P_{k/k-1}^{(u+1)}$) for all k, $u \geq 1$;*

(iii) $\left\| \mathcal{R}_{ei}^{(u+1)}(\mathcal{R}_{ei}^{(u+1)})^H \right\|_2 \leq \left\| \mathcal{R}_{ei}^{(u)}(\mathcal{R}_{ei}^{(u)})^H \right\|_2$ *(or $\left\| \mathcal{R}_{ei}^{(u)}(\mathcal{R}_{ei}^{(u)})^H \right\|_2 \leq \left\| \mathcal{R}_{ei}^{(u+1)}(\mathcal{R}_{ei}^{(u+1)})^H \right\|_2$) for $u \geq 1$.*

Proof: *(i) and (ii) This follows from $S^{(u+1)} \leq S^{(u)}$ within condition (iii) of Theorem 2 of Chapter 8. Since $\mathcal{R}_{ei1}^{(u)}(\mathcal{R}_{ei1}^{(u)})^H$ is common to $\mathcal{R}_{ei}^{(u)}(\mathcal{R}_{ei}^{(u)})^H$ and $\mathcal{R}_{ei}^{(u+1)}(\mathcal{R}_{ei}^{(u+1)})^H$, it suffices to show that*

$$\left\| \mathcal{R}_{ei2}^{(u+1)}(\mathcal{R}_{ei2}^{(u+1)})^H \right\|_2 \leq \left\| \mathcal{R}_{ei2}^{(u)}(\mathcal{R}_{ei2}^{(u)})^H \right\|_2 . \quad (69)$$

Substituting (67) into (68) yields

$$\mathcal{R}_{ei2}^{(u)} = Q\mathcal{G}^H \left(\Delta\Delta^H + C_k \mathcal{G}_0 (P_{k/k-1}^{(u)} - P_{k+1/k}^{(u)} + S^{(u)}) \mathcal{G}_0^H C_k^T)^{-1} - (\Delta\Delta^H)^{-1} \right) \Delta . \quad (70)$$

"We have always been shameless about stealing great ideas." *Steven Paul Jobs*

Note for linear time-invariant systems X, $Y_1 \geq Y_2$, that

$$(XX^H)^{-1} - (XX^H + Y_1)^{-1} \geq (XX^H)^{-1} - (XX^H + Y_2)^{-1}. \tag{71}$$

Since $\left\| \mathcal{G}_0 (P^{(u+1)}_{k/k-1} - P^{(u+1)}_{k+1/k} + S^{(u+1)}) \mathcal{G}_0^H \right\|_2 \leq \left\| \mathcal{G}_0 (P^{(u)}_{k/k-1} - P^{(u)}_{k+1/k} + S^{(u)}) \mathcal{G}_0^H \right\|_2$, *(69) follows from (70) and (71).* □

As is the case for the filtering EM algorithm, the process noise variance estimates asymptotically approach the exact values when the SNR is sufficiently high.

Lemma 10: *Under the conditions of Lemma 9,*

$$\lim_{Q^{-1} \to 0, R \to 0, u \to \infty} \hat{Q}^{(u)} = Q. \tag{72}$$

Proof: *By inspection of the input estimator,* $\mathcal{H}_{IE} = Q\mathcal{G}^H(\Delta\Delta^H)^{-1} = Q\mathcal{G}^H(\mathcal{G}Q\mathcal{G}^H + R)^{-1}$, *it follows that* $\lim_{Q^{-1} \to 0, R \to 0, u \to \infty} \mathcal{H}_{IE} = \mathcal{G}^{-1}$ *and therefore* $\lim_{Q^{-1} \to 0, R \to 0, u \to \infty} \hat{w}^{(u)}_{k/N} = w_k$, *which implies (72), since the MLE (46) is unbiased for large N.* □

It is observed anecdotally that the variance estimates produced by the above smoothing EM algorithm are more accurate than those from the corresponding filtering procedure. This is consistent with the following comparison of approximate CRLBs.

Lemma 11 [26]:

$$-\left(\frac{\partial^2 \log f(\sigma^2_{i,w} \mid \hat{x}_{k/N})}{(\partial \sigma^2_{i,w})^2} \right)^{-1} < -\left(\frac{\partial^2 \log f(\sigma^2_{i,w} \mid \hat{x}_{k/k})}{(\partial \sigma^2_{i,w})^2} \right)^{-1}. \tag{73}$$

Proof: *The vector state elements within (23) can be written in terms of smoothed state estimates,* $x_{i,k+1} = A_i \hat{x}_{k/N} + w_{i,k} = A_i x_k + w_{i,k} - A_i \tilde{x}_{k/N}$, *where* $\tilde{x}_{k/N} = x_k - \hat{x}_{k/N}$. *From the approach of Example 8, the second partial derivative of the corresponding approximate log-likelihood function with respect to the process noise variance is*

$$\frac{\partial^2 \log f(\sigma^2_{i,w} \mid \hat{x}_{k/N})}{(\partial \sigma^2_{i,w})^2} = -\frac{N}{2}(\sigma^2_{i,w} + A_i E\{\tilde{x}_{k/N}\tilde{x}^T_{k/N}\} A_i^T)^{-2}.$$

Similarly, the use of filtered state estimates leads to

$$\frac{\partial^2 \log f(\sigma^2_{i,w} \mid \hat{x}_{k/k})}{(\partial \sigma^2_{i,w})^2} = -\frac{N}{2}(\sigma^2_{i,w} + A_i E\{\tilde{x}_{k/k}\tilde{x}^T_{k/k}\} A_i^T)^{-2}.$$

The minimum-variance smoother minimizes both the causal part and the non-causal part of the estimation error, whereas the Kalman filter only minimizes the causal part. Therefore, $E\{\tilde{x}_{k/N}\tilde{x}^T_{k/N}\} < E\{\tilde{x}_{k/k}\tilde{x}^T_{k/k}\}$. *Thus, the claim (73) follows.* □

"The power of an idea can be measured by the degree of resistance it attracts." *David Yoho*

8.4.2 State Matrix Estimation

8.4.2.1 EM Algorithm

Smoothed state estimates are obtained from the smoothed inputs via

$$\hat{x}^{(u)}_{k+1/N} = A_k \hat{x}^{(u)}_{k/N} + B_k \hat{w}^{(u)}_{k/N} . \tag{74}$$

The resulting $\hat{x}^{(u)}_{k/N}$ are used below to iteratively re-estimate state matrix elements.

***Procedure* 5.** Assume that there exists an initial estimate $\hat{A}^{(1)}$ of A such that $|\lambda_i(\hat{A}^{(1)})| < 1$, i = 1, …, n. Subsequent estimates, $\hat{A}^{(u)}$, $u > 1$, are calculated using the following two-step EM algorithm.

Step 1. Operate the minimum-variance smoother recursions (65), (66), (74) designed with $\hat{A}^{(u)}$ to obtain $\hat{x}^{(u)}_{k/N}$.

Step 2. Copy $\hat{A}^{(u)}$ to $\hat{A}^{(u+1)}$. Use $\hat{x}^{(u)}_{k/N}$ instead of x_k within (53) to obtain candidate estimates $\hat{a}^{(u+1)}_{i,j}$, $i, j = 1, …, n$. Include $\hat{a}^{(u+1)}_{i,j}$ within $\hat{A}^{(u+1)}$ if $|\lambda_i(\hat{A}^{(u+1)})| < 1$, $i = 1, …, n$.

8.4.2.2 Properties

Denote $x = [x_1^T, …, x_N^T]^T$, $\hat{x}^{(u)} = [(\hat{x}^{(u)}_{1/N})^T, …, (\hat{x}^{(u)}_{N/N})^T]^T$ and $\tilde{x}^{(u)} = x - \hat{x}^{(u)} = [(\tilde{x}^{(u)}_{1/N})^T, …, (\tilde{x}^{(u)}_{N/N})^T]^T$. Let $\mathcal{R}^{(u)}$ be redefined as the system that maps the inputs $\begin{bmatrix} v \\ w \end{bmatrix}$ to smoother state estimation error $\tilde{x}^{(u)}$, that is, $\tilde{x}^{(u)} = \mathcal{R}^{(u)} \begin{bmatrix} v \\ w \end{bmatrix}$. It is stated below that the estimated state matrix iterates result in a monotonic sequence of state error covariances.

***Lemma* 12:** *In respect of Procedure 5 for estimating A and x, suppose the following:*

(i) the system (23) – (24) is non-minimum phase, in which B, C, D, Q, R are known, $|\lambda_i(\hat{A}^{(u+1)})| < 1$*, the pair (A, C) is observable and D is of full rank;*

(ii) there exist solutions $P^{(1)}_{1/0}$, $P^{(2)}_{1/0}$ *of (57) for* $AA^T \le A^{(2)}(A^{(2)})^T \le A^{(1)}(A^{(1)})^T$ *satisfying* $P^{(2)}_{1/0} \le P^{(1)}_{1/0}$ *(or the solutions* $P^{(1)}_{1/0}$, $P^{(2)}_{1/0}$ *of (31) for* $A^{(1)}(A^{(1)})^T \le A^{(2)}(A^{(2)})^T \le AA^T$ *satisfying* $P^{(1)}_{1/0} \le P^{(2)}_{1/0}$*).*

Then $\left\| \mathcal{R}^{(u+1)}_{ei} (\mathcal{R}^{(u+1)}_{ei})^H \right\|_2 \le \left\| \mathcal{R}^{(u)}_{ei} (\mathcal{R}^{(u)}_{ei})^H \right\|_2$ *(or* $\left\| \mathcal{R}^{(u)}_{ei} (\mathcal{R}^{(u)}_{ei})^H \right\|_2 \le \left\| \mathcal{R}^{(u+1)}_{ei} (\mathcal{R}^{(u+1)}_{ei})^H \right\|_2$*) for* $u \ge 1$.

"You do not really understand something unless you can explain it to your grandmother." *Albert Einstein*

The proof is omitted since it follows *mutatis mutandis* from that of Lemma 9. Suppose that the smoother (65), (66) designed with the estimates $\hat{a}_{i,j}^{(u)}$ is employed to calculate input estimates $\hat{w}_{k/N}^{(u)}$. An approximate log-likelihood function for the unknown $a_{i,j}$ given samples of $\hat{w}_{k/N}^{(u)}$ is

$$\log f(a_{i,j} \mid \hat{w}_{i,k/K}^{(u)}) = -\frac{N}{2}\log 2\pi - \frac{N}{2}\log(\sigma_{i,w}^{(u)})^2 - \frac{1}{2}(\sigma_{i,w}^{(u)})^{-2}\sum_{k=1}^{N}\hat{w}_{i,k/K}^{(u)}(\hat{w}_{i,k/N}^{(u)})^T. \tag{75}$$

Now let $\mathcal{R}^{(u)}$ denote the map from $\begin{bmatrix} v \\ w \end{bmatrix}$ to the smoother input estimation error $\tilde{w}^{(u)}$ = w – $\hat{w}^{(u)}$ at iteration u. It is argued below that the sequence of state matrix iterates maximises (75).

Lemma 13: *Under the conditions of Lemma 12,* $\left\| \mathcal{R}^{(u+1)}(\mathcal{R}^{(u+1)})^H \right\|_2 \le \left\| \mathcal{R}^{(u)}(\mathcal{R}^{(u)})^H \right\|_2$ *for* $u \ge 1$.

The proof follows *mutatis mutandis* from that of Lemma 9. The above Lemma implies

$$E\{\tilde{w}^{(u+1)}(\tilde{w}^{(u+1)})^T\} \le E\{\tilde{w}^{(u)}(\tilde{w}^{(u)})^T\}. \tag{76}$$

It follows from $\hat{w}^{(u)}$ = w – $\tilde{w}^{(u)}$ that $E\{\tilde{w}^{(u)}(\tilde{w}^{(u)})^T\}$ = $E\{w + \tilde{w}^{(u)})(w + (\tilde{w}^{(u)})^T\}$ = $E\{\tilde{w}^{(u)}(\tilde{w}^{(u)})^T\}$ + Q, which together with (76) implies $E\{\hat{w}^{(u+1)}(\hat{w}^{(u+1)})^T\} \le E\{\hat{w}^{(u)}(\hat{w}^{(u)})^T\}$ and $\log f(a_{i,jw} \mid \hat{w}_{i,k/N}^{(u+1)}) \ge \log f(a_{i,jw} \mid \hat{w}_{i,k/K}^{(u)})$ for all $u \ge 1$. Therefore, it is expected that the sequence of state matrix estimates will similarly vary monotonically. Next, it is stated that the state matrix estimates asymptotically approach the exact values when the SNR is sufficiently high.

Lemma 14: *Under the conditions of Lemma 9,*

$$\lim_{Q^{-1}\to 0, R\to 0, u\to\infty} \hat{A}^{(u)} = A. \tag{77}$$

Proof: *From the proof of Lemma 10,* $\lim_{Q^{-1}\to 0, R\to 0, u\to\infty} \hat{w}_{k/N}^{(u)} = w_k$, *therefore, the states within (74) are reconstructed exactly. Thus, the claim (77) follows since the MLE (53) is unbiased.* □

It is expected that the above EM smoothing algorithm offers improved state matrix estimation accuracy.

Lemma 15:

$$-\left(\frac{\partial^2 \log f(a_{i,j} \mid \hat{x}_{k/N})}{(\partial a_{i,j})^2}\right)^{-1} \le -\left(\frac{\partial^2 \log f(a_{i,j} \mid \hat{x}_{k/k})}{(\partial a_{i,j})^2}\right)^{-1}. \tag{78}$$

"The test of a first-rate intelligence is the ability to hold two opposed ideas in mind at the same time and still retain the ability to function." *Francis Scott Key Fitzgerald*

Proof: *Using smoothed states within (51) yields* $x_{i,k+1} = \sum_{j=1}^{n} a_{i,j}\hat{x}_{i,k/N} + w_{i,k} = \sum_{j=1}^{n} a_{i,j}x_{i,k} + w_{i,k} - \sum_{j=1}^{n} a_{i,j}\tilde{x}_{i,k/N}$, *where* $\tilde{x}_{k/N} = x_k - \hat{x}_{k/N}$. *The second partial derivative of the corresponding log-likelihood function with respect to* $a_{i,j}$ *is*

$$\frac{\partial^2 \log f(a_{i,j} \mid \hat{x}_{k/N})}{(\partial a_{i,j})^2} = -\frac{N}{2}(\sigma_{i,w}^2 + A_i E\{\tilde{x}_{k/N}\tilde{x}_{k/N}^T\}A_i^T)^{-1}\sum_{k=1}^{N} x_{j,k}^2 .$$

Similarly, the use of filtered state estimates leads to

$$\frac{\partial^2 \log f(a_{i,j} \mid \hat{x}_{k/k})}{(\partial a_{i,j})^2} = -\frac{N}{2}(\sigma_{i,w}^2 + A_i E\{\tilde{x}_{k/k}\tilde{x}_{k/k}^T\}A_i^T)^{-1}\sum_{k=1}^{N} x_{j,k}^2 .$$

The result (78) follows since $E\{\tilde{x}_{k/N}\tilde{x}_{k/N}^T\} < E\{\tilde{x}_{k/k}\tilde{x}_{k/k}^T\}$. □

Example 13.: Consider a system where $B = C = D = Q = 1$, $R = \{0.0001, 0.0002, 0.0003\}$ are known and $A = 0.9$ but is unknown. Simulations were conducted using 30 noise realizations with $N = 500{,}000$. The results of the above smoothing EM algorithm and the filtering EM algorithms, initialized with $\hat{A}^{(0)} = 1.03A$, are respectively shown by the dotted and dashed lines within Fig. 6. The figure shows that the estimates improve with increasing u, which is consistent with Lemma 15. The estimates also improve with increasing SNR which illustrates Lemmas 8 and 14. It is observed anecdotally that the smoother EM algorithm outperforms the filter EM algorithm for estimation of A at high signal-to-noise-ratios.

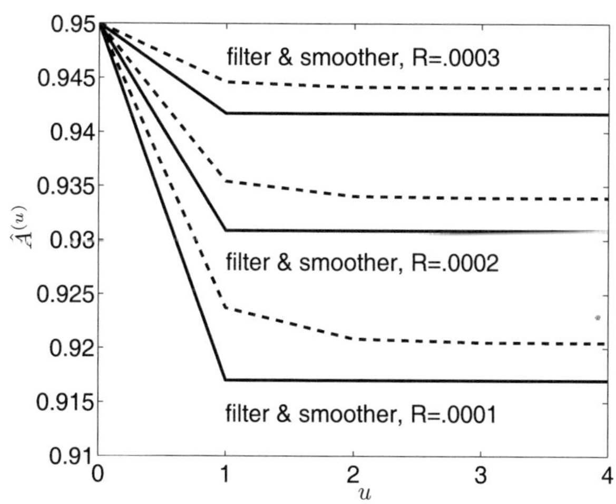

Fig. 6. State matrix estimates calculated by the smoother EM algorithm and filter EM algorithm for Example 13. It can be seen that the $\hat{A}^{(u)}$ better approach the nominal A at higher SNR.

"From the time I was seven, when I purchased my first calculator, I was fascinated by the idea of a machine that could compute things." *Michael Dell*

8.4.3 Measurement Noise Variance Estimation

The discussion of an EM procedure for measurement noise variance estimation is presented in a summary form because it follows analogously to the algorithms described previously.

Procedure 6. Assume that an initial estimate $\hat{R}^{(1)}$ of R is available. Subsequent estimates $\hat{R}^{(u)}$, $u > 1$, are calculated by repeating the following two-step procedure.

Step 1. Operate the minimum-variance smoother (7.66), (7.68), (7.69) designed with $\hat{R}^{(u)}$ to obtain corrected output estimates $\hat{y}_{k/N}^{(u)}$.

Step 2. For $i = 1, \ldots, p$, use $\hat{y}_{k/N}^{(u)}$ instead of y_k within (27) to obtain $\hat{R}^{(u+1)} = \text{diag}((\hat{\sigma}_{1,v}^{(u+1)})^2, (\hat{\sigma}_{2,v}^{(u+1)})^2, \ldots, (\hat{\sigma}_{n,v}^{(u+1)})^2)$.

It can be shown using the approach of Lemma 9 that the sequence of measurement noise variance estimates are either monotonically non-increasing or non-decreasing depending on the initial conditions. When the SNR is sufficiently low, the measurement noise variance estimates converge to the actual value.

Lemma 16: *In respect of Procedure 6,*

$$\lim_{R^{-1}\to 0, Q \to 0, u \to \infty} R^{(u)} = R. \tag{79}$$

Proof: *By inspection of the output,* $\mathcal{H}_{OE} = \mathcal{G}Q\mathcal{G}^H(\mathcal{G}Q\mathcal{G}^H + R)^{-1}$, *it follows that* $\lim_{R^{-1}\to 0, Q \to 0, u \to \infty} \mathcal{H}_{IE} = 0$, *which together with the observation* $\lim_{R^{-1}\to 0, Q \to 0, u \to \infty} E\{zz^T\} = R$ *implies (79), since the MLE (27) is unbiased for large N.* □

Once again, the variance estimates produced by the above procedure are expected to be more accurate than those relying on filtered estimates.

Lemma 17:

$$-\left(\frac{\partial^2 \log f(\sigma_{i,v}^2 \mid \hat{y}_{k/N})}{(\partial \sigma_{i,v}^2)^2}\right)^{-1} < -\left(\frac{\partial^2 \log f(\sigma_{i,v}^2 \mid \hat{y}_{k/k})}{(\partial \sigma_{i,v}^2)^2}\right)^{-1}. \tag{80}$$

Proof: *The second partial derivative of the corresponding log-likelihood function with respect to the process noise variance is*

$$\frac{\partial^2 \log f(\sigma_{i,v}^2 \mid \hat{y}_{i,k/N})}{(\partial \sigma_{i,v}^2)^2} = -\frac{N}{2}(\sigma_{i,v}^2 + E\{\tilde{y}_{i,k/K}\tilde{y}_{i,k/K}^T\})^{-2},$$

"It is unworthy of excellent men to lose hours like slaves in the labor of calculation which could be relegated to anyone else if machines were used." *Gottfried Wilhelm von Leibnitz*

where $\tilde{y}^{(u)}_{k/N} = y - \hat{y}^{(u)}_{k/N}$. *Similarly, the use of filtered state estimates leads to*

$$\frac{\partial^2 \log f(\sigma^2_{i,v} \mid \hat{y}_{i,k/k})}{(\partial \sigma^2_{i,v})^2} = -\frac{N}{2}(\sigma^2_{i,v} + E\{\tilde{y}_{i,k/k}\tilde{y}^T_{i,k/k}\})^{-2},$$

where $\tilde{y}^{(u)}_{k/k} = y - \hat{y}^{(u)}_{k/k}$. *The claim (80) follows since* $E\{\tilde{y}_{k/N}\tilde{y}^T_{k/N}\} < E\{\tilde{y}_{k/k}\tilde{y}^T_{k/k}\}$. □

8.5 Conclusion

From the Central Limit Theorem, the mean of a large sample of independent identically distributed random variables asymptotically approaches a normal distribution. Consequently, parameter estimates are often obtained by maximising Gaussian log-likelihood functions.

Unknown process noise variances and state matrix elements can be estimated by considering i single-input state evolutions of the form $x_{i,k+1} = \sum_{j=1}^{n} a_{i,j}x_{i,k} + w_{i,k}$, $a_{i,j}$, $x_{i,k}$, $w_{i,k} \in \mathbb{R}$. Similarly, unknown measurement noise variances can be estimated by considering i single-output observations of the form $z_{i,k} = y_{i,k} + v_{i,k}$, where $y_{i,k} + v_{i,k} \in \mathbb{R}$. The resulting MLEs are listed in Table 1 and are unbiased provided that the assumed models are correct and the number of samples is large.

The above parameter estimates rely on the availability of complete $x_{i,k}$ and $y_{i,k}$ information. Usually, both states and parameters need to be estimated from measurements. The EM algorithm is a common technique for solving joint state and parameter estimation problems. It has been shown that the estimation sequences vary monotonically and depend on the initial conditions. However, the use of imperfect states from filters or smoothers within the MLE calculations leads to biased parameter estimates. An examination of the approximate Cramér-Rao lower bounds shows that the use of smoothed states as opposed to filtered states is expected to provide improved parameter estimation accuracy.

When the SNR is sufficiently high, the states are recovered exactly and the bias terms diminish to zero, in which case $\lim_{Q^{-1}\to 0, R\to 0} \hat{\sigma}^2_{i,w} = \sigma^2_{i,w}$ and $\lim_{Q^{-1}\to 0, R\to 0} \hat{a}_{i,j} = a_{i,j}$. Therefore, the process noise variance and state matrix estimation procedures described herein are only advocated when the measurement noise is negligible. Conversely, when the SNR is sufficiently low, that is, when the estimation problem is dominated by measurement noise, then $\lim_{Q\to 0, R^{-1}\to 0} \hat{\sigma}^2_{i,v} = \sigma^2_{i,v}$. Thus, measurement noise estimation should only be attempted when the signal is absent. If parameter estimates are desired at intermediate SNRs then the subspace identification techniques such as [13], [14] are worthy of consideration.

"If automobiles had followed the same development cycle as the computer, a Rolls-Royce would today cost $100, get a million miles per gallon, and explode once a year, killing everyone inside." *Mark Stephens*

	ASSUMPTIONS	MAIN RESULTS
Process noise variance	$w_{i,k} \sim \mathcal{N}(0, \sigma_{i,w}^2)$	$\hat{\sigma}_{i,w}^2 = \frac{1}{N}\sum_{k=1}^{N}(x_{i,k+1} - \sum_{j=1}^{n} a_{i,j}x_{i,k})^2$
State matrix elements	$x_{i,k+1} \sim \mathcal{N}(\sum_{j=1}^{n} a_{i,j}x_{i,k},\ \sigma_{i,w}^2)$	$\hat{a}_{i,j} = \frac{\sum_{k=1}^{N}\left(x_{i,k+1} - \sum_{j=1, j\neq i}^{n} a_{i,j}x_{i,k}\right)x_{j,k}}{\sum_{k=1}^{N} x_{j,k}^2}$
Measurement noise variance	$v_{i,k} \sim \mathcal{N}(0, \sigma_{i,v}^2)$	$\hat{\sigma}_{i,v}^2 = \frac{1}{N}\sum_{k=1}^{N}(z_{i,k} - y_{i,k})^2$

Table 1. MLEs for process noise variance, state matrix element and measurement noise variance.

8.6 Problems

Problem 1.

(i) Consider the second order difference equation $x_{k+2} + a_1x_{k+1} + a_0x_k = w_k$. Assuming that $w_k \sim \mathcal{N}(0, \sigma_w^2)$, obtain an equation for the MLEs of the unknown a_1 and a_0.

(ii) Consider the nth order autoregressive system $x_{k+n} + a_{n-1}x_{k+n-1} + a_{n-2}x_{k+n-2} + \ldots + a_0x_k = w_k$, where $a_{n-1}, a_{n-2}, \ldots, a_0$ are unknown. From the assumption $w_k \sim \mathcal{N}(0, \sigma_w^2)$, obtain an equation for MLEs of the unknown coefficients.

Problem 2. Suppose that N samples of $x_{k+1} = Ax_k + w_k$ are available, where $w_k \sim \mathcal{N}(0, \sigma_w^2)$, in which σ_w^2 is an unknown parameter.

(i) Write down a Gaussian log-likelihood function for the unknown parameter, given x_k.

(ii) Derive a formula for the MLE $\hat{\sigma}_w^2$ of σ_w^2.

(iii) Show that $E\{\hat{\sigma}_w^2\} = \sigma_w^2$ provided that N is large.

(iv) Find the Cramér Rao lower bound for $\hat{\sigma}_w^2$.

(v) Replace the actual states x_k with filtered state $\hat{x}_{k/k}$ within the MLE formula. Obtain a high SNR asymptote for this approximate MLE.

"The question of whether computers can think is like the question of whether submarines can swim." *Edsger Wybe Dijkstra*

Problem 3. Consider the state evolution $x_{k+1} = Ax_k + w_k$, where $A \in \mathbb{R}^{n\times n}$ is unknown and $w_k \in \mathbb{R}^n$.

(i) Write down a Gaussian log-likelihood function for the unknown components $a_{i,j}$ of A, given x_k and x_{k+1}.
(ii) Derive a formula for the MLE $\hat{a}_{i,j}$ of $a_{i,j}$.
(iii) Show that $E\{\hat{a}_{i,j}\} = a_{i,j}$. Replace the actual states x_k with the filtered state $\hat{x}_{k/k}$ within the obtained formula to yield an approximate MLE for $a_{i,j}$.
(iv) Obtain a high SNR asymptote for the approximate MLE.

Problem 4. Consider measurements of a sinusoidal signal modelled by $y_k = A\cos(2\pi fk + \varphi) + v_k$, with amplitude $A > 0$, frequency $0 < f < 0.5$, phase φ and Gaussian white measurement noise v_k.

(i) Assuming that φ and f are known, determine the Fisher information and the Cramér Rao lower bound for an unknown A.
(ii) Assuming that A and φ are known, determine the fisher information and the Cramér Rao lower bound for an unknown f_0.
(iii) Assuming that A and f are known, determine the Fisher information and the Cramér Rao lower bound .
(iv) Assuming that the vector parameter $[A^T, f^T, \varphi^T]^T$ is known, determine the Fisher information matrix and the Cramér Rao lower bound. (Hint: use small angle approximations for sine and cosine, see [2].)

8.7 Glossary

SNR	Signal to noise ratio.
MLE	Maximum likelihood estimate.
CRLB	Cramér Rao Lower Bound
$F(\theta)$	The Fisher information of a parameter θ.
$x_k \sim \mathcal{N}(0, \sigma^2)$	The random variable x_k is normally distributed with mean μ and variance σ^2.
$w_{i,k}$, $v_{i,k}$, $z_{i,k}$	i^{th} elements of vectors w_k , v_k , z_k.
$\hat{\sigma}_{i,w}^{(u)}$, $\hat{\sigma}_{i,v}^{(u)}$	Estimates of variances of $w_{i,k}$ and $v_{i,k}$ at iteration u.
$\hat{A}^{(u)}$, $\hat{R}^{(u)}$, $\hat{Q}^{(u)}$	Estimates of state matrix A, covariances R and Q at iteration u.
$\lambda_i(\hat{A}^{(u)})$	The i eigenvalues of $\hat{A}^{(u)}$.
A_i , C_i	i^{th} row of state-space matrices A and C.

"What lies at the heart of every living thing is not a fire, not warm breath, not a 'spark of life' It is information, words, instructions." *Clinton Richard Dawkins*

$K_{i,k}$, $L_{i,k}$	i^{th} row of predictor and filter gain matrices K_k and L_k.
$S_k^{(u)}$	Additive term within the design Riccati difference equation to account for the presence of modelling error at time k and iteration u.
$a_{i,j}$	Element in row i and column j of A.
$C_k^{\#}$	Moore-Penrose pseudo-inverse of C_k.
$\mathcal{R}^{(u)}$	A system (or map) that operates on the filtering/smoothing problem inputs to produce the input, state or output estimation error at iteration u. It is convenient to make use of the factorisation $\mathcal{R}_{ei}^{(u)}(\mathcal{R}_{ei}^{(u)})^H = \mathcal{R}_{ei1}^{(u)}(\mathcal{R}_{ei1}^{(u)})^H + \mathcal{R}_{ei2}^{(u)}(\mathcal{R}_{ei2}^{(u)})^H$, where $\mathcal{R}_{ei2}^{(u)}(\mathcal{R}_{ei2}^{(u)})^H$ includes the filter or smoother solution and $\mathcal{R}_{ei1}^{(u)}(\mathcal{R}_{ei1}^{(u)})^H$ is a lower performance bound.

8.8 References

[1] L. L. Scharf, *Statistical Signal Processing: Detection, Estimation, and Time Series Analysis*, Addison-Wesley Publishing Company Inc., Massachusetts, USA, 1990.

[2] S. M. Kay, *Fundamentals of Statistical Signal Processing: Estimation Theory*, Prentice Hall, Englewood Cliffs, New Jersey, ch. 7, pp. 157 - 204, 1993.

[3] G. J. McLachlan and T. Krishnan, *The EM Algorithm and Extensions*, John Wiley & Sons, Inc., New York, 1997.

[4] H. L. Van Trees and K. L. Bell (Editors), *Baysesian Bounds for Parameter Estimation and Nonlinear Filtering/Tracking*, John Wiley & Sons, Inc., New Jersey, 2007.

[5] A. Van Den Bos, *Parameter Estimation for Scientists and Engineers*, John Wiley & Sons, New Jersey, 2007.

[6] R. K. Mehra, "On the identification of variances and adaptive Kalman filtering", *IEEE Transactions on Automatic Control*, vol. 15, pp. 175 - 184, Apr. 1970.

[7] D. C. Rife and R. R. Boorstyn, "Single-Tone Parameter Estimation from Discrete-time Observations", *IEEE Transactions on Information Theory*, vol. 20, no. 5, pp. 591 - 598, Sep. 1974.

[8] R. P. Nayak and E. C. Foundriat, "Sequential Parameter Estimation Using Pseudoinverse", *IEEE Transactions on Automatic Control*, vol. 19, no. 1, pp. 81 - 83, Feb. 1974.

[9] P. R. Bélanger, "Estimation of Noise Covariance Matrices for a Linear Time-Varying Stochastic Process", *Automatica*, vol. 10, pp. 267 - 275, 1974.

[10] V. Strejc, "Least Squares Parameter Estimation", *Automatica*, vol. 16, pp. 535 - 550, Sep. 1980.

[11] A. P. Dempster, N. M. Laid and D. B. Rubin, "Maximum likelihood from incomplete data via the EM algorithm," *Journal of the Royal Statistical Society*, vol 39, no. 1, pp. 1 - 38, 1977.

[12] P. Van Overschee and B. De Moor, "A Unifying Theorem for Three Subspace System Identification Algorithms", *Automatica*, 1995.

"In my lifetime, we've gone from Eisenhower to George W. Bush. We've gone from John F. Kennedy to Al Gore. If this is evolution, I believe that in twelve years, we'll be voting for plants." *Lewis Niles Black*

[13] T. Katayama and G. Picci, "Realization of stochastic systems with exogenous inputs and subspace identification methods", *Automatica*, vol. 35, pp. 1635 - 1652, 1999.
[14] T. Katayama, *Subspace Methods for System Identification*, Springer-Verlag London Limited, 2005.
[15] R. H. Shumway and D. S. Stoffer, "An approach to time series smoothing and forecasting using the EM algorithm," *Journal of Time Series Analysis*, vol. 3, no. 4, pp. 253 - 264, 1982.
[16] C. F. J. Wu, "On the convergence properties of the EM algorithm," *Annals of Statistics*, vol. 11,no. 1, pp. 95 - 103, Mar. 1983.
[17] M. Feder and E. Weinstein, "Parameter estimation of superimposed signals using the EM algorithm," *IEEE Transactions on Signal Processing*, vol. 36, no. 4, pp. 477 - 489, Apr. 198
[18] G. A. Einicke, "Optimal and Robust Noncausal Filter Formulations", *IEEE Transactions on Signal Processing*, vol. 54, no. 3, pp. 1069 - 1077, Mar. 2006.
[19] G. A. Einicke, J. T. Malos, D. C. Reid and D. W. Hainsworth, "Riccati Equation and EM Algorithm Convergence for Inertial Navigation Alignment", *IEEE Transactions on Signal Processing*, vol 57, no. 1, Jan. 2009.
[20] G. A. Einicke, G. Falco and J. T. Malos, "EM Algorithm State Matrix Estimation for Navigation", *IEEE Signal Processing Letters*, vol. 17, no. 5, pp. 437 - 440, May 2010.
[21] T. K. Moon, "The Expectation-Maximization Algorithm", *IEEE Signal Processing Magazine*, vol. 13, pp. 47 - 60, Nov. 1996.
[22] D. G. Tzikas, A. C. Likas and N. P. Galatsanos, "The Variational Approximation for Bayesian Inference: Life After the EM Algorithm", *IEEE Signal Processing Magazine*, vol. 25, Iss. 6, pp. 131 - 146, Nov. 200
[23] D. M. Titterington, A. F. M. Smith and U. E. Makov, *Statistical Analysis of Finite Mixture Distributions*, Wiley, Chichester and New York, 1985.
[24] R. P. Savage, *Strapdown Analytics*, Strapdown Associates, vol. 2, ch. 15, pp. 15.1 - 15.142, 2000.
[25] P. K. Seidelmann, ed., *Explanatory supplement to the Astronomical Almanac*, Mill Valley, Cal., University Science Books, pp. 52 and 698, 1992.
[26] G. A. Einicke, G. Falco, M. T. Dunn and D. C. Reid, "Iterative Smoother-Based Variance Estimation", IEEE Signal Processing letters, 2012 (to appear).

"The faithful duplication and repair exhibited by the double-stranded DNA structure would seem to be incompatible with the process of evolution. Thus, evolution has been explained by the occurrence of errors during DNA replication and repair." *Tomoyuki Shibata*

9

Robust Prediction, Filtering and Smoothing

9.1 Introduction

The previously-discussed optimum predictor, filter and smoother solutions assume that the model parameters are correct, the noise processes are Gaussian and their associated covariances are known precisely. These solutions are optimal in a mean-square-error sense, that is they provide the best average performance. If the above assumptions are correct, then the filter's mean-square-error equals the trace of design error covariance. The underlying modelling and noise assumptions are a often convenient fiction. They do, however, serve to allow estimated performance to be weighed against implementation complexity.

In general, robustness means "the persistence of a system's characteristic behaviour under perturbations or conditions of uncertainty" [1]. In an estimation context, robust solutions refer to those that accommodate uncertainties in problem specifications. They are also known as worst-case or peak error designs. The standard predictor, filter and smoother structures are retained but a larger design error covariance is used to account for the presence of modelling error.

Designs that cater for worst cases are likely to exhibit poor average performance. Suppose that a bridge designed for average loading conditions returns an acceptable cost benefit. Then a design that is focussed on accommodating infrequent peak loads is likely to provide degraded average cost performance. Similarly, a worst-case shoe design that accommodates rarely occurring large feet would provide poor fitting performance on average. That is, robust designs tend to be conservative. In practice, a trade-off may be desired between optimum and robust designs.

The material canvassed herein is based on the H_∞ filtering results from robust control. The robust control literature is vast, see [2] – [33] and the references therein. As suggested above, the H_∞ solutions of interest here involve observers having gains that are obtained by solving Riccati equations. This Riccati equation solution approach relies on the Bounded Real Lemma – see the pioneering work by Vaidyanathan [2] and Petersen [3]. The Bounded Real Lemma is implicit with game theory [9] – [19]. Indeed, the continuous-time solutions presented in this section originate from the game theoretic approach of Doyle, Glover, Khargonekar, Francis Limebeer, Anderson, Khargonekar, Green, Theodore and Shaked, see [4], [13], [15], [21]. The discussed discrete-time versions stem from the results of Limebeer, Green, Walker, Yaesh, Shaked, Xie, de Souza and Wang, see [5], [11], [18], [19], [21]. In the parlance of game theory: "a statistician is trying to best estimate a linear combination of the states of a system that is driven by nature; nature is trying to cause the statistician's estimate

---

"On a huge hill, Cragged, and steep, Truth stands, and he that will Reach her, about must, and about must go." *John Donne*

to be as erroneous as possible, while trying to minimize the energy it invests in driving the system" [19].

Pertinent state-space H_∞ predictors, filters and smoothers are described in [4] - [19]. Some prediction, filtering and smoothing results are summarised in [13] and methods for accommodating model uncertainty are described in [14], [18], [19]. The aforementioned methods for handling model uncertainty can result in conservative designs (that depart far from optimality). This has prompted the use of linear matrix inequality solvers in [20], [23] to search for optimal solutions to model uncertainty problems.

It is explained in [15], [19], [21] that a saddle-point strategy for the games leads to robust estimators, and the resulting robust smoothing, filtering and prediction solutions are summarised below. While the solution structures remain unchanged, designers need to tweak the scalar within the underlying Riccati equations.

This chapter has two main parts. Section 9.2 describes robust continuous-time solutions and the discrete-time counterparts are presented in Section 9.3. The previously discussed techniques each rely on a trick. The optimum filters and smoothers arise by completing the square. In maximum-likelihood estimation, a function is differentiated with respect to an unknown parameter and then set to zero. The trick behind the described robust estimation techniques is the Bounded Real Lemma, which opens the discussions.

9.2 Robust Continuous-time Estimation

9.2.1 Continuous-Time Bounded Real Lemma

First, consider the unforced system

$$\dot{x}(t) = A(t)x(t) \tag{1}$$

over a time interval $t \in [0, T]$, where $A(t) \in \mathbb{R}^{n \times n}$. For notational convenience, define the stacked vector $x = \{x(t), t \in [0, T]\}$. From Lyapunov stability theory [36], the system (1) is asymptotically stable if there exists a function $V(x(t)) > 0$ such that $\dot{V}(x(t)) < 0$. A possible Lyapunov function is $V(x(t)) = x^T(t)P(t)x(t)$, where $P(t) = P^T(t) \in \mathbb{R}^{n \times n}$ is positive definite. To ensure $x \in \mathcal{L}_2$ it is required to establish that

$$\dot{V}(x(t)) = \dot{x}^T(t)P(t)x(t) + x^T(t)\dot{P}(t)x(t) + x^T(t)P(t)\dot{x}(t) < 0\,. \tag{2}$$

Now consider the output of a linear time varying system, $y = \mathcal{G} w$, having the state-space representation

$$\dot{x}(t) = A(t)x(t) + B(t)w(t)\,, \tag{3}$$

"Uncertainty is one of the defining features of Science. Absolute proof only exists in mathematics. In the real world, it is impossible to prove that theories are right in every circumstance; we can only prove that they are wrong. This provisionality can cause people to lose faith in the conclusions of science, but it shouldn't. The recent history of science is not one of well-established theories being proven wrong. Rather, it is of theories being gradually refined." *New Scientist vol. 212 no. 2835*

$$y(t) = C(t)x(t), \tag{4}$$

where $w(t) \in \mathbb{R}^m$, $B(t) \in \mathbb{R}^{n \times m}$ and $C(t) \in \mathbb{R}^{p \times n}$. Assume temporarily that $E\{w(t)w^T(\tau)\} = I\delta(t-\tau)$. The Bounded Real Lemma [13], [15], [21], states that $w \in \mathcal{L}_2$ implies $y \in \mathcal{L}_2$ if

$$\dot{V}(x(t)) + y^T(t)y(t) - \gamma^2 w^T(t)w(t) < 0 \tag{5}$$

for a $\gamma \in \mathbb{R}$. Integrating (5) from $t = 0$ to $t = T$ gives

$$\int_0^T \dot{V}(x(t))\, dt + \int_0^T y^T(t)y(t)\, dt - \gamma^2 \int_0^T w^T(t)w(t)\, dt < 0 \tag{6}$$

and noting that $\int_0^T \dot{V}(x(t))\, dt = x^T(T)P(T)x(T) - x^T(0)P(0)x(0)$, another objective is

$$\frac{x^T(T)P(T)x(T) - x^T(0)P(0)x(0) + \int_0^T y^T(t)y(t)\, dt}{\int_0^T w^T(t)w(t)\, dt} \le \gamma^2 . \tag{7}$$

Under the assumptions $x(0) = 0$ and $P(T) = 0$, the above inequality simplifies to

$$\frac{\|y(t)\|_2^2}{\|w(t)\|_2^2} = \frac{\int_0^T y^T(t)y\,(t)dt}{\int_0^T w^T(t)w(t)\, dt} \le \gamma^2 . \tag{8}$$

The ∞-norm of $\mathcal{G}$ is defined as

$$\|\mathcal{G}\|_\infty = \frac{\|y\|_2}{\|w\|_2} = \frac{\|\mathcal{G}w\|_2}{\|w\|_2} . \tag{9}$$

The Lebesgue ∞-space is the set of systems having finite ∞-norm and is denoted by $\mathcal{L}_\infty$. That is, $\mathcal{G} \in \mathcal{L}_\infty$, if there exists a $\gamma \in \mathbb{R}$ such that

$$\sup_{\|w\|_2 \neq 0} \|\mathcal{G}\|_\infty = \sup_{\|w\|_2 \neq 0} \frac{\|y\|_2}{\|w\|_2} \le \gamma , \tag{10}$$

namely, the supremum (or maximum) ratio of the output and input 2-norms is finite. The conditions under which $\mathcal{G} \in \mathcal{L}_\infty$ are specified below. The accompanying sufficiency proof combines the approaches of [15], [31]. A further five proofs for this important result appear in [21].

Lemma 1: *The continuous-time Bounded Real Lemma [15], [13], [21]: In respect of the above system $\mathcal{G}$, suppose that the Riccati differential equation*

$$-\dot{P}(t) = P(t)A(t) + A^T(t)P(t) + C^T(t)C(t) + \gamma^{-2}P(t)B(t)B^T(t)P(t) , \tag{11}$$

has a solution on [0, T]. Then $\|\mathcal{G}\|_\infty \le \gamma$ for any $w \in \mathcal{L}_2$.

"Information is the resolution of uncertainty." *Claude Elwood Shannon*

Proof: *From (2) – (5),*

$$\dot{V}(t) + y^T(t)y(t) - \gamma^2 w^T(t)w(t)$$

$$= x^T(t)C^T(t)C(t)x(t) - \gamma^2 w^T(t)w(t) + x^T(t)\dot{P}(t)x(t)$$

$$+(A(t)x(t) + B(t)w(t))^T P(t)x(t) + x^T(t)P(t)(A(t)x^T(t) + B(t)w(t))$$

$$= \gamma^{-2} x^T(t)P(t)B(t)B^T(t)P(t)x(t) - \gamma^2 w^T(t)w(t)) + w^T(t)B^T(t)P(t)x(t) + x^T(t)P(t)B(t)w(t)$$

$$= -\gamma^2 (w(t) - \gamma^{-2} B(t)P(t)x(t))^T (w(t) - \gamma^{-2} B(t)P(t)x(t)),$$

which implies (6) and (7). Inequality (8) is established under the assumptions x(0) = 0 and P(T) = 0. □

In general, where $E\{w(t)w^T(\tau)\} = Q(t)\delta(t-\tau)$, the scaled matrix $\overline{B}(t) = B(t)Q^{1/2}(t)$ may be used in place of $B(t)$ above. When the plant $\mathcal{G}$ has a direct feedthrough matrix, that is,

$$y(t) = C(t)x(t) + D(t)w(t), \tag{12}$$

$D(t) \in \mathbb{R}^{p \times m}$, the above Riccati differential equation is generalised to

$$\begin{aligned} -\dot{P}_1(t) = P_1(t)(A(t) + B(t)M^{-1}(t)D^T(t)C(t)) + (A(t) + B(t)M^{-1}(t)D^T(t)C(t))^T P_1(t) \\ + \gamma^{-2} B(t)M^{-1}(t)B^T(t) + C^T(t)(I + D(t)M^{-1}(t)D^T(t))C(t), \end{aligned} \tag{13}$$

where $M(t) = \gamma^2 I - D^T(t)D(t) > 0$. A proof is requested in the problems.

Criterion (8) indicates that the ratio of the system's output and input energies is bounded above by γ^2 for any $w \in \mathcal{L}_2$, including worst-case w. Consequently, solutions satisfying (8) are often called worst-case designs.

9.2.2 Continuous-Time H$_\infty$ Filtering

9.2.2.1 Problem Definition

Now that the Bounded Real Lemma has been defined, the H$_\infty$ filter can be set out. The general filtering problem is depicted in Fig. 1. It is assumed that the system $\mathcal{G}_2$ has the state-space realisation

$$\dot{x}(t) = A(t)x(t) + B(t)w(t), \quad x(0) = 0, \tag{14}$$

$$y_2(t) = C_2(t)x(t). \tag{15}$$

Suppose that the system $\mathcal{G}_1$ has the realisation (14) and

$$y_1(t) = C_1(t)x(t). \tag{16}$$

"All exact science is dominated by the idea of approximation." *Earl Bertrand Arthur William*

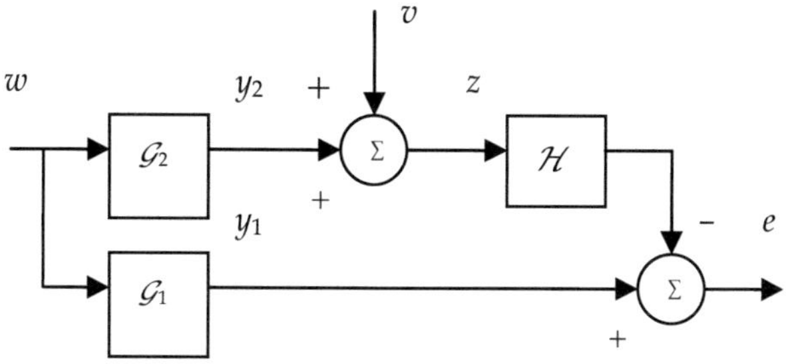

Figure 1. The general filtering problem. The objective is to estimate the output of $\mathcal{G}_1$ from noisy measurements of $\mathcal{G}_2$.

It is desired to find a causal solution $\mathcal{H}$ that produces estimates $\hat{y}_1(t\,|\,t)$ of $y_1(t)$ from the measurements,

$$z(t) = y_2(t) + v(t)\,, \tag{17}$$

at time t so that the output estimation error,

$$e(t\,|\,t) = y_1(t) - \hat{y}_1(t\,|\,t)\,, \tag{18}$$

is in $\mathcal{L}_2$. The error signal (18) is generated by a system denoted by $e = \mathcal{R}_{ei}$, where $i = \begin{bmatrix} v \\ w \end{bmatrix}$ and $\mathcal{R}_{ei} = -[\mathcal{H} \quad \mathcal{H}\mathcal{G}_2 - \mathcal{G}_1]$. Hence, the objective is to achieve $\int_0^T e^T(t\,|\,t)e(t\,|\,t)\,dt$ - $\gamma^2 \int_0^T i^T(t)i(t)\,dt < 0$ for some $\gamma \in \mathbb{R}$. For convenience, it is assumed here that $w(t) \in \mathbb{R}^m$, $E\{w(t)\} = 0$, $E\{w(t)w^T(\tau)\} = Q(t)\delta(t-\tau)$, $v(t) \in \mathbb{R}^p$, $E\{v(t)\} = 0$, $E\{v(t)v^T(\tau)\} = R(t)\delta(t-\tau)$ and $E\{w(t)v^T(\tau)\} = 0$.

9.2.2.2 H$_\infty$ Solution

A parameterisation of all solutions for the H$_\infty$ filter is developed in [21]. A minimum-entropy filter arises when the contractive operator within [21] is zero and is given by

$$\dot{\hat{x}}(t\,|\,t) = \big(A(t) - K(t)C_2(t)\big)\hat{x}(t\,|\,t) + K(t)z(t), \quad \hat{x}(0) = 0, \tag{19}$$

$$\hat{y}_1(t\,|\,t) = C_1(t\,|\,t)\hat{x}(t\,|\,t), \tag{20}$$

where

$$K(t) = P(t)C_2^T(t)R^{-1}(t) \tag{21}$$

"Uncertainty and expectation are the joys of life. Security is an insipid thing, through the overtaking and possessing of a wish discovers the folly of the chase." *William Congreve*

is the filter gain and $P(t) = P^T(t) > 0$ is the solution of the Riccati differential equation

$$\dot{P}(t) = A(t)P(t) + P(t)A^T(t) + B(t)Q(t)B^T(t) - P(t)(C_2^T(t)R^{-1}(t)C_2(t) - \gamma^{-2}C_1^T(t)C_1(t))P(t), \; P(0) = 0. \tag{22}$$

It can be seen that the H_∞ filter has a structure akin to the Kalman filter. A point of difference is that the solution to the above Riccati differential equation solution depends on $C_1(t)$, the linear combination of states being estimated.

9.2.2.3 Properties

Define $\bar{A}(t) = A(t) - K(t)C_2(t)$. Subtracting (19) – (20) from (14) – (15) yields the error system

$$\begin{bmatrix} \dot{\tilde{x}}(t|t) \\ e(t|t) \end{bmatrix} = \begin{bmatrix} \bar{A}(t) & [-K(t) & B(t)] \\ C_1(t) & [0 & 0] \end{bmatrix} \begin{bmatrix} \tilde{x}(t|t) \\ \begin{bmatrix} v(t) \\ w(t) \end{bmatrix} \end{bmatrix}, \; \tilde{x}(0) = 0, \quad = \mathcal{R}_{ei} i, \tag{23}$$

where $\tilde{x}(t|t) = x(t) - \hat{x}(t|t)$ and $\mathcal{R}_{ei} = \begin{bmatrix} \bar{A}(t) & [-K(t) & B(t)] \\ C_1(t) & [0 & 0] \end{bmatrix}$. The adjoint of $\mathcal{R}_{ei}$ is given by

$\mathcal{R}_{ei}^H = \begin{bmatrix} -\bar{A}^T(t) & C_1^T(t) \\ \begin{bmatrix} K^T(t) \\ -B^T(t) \end{bmatrix} & \begin{bmatrix} 0 \\ 0 \end{bmatrix} \end{bmatrix}$. It is shown below that the estimation error satisfies the desired performance objective.

Lemma 2: *In respect of the H_∞ problem (14) – (18), the solution (19) – (20) achieves the performance* $x^T(T)P(T)x(T) - x^T(0)P(0)x(0) + \int_0^T e^T(t|t)e(t|t)\,dt - \gamma^2 \int_0^T i^T(t)i(t)\,dt < 0$.

Proof: *Following the approach in [15], [21], by applying Lemma 1 to the adjoint of (23), it is required that there exists a positive definite symmetric solution to*

$$-\dot{P}(\tau) = \bar{A}(\tau)P(\tau) + P(\tau)\bar{A}^T(\tau) + B(\tau)Q(\tau)B^T(\tau) + K(\tau)R(\tau)K^T(\tau) + \gamma^{-2}P(\tau)C_1^T(\tau)C_1(\tau))P(\tau), \; P(\tau)\big|_{\tau=T} = 0,$$

"Although economists have studied the sensitivity of import and export volumes to changes in the exchange rate, there is still much uncertainty about just how much the dollar must change to bring about any given reduction in our trade deficit." *Martin Stuart Feldstein*

on [0, T] for some $\gamma \in \mathbb{R}$, in which $\tau = T - t$ is a time-to-go variable. Substituting $K(\tau) = P(\tau)C_2^T(\tau)R^{-1}(\tau)$ into the above Riccati differential equation yields

$$-\dot{P}(\tau) = A(\tau)P(\tau) + P(\tau)A^T(\tau) + B(\tau)Q(\tau)B^T(\tau) - P(\tau)(C_2^T(\tau)R^{-1}(\tau)(C_2(\tau) - \gamma^{-2}C_1^T(\tau)C_1(\tau))P(\tau),$$

$$P(\tau)\big|_{\tau=T} = 0.$$

Taking adjoints to address the problem (23) leads to (22), for which the existence of a positive define solution implies $x^T(T)P(T)x(T) - x^T(0)P(0)x(0) + \int_0^T e^T(t|t)e(t|t)\,dt - \gamma^2\int_0^T i^T(t)i(t)\,dt < 0$. Thus, under the assumption x(0) = 0, $\int_0^T e^T(t|t)e(t|t)\,dt - \gamma^2\int_0^T i^T(t)i(t)\,dt < -x^T(T)P(T)x(T) < 0$. Therefore, $\mathcal{R}_{ei} \in \mathcal{L}_\infty$, that is, $w, v \in \mathcal{L}_2 \Rightarrow e \in \mathcal{L}_2$. □

9.2.2.4 Trading-Off H_∞ Performance

In a robust filter design it is desired to meet an H_∞ performance objective for a minimum possible γ. A minimum γ can be found by conducting a search and checking for the existence of positive definite solutions to the Riccati differential equation (22). This search is tractable because $\dot{P}(t)$ is a convex function of γ^2, since $\frac{\partial^2 \dot{P}(t)}{\partial^2 \gamma^2} = \gamma^{-6}P(t)C_1^T(t)C_1(t))P(t) > 0$.

In some applications it may be possible to estimate *a priori* values for γ. Recall for output estimation problems that the error is generated by $e = \mathcal{R}_{ei} i$, where $\mathcal{R}_{ei} = -[\mathcal{H} \ \ (\mathcal{H} - I)\mathcal{G}_1]$. From the arguments of Chapters 1 - 2 and [28], for single-input-single-output plants $\lim_{\sigma_v^2 \to 0} |\mathcal{H}| = 1$ and $\lim_{\sigma_v^2 \to 0} |\mathcal{R}_{ei}| = 1$, which implies $\lim_{\sigma_v^2 \to 0} \|\mathcal{R}_{ei}\mathcal{R}_{ei}^H\|_\infty = \sigma_v^2$. Since the H_∞ filter achieves the performance $\|\mathcal{R}_{ei}\mathcal{R}_{ei}^H\|_\infty < \gamma^2$, it follows that an *a priori* design estimate is $\gamma = \sigma_v$ at high signal-to-noise-ratios.

When the problem is stationary (or time-invariant), the filter gain is precalculated as $K = PC^TR^{-1}$, where P is the solution of the algebraic Riccati equation

$$0 = AP + PA^T - P(C_2^TR^{-1}C_2 - \gamma^{-2}C_1^TC_1)P + BQB^T \qquad (24)$$

Suppose that $\mathcal{G}_2 = \mathcal{G}_1$ is a time-invariant single-input-single-output system and let $R_{ei}(s)$ denote the transfer function of $\mathcal{R}_{ei}$. Then Parseval's Theorem states that the average total energy of $e(t|t)$ is

$$\|e(t|t)\|_2^2 = \int_{-\infty}^{\infty} |e(t|t)|^2\,dt = \int_{-j\infty}^{j\infty} R_{ei}R_{ei}^H(s)\,ds = \int_{-j\infty}^{j\infty} |R_{ei}(s)|^2 ds, \qquad (25)$$

"Life is uncertain. Eat dessert first." *Ernestine Ulmer*

which equals the area under the error power spectral density, $R_{ei}R_{ei}^{H}(s)$. Recall that the optimal filter (in which $\gamma = \infty$) minimises (25), whereas the H$_\infty$ filter minimises

$$\sup_{\|i\|_2 \neq 0} \left\| R_{ei}R_{ei}^{H} \right\|_{\infty} = \sup_{\|i\|_2 \neq 0} \frac{\|e\|_2^2}{\|i\|_2^2} < \gamma^2 . \tag{26}$$

In view of (25) and (26), it follows that the H$_\infty$ filter minimises the maximum magnitude of $R_{ei}R_{ei}^{H}(s)$. Consequently, it is also called a 'minimax filter'. However, robust designs, which accommodate uncertain inputs tend to be conservative. Therefore, it is prudent to investigate using a larger γ to achieve a trade-off between H$_\infty$ and minimum-mean-square-error performance criteria.

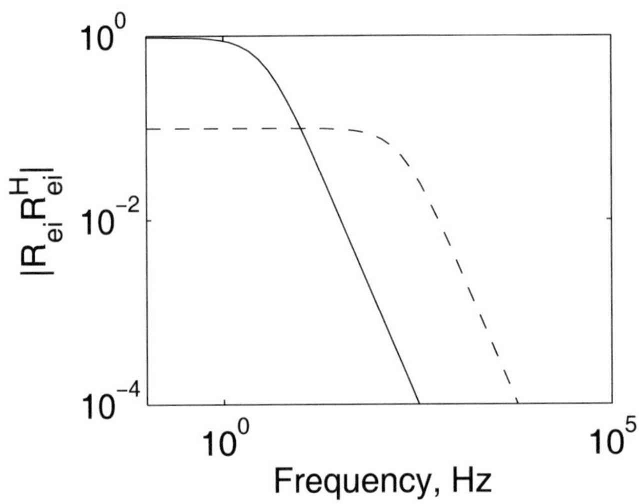

Figure 2. $\left|R_{ei}R_{ei}^{H}(s)\right|$ versus frequency for Example 1: optimal filter (solid line) and H$_\infty$ filter (dotted line).

Example 1. Consider a time-invariant output estimation problem where A = -1, $B = C_2 = C_1$ = 1, σ_w^2 = 10 and σ_v^2 = 0.1. The magnitude of the error spectrum exhibited by the optimal filter (designed with $\gamma^2 = 10^8$) is indicated by the solid line of Fig. 2. From a search, a minimum of $\gamma^2 = 0.099$ was found such that the algebraic Riccati equation (24) has a positive definite solution, which concurs with the *a priori* estimate of $\gamma^2 \approx \sigma_v^2$. The magnitude of the error spectrum exhibited by the H$_\infty$ filter is indicated by the dotted line of Fig. 2. The figure demonstrates that the filter achieves $\left|R_{ei}R_{ei}^{H}(s)\right| < \gamma^2$. Although the H$_\infty$ filter reduces the peak of the error spectrum by 10 dB, it can be seen that the area under the curve is larger, that is, the mean square error increases. Consequently, some intermediate value of γ may need to be considered to trade off peak error (spectrum) and average error performance.

"If the uncertainty is larger than the effect, the effect itself becomes moot." *Patrick Frank*

9.2.3 Accommodating Uncertainty

The above filters are designed for situations in which the inputs $v(t)$ and $w(t)$ are uncertain. Next, problems in which model uncertainty is present are discussed. The described approaches involve converting the uncertainty into a fictitious noise source and solving an auxiliary H_∞ filtering problem.

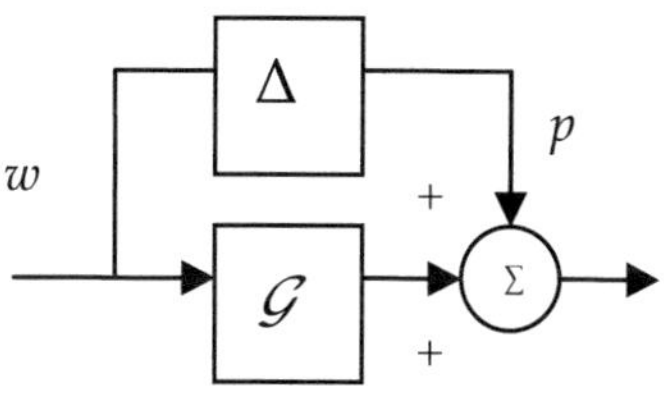

Figure 3. Representation of additive model uncertainty.

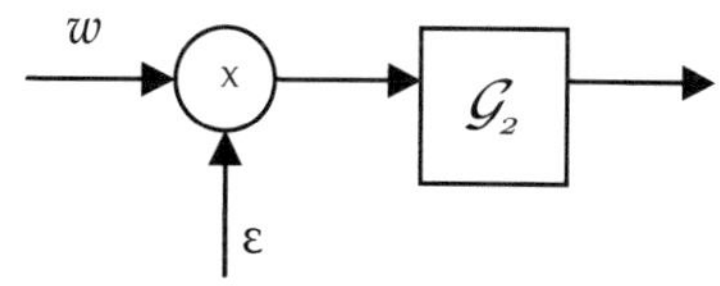

Figure 4. Input scaling in lieu of a problem that possesses an uncertainty.

9.2.3.1 Additive Uncertainty

Consider a time-invariant output estimation problem in which the nominal model is $\mathcal{G}_2 + \Delta$, where $\mathcal{G}_2$ is known and Δ is unknown, as depicted in Fig. 3. The $p(t)$ represents a fictitious signal to account for discrepancies due to the uncertainty. It is argued below that a solution to the H_∞ filtering problem can be found by solving an auxiliary problem in which the input is scaled by $\varepsilon \in \mathbb{R}$ as shown in Fig. 4. In lieu of the filtering problem possessing the uncertainty Δ, an auxiliary problem is defined as

$$\dot{x}(t) = Ax(t) + Bw(t) + Bp(t)\,,\ x(0) = 0\,, \tag{27}$$

$$z(t) = C_2(t)x(t) + v(t)\,, \tag{28}$$

$$e(t\,|\,t) = C_1(t)x(t) - C_1(t)\hat{x}(t)\,, \tag{29}$$

where $p(t)$ is an additional exogenous input satisfying

$$\|p\|_2^2 < \delta^2 \|w\|_2^2\,,\ \ \delta \in \mathbb{R}\,. \tag{30}$$

Consider the scaled H_∞ filtering problem where

$$\dot{x}(t) = Ax(t) + B\varepsilon w(t)\,,\ x(0) = 0\,, \tag{31}$$

$$z(t) = C_2(t)x(t) + v(t)\,, \tag{32}$$

$$e(t\,|\,t) = C_1(t)x(t) - C_1(t)\hat{x}(t)\,, \tag{33}$$

in which $\varepsilon^2 = (1 + \delta^2)^{-1}$.

"A theory has only the alternative of being right or wrong. A model has a third possibility - it may be right but irrelevant." *Manfred Eigen*

Lemma 3 [26]: *Suppose for a $\gamma \neq 0$ that the scaled H_∞ problem (31) – (33) is solvable, that is, $\|e\|_2^2 < \gamma^2(\varepsilon^{-2}\|w\|_2^2 + \|v\|_2^2)$. Then, this guarantees the performance*

$$\|e\|_2^2 < \gamma^2(\|w\|_2^2 + \|p\|_2^2 + \|v\|_2^2) \tag{34}$$

for the solution of the auxiliary problem (27) – (29).

Proof: *From the assumption that problem (31) – (33) is solvable, it follows that $\|e\|_2^2 < \gamma^2(\varepsilon^{-2}\|w\|_2^2 + \|v\|_2^2)$. Substituting for ε, using (30) and rearranging yields (34).* □

9.2.4 Multiplicative Uncertainty

Next, consider a filtering problem in which the model is $G(I + \Delta)$, as depicted in Fig. 5. It is again assumed that G and Δ are known and unknown transfer function matrices, respectively. This problem may similarly be solved using Lemma 3. Thus a filter that accommodates additive or multiplicative uncertainty simply requires scaling of an input. The above scaling is only sufficient for a H_∞ performance criterion to be met. The design may well be too conservative and it is worthwhile to explore the merits of using values for δ less than the uncertainty's assumed norm bound.

9.2.5 Parametric Uncertainty

Finally, consider a time-invariant output estimation problem in which the state matrix is uncertain, namely,

$$\dot{x}(t) = (A + \Delta_A)x(t) + Bw(t), \quad x(0) = 0, \tag{35}$$

$$z(t) = C_2(t)x(t) + v(t), \tag{36}$$

$$e(t \mid t) = C_1(t)x(t) - C_1(t)\hat{x}(t), \tag{37}$$

where $\Delta_A \in \mathbb{R}^{n \times n}$ is unknown. Define an auxiliary H_∞ filtering problem by

$$\dot{x}(t) = Ax(t) + Bw(t) + p(t), \quad x(0) = 0, \tag{38}$$

(36) and (37), where $p(t) = \Delta_A x(t)$ is a fictitious exogenous input. A solution to this problem would achieve

$$\|e\|_2^2 < \gamma^2(\|w\|_2^2 + \|p\|_2^2 + \|v\|_2^2) \tag{39}$$

for a $\gamma \neq 0$. From the approach of [14], [18], [19], consider the scaled filtering problem

$$\dot{x}(t) = Ax(t) + \bar{B}\bar{w}(t), \quad x(0) = 0, \tag{40}$$

"Remember that all models are wrong; the practical question is how wrong do they have to be to not be useful." *George Edward Pelham Box*

(36), (37), where $\bar{B} = \begin{bmatrix} B & \varepsilon^{-1} \end{bmatrix}$, $\bar{w}(t) = \begin{bmatrix} w(t) \\ \varepsilon p(t) \end{bmatrix}$ and 0 < ε < 1. Then the solution of this H∞ filtering problem satisfies

$$\|e\|_2^2 < \gamma^2(\|w\|_2^2 + \varepsilon^2\|p\|_2^2 + \|v\|_2^2), \tag{41}$$

which implies (39). Thus, state matrix parameter uncertainty can be accommodated by including a scaled input in the solution of an auxiliary H∞ filtering problem. Similar solutions to problems in which other state-space parameters are uncertain appear in [14], [18], [19].

9.2.6 Continuous-Time H∞ Smoothing

9.2.6.1 Background

There are three kinds of H∞ smoothers: fixed point, fixed lag and fixed interval (see the tutorial [13]). The next development is concerned with continuous-time H∞ fixed-interval smoothing. The smoother in [10] arises as a combination of forward states from an H∞ filter and adjoint states that evolve according to a Hamiltonian matrix. A different fixed-interval smoothing problem to [10] is found in [16] by solving for saddle conditions within differential games. A summary of some filtering and smoothing results appears in [13]. Robust prediction, filtering and smoothing problems are addressed in [22]; the H∞ predictor, filter and smoother require the solution of a Riccati differential equation that evolves forward in time, whereas the smoother additionally requires another to be solved in reverse-time. Another approach for combining forward and adjoint estimates is described [32] where the Fraser-Potter formula is used to construct a smoothed estimate.

Continuous-time, fixed-interval smoothers that differ from the formulations within [10], [13], [16], [22], [32] are reported in [34] - [35]. A robust version of [34] - [35] appears in [33], which is described below.

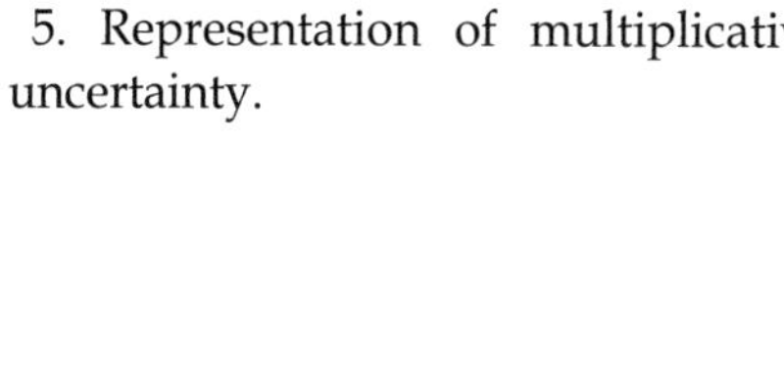

Figure 5. Representation of multiplicative model uncertainty.

Figure 6. Robust smoother error structure.

"The purpose of models is not to fit the data but to sharpen the questions." *Samuel Karlin*

9.2.6.2 Problem Definition

Once again, it is assumed that the data is generated by (14) – (17). For convenience, attention is confined to output estimation, namely $\mathcal{G}_2 = \mathcal{G}_1$ within Fig. 1. Input and state estimation problems can be handled similarly using the solution structures described in Chapter 6. It is desired to find a fixed-interval smoother solution $\mathcal{H}$ that produces estimates $\hat{y}_1(t|T)$ of $y_1(t)$ so that the output estimation error

$$e(t|T) = y_1(t) - \hat{y}_1(t|T) \tag{42}$$

is in $\mathcal{L}_2$. As before, the map from the inputs $i = \begin{bmatrix} v \\ w \end{bmatrix}$ to the error is denoted by $\mathcal{R}_{ei} = -[\mathcal{H} \quad \mathcal{H}\mathcal{G}_1 - \mathcal{G}_1]$ and the objective is to achieve $\int_0^T e^T(t|T)e(t|T)\,dt - \gamma^2 \int_0^T i^T(t)i(t)\,dt < 0$ for some $\gamma \in \mathbb{R}$.

9.2.6.3 H∞ Solution

The following H∞ fixed-interval smoother exploits the structure of the minimum-variance smoother but uses the gain (21) calculated from the solution of the Riccati differential equation (22) akin to the H∞ filter. An approximate Wiener-Hopf factor inverse, $\hat{\Delta}^{-1}$, is given by

$$\begin{bmatrix} \dot{\hat{x}}(t|t) \\ \alpha(t) \end{bmatrix} = \begin{bmatrix} A(t) - K(t)C(t) & K(t) \\ -R^{-1/2}(t)C(t) & R^{-1/2}(t) \end{bmatrix} \begin{bmatrix} \hat{x}(t|t) \\ z(t) \end{bmatrix}. \tag{43}$$

An inspection reveals that the states within (43) are the same as those calculated by the H∞ filter (19). The adjoint of $\hat{\Delta}^{-1}$, which is denoted by $\hat{\Delta}^{-H}$, has the realisation

$$\begin{bmatrix} -\dot{\xi}(t) \\ \beta(t) \end{bmatrix} = \begin{bmatrix} A^T(t) - C^T(t)K^T(t) & -C^T(t)R^{-1/2}(t) \\ K^T(t) & R^{-1/2}(t) \end{bmatrix} \begin{bmatrix} \xi(t) \\ \alpha(t) \end{bmatrix}. \tag{44}$$

Output estimates are obtained as

$$\hat{y}(t|T) = z(t) - R(t)\beta(t). \tag{45}$$

However, an additional condition requires checking in order to guarantee that the smoother actually achieves the above performance objective; the existence of a solution $P_2(t) = P_2^T(t) > 0$ is required for the auxiliary Riccati differential equation

$$\begin{aligned} -\dot{P}_2(t) &= \bar{A}(t)P_2(t) + P_2(t)\bar{A}^T(t) + K(t)R^2(t)K^T(t) \\ &\quad + \gamma_2^{-2}P_2(t)C^T(t)R^{-1}(t)\big(C(t)P(t)C^T(t) + R(t)\big)R^{-1}(t)C(t)P_2(t), \; P_2(T) = 0, \end{aligned} \tag{46}$$

where $\bar{A}(t) = A(t) - K(t)C(t)$.

"Certainty is the mother of quiet and repose, and uncertainty the cause of variance and contentions." *Edward Coke*

9.2.7 Performance

It will be shown subsequently that the robust fixed-interval smoother (43) – (45) has the error structure shown in Fig. 6, which is examined below.

Lemma 4 [33]: *Consider the arrangement of two linear systems* $f = \mathcal{R}_{fi} i$ *and* $u = \mathcal{R}_{uj}^{H} j$ *shown in Fig. 6, in which* $i = \begin{bmatrix} w \\ v \end{bmatrix}$ *and* $j = \begin{bmatrix} f \\ v \end{bmatrix}$. *Let* $\mathcal{R}_{ei}$ *denote the map from i to e. Assume that w and v* $\in \mathcal{L}_2$. *If and only if: (i)* $\mathcal{R}_{fi} \in \mathcal{L}_\infty$ *and (ii)* $\mathcal{R}_{uj}^{H} \in \mathcal{L}_\infty$, *then (i) f, u, e* $\in \mathcal{L}_2$ *and (ii)* $\mathcal{R}_{ei} \in \mathcal{L}_\infty$.

Proof: *(i) To establish sufficiency, note that* $\|i\|_2 \le \|w\|_2 + \|v\|_2$ => $d \in \mathcal{L}_2$, *which with Condition (i) =>* $f \in \mathcal{L}_2$. *Similarly,* $\|j\|_2 \le \|f\|_2 + \|v\|_2$ => $j \in \mathcal{L}_2$, *which with Condition (ii) =>* $u \in \mathcal{L}_2$. *Also,* $\|e\|_2 \le \|f\|_2 + \|u\|_2$ => $e \in \mathcal{L}_2$. *The necessity of (i) follows from the assumption* $i \in \mathcal{L}_2$ *together with the property* $\mathcal{R}_{fi} \mathcal{L}_2 \subset \mathcal{L}_2$ => $\mathcal{R}_{fi} \in \mathcal{L}_\infty$ *(see [p. 83, 21]). Similarly,* $j \in \mathcal{L}_2$ *together with the property* $\mathcal{R}_{uj}^{H} \mathcal{L}_2 \subset \mathcal{L}_2$ => $\mathcal{R}_{uj}^{H} \in \mathcal{L}_\infty$.

(ii) Finally, $i \in \mathcal{L}_2$, $e = \mathcal{R}_{ei} i \in \mathcal{L}_2$ *together with the property* $\mathcal{R}_{ei} \mathcal{L}_2 \subset \mathcal{L}_2$ => $\mathcal{R}_{ei} \in \mathcal{L}_\infty$. □

It is easily shown that the error system, $\mathcal{R}_{ei}$, for the model (14) – (15), the data (17) and the smoother (43) – (45), is given by

$$\begin{bmatrix} \dot{\tilde{x}}(t) \\ -\dot{\xi}(t) \\ e(t \mid T) \end{bmatrix} = \begin{bmatrix} \bar{A}(t) & 0 & B(t) & -K(t) \\ -C^T(t)R^{-1}(t)C(t) & \bar{A}^T(t) & 0 & -C^T(t)R^{-1}(t) \\ C(t) & R(t)K^T(t) & 0 & 0 \end{bmatrix} \begin{bmatrix} \tilde{x}(t) \\ \xi(t) \\ w(t) \\ v(t) \end{bmatrix}, \tilde{x}(0) = 0, \tag{47}$$

$$\xi(T) = 0,$$

where $\tilde{x}(t \mid t) = x(t) - \hat{x}(t \mid t)$. The conditions for the smoother attaining the desired performance objective are described below.

Lemma 5 [33]: *In respect of the smoother error system (47), if there exist symmetric positive define solutions to (22) and (46) for* γ, $\gamma_2 > 0$, *then the smoother (43) – (45) achieves* $\mathcal{R}_{ei} \in \mathcal{L}_\infty$, *that is,* $i \in \mathcal{L}_2$ *implies* $e \in \mathcal{L}_2$.

Proof: *Since* $\tilde{x}(t \mid t)$ *is decoupled from* $\xi(t)$, $\mathcal{R}_{ei}$ *is equivalent to the arrangement of two systems* $\mathcal{R}_{fi}$ *and* $\mathcal{R}_{uj}^{H}$ *shown in Fig. 6. The* $\mathcal{R}_{fi}$ *is defined by (23) in which* $C_2(t) = C(t)$. *From Lemma 2, the existence of a positive definite solution to (22) implies* $\mathcal{R}_{fi} \in \mathcal{L}_\infty$. *The* $\mathcal{R}_{uj}^{H}$ *is given by the system*

$$-\dot{\xi}(\tau) = \bar{A}^T(\tau)\xi(\tau) - C^T(\tau)R^{-1}(\tau)\tilde{y}(\tau \mid \tau) - C^T(\tau)R^{-1}(\tau)v(\tau), \ \xi(T) = 0, \tag{48}$$

$$u(\tau) = R(\tau)K^T(\tau)\xi(\tau). \tag{49}$$

"Doubt is uncomfortable, certainty is ridiculous." *François-Marie Arouet de Voltaire*

For the above system to be in $\mathcal{L}_\infty$, *from Lemma 4, it is required that there exists a solution to (46) for which the existence of a positive definite solution implies* $\mathcal{R}_{uj}^H \in \mathcal{L}_\infty$. *The claim* $\mathcal{R}_{ei} \in \mathcal{L}_\infty$ *follows from Lemma 4.* □

The H$_\infty$ solution can be derived as a solution to a two-point boundary value problem, which involves a trade-off between causal and noncausal processes (see [10], [15], [21]). This suggests that the H$_\infty$ performance of the above smoother would not improve on that of the filter. Indeed, from Fig. 6, $e = f + u$ and the triangle rule yields $\|e\|_2 \le \|f\|_2 + \|u\|_2$, where f is the H$_\infty$ filter error. That is, the error upper bound for the H$_\infty$ fixed-interval smoother (43) – (45) is greater than that for the H$_\infty$ filter (19) – (20). It is observed below that compared to the minimum-variance case, the H$_\infty$ solution exhibits an increased mean-square error.

Lemma 6 [33]: *For the output estimation problem (14) – (18), in which* $C_2(t) = C_1(t) = C(t)$, *the smoother solution (43) – (45) results in*

$$\left\| \mathcal{R}_{ei}\mathcal{R}_{ei}^H \right\|_{2,\gamma^{-2} > 0} > \left\| \mathcal{R}_{ei}\mathcal{R}_{ei}^H \right\|_{2,\gamma^{-2} = 0} . \tag{50}$$

Proof: *By expanding* $\mathcal{R}_{ei}\mathcal{R}_{ei}^H$ *and completing the squares, it can be shown that* $\mathcal{R}_{ei}\mathcal{R}_{ei}^H = \mathcal{R}_{ei1}\mathcal{R}_{ei1}^H + \mathcal{R}_{ei2}\mathcal{R}_{ei2}^H$, *where* $\mathcal{R}_{ei2}\mathcal{R}_{ei2}^H = \mathcal{G}_1 Q(t)\mathcal{G}_1^H - \mathcal{G}_1 Q(t)\mathcal{G}_1^H\Delta^{-H}\Delta^{-1}\mathcal{G}_1 Q(t)\mathcal{G}_1^H$ *and* $\mathcal{R}_{ei1} = \mathcal{H}\Delta - \mathcal{G}_1 Q(t)\mathcal{G}_1^H\Delta^{-H} = [\mathcal{H} - I + R(t)(\Delta\Delta^H)^{-1}]\Delta$. *Substituting* $\mathcal{H} = I - R(t)(\hat{\Delta}\hat{\Delta}^H)^{-1}$ *into* $\mathcal{R}_{ei1}$ *yields*

$$\mathcal{R}_{ei1} = R(t)[(\Delta\Delta^H)^{-1} - (\hat{\Delta}\hat{\Delta}^H)^{-1}]\Delta , \tag{51}$$

which suggests $\hat{\Delta} = C(t)\mathcal{G}_0 K(t)R^{1/2}(t) + R^{1/2}(t)$, *where* $\mathcal{G}_0$ *denotes an operator having the state-space realization* $\begin{bmatrix} A(t) & I \\ I & 0 \end{bmatrix}$. *Constructing* $\hat{\Delta}\hat{\Delta}^H = C(t)\mathcal{G}_0[K(t)R(t)K^T(t) - P(t)A^T(t) - A(t)P(t)]\mathcal{G}_0^H C^T(t) + R(t)$ *and using (22) yields* $\hat{\Delta}\hat{\Delta}^H = C(t)\mathcal{G}_0[B(t)Q(t)B^T(t) - \dot{P}(t) + \gamma^{-2}P(t)C^T(t)C(t)P(t)]\mathcal{G}_0^H C^T(t) + R(t)$. *Comparison with* $\Delta\Delta^H = C(t)\mathcal{G}_0 B(t)Q(t)B^T(t)\mathcal{G}_0^H C^T(t) + R(t)$ *leads to* $\hat{\Delta}\hat{\Delta}^H = \Delta\Delta^H - C(t)\mathcal{G}_0(\dot{P}(t) + \gamma^{-2}P(t)C^T(t)C(t)P(t))\mathcal{G}_0^H C^T(t)$. *Substituting for* $\hat{\Delta}\hat{\Delta}^H$ *into (51) yields*

$$\mathcal{R}_{ei1} = R(t)[(\Delta\Delta^H)^{-1} - (\Delta\Delta^H - C(t)\mathcal{G}_0(\dot{P}(t) - \gamma^{-2}P(t)C^T(t)C(t)P(t))\mathcal{G}_0^H C^T(t))^{-1}]\Delta . \tag{52}$$

The observation (50) follows by inspection of (52). □

Thus, the cost of designing for worst case input conditions is a deterioration in the mean performance. Note that the best possible average performance $\left\| R_{ei}R_{ei}^H \right\|_2 = \left\| R_{ei2}R_{ei2}^H \right\|_2$ can be attained in problems where there are no uncertainties present, $\gamma^{-2} = 0$ and the Riccati equation solution has converged, that is, $\dot{P}(t) = 0$, in which case $\hat{\Delta}\hat{\Delta}^H = \Delta\Delta^H$ and $\mathcal{R}_{ei1}$ is a zero matrix.

"We know accurately only when we know little, with knowledge doubt increases." *Johann Wolfgang von Goethe*

9.2.8 Performance Comparison

It is of interest to compare to compare the performance of (43) - (45) with the H$_\infty$ smoother described in [10], [13], [16], namely,

$$\begin{bmatrix} \dot{\hat{x}}(t\,|\,T) \\ \dot{\xi}(t) \end{bmatrix} = \begin{bmatrix} A(t) & B(t)Q(t)B^T(t) \\ C^T(t)R^{-1}(t)C(t) & -A'(t) \end{bmatrix} \begin{bmatrix} \hat{x}(t\,|\,T) \\ \xi(t) \end{bmatrix} + \begin{bmatrix} 0 \\ -C^T(t)R^{-1}(t) \end{bmatrix} z(t) \,, \tag{53}$$

$$\hat{x}(t\,|\,T) = \hat{x}(t) + P(t)\xi(t) \tag{54}$$

and (22). Substituting (54) and its differential into the first row of (53) together with (21) yields

$$\dot{\hat{x}}(t) = A(t)\hat{x}(t) + K(t)(z(t) - C(t)\hat{x}(t)) \,, \tag{55}$$

which reverts to the Kalman filter at γ^{-2} = 0. Substituting $\xi(t) = P^{-1}(t)(\hat{x}(t\,|\,T) - \hat{x}(t))$ into the second row of (53) yields

$$\dot{\hat{x}}(t\,|\,T) = A(t)\hat{x}(t) + G(t)(\hat{x}(t\,|\,T) - \hat{x}(t)) \,, \tag{56}$$

where $G(t) = B(t)Q(t)B^T(t)P_2^{-1}(t)$, which reverts to the maximum-likelihood smoother at γ^{-2} = 0. Thus, the Hamiltonian form (53) - (54) can be realised by calculating the filtered estimate (55) and then obtaining the smoothed estimate from (56).

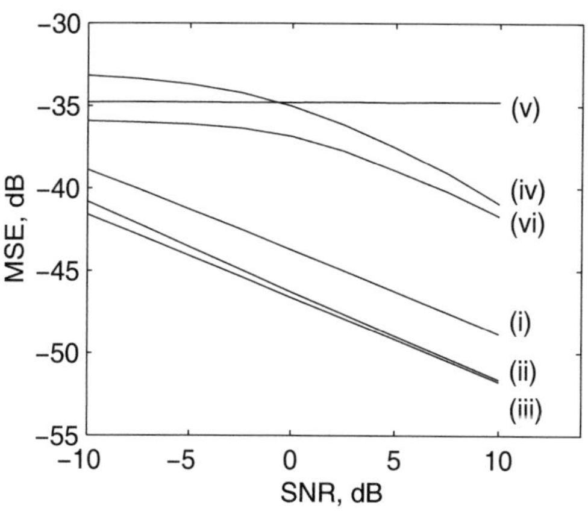

Figure 7. Fixed-interval smoother performance comparison for Gaussian process noise: (i) Kalman filter; (ii) Maximum likelihood smoother; (iii) Minimum-variance smoother; (iv) H$_\infty$ filter; (v) H$_\infty$ smoother [10], [13], [16]; and (vi) H$_\infty$ smoother (43) - (45).

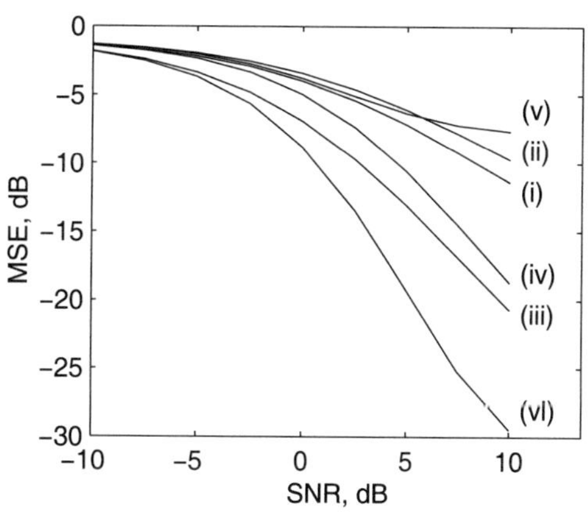

Figure 8. Fixed-interval smoother performance comparison for sinusoidal process noise: (i) Kalman filter; (ii) Maximum likelihood smoother; (iii) Minimum-variance smoother; (iv) H$_\infty$ filter; (v) H$_\infty$ smoother [10], [13], [16]; and (vi) H$_\infty$ smoother (43) - (45).

"Inquiry is fatal to certainty." *William James Durant*

Example: 2 [35]. Let $A = \begin{bmatrix} -1 & 0 \\ 0 & -1 \end{bmatrix}$, $B = C = Q = \begin{bmatrix} 1 & 0 \\ 0 & 1 \end{bmatrix}$, $D = \begin{bmatrix} 0 & 0 \\ 0 & 0 \end{bmatrix}$ and $R = \begin{bmatrix} \sigma_v^2 & 0 \\ 0 & \sigma_v^2 \end{bmatrix}$ denote time-invariant parameters for an output estimation problem. Simulations were conducted for the case of $T = 100$ seconds, $\delta t = 1$ millisecond, using 500 realizations of zero-mean, Gaussian process noise and measurement noise. The resulting mean-square-error (MSE) versus signal-to-noise ratio (SNR) are shown in Fig. 7. The H_∞ solutions were calculated using *a priori* designs of $\gamma^{-2} = \sigma_v^{-2}$ within (22). It can be seen from trace (vi) of Fig. 7 that the H_∞ smoothers exhibit poor performance when the exogenous inputs are in fact Gaussian, which illustrates Lemma 6. The figure demonstrates that the minimum-variance smoother out-performs the maximum-likelihood smoother. However, at high SNR, the difference in smoother performance is inconsequential. Intermediate values for γ^{-2} may be selected to realise a smoother design that achieves a trade-off between minimum-variance performance (trace (iii)) and H_∞ performance (trace (v)).

Example 3 [35]. Consider the non-Gaussian process noise signal $w(t) = \sin(t)\sigma_{\sin(t)}^{-1}$, where $\sigma_{\sin(t)}^{2}$ denotes the sample variance of sin(t). The results of a simulation study appear in Fig. 8. It can be seen that the H_∞ solutions, which accommodate input uncertainty, perform better than those relying on Gaussian noise assumptions. In this example, the developed H_∞ smoother (43) - (45) exhibits the best mean-square-error performance.

9.3 Robust Discrete-time Estimation

9.3.1 Discrete-Time Bounded Real Lemma

The development of discrete-time H_∞ filters and smoothers proceeds analogously to the continuous-time case. From Lyapunov stability theory [36], for the unforced system

$$x_{k+1} = A_k x_k , \tag{57}$$

$A_k \in \mathbb{R}^{n\times n}$, to be asymptotically stable over the interval $k \in [1, N]$, a Lyapunov function, $V_k(x_k)$, is required to satisfy $\Delta V_k(x_k) < 0$, where $\Delta V_k(x_k) = V_{k+1}(x_k) - V_k(x_k)$ denotes the first backward difference of $V_k(x_k)$. Consider the candidate Lyapunov function $V_k(x_k) = x_k^T P_k x_k$, where $P_k = P_k^T \in \mathbb{R}^{n\times n}$ is positive definite. To guarantee $x_k \in \ell_2$, it is required that

$$\Delta V_k(x_k) = x_{k+1}^T P_{k+1} x_{k+1} - x_k^T P_k x_k < 0 . \tag{58}$$

Now let $y = \mathcal{G} w$ denote the output of the system

$$x_{k+1} = A_k x_k + B_k w_k , \tag{59}$$

$$y_k = C_k x_k , \tag{60}$$

where $w_k \in \mathbb{R}^m$, $B_k \in \mathbb{R}^{n\times m}$ and $C_k \in \mathbb{R}^{p\times n}$.

"Education is the path from cocky ignorance to miserable uncertainty." *Samuel Langhorne Clemens aka. Mark Twain*

The Bounded Real Lemma [18] states that $w \in \ell_2$ implies $y \in \ell_2$ if

$$x_{k+1}^T P_{k+1} x_{k+1} - x_k^T P_k x_k + y_k^T y_k - \gamma^2 w_k^T w_k < 0 \tag{61}$$

for a $\gamma \in \mathbb{R}$. Summing (61) from $k = 0$ to $k = N - 1$ yields the objective

$$-x_0^T P_0 x_0 + \sum_{k=0}^{N-1} y_k^T y_k - \gamma^2 \sum_{k=0}^{N-1} w_k^T w_k < 0 , \tag{62}$$

that is,

$$\frac{-x_0^T P_0 x_0 + \sum_{k=0}^{N-1} y_k^T y_k}{\sum_{k=0}^{N-1} w_k^T w_k} < \gamma^2 . \tag{63}$$

Assuming that $x_0 = 0$,

$$\left\| \mathcal{G} \right\|_\infty = \frac{\left\| y \right\|_2}{\left\| w \right\|_2} = \frac{\left\| \mathcal{G} w \right\|_2}{\left\| w \right\|_2} = \frac{\sqrt{\sum_{k=0}^{N-1} y_k^T y_k}}{\sqrt{\sum_{k=0}^{N-1} w_k^T w_k}} < \gamma . \tag{64}$$

Conditions for achieving the above objectives are established below.

Lemma 7: *The discrete-time Bounded Real Lemma [18]: In respect of the above system $\mathcal{G}$, suppose that the Riccati difference equation*

$$P_k = A_k^T P_{k+1} A_k + \gamma^{-2} A_k^T P_{k+1} B_k (I - \gamma^{-2} B_k^T P_{k+1} B_k)^{-1} B_k^T P_{k+1} A_k + C_k^T C_k , \tag{65}$$

with $P_T = 0$, has a positive definite symmetric solution on [0, N]. Then $\left\| \mathcal{G} \right\|_\infty \le \gamma$ for any $w \in \ell_2$.

Proof: *From the approach of Xie et al [18], define*

$$p_k = w_k - \gamma^{-2} (I - \gamma^{-2} B_k^T P_{k+1} B_k)^{-1} B_k^T P_{k+1} A_k x_k . \tag{66}$$

It is easily verified that

$$x_{k+1}^T P_{k+1} x_{k+1} - x_k^T P_k x_k + y_k^T y_k - \gamma^2 w_k^T w_k = -\gamma^{-2} p_k^T (I - \gamma^{-2} B_k^T P_{k+1} B_k)^{-1} p_k - x_k^T A_k^T P_{k+1} A_k x_k ,$$

which implies (61) – (62) and (63) under the assumption $x_0 = 0$. □

The above lemma relies on the simplifying assumption $E\{w_j w_k^T\} = I\delta_{jk}$. When $E\{w_j w_k^T\} = Q_k \delta_{jk}$, the scaled matrix $\bar{B}_k = B_k Q_k^{1/2}$ may be used in place of B_k above. In the case where $\mathcal{G}$ possesses a direct feedthrough matrix, namely, $y_k = C_k x_k + D_k w_k$, the Riccati difference equation within the above lemma becomes

$$\begin{aligned} P_k &= A_k^T P_{k+1} A_k + C_k^T C_k \\ &\quad + \gamma^{-2} (A_k^T P_{k+1} B_k + C_k^T D_k)(I - \gamma^{-2} B_k^T P_{k+1} B_k - \gamma^{-2} D_k^T D_k)^{-1} (B_k^T P_{k+1} A_k + D_k^T C_k) . \end{aligned} \tag{67}$$

"And as he thus spake for himself, Festus said with a loud voice, Paul, thou art beside thyself, much learning doth make thee mad." *Acts 26: 24*

A verification is requested in the problems. It will be shown that predictors, filters and smoothers satisfy a H∞ performance objective if there exist solutions to Riccati difference equations arising from the application of Lemma 7 to the corresponding error systems. A summary of the discrete-time results from [5], [11], [13] and the further details described in [21], [30], is presented below.

9.3.2 Discrete-Time H∞ Prediction

9.3.2.1 Problem Definition

Consider a nominal system $\mathcal{G}_2$

$$x_{k+1} = A_k x_k + B_k w_k, \tag{68}$$

$$y_{2,k} = C_{2,k} x_k, \tag{69}$$

together with a fictitious reference system $\mathcal{G}_1$ realised by (68) and

$$y_{1,k} = C_{1,k} x_k, \tag{70}$$

where A_k, B_k, $C_{2,k}$ and $C_{1,k}$ are of appropriate dimensions. The problem of interest is to find a solution $\mathcal{H}$ that produces one-step-ahead predictions, $\hat{y}_{1,k/k-1}$, given measurements

$$z_k = y_{2,k} + v_k \tag{71}$$

at time k - 1. The prediction error is defined as

$$e_{k/k-1} = y_{1,k} - \hat{y}_{1,k/k-1}. \tag{72}$$

The error sequence (72) is generated by $e = \mathcal{R}_{ei} i$, where $\mathcal{R}_{ei} = -[\mathcal{H} \quad \mathcal{H}\mathcal{G}_2 - \mathcal{G}_1]$, $i = \begin{bmatrix} v \\ w \end{bmatrix}$ and the objective is to achieve $\sum_{k=0}^{N-1} e_{k/k-1}^T e_{k/k-1} - \gamma^2 \sum_{k=0}^{N-1} i_k^T i_k < 0$, for some $\gamma \in \mathbb{R}$. For convenience, it is assumed that $w_k \in \mathbb{R}^m$, $E\{w_k\} = 0$, $E\{w_j w_k^T\} = Q_k \delta_{jk}$, $v_k \in \mathbb{R}^p$, $E\{v_k\} = 0$, $E\{v_j v_k^T\} = R_k \delta_{jk}$ and $E\{w_j v_k^T\} = 0$.

9.3.2.2 H∞ Solution

The H∞ predictor has the same structure as the optimum minimum-variance (or Kalman) predictor. It is given by

$$\hat{x}_{k+1/k} = \left(A_k - K_k C_{2,k}\right)\hat{x}_{k/k-1} + K_k z_k, \tag{73}$$

$$\hat{y}_{1,k/k-1} = C_{1,k}\hat{x}_{k/k-1}, \tag{74}$$

"Why waste time learning when ignorance is instantaneous?" *William Boyd Watterson II*

where

$$K_k = A_k P_{k/k-1} C_{2,k}^T (C_{2,k} P_{k/k-1} C_{2,k}^T + R_k)^{-1} \tag{75}$$

is the one-step-ahead predictor gain,

$$P_{k/k-1} = (M_k^{-1} - \gamma^{-2} C_{1,k+1}^T C_{1,k+1})^{-1}, \tag{76}$$

and $M_k = M_k^T > 0$ satisfies the Riccati differential equation

$$M_{k+1} = A_k M_k A_k^T + B_k Q_k B_k^T - A_k M_k \begin{bmatrix} C_{1,k}^T & C_{2,k}^T \end{bmatrix} \begin{bmatrix} C_{1,k} M_k C_{1,k}^T - \gamma^2 I & C_{1,k} M_k C_{2,k}^T \\ C_{2,k} M_k C_{1,k}^T & R_k + C_{2,k} M_k C_{2,k}^T \end{bmatrix}^{-1} \begin{bmatrix} C_{1,k} \\ C_{2,k} \end{bmatrix} M_k A_k^T \tag{77}$$

such that $\begin{bmatrix} C_{1,k} M_k C_{1,k}^T - \gamma^2 I & C_{1,k} M_k C_{2,k}^T \\ C_{2,k} M_k C_{1,k}^T & R_k + C_{2,k} M_k C_{2,k}^T \end{bmatrix} > 0$. The above predictor is also known as an *a priori* filter within [11], [13], [30].

9.3.2.3 Performance

Following the approach in the continuous-time case, by subtracting (73) – (74) from (68), (70), the predictor error system is

$$\begin{bmatrix} \tilde{x}_{k+1/k} \\ e_{k/k-1} \end{bmatrix} = \begin{bmatrix} A_k - K_k C_{2,k} & [-K_k \quad B_k] \\ C_{1,k} & [0 \quad 0] \end{bmatrix} \begin{bmatrix} \tilde{x}_{k/k-1} \\ \begin{bmatrix} v_k \\ w_k \end{bmatrix} \end{bmatrix}, \quad \tilde{x}_0 = 0, \tag{78}$$

$$= \mathcal{R}_{ei} i,$$

where $\tilde{x}_{k/k-1} = x_k - \hat{x}_{k/k-1}$, $\mathcal{R}_{ei} = \begin{bmatrix} A_k - K_k C_{2,k} & [-K_k \quad B_k] \\ C_{1,k} & [0 \quad 0] \end{bmatrix}$ and $i = \begin{bmatrix} v \\ w \end{bmatrix}$. It is shown below that the prediction error satisfies the desired performance objective.

Lemma 8 [11], [13], [30]: *In respect of the H_∞ prediction problem (68) – (72), the existence of $M_k = M_k^T > 0$ for the Riccati differential equation (77) ensures that the solution (73) – (74) achieves the performance objective $\sum_{k=0}^{N-1} e_{k/k-1}^T e_{k/k-1} - \gamma^2 \sum_{k=0}^{N-1} i_k^T i_k < 0$.*

Proof: *By applying the Bounded Real Lemma to $\mathcal{R}_{ei}^H$ and taking the adjoint to address $\mathcal{R}_{ei}$, it is required that there exists a positive define symmetric solution to*

"Give me a fruitful error any time, full of seeds bursting with its own corrections. You can keep your sterile truth for yourself." *Vilfredo Federico Damaso Pareto*

$$P_{k+1} = (A_k - K_kC_{2,k})P_k(A_k - K_kC_{2,k})^T$$
$$+\gamma^{-2}(A_k - K_kC_{2,k})P_kC_{1,k}^T(I - \gamma^{-2}C_{1,k}P_kC_{1,k}^T)^{-1}C_{2,k}P_k(A_k - K_kC_{2,k})^T + K_kR_kK_k^T + B_kQ_kB_k^T$$
$$= (A_k - K_kC_{2,k})(P_k + \gamma^{-2}P_kC_{1,k}^T(I - \gamma^{-2}C_{1,k}P_kC_{1,k}^T)^{-1}C_{1,k}P_k)(A_k - K_kC_{2,k})^T + K_kR_kK_k^T + B_kQ_kB_k^T$$
$$= (A_k - K_kC_{2,k})(P_k^{-1} + \gamma^{-2}C_{1,k}^TC_{1,k})^{-1}(A_k - K_kC_{2,k})^T + K_kR_kK_k^T + B_kQ_kB_k^T \quad (79)$$

in which use was made of the Matrix Inversion Lemma. Defining $P_{k/k-1} = (P_k^{-1} + \gamma^{-2}C_{1,k}^TC_{1,k})^{-1}$ *leads to*

$$(P_{k+1/k}^{-1} + \gamma^{-2}C_{1,k+1}^TC_{1,k+1})^{-1} = (A_k - K_kC_{2,k})P_{k/k-1}(A_k - K_kC_{2,k})^T + K_kR_kK_k^T + B_kQ_kB_k^T$$
$$= A_kP_{k/k-1}A_k^T + B_kQ_kB_k^T - A_kP_{k/k-1}C_{2,k}^T(R + C_kP_{k/k-1}C_{2,k}^T)^{-1}C_{2,k}P_{k/k-1}A_k^T.$$

and applying the Matrix Inversion Lemma gives

$$(P_{k+1/k}^{-1} + \gamma^{-2}C_{1,k+1}^TC_{1,k+1})^{-1} = A_kP_{k/k-1}A_k^T + B_kQ_kB_k^T - A_kP_{k/k-1}C_{2,k}^T(R + C_{2,k}P_{k/k-1}C_{2,k}^T)^{-1}C_{2,k}P_{k/k-1}A_k^T$$
$$= A_k(P_{k/k-1} + C_{2,k}^TR_k^{-1}C_{2,k})^{-1}A_k^T + B_kQ_kB_k^T .$$

The change of variable (76), namely, $P_{k/k-1}^{-1} = M_k^{-1} - \gamma^{-2}C_{1,k}^TC_{1,k}$, *results in*

$$M_{k+1} = A_k(M_k^{-1} + C_{2,k}^TR_k^{-1}C_{2,k} - \gamma^{-2}C_{1,k}^TC_{1,k})^{-1}A_k^T + B_kQ_kB_k^T$$
$$= A_k(M_k^{-1} + \bar{C}_k\bar{R}_k\bar{C}_k^T)^{-1}A_k^T + B_kQ_kB_k^T . \quad (80)$$

where $\bar{C}_k = \begin{bmatrix} C_{1,k} \\ C_{2,k} \end{bmatrix}$ *and* $\bar{R}_k = \begin{bmatrix} -\gamma^{-2}I & 0 \\ 0 & R_k \end{bmatrix}$. *Applying the Matrix Inversion Lemma within (80) gives*

$$M_{k+1} = A_kMA_k^T - A_kM_k\bar{C}_k^T(\bar{R}_k + \bar{C}_kM_k\bar{C}_k^T)^{-1}\bar{C}_kM_kA_k^T + B_kQ_kB_k^T , \quad (81)$$

Expanding (81) yields (77). The existence of $M_k > 0$ for the above Riccati differential equation implies $P_k > 0$ for (79). Thus, it follows from Lemma 7 that the stated performance objective is achieved. □

9.3.3 Discrete-Time H∞ Filtering

9.3.3.1 Problem Definition

Consider again the configuration of Fig. 1. Assume that the systems $\mathcal{G}_2$ and $\mathcal{G}_1$ have the realisations (68) - (69) and (68), (70), respectively. It is desired to find a solution $\mathcal{H}$ that operates on the measurements (71) and produces the filtered estimates $\hat{y}_{1,k/k}$. The filtered error sequence,

$$e_{k/k} = y_{1,k} - \hat{y}_{1,k/k} , \quad (82)$$

"Never interrupt your enemy when he is making a mistake." *Napoléon Bonaparte* is generated by $e = \mathcal{R}_{ei}i$, where $\mathcal{R}_{ei} = -[\mathcal{H} \quad \mathcal{H}\mathcal{G}_2 - \mathcal{G}_1]$, $i = \begin{bmatrix} v \\ w \end{bmatrix}$. The H∞ performance objective is to achieve $\sum_{k=0}^{N-1} e_{k/k}^T e_{k/k} - \gamma^2 \sum_{k=0}^{N-1} i_k^T i_k < 0$, for some $\gamma \in \mathbb{R}$.

9.3.3.2 H∞ Solution

As explained in Chapter 4, filtered states can be evolved from

$$\hat{x}_{k/k} = A_{k-1}\hat{x}_{k-1/k-1} + L_k(z_k - C_{2,k}A_{k-1}\hat{x}_{k-1/k-1}), \tag{83}$$

where $L_k \in \mathbb{R}^{n\times p}$ is a filter gain. The above recursion is called an *a posteriori* filter in [11], [13], [30]. Output estimates are obtained from

$$\hat{y}_{1,k-1/k-1} = C_{1,k-1}\hat{x}_{k-1/k-1}. \tag{84}$$

The filter gain is calculated as

$$L_k = M_k C_k^T (C_k M_k C_k^T + R_k)^{-1}, \tag{85}$$

where $M_k = M_k^T > 0$ satisfies the Riccati differential equation

$$M_k = A_{k-1}M_{k-1}A_{k-1}^T + B_{k-1}Q_{k-1}B_{k-1}^T - A_{k-1}M_{k-1}\begin{bmatrix} C_{1,k-1}^T & C_{2,k-1}^T \end{bmatrix} \times \begin{bmatrix} C_{1,k-1}M_{k-1}C_{1,k-1}^T - \gamma^2 I & C_{1,k-1}M_{k-1}C_{2,k-1}^T \\ C_{2,k-1}M_{k-1}C_{1,k-1}^T & R_{k-1} + C_{2,k-1}M_{k-1}C_{2,k-1}^T \end{bmatrix}^{-1} \begin{bmatrix} C_{1,k-1} \\ C_{2,k-1} \end{bmatrix} M_{k-1}A_{k-1}^T \tag{86}$$

such that $\begin{bmatrix} C_{1,k-1}M_{k-1}C_{1,k-1}^T - \gamma^2 I & C_{1,k-1}M_{k-1}C_{2,k-1}^T \\ C_{2,k-1}M_{k-1}C_{1,k-1}^T & R_{k-1} + C_{2,k-1}M_{k-1}C_{2,k-1}^T \end{bmatrix} > 0$.

9.3.3.3 Performance

Subtracting from (83) from (68) gives $\tilde{x}_{k/k} = A_{k-1}\hat{x}_{k-1/k-1} + B_{k-1}w_{k-1} - A_{k-1}\hat{x}_{k-1/k-1} + L_k C_{2,k} A_{k-1}\hat{x}_{k-1/k-1} + L_k(C_{2,k}(A_{k-1}x_{k-1} + B_{k-1}w_{k-1}) + v_k)$. Denote $i_k = \begin{bmatrix} v_k \\ w_{k-1} \end{bmatrix}$, then the filtered error system may be written as

$$\begin{bmatrix} \tilde{x}_{k/k} \\ e_{k-1/k-1} \end{bmatrix} = \begin{bmatrix} (I - L_k C_{2,k})A_{k-1} & [-L_k \quad (I - L_k C_{2,k})B_{k-1}] \\ C_{1,k} & [0 \quad 0] \end{bmatrix} \begin{bmatrix} \tilde{x}_{k-1/k-1} \\ i_k \end{bmatrix} = \mathcal{R}_{ei} i, \tag{87}$$

"I believe the most solemn duty of the American president is to protect the American people. If America shows uncertainty and weakness in this decade, the world will drift toward tragedy. This will not happen on my watch." *George Walker Bush*

with $\tilde{x}_0 = 0$, where $\mathcal{R}_{ei} = \begin{bmatrix} (I - L_k C_{2,k}) A_{k-1} & [-L_k \quad (I - L_k C_{2,k}) B_{k-1}] \\ C_{1,k} & [0 \quad 0] \end{bmatrix}$. It is shown below that the filtered error satisfies the desired performance objective.

Lemma 9 [11], [13], [30]: *In respect of the H_∞ problem (68) – (70), (82), the solution (83) – (84) achieves the performance* $\sum_{k=0}^{N-1} e_{k/k}^T e_{k/k} - \gamma^2 \sum_{k=0}^{N-1} i_k^T i_k < 0$.

Proof: *By applying the Bounded Real Lemma to $\mathcal{R}_{ei}^H$ and taking the adjoint to address $\mathcal{R}_{ei}$, it is required that there exists a positive define symmetric solution to*

$$\begin{aligned} P_{k+1} &= (I - L_k C_{2,k}) A_{k-1} P_k A_{k-1}^T (I - C_{2,k}^T L_k^T) \\ &\quad + \gamma^{-2} (I - L_k C_{2,k}) A_{k-1} P_k C_{1,k}^T (I - \gamma^{-2} C_{1,k} P_k C_{1,k}^T)^{-1} C_{1,k} P_k A_{k-1}^T (I - L_k C_{2,k})^T \\ &\quad + (I - L_k C_{2,k}) B_{k-1} Q_{k-1} B_{k-1}^T (I - C_{2,k}^T L_k^T) + L_k R_k L_k^T \\ &= (I - L_k C_{2,k}) A_{k-1} (P_k^{-1} - \gamma^{-2} C_{1,k}^T C_{1,k}) A_{k-1}^T (I - C_{2,k}^T L_k^T) \\ &\quad + (I - L_k C_{2,k}) B_{k-1} Q_{k-1} B_{k-1}^T (I - C_{2,k}^T L_k^T) + L_k R_k L_k^T, \end{aligned} \tag{88}$$

in which use was made of the Matrix Inversion Lemma. Defining

$$P_{k/k-1}^{-1} = P_k^{-1} - \gamma^{-2} C_{1,k}^T C_{1,k}, \tag{89}$$

using (85) and applying the Matrix Inversion Lemma leads to

$$\begin{aligned} (P_{k+1/k}^{-1} + \gamma^{-2} C_{1,k}^T C_{1,k}) &= (I - L_k C_{2,k})(A_{k-1} P_{k/k-1} A_{k-1}^T + B_{k-1} Q_{k-1} B_{k-1}^T)(I - C_{2,k}^T L_k^T) + L_k R_k L_k^T \\ &= (I - L_k C_{2,k}) M_k (I - C_{2,k}^T L_k^T) + L_k R_k L_k^T \\ &= M_k - M_k C_{2,k}^T (R_k + C_{2,k} M_k C_{2,k}^T)^{-1} C_{2,k} M_k \\ &= (M_k^{-1} + C_{2,k}^T R_k^{-1} C_{2,k})^{-1}, \end{aligned} \tag{90}$$

where

$$M_k = A_{k-1} P_{k/k-1} A_{k-1}^T + B_{k-1} Q_{k-1} B_{k-1}^T. \tag{91}$$

It follows from (90) that $P_{k+1/k}^{-1} + \gamma^{-2} C_{1,k}^T C_{1,k} = M_k^{-1} + C_{2,k}^T R_k^{-1} C_{2,k}$ *and*

$$\begin{aligned} P_{k/k-1}^{-1} &= M_{k-1}^{-1} + C_{2,k-1}^T R_{k-1}^{-1} C_{2,k-1} - \gamma^{-2} C_{1,k-1}^T C_{1,k-1} \\ &= M_{k-1}^{-1} + \bar{C}_{k-1}^T \bar{R}_{k-1}^{-1} \bar{C}_{k-1}, \end{aligned} \tag{92}$$

where $\bar{C}_k = \begin{bmatrix} C_{1,k} \\ C_{2,k} \end{bmatrix}$ *and* $\bar{R}_k = \begin{bmatrix} -\gamma^{-2} I & 0 \\ 0 & R_k \end{bmatrix}$. *Substituting (92) into (91) yields*

"Hell, there are no rules here – we're trying to accomplish something." *Thomas Alva Edison*

$$M_k = A_{k-1}(M_{k-1}^{-1} + \bar{C}_{k-1}\bar{R}_{k-1}\bar{C}_{k-1}^T)^{-1}A_{k-1}^T + B_{k-1}Q_{k-1}B_{k-1}^T, \tag{93}$$

which is the same as (86). The existence of $M_k > 0$ for the above Riccati difference equation implies the existence of a $P_k > 0$ for (88). Thus, it follows from Lemma 7 that the stated performance objective is achieved. □

9.3.4 Solution to the General Filtering Problem

Limebeer, Green and Walker express Riccati difference equations such as (86) in a compact form using J-factorisation [5], [21]. The solutions for the general filtering problem follow immediately from their results. Consider

$$\begin{bmatrix} x_{k+1} \\ e_{k/k} \\ z_k \end{bmatrix} = \begin{bmatrix} A_k & B_{1,1,k} & 0 \\ C_{1,1,k} & D_{1,1,k} & D_{1,2,k} \\ C_{2,1,k} & D_{2,1,k} & 0 \end{bmatrix} \begin{bmatrix} x_k \\ i_k \\ -\hat{y}_{1,k/k} \end{bmatrix}. \tag{94}$$

Let $J_k = \begin{bmatrix} E\{i_k i_k^T\} & 0 \\ 0 & -\gamma^2 \end{bmatrix}$, $\bar{C}_k = \begin{bmatrix} C_{1,1,k} \\ C_{2,1,k} \end{bmatrix}$, $\bar{D}_k = \begin{bmatrix} D_{1,1,k} & D_{1,2,k} \\ D_{2,1,k} & 0 \end{bmatrix}$ and $\bar{B}_k = \begin{bmatrix} B_{1,1,k} & 0 \end{bmatrix}$. From the approach of [5], [21], the Riccati difference equation corresponding to the H_∞ problem (94) is

$$\begin{aligned} M_{k+1} &= A_k M_k A_k^T + \bar{B}_k J_k \bar{B}_k^T \\ &\quad -(A_k M_k \bar{C}_k^T + \bar{B}_k J_k \bar{D}_k^T)(\bar{C}_k M_k \bar{C}_k^T + \bar{D}_k J_k \bar{D}_k^T)^{-1}(A_k M_k \bar{C}_k^T + \bar{B}_k J_k \bar{D}_k^T)^T. \end{aligned} \tag{95}$$

Suppose in a general filtering problem that $\mathcal{G}_2$ is realised by (68), $y_{2,k} = C_{2,k}x_k + D_{2,k}w_k$, $\mathcal{G}_1$ is realised by (68) and $y_{1,k} = C_{1,k}x_k + D_{1,k}w_k$. Then substituting $B_{1,1,k} = \begin{bmatrix} 0 & B_k \end{bmatrix}$, $C_{1,1,k} = C_{1,k}$, $C_{2,1,k} = C_{2,k}$, $D_{1,1,k} = \begin{bmatrix} 0 & D_{1,k} \end{bmatrix}$, $D_{1,2,k} = I$ and $D_{2,1,k} = \begin{bmatrix} I & D_{2,k} \end{bmatrix}$ into (95) yields

$$\begin{aligned} M_{k+1} &= A_k M_k A_k^T - \begin{bmatrix} A_k M_k C_{1,k}^T + B_k Q_k D_{1,k}^T \\ A_k M_k C_{2,k}^T + B_k Q_k D_{2,k}^T \end{bmatrix} \\ &\quad \times \begin{bmatrix} C_{1,k} M_k C_{1,k}^T + D_{1,k} Q_k D_{1,k}^T - \gamma^2 I & C_{1,k} M_k C_{2,k}^T + D_{1,k} Q_k D_{2,k}^T \\ C_{2,k} M_k C_{1,k}^T + D_{2,k} Q_k D_{1,k}^T & R_k + C_{2,k} M_k C_{2,k}^T + D_{2,k} Q_k D_{2,k}^T \end{bmatrix}^{-1} \\ &\quad \times \begin{bmatrix} C_{1,k} M_k A_k^T + D_{1,k} Q_k B_{1,k}^T & C_{2,k} M_k A_k^T + D_{2,k} Q_k B_k^T \end{bmatrix} + B_k Q_k B_k^T. \end{aligned} \tag{96}$$

The filter solution is given by

$$\hat{x}_{k+1/k} = A_k \hat{x}_{k/k-1} + K_k (z_k - C_{2,1,k} \hat{x}_{k/k-1}), \tag{97}$$

$$\hat{y}_{1,k/k} = C_{1,1,k} \hat{x}_{k/k-1} + L_k (z_k - C_{2,1,k} \hat{x}_{k/k-1}), \tag{98}$$

where $K_k = (A_k M_k C_{2,k}^T + B_k Q_k D_{2,k}^T)\Omega_k^{-1}$, $L_k = (C_{1,k} M_k C_{2,k}^T + D_{1,k} Q_k D_{2,k}^T)\Omega_k^{-1}$ and $\Omega_k = C_{2,k} M_k C_{2,k}^T + D_{2,k} Q_k D_{2,k}^T + R_k$.

"If we knew what it is we were doing, it would not be called research, would it?" *Albert Einstein*

9.3.5 Discrete-Time H$_\infty$ Smoothing

9.3.5.1 Problem Definition

Suppose that measurements (72) of a system (68) – (69) are available over an interval $k \in [1, N]$. The problem of interest is to calculate smoothed estimates $\hat{y}_{k/N}$ of y_k such that the error sequence

$$e_{k/N} = y_k - \hat{y}_{k/N} \tag{99}$$

is in ℓ_2.

9.3.5.2 H$_\infty$ Solution

The following fixed-interval smoother for output estimation [28] employs the gain for the H$_\infty$ predictor,

$$K_k = A_k P_{k/k-1} C_{2,k}^T \Omega_k^{-1}, \tag{100}$$

where $\Omega_k = C_{2,k} P_{k/k-1} C_{2,k}^T + R_k$, in which $P_{k/k-1}$ is obtained from (76) and (77). The gain (100) is used in the minimum-variance smoother structure described in Chapter 7, *viz.*,

$$\begin{bmatrix} \hat{x}_{k+1/k} \\ \alpha_k \end{bmatrix} = \begin{bmatrix} A_k - K_k C_{2,k} & K_k \\ -\Omega_k^{-1/2} C_{2,k} & \Omega_k^{-1/2} \end{bmatrix} \begin{bmatrix} \hat{x}_{k/k-1} \\ z_k \end{bmatrix}, \tag{101}$$

$$\begin{bmatrix} \xi_{k-1} \\ \beta_k \end{bmatrix} = \begin{bmatrix} A_k^T - C_{2,k}^T K_k^T & C_{2,k}^T \Omega_k^{-1/2} \\ -K_k^T & \Omega_k^{-1/2} \end{bmatrix} \begin{bmatrix} \xi_k \\ \alpha_k \end{bmatrix}, \xi_N = 0, \tag{102}$$

$$\hat{y}_{k/N} = z_k - R_k \beta_k . \tag{103}$$

It is argued below that this smoother meets the desired H$_\infty$ performance objective.

9.3.5.3 H$_\infty$ Performance

It is easily shown that the smoother error system is

$$\begin{bmatrix} \tilde{x}_{k+1/k} \\ \lambda_{k-1} \\ e_{k/N} \end{bmatrix} = \begin{bmatrix} \begin{bmatrix} A_k - K_k C_{2,k} & 0 \\ C_{2,k}^T \Omega_k^{-1} C_{2,k} & A_k^T - C_{2,k}^T K_k^T \end{bmatrix} & \begin{bmatrix} -K_k & B_k \\ C_{2,k}^T \Omega_k^{-1} & 0 \end{bmatrix} \\ \begin{bmatrix} R_k \Omega_k^{-1} C_{2,k} & -R_k K_k^T \end{bmatrix} & \begin{bmatrix} R_k \Omega_k^{-1} - I & 0 \end{bmatrix} \end{bmatrix} \begin{bmatrix} \tilde{x}_{k/k-1} \\ \lambda_k \\ v_k \\ w_k \end{bmatrix}, \tag{104}$$

$$= \boldsymbol{\mathcal{R}}_{ei} i ,$$

with $\tilde{x}_0 = 0$, where $\tilde{x}_{k/k-1} = x_k - \hat{x}_{k/k-1}$, $i = \begin{bmatrix} v \\ w \end{bmatrix}$ and

---

"I have had my results for a long time: but I do not yet know how I am to arrive at them." *Karl Friedrich Gauss*

$$\mathcal{R}_{ei} = \begin{bmatrix} \begin{bmatrix} A_k - K_k C_{2,k} & 0 \\ C_{2,k}^T \Omega_k^{-1} C_{2,k} & A_k^T - C_{2,k}^T K_k^T \end{bmatrix} & \begin{bmatrix} -K_k & B_k \\ C_{2,k}^T \Omega_k^{-1} & 0 \end{bmatrix} \\ \begin{bmatrix} R_k \Omega_k^{-1} C_{2,k} & -R_k K_k^T \end{bmatrix} & \begin{bmatrix} R_k \Omega_k^{-1} - I & 0 \end{bmatrix} \end{bmatrix}.$$

Lemma 10: *In respect of the smoother error system (104), if there exists a symmetric positive definite solutions to (77) for* $\gamma > 0$*, then the smoother (101) – (103) achieves* $\mathcal{R}_{ei} \in \ell_\infty$*, that is,* $i \in \ell_2$ *implies* $e \in \ell_2$.

Outline of Proof: *From Lemma 8,* $\tilde{x} \in \ell_2$*, since it evolves within the predictor error system. Therefore,* $\lambda \in \ell_2$*, since it evolves within the adjoint predictor error system. Then* $e \in \ell_2$*, since it is a linear combination of* $\tilde{x}$*,* λ *and* $i \in \ell_2$. □

9.3.5.4 Performance Comparison

Example 4 [28]. A voiced speech utterance "a e i o u" was sampled at 8 kHz for the purpose of comparing smoother performance. Simulations were conducted with the zero-mean, unity-variance speech sample interpolated to a 16 kHz sample rate, to which 200 realizations of Gaussian measurement noise were added and the signal to noise ratio was varied from -5 to 5 dB. The speech sample is modelled as a first-order autoregressive process

$$x_{k+1} = A x_k + w_k, \tag{105}$$

where $A \in \mathbb{R}$, $0 < A < 1$. Estimates for σ_w^2 and A were calculated at 20 dB SNR using an EM algorithm, see Chapter 8.

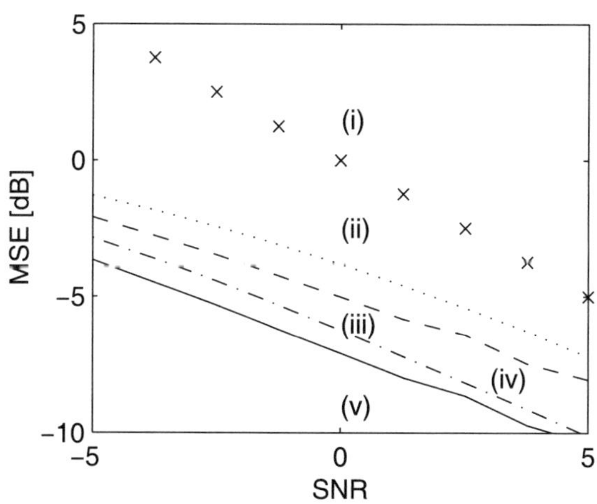

Fig. 9. Speech estimate performance comparison: (i) data (crosses), (ii) Kalman filter (dotted line), (iii) H $_\infty$ filter (dashed line), (iv) minimum-variance smoother (dot-dashed line) and (v) H $_\infty$ smoother (solid line).

"If I have seen further it is only by standing on the shoulders of giants." *Isaac Newton*

Simulations were conducted in which a minimum-variance filter and a fixed-interval smoother were employed to recover the speech message from noisy measurements. The results are provided in Fig. 9. As expected, the smoother out-performs the filter. Searches were conducted for minimum values of γ such that solutions to the design Riccati difference equations were positive definite for each noise realisation. The performance of the resulting H_∞ filter and smoother are indicated by the dashed line and solid line of the figure. It can be seen for this example that the H_∞ filter out-performs the Kalman filter. The figure also indicates that the robust smoother provides the best performance and exhibits about 4 dB reduction in mean-square-error compared to the Kalman filter at 0 dB SNR. This performance benefit needs to be reconciled against the extra calculation cost of combining robust forward and backward state predictors within (101) – (103).

9.3.5.5 High SNR and Low SNR Asymptotes

An understanding of why robust solutions are beneficial in the presence of uncertainties can be gleaned by examining single-input-single-output filtering and equalisation. Consider a time-invariant plant having the canonical form

$$A = \begin{bmatrix} 0 & 1 & \cdots & 0 \\ 0 & & \ddots & 0 \\ \vdots & & & \\ -a_0 & -a_1 & & -a_{n-1} \end{bmatrix}, \; B = \begin{bmatrix} 0 \\ \vdots \\ 0 \\ 1 \end{bmatrix}, \; C_2 = \begin{bmatrix} c & 0 & \cdots & 0 \end{bmatrix},$$

$a_0, \ldots a_{n-1}, c \in \mathbb{R}$. Since the plant is time-invariant, the transfer function exists and is denoted by $G(z)$. Some notation is defined prior to stating some observations for output estimation problems. Suppose that an H_∞ filter has been constructed for the above plant. Let the H_∞ algebraic Riccati equation solution, predictor gain, filter gain, predictor, filter and smoother transfer function matrices be denoted by $P^{(\infty)}$, $K^{(\infty)}$, $L^{(\infty)}$, $H_P^{(\infty)}(z)$, $H_F^{(\infty)}(z)$ and $H_S^{(\infty)}(z)$ respectively. The H_∞ filter transfer function matrix may be written as $H_F^{(\infty)}(z) = L^{(\infty)} + (I - L^{(\infty)})H_P^{(\infty)}(z)$ where $L^{(\infty)} = I - R(\Omega^{(\infty)})^{-1}$. The transfer function matrix of the map from the inputs to the filter output estimation error is

$$R_{ei}^{(\infty)}(z) = -[H_F^{(\infty)}(z)\sigma_v \quad (H_F^{(\infty)}(z) - I)G(z)\sigma_w]. \tag{106}$$

The H_∞ smoother transfer function matrix can be written as $H_S^{(\infty)}(z) = I - R(I - (H_P^{(\infty)}(z))^H)(\Omega^{(\infty)})^{-1}(I - H_P^{(\infty)}(z))$. Similarly, let $P^{(2)}$, $K^{(2)}$, $L^{(2)}$, $H_F^{(2)}(z)$ and $H_S^{(2)}(z)$ denote the minimum-variance algebraic Riccati equation solution, predictor gain, filter gain, filter and smoother transfer function matrices respectively.

"In computer science, we stand on each other's feet." *Brian K. Reid*

Proposition 1 [28]: *In the above output estimation problem:*

(i)

$$\lim_{\sigma_v^2 \to 0} \sup_{\omega \in \{-\pi,\pi\}} \left| H_F^{(\infty)}(e^{j\omega}) \right| = 1. \tag{107}$$

(ii)

$$\lim_{\sigma_v^2 \to 0} \sup_{\omega \in \{-\pi,\pi\}} \left| H_F^{(2)}(e^{j\omega}) \right| < \lim_{\sigma_v^2 \to 0} \sup_{\omega \in \{-\pi,\pi\}} \left| H_F^{(\infty)}(e^{j\omega}) \right|. \tag{108}$$

(iii)

$$\lim_{\sigma_v^2 \to 0} \sup_{\omega \in \{-\pi,\pi\}} \left| R_{ei}^{(\infty)}(R_{ei}^{(\infty)})^H(e^{j\omega}) \right| = \lim_{\sigma_v^2 \to 0} \sup_{\omega \in \{-\pi,\pi\}} \left| H_F^{(\infty)}(H_F^{(\infty)})^H(e^{j\omega}) \right| \sigma_v^2. \tag{109}$$

(iv)

$$\lim_{\sigma_v^2 \to 0} \sup_{\omega \in \{-\pi,\pi\}} \left| H_S^{(\infty)}(e^{j\omega}) \right| = 1. \tag{110}$$

(v)

$$\lim_{\sigma_v^2 \to 0} \sup_{\omega \in \{-\pi,\pi\}} \left| H_S^{(2)}(e^{j\omega}) \right| < \lim_{\sigma_v^2 \to 0} \sup_{\omega \in \{-\pi,\pi\}} \left| H_S^{(\infty)}(e^{j\omega}) \right|. \tag{111}$$

Outline of Proof: *(i) Let* $p_{(1,1)}^{(\infty)}$ *denote the (1,1) component of* $P^{(\infty)}$. *The low measurement noise observation (107) follows from* $L^{(\infty)} = 1 - \sigma_v^2 (c^2 p_{(1,1)}^{(\infty)} + \sigma_v^2)^{-1}$ *which implies* $\lim_{\sigma_v^2 \to 0} L^{(\infty)} = 1$.

(ii) Observation (108) follows from $p_{(1,1)}^{(\infty)} > p_{(1,1)}^{(2)}$, *which results in* $\lim_{\sigma_v^2 \to 0} L^{(\infty)} > \lim_{\sigma_v^2 \to 0} L^{(2)}$.

(iii) Observation (109) follows immediately from the application of (107) in (106).

(iv) Observation (110) follows from $\lim_{\sigma_v^2 \to 0} \sigma_v^2 (c^2 p_{(1,1)}^{(\infty)} + \sigma_v^2)^{-1} = 0$.

(v) Observation (111) follows from $p_{(1,1)}^{(\infty)} > p_{(1,1)}^{(2)}$ *which results in* $\lim_{\sigma_v^2 \to 0} \Omega_3^{(\infty)} > \lim_{\sigma_v^2 \to 0} \Omega^{(2)}$. □

An interpretation of (107) and (110) is that the maximum magnitudes of the filters and smoothers asymptotically approach a short circuit (or zero impedance) when $\sigma_v^2 \to 0$. From (108) and (111), as $\sigma_v^2 \to 0$, the maximum magnitudes of the H_∞ solutions approach the short circuit asymptote closer than the optimal minimum-variance solutions. That is, for low measurement noise, the robust solutions accommodate some uncertainty by giving greater weighting to the data. Since $\lim_{\sigma_v^2 \to 0} \left\| R_{ei} \right\|_\infty \to \sigma_v$ and the H_∞ filter achieves the performance $\left\| R_{ei} \right\|_\infty < \gamma$, it follows from (109) that an *a priori* design estimate is $\gamma = \sigma_v$.

"All programmers are optimists." *Frederick P. Brooks, Jr*

Suppose now that a time-invariant plant has the transfer function $G(z) = C(zI - A)^{-1}B + D$, where A, B and C are defined above together with $D \in \mathbb{R}$. Consider an input estimation (or equalisation) problem in which the transfer function matrix of the causal H_∞ solution that estimates the input of the plant is

$$H_F^{(\infty)}(z) = QD^T\left(\Omega^{(\infty)}\right)^{-1} - QD^T\left(\Omega^{(\infty)}\right)^{-1} H_P^{(\infty)}(z). \tag{112}$$

The transfer function matrix of the map from the inputs to the input estimation error is

$$R_{ei}^{(\infty)}(z) = -[H_F^{(\infty)}(z)\sigma_v \quad (H_F^{(\infty)}G(z) - I)\sigma_w]. \tag{113}$$

The noncausal H_∞ transfer function matrix of the input estimator can be written as $H_S^{(\infty)}(z)$ = $QG^{-H}(z)(I - (H_P^{(\infty)}(z))^H)(\Omega_3^{(\infty)})^{-1}(I - H_P^{(\infty)}(z))$.

Proposition 2 [28]: *For the above input estimation problem:*

(i)

$$\lim_{\sigma_v^{-2} \to 0} \sup_{\omega \in \{-\pi,\pi\}} \left|H_F^{(\infty)}(e^{j\omega})\right| = 0. \tag{114}$$

(ii)

$$\lim_{\sigma_v^{-2} \to 0} \sup_{\omega \in \{-\pi,\pi\}} \left|H_F^{(2)}(e^{j\omega})\right| > \lim_{\sigma_v^{-2} \to 0} \sup_{\omega \in \{-\pi,\pi\}} \left|H_F^{(\infty)}(e^{j\omega})\right|. \tag{115}$$

(iii)

$$\begin{aligned}&\lim_{\sigma_v^{-2} \to 0} \sup_{\omega \in \{-\pi,\pi\}} \left|R_{ei}^{(\infty)}(R_{ei}^{(\infty)})^H(e^{j\omega})\right| \\ &\quad = \lim_{\sigma_v^{-2} \to 0} \sup_{\omega \in \{-\pi,\pi\}} \left|(H_F^{(\infty)}G^{(\infty)}(e^{j\omega}) - 1)(H_F^{(\infty)}G^{(\infty)}(e^{j\omega}) - 1)^H\right|\sigma_w^2.\end{aligned} \tag{116}$$

(iv)

$$\lim_{\sigma_v^{-2} \to 0} \sup_{\omega \in \{-\pi,\pi\}} \left|H_S^{(\infty)}(e^{j\omega})\right| = 0. \tag{117}$$

(v)

$$\lim_{\sigma_v^{-2} \to 0} \sup_{\omega \in \{-\pi,\pi\}} \left|H_S^{(2)}(e^{j\omega})\right| > \lim_{\sigma_v^{-2} \to 0} \sup_{\omega \in \{-\pi,\pi\}} \left|H_S^{(\infty)}(e^{j\omega})\right|. \tag{118}$$

Outline of Proof: *(i) and (iv) The high measurement noise observations (114) and (117) follow from* $\Omega^{(\infty)} = c^2 p_{(1,1)}^{(\infty)} + D\sigma_w^2 + \sigma_v^2$ *which implies* $\lim_{\sigma_v^{-2} \to 0} (\Omega_3^{(\infty)})^{-1} = 0$.

(ii) and (v) The observations (115) and (118) follow from $p_{(1,1)}^{(\infty)} > p_{(1,1)}^{(2)}$, *which results in* $\lim_{\sigma_v^2 \to 0} \Omega_3^{(\infty)} >$ $\lim_{\sigma_v^2 \to 0} \Omega^{(2)}$.

"Always code as if the guy who ends up maintaining your code will be a violent psychopath who knows where you live." *Damian Conway*

(iii) The observation (116) follows immediately from the application of (114) in (113). □

An interpretation of (114) and (117) is that the maximum magnitudes of the equalisers asymptotically approach an open circuit (or infinite impedance) when $\sigma_v^{-2} \to 0$. From (115) and (118), as $\sigma_v^{-2} \to 0$, the maximum magnitude of the H$_\infty$ solution approaches the open circuit asymptote closer than that of the optimum minimum-variance solution. That is, under high measurement noise conditions, robust solutions accommodate some uncertainty by giving less weighting to the data. Since $\lim_{\sigma_v^{-2} \to 0} \left\| R_{ei} \right\|_\infty \to \sigma_w$, the H$_\infty$ solution achieves the performance $\left\| R_{ei} \right\|_\infty < \gamma$, it follows from (116) than an *a priori* design estimate is $\gamma = \sigma_w$.

Proposition 1 follows intuitively. Indeed, the short circuit asymptote is sometimes referred to as the singular filter. Proposition 2 may appear counter-intuitive and warrants further explanation. When the plant is minimum phase and the measurement noise is negligible, the equaliser inverts the plant. Conversely, when the equalisation problem is dominated by measurement noise, the solution is a low gain filter; that is, the estimation error is minimised by giving less weighting to the data.

9.4 Conclusion

Uncertainties are invariably present within the specification of practical problems. Consequently, robust solutions have arisen to accommodate uncertain inputs and plant models. The H$_\infty$ performance objective is to minimise the ratio of the output energy to the input energy of an error system, that is, minimise

$$\sup_{\|i\|_2 \neq 0} \left\| \mathcal{R}_{ei} \right\|_\infty = \sup_{\|i\|_2 \neq 0} \frac{\|e\|_2}{\|i\|_2} \le \gamma$$

for some $\gamma \in \mathbb{R}$. In the time-invariant case, the objective is equivalent to minimising the maximum magnitude of the error power spectrum density.

Predictors, filters and smoothers that satisfy the above performance objective are found by applying the Bounded Real Lemma. The standard solution structures are retained but larger design error covariances are employed to account for the presence of uncertainty. In continuous time output estimation, the error covariance is found from the solution of

$$\dot{P}(t) = A(t)P(t) + P(t)A^T(t) - P(t)(C^T(t)R^{-1}(t)C(t) - \gamma^{-2}C^T(t)C(t))P(t) + B(t)Q(t)B^T(t) .$$

Discrete-time predictors, filters and smoothers for output estimation rely on the solution of

$$P_{k+1} = A_k P_k A_k^T - A_k P_k \begin{bmatrix} C_k^T & C_k^T \end{bmatrix} \begin{bmatrix} C_k P_k C_k^T - \gamma^2 I & C_k P_k C_k^T \\ C_k P_k C_k^T & R_k + C_k P_k C_k^T \end{bmatrix}^{-1} \begin{bmatrix} C_k \\ C_k \end{bmatrix} P_k A_k^T + B_k Q_k B_k^T .$$

"Your most unhappy customers are your greatest source of learning." *William Henry (Bill) Gates III*

It follows that the H_∞ designs revert to the optimum minimum-variance solutions as $\gamma^{-2} \to 0$. Since robust solutions are conservative, the art of design involves finding satisfactory trade-offs between average and worst-case performance criteria, namely, tweaking the γ.

A summary of suggested approaches for different linear estimation problem conditions is presented in Table 1. When the problem parameters are known precisely then the optimum minimum-variance solutions cannot be improved upon. However, when the inputs or the models are uncertain, robust solutions may provide improved mean-square-error performance. In the case of low measurement noise output-estimation, the benefit arises because greater weighting is given to the data. Conversely, for high measurement noise input estimation, robust solutions accommodate uncertainty by giving less weighting to the data.

PROBLEM CONDITIONS	SUGGESTED APPROACHES
Gaussian process and measurement noises, known 2nd-order statistics. Known system model parameters.	1. Optimal minimum-variance (or Kalman) filter. 2. Fixed-lag smoothers, which improve on filter performance (see Lemma 3 and Example 1 of Chapter 7). They suit on-line applications and have low additional complexity. A sufficiently large smoothing lag results in optimal performance (see Example 3 of Chapter 7). 3. Maximum-likelihood (or Rauch-Tung-Striebel) smoothers, which also improve on filter performance (see Lemma 6 of Chapter 6 and Lemma 4 of Chapter 7). They can provide close to optimal performance (see Example 5 of Chapter 6). 4. The minimum-variance smoother provides the best performance (see Lemma 12 of Chapter 6 and Lemma 8 of Chapter 7) at the cost of increased complexity (see Example 5 of Chapter 6 and Example 2 of Chapter 7).
Uncertain process and measurement noises, known 2nd-order statistics. Known system model parameters.	1. Optimal minimum-variance filter, which does not rely on Gaussian noise assumptions. 2. Optimal minimum-variance smoother, which similarly does not rely on Gaussian noise assumptions (see Example 6 of Chapter 6). 3. Robust filter which trades off H_∞ performance (see Lemmas 2, 9) and mean-square-error performance (see Example 3). 4. Robust smoother which trades off H_∞ performance (see Lemmas 5, 10) and mean-square-error performance (see Example 3).
Uncertain processes and measurement noises. Uncertain system model parameters.	1. Robust filter (see Example 4). 2. Robust smoother (see Example 4). 3. Robust filter or smoother with scaled inputs (see Lemma 3).

Table 1. Suggested approaches for different linear estimation problem conditions.

"A computer lets you make more mistakes than almost any invention in history, with the possible exceptions of tequila and hand guns." *Mitch Ratcliffe*

9.5 Problems

Problem 1 [31].

(i) Consider a system $\mathcal{G}$ having the state-space representation $\dot{x}(t) = Ax(t) + Bw(t)$, $y(t) = Cx(t)$. Show that if there exists a matrix $P = P^T > 0$ such that $\begin{bmatrix} A^TP + PA + C^TC & PB \\ B^TP & -\gamma^2 I \end{bmatrix} < 0$ then $x^T(T)Px(T) - x^T(0)Px(0) + \int_0^T y^T(t)y(t)dt \le \gamma^2 \int_0^T w^T(t)w(t)\, dt$.

(ii) Generalise (i) for the case where $y(t) = Cx(t) + Dw(t)$.

Problem 2. Consider a system $\mathcal{G}$ modelled by $\dot{x}(t) = A(t)x(t) + B(t)w(t)$, $y(t) = C(t)x(t) + D(t)w(t)$. Suppose that the Riccati differential equation

$$-\dot{P}(t) = P(t)(A(t) + B(t)M^{-1}(t)D^T(t)C(t)) + (A(t) + B(t)M^{-1}(t)D^T(t)C(t))^T P(t)$$
$$+\gamma^{-2}B(t)M^{-1}(t)B^T(t) + C^T(t)(I + D(t)M^{-1}(t)D^T(t))C(t),$$

$M(t) = \gamma^2 I - D^T(t)D(t) > 0$, has a solution on $[0, T]$. Show that $\|\mathcal{G}\|_\infty \le \gamma$ for any $w \in \mathcal{L}_2$. (Hint: define $V(x(t)) = x^T(t)P(t)\, x(t)$ and show that $\dot{V}(x(t)) + y^T(t)y(t) - \gamma^2 w^T(t)w(t) < 0$.)

Problem 3. For measurements $z(t) = y(t) + v(t)$ of a system realised by $\dot{x}(t) = A(t)x(t) + B(t)w(t)$, $y(t) = C(t)x(t)$, show that the map from the inputs $i = \begin{bmatrix} v \\ w \end{bmatrix}$ to the H$_\infty$ fixed-interval smoother error $e(t\,|\,T)$ is

$$\begin{bmatrix} \dot{\tilde{x}}(t) \\ -\dot{\xi}(t) \\ e(t\,|\,T) \end{bmatrix} = \begin{bmatrix} A(t) - K(t)C(t) & 0 & B(t) & -K(t) \\ -C^T(t)R^{-1}(t)C(t) & A^T(t) - C^T(t)K^T(t) & 0 & -C^T(t)R^{-1}(t) \\ C(t) & R(t)K^T(t) & 0 & 0 \end{bmatrix} \begin{bmatrix} \tilde{x}(t) \\ \xi(t) \\ w(t) \\ v(t) \end{bmatrix}.$$

Problem 4 [18].

(i) For a $\mathcal{G}$ modelled by $x_{k+1} = A_k x_k + B_k w_k$, $y_k = C_k x_k\ D_k w_k$, show that the existence of a solution to the Riccati difference equation

$$P_k = A_k^T P_{k+1} A_k + \gamma^{-2} A_k^T P_{k+1} B_k (I - \gamma^{-2} B_k^T P_{k+1} B_k)^{-1} B_k^T P_{k+1} A_k + C_k^T C_k$$

is sufficient for $x_k^T P_k x_k - x_{k+1}^T P_{k+1} x_{k+1} + y_k^T y_k - \gamma^2 w_k^T w_k < 0$. Hint: construct $x_{k+1}^T P_{k+1} x_{k+1} - x_k^T P_k x_k$ and show that

$$x_{k+1}^T P_{k+1} x_{k+1} - x_k^T P_k x_k + y_k^T y_k - \gamma^2 w_k^T w_k = -\gamma^{-2} p_k^T (I - \gamma^{-2} B_k^T P_{k+1} B_k)^{-1} p_k - x_k^T A_k^T P_{k+1} A_k x_k,$$

"A computer once beat me at chess, but it was no match for me at kick boxing." *Emo Philips*

where $p_k = w_k - \gamma^{-2}(I - \gamma^{-2}B_k^T P_{k+1} B_k)^{-1} B_k^T P_{k+1} A_k x_k$.

(ii) Show that $-x_0^T P_0 x_0 + \sum_{k=0}^{N-1} y_k^T y_k - \gamma^2 \sum_{k=0}^{N-1} w_k^T w_k < 0$.

Problem 5. Now consider the model $x_{k+1} = A_k x_k + B_k w_k$, $y_k = C_k x_k + D_k w_k$ and show that the existence of a solution to the Riccati difference equation

$$P_k = A_k^T P_{k+1} A_k + \gamma^{-2}(A_k^T P_{k+1} B_k + C_k^T D_k)(I - \gamma^{-2} B_k^T P_{k+1} B_k - \gamma^{-2} D_k^T D_k)^{-1}(B_k^T P_{k+1} A_k + D_k^T C_k) + C_k^T C_k$$

is sufficient for $x_k^T P_k x_k - x_{k+1}^T P_{k+1} x_{k+1} + y_k^T y_k - \gamma^2 w_k^T w_k < 0$. Hint: define

$$p_k = w_k - \gamma^{-2}(I - \gamma^{-2} B_k^T P_{k+1} B_k - \gamma^{-2} D_k^T D_k)^{-1}(B_k^T P_{k+1} A_k + D_k^T C_k).$$

Problem 6. Suppose that a predictor attains a H_∞ performance objective, that is, the conditions of Lemma 8 are satisfied. Show that using the predicted states to construct filtered output estimates $\hat{y}_{k/k}$ results in $\tilde{y}_{k/k} = y - \hat{y}_{k/k} \in \ell_2$.

9.6 Glossary

$\mathcal{L}_\infty$ — The Lebesgue ∞-space defined as the set of continuous-time systems having finite ∞-norm.

$\mathcal{R}_{ei} \in \mathcal{L}_\infty$ — The map $\mathcal{R}_{ei}$ from the inputs $i(t)$ to the estimation error $e(t)$ satisfies $\int_0^T e^T(t)e(t)dt - \gamma^2 \int_0^T i^T(t)i(t)dt < 0$. Therefore, $i \in \mathcal{L}_2$ implies $e \in \mathcal{L}_2$.

ℓ_∞ — The Lebesgue ∞-space defined as the set of discrete-time systems having finite ∞-norm.

$\mathcal{R}_{ei} \in \ell_\infty$ — The map $\mathcal{R}_{ei}$ from the inputs i_k to the estimation error e_k satisfies $\sum_{k=0}^{N-1} e_k^T e_k - \gamma^2 \sum_{k=0}^{N-1} i_k^T i_k < 0$. Therefore, $i \in \ell_2$ implies $e \in \ell_2$.

9.7 References

[1] J. Stelling, U. Sauer, Z. Szallasi, F. J. Doyle and J. Doyle, "Robustness of Cellular Functions", *Cell*, vol. 118, pp. 675 – 685, Dep. 2004.

[2] P. P. Vaidyanathan, "The Discrete-Time Bounded-Real Lemma in Digital Filtering", *IEEE Transactions on Circuits and Systems*, vol. 32, no. 9, pp. 918 – 924, Sep. 1985.

[3] I. Petersen, "A Riccati equation approach to the design of stabilizing controllers and observers for a class of uncertain linear systems", *IEEE Transactions on Automatic Control*, vol. 30, iss. 9, pp. 904 – 907, 1985.

"On two occasions I have been asked, 'If you put into the machine wrong figures, will the right answers come out?' I am not able rightly to apprehend the kind of confusion of ideas that could provoke such a question." *Charles Babbage*

[4] J. C. Doyle, K. Glover, P. P. Khargonekar and B. A. Francis, "State-Space Solutions to Standard H_2 and H_∞ Control Problems", *IEEE Transactions on Automatic Control*, vol. 34, no. 8, pp. 831 - 847, Aug. 198
[5] D. J. N. Limebeer, M. Green and D. Walker, "Discrete-Time H_∞ Control, *Proceedings 28th IEEE Conference on Decision and Control*, Tampa, Florida, pp. 392 - 396, Dec. 198
[6] T. Basar, "Optimum performance levels for minimax filters, predictors and smoothers" *Systems and Control Letters*, vol. 16, pp. 309 - 317, 198
[7] D. S. Bernstein and W. M. Haddad, "Steady State Kalman Filtering with an H_∞ Error Bound", *Systems and Control Letters*, vol. 12, pp. 9 - 16, 198
[8] U. Shaked, "H_∞-Minimum Error State Estimation of Linear Stationary Processes", *IEEE Transactions on Automatic Control*, vol. 35, no. 5, pp. 554 - 558, May, 1990.
[9] T. Başar and P. Bernhard, *H^∞-Optimal Control and Related Minimax Design Problems: A Dynamic Game Approach*, Series in Systems & Control: Foundations & Applications, Birkhäuser, Boston, 1991.
[10] K. M. Nagpal and P. P. Khargonekar, "Filtering and Smoothing in an H_∞ Setting", *IEEE Transactions on Automatic Control*, vol. 36, no. 2, pp 152 - 166, Feb. 1991.
[11] I. Yaesh and U. Shaked, "H_∞-Optimal Estimation - The Discrete Time Case", *Proceedings of the MTNS*, pp. 261 - 267, Jun. 1991.
[12] A. Stoorvogel, *The H_∞ Control Problem*, Series in Systems and Control Engineering, Prentice Hall International (UK) Ltd, Hertfordshire, 1992.
[13] U. Shaked and Y. Theodor, "H_∞ Optimal Estimation: A Tutorial", *Proceedings 31st IEEE Conference on Decision and Control*, pp. 2278 - 2286, Tucson, Arizona, Dec. 1992.
[14] C. E. de Souza, U. Shaked and M. Fu, "Robust H_∞ Filtering with Parametric Uncertainty and Deterministic Input Signal", *Proceedings 31st IEEE Conference on Decision and Control*, Tucson, Arizona, pp. 2305 - 2310, Dec. 1992.
[15] D. J. N. Limebeer, B. D. O. Anderson, P. P. Khargonekar and M. Green, "A Game Theoretic Approach to H^∞ Control for Time-Varying Systems", *SIAM Journal on Control and Optimization*, vol. 30, no. 2, pp. 262 - 283, Mar. 1992.
[16] I. Yaesh and Shaked, "Game Theory Approach to Finite-Time Horizon Optimal Estimation", *IEEE Transactions on Automatic Control*, vol. 38, no. 6, pp. 957 - 963, Jun. 1993.
[17] B. van Keulen, *H_∞ Control for Distributed Parameter Systems: A State-Space Approach*, Series in Systems & Control: Foundations & Applications, Birkhäuser, Boston, 1993.
[18] L. Xie, C. E. De Souza and Y. Wang, "Robust Control of Discrete Time Uncertain Dynamical Systems", *Automatica*, vol. 29, no. 4, pp. 1133 - 1137, 1993.
[19] Y. Theodore, U. Shaked and C. E. de Souza, "A Game Theory Approach To Robust Discrete-Time H_∞-Estimation", *IEEE Transactions on Signal Processing*, vol. 42, no. 6, pp. 1486 - 1495, Jun. 1994.
[20] S. Boyd, L. El Ghaoui, E. Feron and V. Balakrishnan, *Linear Matrix Inequalities in System and Control Theory*, SIAM Studies in Applied Mathematics, vol. 15, SIAM, Philadelphia, 1994.
[21] M. Green and D. J. N. Limebeer, *Linear Robust Control*, Prentice-Hall Inc., Englewood Cliffs, New Jersey, 1995.

"Never trust a computer you can't throw out a window." *Stephen Gary Wozniak*

[22] S. O. R. Moheimani, A. V. Savkin and I. R. Petersen, "Robust Filtering, Prediction, Smoothing and Observability of Uncertain Systems", *IEEE Transactions on Circuits and Systems*, vol. 45, no. 4, pp. 446 - 457, Apr. 1998.
[23] J. C. Geromel, "Optimal Linear Filtering Under Parameter Uncertainty", *IEEE Transactions on Signal Processing*, vol. 47, no. 1, pp. 168 - 175, Jan. 199
[24] T. Başar and G. J. Oldsder, *Dynamic Noncooperative Game Theory*, Second Edition, SIAM, Philadelphia, 199
[25] B. Hassibi, A. H. Sayed and T. Kailath, *Indefinite-Quadratic Estimation and Control: A Unified Approach to H^{∞} and H^2 Theories*, SIAM, Philadelphia, 199
[26] G. A. Einicke and L. B. White, "Robust Extended Kalman Filtering", *IEEE Transactions on Signal Processing*, vol. 47, no. 9, pp. 2596 - 2599, Sep., 199
[27] Z. Wang and B. Huang, "Robust H_2/H_{∞} Filtering for Linear Systems with Error Variance Constraints", *IEEE Transactions on Signal Processing*, vol. 48, no. 9, pp. 2463 - 2467, Aug. 2000.
[28] G. A. Einicke, "Optimal and Robust Noncausal Filter Formulations", *IEEE Transactions on Signal Processing*, vol. 54, no. 3, pp. 1069 - 1077, Mar. 2006.
[29] A. Saberi, A. A. Stoorvogel and P. Sannuti, *Filtering Theory With Applications to Fault Detection, Isolation, and Estimation*, Birkhäuser, Boston, 2007.
[30] F. L. Lewis, L. Xie and D. Popa, *Optimal and Robust Estimation: With an Introduction to Stochastic Control Theory*, Second Edition, Series in Automation and Control Engineering, Taylor & Francis Group, LLC, 2008.
[31] J.-C. Lo and M.-L. Lin, "Observer-Based Robust H_{∞} Control for Fuzzy Systems Using Two-Step Procedure", *IEEE Transactions on Fuzzy Systems*, vol. 12, no. 3, pp. 350 - 359, Jun. 2004.
[32] E. Blanco, P. Neveux and H. Thomas, "The H_{∞} Fixed-Interval Smoothing Problem for Continuous Systems", *IEEE Transactions on Signal Processing*, vol. 54, no. 11, pp. 4085 - 4090, Nov. 2006.
[33] G. A. Einicke, "A Solution to the Continuous-Time H-infinity Fixed-Interval Smoother Problem", *IEEE Transactions on Automatic Control*, vol. 54, no. 12, pp. 2904 - 2908, Dec. 200
[34] G. A. Einicke, "Asymptotic Optimality of the Minimum-Variance Fixed-Interval Smoother", *IEEE Transactions on Signal Processing*, vol. 55, no. 4, pp. 1543 - 1547, Apr. 2007.
[35] G. A. Einicke, J. C. Ralston, C. O. Hargrave, D. C. Reid and D. W. Hainsworth, "Longwall Mining Automation, An Application of Minimum-Variance Smoothing", *IEEE Control Systems Magazine*, vol. 28, no. 6, pp. 28 - 37, Dec. 2008.
[36] K. Ogata, *Discrete-time Control Systems*, Prentice-Hall, Inc., Englewood Cliffs, New Jersey, 1987.

"The most amazing achievement of the computer software industry is its continuing cancellation of the steady and staggering gains made by the computer hardware industry." *Henry Petroski*

10

Nonlinear Prediction, Filtering and Smoothing

10.1 Introduction

The Kalman filter is widely used for linear estimation problems where its behaviour is well-understood. Under prescribed conditions, the estimated states are unbiased and stability is guaranteed. Many real-world problems are nonlinear which requires amendments to linear solutions. If the nonlinear models can be expressed in a state-space setting then the Kalman filter may find utility by applying linearisations at each time step. Linearising means finding tangents to the curves of interest about the current estimates, so that the standard filter recursions can be employed in tandem to produce predictions for the next step. This approach is known as extended Kalman filtering - see [1] - [5].

Extended Kalman filters (EKFs) revert to optimal Kalman filters when the problems become linear. Thus, EKFs can yield approximate minimum-variance estimates. However, there are no accompanying performance guarantees and they fall into the try-at-your-own-risk category. Indeed, Anderson and Moore [3] caution that the EKF "can be satisfactory on occasions". A number of compounding factors can cause performance degradation. The approximate linearisations may be crude and are carried out about estimated states (as opposed to true states). Observability problems occur when the variables do not map onto each other, giving rise to discontinuities within estimated state trajectories. Singularities within functions can result in non-positive solutions to the design Riccati equations and lead to instabilities.

The discussion includes suggestions for performance improvement and is organised as follows. The next section begins with Taylor series expansions, which are prerequisites for linearisation. First, second and third-order EKFs are then derived. EKFs tend be prone to instability and a way of enforcing stability is to masquerade the design Riccati equation by a faux version. This faux algebraic Riccati equation technique [6] - [10] is presented in Section 10.3. In Section 10.4, the higher order terms discarded by an EKF are treated as uncertainties. It is shown that a robust EKF arises by solving a scaled H_∞ problem in lieu of one possessing uncertainties. Nonlinear smoother procedures can be designed similarly. The use of fixed-lag and Rauch-Tung-Striebel smoothers may be preferable from a complexity perspective. However, the approximate minimum-variance and robust smoothers, which are presented in Section 10.5, revert to optimal solutions when the nonlinearities and uncertainties diminish. Another way of guaranteeing stability is to by imposing constraints and one such approach is discussed in Section 10.6.

"It is the mark of an instructed mind to rest satisfied with the degree of precision to which the nature of the subject admits and not to seek exactness when only an approximation of the truth is possible." *Aristotle*

10.2 Extended Kalman Filtering

10.2.1 Taylor Series Expansion

A nonlinear function $a_k(x):\mathbb{R}^n \to \mathbb{R}$ having n continuous derivatives may be expanded as a Taylor series about a point x_0

$$\begin{aligned} a_k(x) &= a_k(x_0) + \frac{1}{1!}(x - x_0)^T \nabla a_k(x_0) \\ &+ \frac{1}{2!}(x - x_0)^T \nabla^T \nabla a_k(x_0)(x - x_0) \\ &+ \frac{1}{3!}(x - x_0)^T \nabla^T \nabla (x - x_0) \nabla a_k(x_0)(x - x_0) \\ &+ \frac{1}{4!}(x - x_0)^T \nabla^T \nabla (x - x_0) \nabla (x - x_0) \nabla a_k(x_0)(x - x_0) + \ldots, \end{aligned} \tag{1}$$

where $\nabla a_k = \begin{bmatrix} \dfrac{\partial a_k}{\partial x_1} & \cdots & \dfrac{\partial a_k}{\partial x_n} \end{bmatrix}$ is known as the gradient of $a_k(.)$ and

$$\nabla^T \nabla a_k = \begin{bmatrix} \dfrac{\partial^2 a_k}{\partial x_1^2} & \dfrac{\partial^2 a_k}{\partial x_1 \partial x_2} & \cdots & \dfrac{\partial^2 a_k}{\partial x_1 \partial x_n} \\ \dfrac{\partial^2 a_k}{\partial x_2 \partial x_1} & \dfrac{\partial^2 a_k}{\partial x_2^2} & \cdots & \dfrac{\partial^2 a_k}{\partial x_2 \partial x_n} \\ \vdots & \vdots & \ddots & \vdots \\ \dfrac{\partial^2 a_k}{\partial x_n \partial x_1} & \dfrac{\partial^2 a_k}{\partial x_n \partial x_2} & \cdots & \dfrac{\partial^2 a_k}{\partial x_n^2} \end{bmatrix}$$

is called a Hessian matrix.

10.2.2 Nonlinear Signal Models

Consider nonlinear systems having state-space representations of the form

$$x_{k+1} = a_k(x_k) + b_k(x_k)w_k, \tag{2}$$

$$y_k = c_k(x_k), \tag{3}$$

where $a_k(.)$, $b_k(.)$ and $c_k(.)$ are continuous differentiable functions. For a scalar function, $a_k(x):\mathbb{R} \to \mathbb{R}$, its Taylor series about $x = x_0$ may be written as

"In the real world, nothing happens at the right place at the right time. It is the job of journalists and historians to correct that." *Samuel Langhorne Clemens aka. Mark Twain*

$$a_k(x) = a_k(x_0) + (x - x_0)\left.\frac{\partial a_k}{\partial x}\right|_{x=x_0} + \frac{1}{2}(x - x_0)^2\left.\frac{\partial^2 a_k}{\partial x^2}\right|_{x=x_0}$$
$$+ \frac{1}{6}(x - x_0)^3\left.\frac{\partial^3 a_k}{\partial x^3}\right|_{x=x_0} + \cdots + \frac{1}{n!}(x - x_0)^n\left.\frac{\partial^n a_k}{\partial x^n}\right|_{x=x_0} . \tag{4}$$

Similarly, Taylor series for $b_k(x): \mathbb{R} \to \mathbb{R}$ and $c_k(x): \mathbb{R} \to \mathbb{R}$ about $x = x_0$ are

$$b_k(x) = b_k(x_0) + (x - x_0)\left.\frac{\partial b_k}{\partial x}\right|_{x=x_0} + \frac{1}{2}(x - x_0)^2\left.\frac{\partial^2 b_k}{\partial x^2}\right|_{x=x_0}$$
$$+ \frac{1}{6}(x - x_0)^3\left.\frac{\partial^3 b_k}{\partial x^3}\right|_{x=x_0} + \cdots + \frac{1}{n!}(x - x_0)^n\left.\frac{\partial^n b_k}{\partial x^n}\right|_{x=x_0} , \tag{5}$$

and

$$c_k(x) = c_k(x_0) + (x - x_0)\left.\frac{\partial c_k}{\partial x}\right|_{x=x_0} + \frac{1}{2}(x - x_0)^2\left.\frac{\partial^2 c_k}{\partial x^2}\right|_{x=x_0}$$
$$+ \frac{1}{6}(x - x_0)^3\left.\frac{\partial^3 c_k}{\partial x^3}\right|_{x=x_0} + \cdots + \frac{1}{n!}(x - x_0)^n\left.\frac{\partial^n c_k}{\partial x^n}\right|_{x=x_0} , \tag{6}$$

respectively.

10.2.3 First-Order Extended Kalman Filter

Suppose that filtered estimates $\hat{x}_{k/k}$ of x_k are desired given observations

$$z_k = c_k(x_k) + v_k , \tag{7}$$

where v_k is a measurement noise sequence. A first-order EKF for the above problem is developed below. Following the approach within [3], the nonlinear system (2) - (3) is approximated by

$$x_{k+1} = A_k x_k + B_k w_k + \mu_k , \tag{8}$$

$$y_k = C_k x_k + \pi_k , \tag{9}$$

where A_k, B_k, C_k, μ_k and π_k are found from suitable truncations of the Taylor series for each nonlinearity. From Chapter 4, a filter for the above model is given by

$$\hat{x}_{k/k} = \hat{x}_{k/k-1} + L_k(z_k - C_k\hat{x}_{k/k-1} - \pi_k) , \tag{10}$$

$$\hat{x}_{k+1/k} = A_k\hat{x}_{k/k} + \mu_k , \tag{11}$$

"You will always define events in a manner which will validate your agreement with reality." *Steve Anthony Maraboli*

where $L_k = P_{k/k-1}C_k^T\Omega_k^{-1}$ is the filter gain, in which $\Omega_k = C_kP_{k/k-1}C_k^T + R_k$, $P_{k/k} = P_{k/k-1} - P_{k/k-1}C_k^T(C_kP_{k/k-1}C_k^T + R_k)^{-1}C_kP_{k/k-1}$ and $P_{k+1/k} = A_kP_{k/k}A_k^T + B_kQ_kB_k^T$. It is common practice (see [1] – [5]) to linearise about the current conditional mean estimate, retain up to first order terms within the corresponding Taylor series and assume $B_k = b_k(\hat{x}_{k/k})$. This leads to

$$\begin{aligned} a_k(x) &\approx a_k(\hat{x}_{k/k}) + (x - \hat{x}_{k/k})^T \nabla a_k\big|_{x=\hat{x}_{k/k}} \\ &= A_k x_k + \mu_k \end{aligned} \tag{12}$$

and

$$\begin{aligned} c_k(x_k) &\approx c_k(\hat{x}_{k/k-1}) + (x - \hat{x}_{k/k-1})^T \nabla c_k\big|_{x=\hat{x}_{k/k-1}} \\ &= C_k x_k + \pi_k , \end{aligned} \tag{13}$$

where $A_k = \nabla a_k(x)\big|_{x=\hat{x}_{k/k}}$, $C_k = \nabla c_k(x)\big|_{x=\hat{x}_{k/k-1}}$, $\mu_k = a_k(\hat{x}_{k/k}) - A_k\hat{x}_{k/k}$ and $\pi_k = c_k(\hat{x}_{k/k-1}) - C_k\hat{x}_{k/k-1}$. Substituting for μ_k and π_k into (10) – (11) gives

$$\hat{x}_{k/k} = \hat{x}_{k/k-1} + L_k(z_k - c_k(\hat{x}_{k/k-1})) , \tag{14}$$

$$\hat{x}_{k+1/k} = a_k(\hat{x}_{k/k}) . \tag{15}$$

Note that nonlinearities enter into the state correction (14) and prediction (15), whereas linearised matrices A_k, B_k and C_k are employed in the Riccati equation and gain calculations.

In the case of scalar states, the linearisations are $A_k = \left.\dfrac{\partial a_k}{\partial x}\right|_{x=\hat{x}_{k/k}}$ and $C_k = \left.\dfrac{\partial c_k}{\partial x}\right|_{x=\hat{x}_{k/k-1}}$. In texts on optimal filtering, the recursions (14) – (15) are either called a first-order EKF or simply an EKF, see [1] – [5]. Two higher order versions are developed below.

10.2.4 Second-Order Extended Kalman Filter

Truncating the series (1) after the second-order term and observing that $(x - \hat{x}_{k/k})^T \nabla^T$ is a scalar yields

$$\begin{aligned} a_k(x) &\approx a_k(\hat{x}_{k/k}) + (x - \hat{x}_{k/k})^T \nabla a_k\big|_{x=\hat{x}_{k/k}} + \frac{1}{2}(x - \hat{x}_{k/k})^T \nabla^T \nabla a_k\big|_{x=\hat{x}_{k/k}} (x - \hat{x}_{k/k}) , \\ &= a_k(\hat{x}_{k/k}) + (x - \hat{x}_{k/k})^T \nabla a_k\big|_{x=\hat{x}_{k/k}} + \frac{1}{2}\nabla P_{k/k} \nabla^T a_k\big|_{x=\hat{x}_{k/k}} \\ &= A_k x_k + \mu_k , \end{aligned} \tag{16}$$

"People take the longest possible paths, digress to numerous dead ends, and make all kinds of mistakes. Then historians come along and write summaries of this messy, nonlinear process and make it appear like a simple straight line." *Dean L. Kamen*

where $A_k = \nabla a_k(x)\big|_{x=\hat{x}_{k/k}}$ and $\mu_k = a_k(\hat{x}_{k/k}) - A_k\hat{x}_{k/k} + \frac{1}{2}\nabla P_{k/k}\nabla^T a_k\big|_{x=\hat{x}_{k/k}}$. Similarly for the system output,

$$\begin{aligned} c_k(x) &\approx c_k(\hat{x}_{k/k-1}) + (x_k - \hat{x}_{k/k-1})^T \nabla c_k\big|_{x=\hat{x}_{k/k-1}} + \frac{1}{2}(x_k - \hat{x}_{k/k-1})^T \nabla^T \nabla c_k\big|_{x=\hat{x}_{k/k-1}} (x_k - \hat{x}_{k/k-1}) \\ &= c_k(\hat{x}_{k/k-1}) + (x_k - \hat{x}_{k/k-1})^T \nabla c_k\big|_{x=\hat{x}_{k/k-1}} + \frac{1}{2}\nabla P_{k/k-1}\nabla^T c_k\big|_{x=\hat{x}_{k/k-1}} \\ &= C_k x_k + \pi_k , \end{aligned} \tag{17}$$

where $C_k = \nabla c_k(x)\big|_{x=\hat{x}_{k/k-1}}$ and $\pi_k = c_k(\hat{x}_{k/k-1}) - C_k\hat{x}_{k/k-1} + \frac{1}{2}\nabla P_{k/k-1}\nabla^T c_k\big|_{x=\hat{x}_{k/k-1}}$. Substituting for μ_k and π_k into the filtering and prediction recursions (10) – (11) yields the second-order EKF

$$\hat{x}_{k/k} = \hat{x}_{k/k-1} + L_k\left(z_k - c_k(\hat{x}_{k/k-1}) - \frac{1}{2}\nabla P_{k/k-1}\nabla^T c_k\big|_{x=\hat{x}_{k/k-1}} \right), \tag{18}$$

$$\hat{x}_{k+1/k} = a_k(\hat{x}_{k/k}) + \frac{1}{2}\nabla P_{k/k}\nabla^T a_k\big|_{x=\hat{x}_{k/k}} . \tag{19}$$

The above form is described in [2]. The further simplifications $\nabla P_{k/k}\nabla^T a_k\big|_{x=\hat{x}_{k/k}} \approx tr\left(\nabla P_{k/k}\nabla^T a_k\big|_{x=\hat{x}_{k/k}}\right)$ and $\nabla P_{k/k-1}\nabla^T c_k\big|_{x=\hat{x}_{k/k-1}} \approx tr\left(\nabla P_{k/k-1}\nabla^T c_k\big|_{x=\hat{x}_{k/k-1}}\right)$ are assumed in [4], [5].

10.2.5 Third-Order Extended Kalman Filter

Higher order EKFs can be realised just as elegantly as its predecessors. Retaining up to third-order terms within (1) results in

$$\begin{aligned} a_k(x) &\approx a_k(\hat{x}_{k/k}) + (x - \hat{x}_{k/k})\nabla a_k\big|_{x=\hat{x}_{k/k}} + \frac{1}{2}\nabla P_{k/k}\nabla^T a_k\big|_{x=\hat{x}_{k/k}} \\ &\quad + \frac{1}{6}\nabla P_{k/k}\nabla^T a_k\big|_{x=\hat{x}_{k/k}} (x_k - \hat{x}_{k/k})\nabla a_k\big|_{x=\hat{x}_{k/k}} \\ &= A_k x_k + \mu_k , \end{aligned} \tag{20}$$

where

$$A_k = \nabla a_k(x)\big|_{x=\hat{x}_{k/k}} + \frac{1}{6}\nabla P_{k/k}\nabla^T a_k\big|_{x=\hat{x}_{k/k}} \tag{21}$$

"It might be a good idea if the various countries of the world would occasionally swap history books, just to see what other people are doing with the same set of facts." *William E. Vaughan*

and $\mu_k = a_k(\hat{x}_{k/k}) - A_k\hat{x}_{k/k} + \frac{1}{2}\nabla P_{k/k}\nabla^T a_k\big|_{x=\hat{x}_{k/k}}$. Similarly, for the output nonlinearity it is assumed that

$$\begin{aligned} c_k(x_k) &\approx c_k(\hat{x}_{k/k-1}) + (x - \hat{x}_{k/k-1})\nabla c_k\big|_{x=\hat{x}_{k/k-1}} + \frac{1}{2}\nabla P_{k/k-1}\nabla^T c_k\big|_{x=\hat{x}_{k/k-1}} \\ &+ \frac{1}{6}\nabla P_{k/k-1}\nabla^T c_k\big|_{x=\hat{x}_{k/k-1}}(x_k - \hat{x}_{k/k-1})\nabla c_k\big|_{x=\hat{x}_{k/k-1}} \\ &= C_k x_k + \pi_k , \end{aligned} \tag{22}$$

where

$$C_k = \nabla c_k(x)\big|_{x=\hat{x}_{k/k-1}} + \frac{1}{6}\nabla P_{k/k-1}\nabla^T c_k\big|_{x=\hat{x}_{k/k-1}} \tag{23}$$

and $\pi_k = c_k(\hat{x}_{k/k-1}) - C_k\hat{x}_{k/k-1} + \frac{1}{6}\nabla P_{k/k-1}\nabla^T c_k\big|_{x=\hat{x}_{k/k-1}}$. The resulting third-order EKF is defined by (18) – (19) in which the gain is now calculated using (21) and (23).

Example 1. Consider a linear state evolution $x_{k+1} = Ax_k + w_k$, with $A = 0.5$, $w_k \in \mathbb{R}$, $Q = 0.05$, a nonlinear output mapping $y_k = \sin(x_k)$ and noisy observations $z_k = y_k + v_k$, $v_k \in \mathbb{R}$. The first-order EKF for this problem is given by

$$\hat{x}_{k/k} = \hat{x}_{k/k-1} + L_k(z_k - \sin(\hat{x}_{k/k-1})) ,$$

$$\hat{x}_{k+1/k} = A\hat{x}_{k/k} ,$$

where $L_k = P_{k/k-1}C_k^T\Omega_k^{-1}$, $\Omega_k = C_kP_{k/k-1}C_k^T + R_k$, $C_k = \cos(\hat{x}_{k/k-1})$, $P_{k/k} = P_{k/k-1} - P_{k/k-1}C_k^T(C_kP_{k/k-1}C_k^T + R_k)^{-1}C_kP_{k/k-1}$ and $P_{k+1/k} = A_kP_{k/k}A_k^T + Q_k$. The filtering step within the second-order EKF is amended to

$$\hat{x}_{k/k} = \hat{x}_{k/k-1} + L_k(z_k - \sin(\hat{x}_{k/k-1}) + \sin(\hat{x}_{k/k-1})P_{k/k-1}/2) .$$

The modified output linearisation for the third-order EKF is

$$C_k = \cos(\hat{x}_{k/k-1}) + \sin(\hat{x}_{k/k-1})P_{k/k-1}/6 .$$

Simulations were conducted in which the signal-to-noise-ratio was varied from 20 dB to 40 dB for N = 200,000 realisations of Gaussian noise sequences. The mean-square-errors exhibited by the first, second and third-order EKFs are plotted in Fig. 1. The figure demonstrates that including higher-order Taylor series terms within the filter can provide small performance improvements but the benefit diminishes with increasing measurement noise.

"No two people see the external world in exactly the same way. To every separate person a thing is what he thinks it is – in other words, not a thing, but a think." *Penelope Fitzgerald*

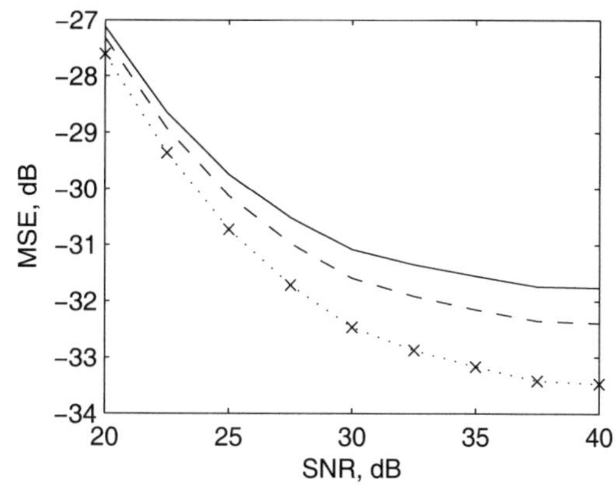

Figure 1. Mean-square-error (MSE) versus signal-to-noise-ratio (SNR) for Example 1: first-order EKF (solid line), second-order EKF (dashed line) and third-order EKF (dotted-crossed line).

10.3 The Faux Algebraic Riccati Equation Technique

10.3.1 A Nonlinear Observer

The previously-described Extended-Kalman filters arise by linearising the signal model about the current state estimate and using the linear Kalman filter to predict the next estimate. This attempts to produce a locally optimal filter, however, it is not necessarily stable because the solutions of the underlying Riccati equations are not guaranteed to be positive definite. The faux algebraic Riccati technique [6] - [10] seeks to improve on EKF performance by trading off approximate optimality for stability. The familiar structure of the EKF is retained but stability is achieved by selecting a positive definite solution to a faux Riccati equation for the gain design.

Assume that data is generated by the following signal model comprising a stable, linear state evolution together with a nonlinear output mapping

$$x_{k+1} = Ax_k + Bw_k , \tag{24}$$

$$z_k = c_k(x_k) + v_k , \tag{25}$$

where the components of $c_k(.)$ are assumed to be continuous differentiable functions. Suppose that it is desired to calculate estimates of the states from the measurements. A nonlinear observer may be constructed having the form

$$\hat{x}_{k+1/k} = A\hat{x}_k + g_k(z_k - c(\hat{x}_{k/k-1})) , \tag{26}$$

where $g_k(.)$ is a gain function to be designed. From (24) - (26), the state prediction error is given by

"The observer, when he seems to himself to be observing a stone, is really, if physics is to be believed, observing the effects of the stone upon himself." *Bertrand Arthur William Russell*

$$\tilde{x}_{k+1/k} = A\tilde{x}_{k/k-1} - g_k(\varepsilon_k) + w_k , \tag{27}$$

where $\tilde{x}_k = x_k - \hat{x}_{k/k-1}$ and $\varepsilon_k = z_k - c(\hat{x}_{k/k-1})$. The Taylor series expansion of $c_k(.)$ to first order terms leads to $\varepsilon_k \approx C_k\tilde{x}_{k/k-1} + v_k$, where $C_k = \nabla c_k(x)\big|_{x=\hat{x}_{k/k-1}}$. The objective here is to design $g_k(\varepsilon_k)$ to be a linear function of $\tilde{x}_{k/k-1}$ to first order terms. It will be shown that for certain classes of problems, this objective can be achieved by a suitable choice of a linear bounded matrix function of the states D_k, resulting in the time-varying gain function $g_k(\varepsilon_k) = K_kD_k\varepsilon_k$, where K_k is a gain matrix of appropriate dimension. For example, consider $x_k \in \mathbb{R}^n$ and $z_k \in \mathbb{R}^m$, which yield $\varepsilon_k \in \mathbb{R}^m$ and $C_k \in \mathbb{R}^{m\times n}$. Suppose that a linearisation $D_k \in \mathbb{R}^{p\times m}$ can be found so that $\bar{C}_k = D_kC_k \in \mathbb{R}^{p\times m}$ possesses approximately constant terms. Then the locally linearised error (27) may be written as

$$\tilde{x}_{k+1/k} = (A - K_k\bar{C}_k)\tilde{x}_{k/k-1} - K_kD_kv_k + w_k . \tag{28}$$

If $|\lambda_i(A)| < 1$, $i = 1 \ldots n$, and if the pair $(A,\bar{C}_k)$ is completely observable, then the asymptotic stability of (28) can be guaranteed by selecting the gain such that $|\lambda_i(A - K_k\bar{C}_k)| < 1$. A method for selecting the gain is described below.

10.3.2 Gain Selection

From (28), an approximate equation for the error covariance $P_{k/k-1} = E\{\tilde{x}_{k/k-1}\tilde{x}^T_{k/k-1}\}$ is

$$P_{k+1/k} = (A - K_k\bar{C}_k)P_{k/k-1}(A - K_k\bar{C}_k)^T + K_kD_kRD_k^TK_k^T + Q , \tag{29}$$

which can be written as

$$P_{k/k} = P_{k/k-1} - P_{k/k-1}\bar{C}_k^T(\bar{C}_kP_{k/k-1}\bar{C}_k^T + D_kRD_k^T)^{-1}\bar{C}_kP_{k/k-1} , \tag{30}$$

$$P_{k+1/k} = AP_{k/k}A + Q . \tag{31}$$

In an EKF for the above problem, the gain is obtained by solving the above Riccati difference equation and calculating

$$K_k = P_{k/k-1}\bar{C}_k^T(\bar{C}_kP_{k/k-1}\bar{C}_k^T + D_kRD_k^T)^{-1} . \tag{32}$$

The faux algebraic Riccati equation approach [6] – [10] is motivated by connections between Riccati difference equation and algebraic Riccati equation solutions. Indeed, it is noted for some nonlinear problems that the gains can converge to a steady-state matrix [3]. This technique is also known as 'covariance setting'. Following the approach of [10], the Riccati difference equation (30) may be masqueraded by the faux algebraic Riccati equation

$$\Sigma_k = \Sigma_k - \Sigma_k\bar{C}_k^T(\bar{C}_k\Sigma_k\bar{C}_k^T + D_kRD_k^T)^{-1}\bar{C}_k\Sigma_k . \tag{33}$$

"The universe as we know it is a joint product of the observer and the observed." *Pierre Teilhard De Chardin*

That is, rather than solve (30), an arbitrary positive definite solution Σ_k is assumed instead and then the gain at each time k is calculated from (31) - (32) using Σ_k in place of $P_{k/k-1}$.

10.3.3 Tracking Multiple Signals

Consider the problem of tracking two frequency or phase modulated signals which may be modelled by equation (34), where $a_k^{(1)}$, $a_k^{(2)}$, $\omega_k^{(1)}$, $\omega_k^{(2)}$, $\phi_k^{(1)}$, $\phi_k^{(2)}$, $\mu_a^{(1)}$, $\mu_a^{(2)}$, $\mu_\omega^{(1)}$, $\mu_\omega^{(2)}$ $\in \mathbb{R}$ and $w_k^{(1)}$, … $w_k^{(6)}$ $\in \mathbb{R}$ are zero-mean, uncorrelated, white processes with covariance Q = diag($\sigma^2_{w^{(1)}},\ldots,\sigma^2_{w^{(6)}}$). The states $a_k^{(i)}$, $\omega_k^{(i)}$ and $\phi_k^{(i)}$, i = 1, 2, represent the signals' instantaneous amplitude, frequency and phase components, respectively.

$$\begin{bmatrix} a_{k+1}^{(1)} \\ \omega_{k+1}^{(1)} \\ \phi_{k+1}^{(1)} \\ a_{k+1}^{(2)} \\ \omega_{k+1}^{(2)} \\ \phi_{k+1}^{(2)} \end{bmatrix} = \begin{bmatrix} \mu_a^{(1)} & 0 & 0 & 0 & 0 & 0 \\ 0 & \mu_\omega^{(1)} & 0 & 0 & 0 & 0 \\ 0 & 1 & 1 & 0 & 0 & 0 \\ 0 & 0 & 0 & \mu_a^{(2)} & 0 & 0 \\ 0 & 0 & 0 & 0 & \mu_\omega^{(2)} & 0 \\ 0 & 0 & 0 & 0 & 1 & 1 \end{bmatrix} \begin{bmatrix} a_k^{(1)} \\ \omega_k^{(1)} \\ \phi_k^{(1)} \\ a_k^{(2)} \\ \omega_k^{(2)} \\ \phi_k^{(2)} \end{bmatrix} + \begin{bmatrix} w_k^{(1)} \\ w_k^{(2)} \\ w_k^{(3)} \\ w_k^{(4)} \\ w_k^{(5)} \\ w_k^{(6)} \end{bmatrix}. \tag{34}$$

Let

$$\begin{bmatrix} z_k^{(1)} \\ z_k^{(2)} \\ z_k^{(3)} \\ z_k^{(4)} \end{bmatrix} = \begin{bmatrix} a_k^{(1)}\cos\phi_k^{(1)} \\ a_k^{(1)}\sin\phi_k^{(1)} \\ a_k^{(2)}\cos\phi_k^{(2)} \\ a_k^{(2)}\sin\phi_k^{(2)} \end{bmatrix} + \begin{bmatrix} v_k^{(1)} \\ v_k^{(2)} \\ v_k^{(3)} \\ v_k^{(4)} \end{bmatrix} \tag{35}$$

denote the complex baseband observations, where $v_k^{(1)}$, …, $v_k^{(4)}$ $\in \mathbb{R}$ are zero-mean, uncorrelated, white processes with covariance R = $diag(\sigma^2_{v^{(1)}},\ldots,\sigma^2_{v^{(4)}})$. Expanding the prediction error to linear terms yields $C_k = [C_k^{(1)} \;\; C_k^{(2)}]$, where

$$C_k^{(i)} = \begin{bmatrix} \cos\hat{\phi}_{k/k-1}^{(i)} & 0 & -\hat{a}_{k/k-1}^{(i)}\sin\hat{\phi}_{k/k-1}^{(i)} \\ \sin\hat{\phi}_{k/k-1}^{(i)} & 0 & \hat{a}_{k/k-1}^{(i)}\cos\hat{\phi}_{k/k-1}^{(i)} \end{bmatrix}.$$

This form suggests the choice $D_k = \begin{bmatrix} D_k^{(1)} \\ D_k^{(2)} \end{bmatrix}$, where

$$D_k^{(i)} = \begin{bmatrix} \cos\hat{\phi}_{k/k-1}^{(i)} & \sin\hat{\phi}_{k/k-1}^{(i)} \\ -\sin\hat{\phi}_{k/k-1}^{(i)}/\hat{a}_{k/k-1}^{(i)} & \cos\hat{\phi}_{k/k-1}^{(i)}/\hat{a}_{k/k-1}^{(i)} \end{bmatrix}.$$

"If you haven't found something strange during the day, it hasn't been much of a day." *John Archibald Wheeler*

In the multiple signal case, the linearization $\bar{C}_k = D_k C_k$ does not result in perfect decoupling. While the diagonal blocks reduce to $\bar{C}_k^{(i,i)} = \begin{bmatrix} 1 & 0 & 0 \\ 0 & 0 & 1 \end{bmatrix}$, the off-diagonal blocks are

$$\bar{C}_k^{(i,j)} = \begin{bmatrix} \cos(\hat{\phi}_{k/k-1}^{(i)} - \hat{\phi}_{k/k-1}^{(j)}) & 0 & \hat{a}_{k/k-1}^{(j)} \sin(\hat{\phi}_{k/k-1}^{(i)} - \hat{\phi}_{k/k-1}^{(j)}) \\ -\dfrac{1}{\hat{a}_{k/k-1}^{(i)}} \cos(\hat{\phi}_{k/k-1}^{(i)} - \hat{\phi}_{k/k-1}^{(j)}) & 0 & \dfrac{\hat{a}_{k/k-1}^{(j)}}{\hat{a}_{k/k-1}^{(i)}} \cos(\hat{\phi}_{k/k-1}^{(i)} - \hat{\phi}_{k/k-1}^{(j)}) \end{bmatrix}.$$

Assuming a symmetric positive definite solution to (33) of the form $\Sigma_k = \begin{bmatrix} \Sigma_k^a & 0 & 0 \\ 0 & \Sigma_k^{\omega} & \Sigma_k^{\omega\phi} \\ 0 & \Sigma_k^{\phi\omega} & \Sigma_k^{\phi} \end{bmatrix}$, with Σ_k^a, Σ_k^{ω}, $\Sigma_k^{\omega\phi}$, $\Sigma_k^{\phi} \in \mathbb{R}$ and choosing the gains according to (32) yields $K_k = \begin{bmatrix} K_k^a & 0 \\ 0 & K_k^{\omega} \\ 0 & K_k^{\phi} \end{bmatrix}$, where $K_k^a = \Sigma_k^a(\Sigma_k^a + \sigma_v^2)^{-1}$, $K_k^{\omega} = \Sigma_k^{\omega\phi}(\Sigma_k^{\phi} + \sigma_v^2 \hat{a}_{k/k}^{-2})^{-1}$ and $K_k^{\phi} = \Sigma_k^{\phi}(\Sigma_k^{\phi} + \sigma_v^2 \hat{a}_{k/k}^{-2})^{-1}$. The nonlinear observer then becomes

$$\hat{a}_{k/k}^{(i)} = \hat{a}_{k/k-1}^{(i)} + \Sigma_k^a (z_k^{(1)} \cos \hat{\phi}_{k/k-1}^{(i)} + z_k^{(2)} \sin \hat{\phi}_{k/k-1}^{(i)})(\Sigma_k^a + \sigma_v^2)^{-1},$$

$$\hat{\omega}_{k/k}^{(i)} = \hat{\omega}_{k/k-1}^{(i)} + \Sigma_k^{\omega\phi} (z_k^{(1)} \cos \hat{\phi}_{k/k-1}^{(i)} + z_k^{(2)} \sin \hat{\phi}_{k/k-1}^{(i)})(\hat{a}_{k/k-1}^{(i)} \Sigma_k^{\phi} + \sigma_v^2 / a_{k/k-1}^{(i)})^{-1},$$

$$\hat{\phi}_{k/k}^{(i)} = \hat{\phi}_{k/k-1}^{(i)} + \Sigma_k^{\phi} (z_k^{(1)} \cos \hat{\phi}_{k/k-1}^{(i)} + z_k^{(2)} \sin \hat{\phi}_{k/k-1}^{(i)})(\hat{a}_{k/k-1}^{(i)} \Sigma_k^{\phi} + \sigma_v^2 / a_{k/k-1}^{(i)})^{-1}.$$

10.3.4 Stability Conditions

In order to establish conditions for the error system (28) to be asymptotically stable, the problem is recast in a passivity framework as follows. Let $w = \begin{bmatrix} w_k^{(1)} \\ w_k^{(2)} \\ \vdots \\ w_k^{(m)} \end{bmatrix}$, $e = \begin{bmatrix} e_k^{(1)} \\ e_k^{(2)} \\ \vdots \\ e_k^{(m)} \end{bmatrix} \in \mathbb{R}^m$.

Consider the configuration of Fig. 2, in which there is a cascade of a stable linear system $\mathcal{G}$ and a nonlinear function matrix $\gamma(.)$ acting on e. It follows from the figure that

$$e = w - \mathcal{G}\gamma(e). \tag{36}$$

Let Δ_f denote a forward difference operator with $\Delta_f e_k = e_k^{(i)} - e_{k-1}^{(i)}$. It is assumed that $\gamma(.)$ satisfies some sector conditions which may be interpreted as bounds existing on the slope of the components of $\gamma(.)$; see Theorem 14, p. 7 of [11].

"Discovery consists of seeing what everyone has seen and thinking what nobody has thought." *Albert Szent-Görgyi*

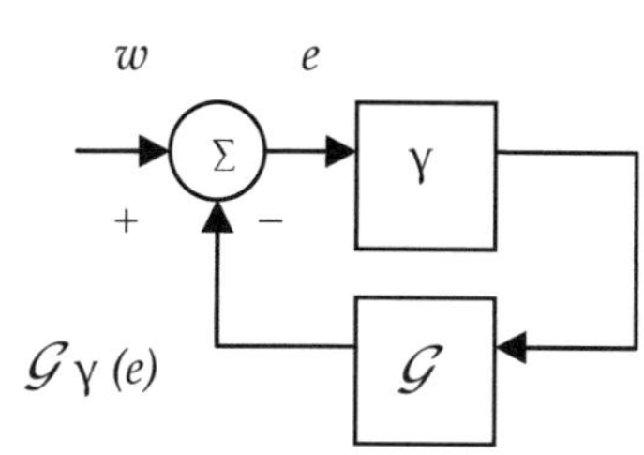

Figure 2. Nonlinear error system configuration.

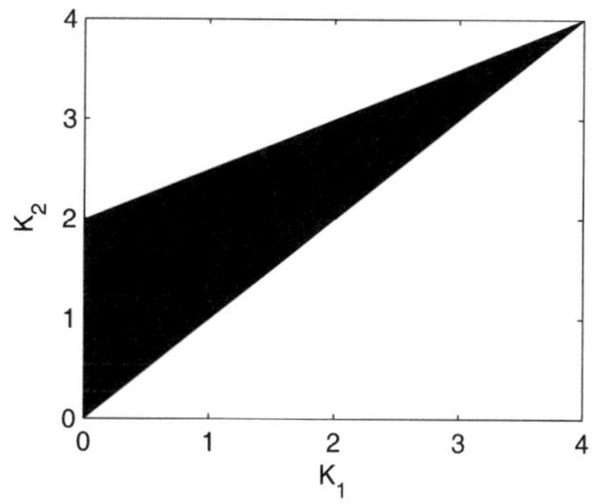

Figure 3. Stable gain space for Example 2.

Lemma 1 [10]: *Consider the system (36), where w, e* $\in \mathbb{R}^m$. *Suppose that* $\gamma(.)$ *consists of m identical, noninteracting nonlinearities, with* $\gamma(e_k^{(i)})$ *monotonically increasing in the sector* $[0,\beta]$, $\beta \ge 0$, $\beta \in \mathbb{R}$, *that is,*

$$0 \le \gamma(e_k^{(i)}) / e_k^{(i)} \le \beta \tag{37}$$

for all $e_k^{(i)} \in \mathbb{R}$, $e_k^{(i)} \neq 0$. *Assume that* $\mathcal{G}$ *is a causal, stable, finite-gain, time-invariant map* $\mathbb{R}^m \to \mathbb{R}^m$, *having a z-transform G(z), which is bounded on the unit circle. Let I denote an* $m \times m$ *identity matrix. Suppose that for some* $q > 0$, $q \in \mathbb{R}$, *there exists a* $\delta \in \mathbb{R}$, *such that*

$$\left\langle (G(z) + q\Delta_f G(z) + I\beta^{-1})e, e \right\rangle \ge \delta \left\langle e, e \right\rangle \tag{38}$$

for all $e_k^{(i)} \in \mathbb{R}$. *Under these conditions* $w \in \ell_2$ *implies e,* $\gamma(e_k^{(i)}) \in \ell_2$.

Proof: *From (36),* $\Delta_f w = \Delta_f e + \Delta_f G(z)\gamma(e)$ *and* $w + q\Delta_f w = (G(z) + q\Delta_f G(z) + I\beta^{-1})\gamma(e) + e - I\beta^{-1}\gamma(e) + e - I\beta^{-1}\gamma(e) + q\Delta_f e$. *Then*

$$\begin{aligned} \left\langle w + q\Delta_f w, \gamma(e) \right\rangle &\ge \left\langle e - I\beta^{-1}\gamma(e), \gamma(e) \right\rangle + \left\langle q\Delta_f e, \gamma(e) \right\rangle \\ &\quad + \left\langle (G(z) + q\Delta_f G(z) + I\beta^{-1})\gamma(e), \gamma(e) \right\rangle. \end{aligned} \tag{39}$$

Consider the first term on the right hand side of (39). Since the $\gamma(e)$ *consists of noninteracting nonlinearities,* $\left\langle \gamma(e), e \right\rangle = \sum_{i=1}^{m} \left\langle \gamma(e^{(i)}), e^{(i)} \right\rangle$ *and* $\left\langle e - I\beta^{-1}\gamma(e), \gamma(e) \right\rangle = \sum_{i=1}^{m} \left\langle e^{(i)} - \gamma(e^{(i)}) I\beta^{-1}, e^{(i)} \right\rangle \ge 0$. *Using the approach of [11] together with the sector conditions on the identical noninteracting nonlinearities (37), it can be shown that expanding out the second term of (39) yields* $\left\langle \Delta_f e, \gamma(e) \right\rangle \ge$

"The intelligent man finds almost everything ridiculous, the sensible man hardly anything." *Johann Wolfgang von Goethe*

0. Using $\left\|\Delta_f w\right\|_2 \le 2\left\|w\right\|_2$ *(from p. 192 of [11]), the Schwartz inequality and the triangle inequality, it can be shown that*

$$\langle w + q\nabla w, \gamma(e)\rangle \le (1+2q)\left\|w\right\|_2 . \tag{40}$$

It follows from (38) – (40) that $\left\|\gamma(e)\right\|_2^2 \le (1 + 2q)\delta^{-1}\left\|w\right\|_2$ *; hence* $\gamma(e_k^{(i)}) \in \ell_2$*. Since the gain of G(z) is finite, it also follows that* $G(z)\gamma(e_k^{(i)}) \in \ell_2$. □

If $G(z)$ is stable and bounded on the unit circle, then the test condition (38) becomes

$$\lambda_{\min}\{I + q(I - z^{-1}I)(G(z) + G^H(z)) + \beta^{-1}\} \ge \delta , \tag{41}$$

see pp. 175 and 194 of [11].

10.3.5 Applications

Example 2 [10]. Consider a unity-amplitude frequency modulated (FM) signal modelled as $\omega_{k+1} = \mu_\omega \omega_k + w_k$, $\phi_{k+1} = \phi_k + \omega_k$, $z_k^{(1)} = \cos(\phi_k) + v_k^{(1)}$ and $z_k^{(2)} = \sin(\phi_k) + v_k^{(2)}$. The error system for an FM demodulator may be written as

$$\begin{bmatrix} \tilde{\omega}_{k+1} \\ \tilde{\phi}_{k+1} \end{bmatrix} = \begin{bmatrix} \mu_\omega & 0 \\ 1 & 1 \end{bmatrix} \begin{bmatrix} \tilde{\omega}_k \\ \tilde{\phi}_k \end{bmatrix} - \begin{bmatrix} K_1 \\ K_2 \end{bmatrix} \sin(\tilde{\phi}_k) + w_k \tag{42}$$

for gains K_1, $K_2 \in \mathbb{R}$ to be designed. In view of the form (36), the above error system is reformatted as

$$\begin{bmatrix} \tilde{\omega}_{k+1} \\ \tilde{\phi}_{k+1} \end{bmatrix} = \begin{bmatrix} \mu_\omega & -K_1 \\ 1 & 1-K_2 \end{bmatrix} \begin{bmatrix} \tilde{\omega}_k \\ \tilde{\phi}_k \end{bmatrix} + \gamma\left(\begin{bmatrix} 0 & 1 \end{bmatrix} \begin{bmatrix} \tilde{\omega}_k \\ \tilde{\phi}_k \end{bmatrix} \right) + w_k , \tag{43}$$

where $\gamma(x) = x - \sin(x)$. The z-transform of the linear part of (43) is $G(z) = (K_2 z + K_2 + \mu_\omega K_1)(z^2 + (K_2 - 1 - \mu_\omega)z + K_1 + 1 - \mu_\omega K_2)^{-1}$. The nonlinearity satisfies the sector condition (37) for $\beta = 1.22$. Candidate gains may be assessed by checking that $G(z)$ is stable and the test condition (41). The stable gain space calculated for the case of $\mu_\omega = 0.9$ is plotted in Fig. 3. The gains are required to lie within the shaded region of the plot for the error system (42) to be asymptotically stable.

"He that does not offend cannot be honest." *Thomas Paine*

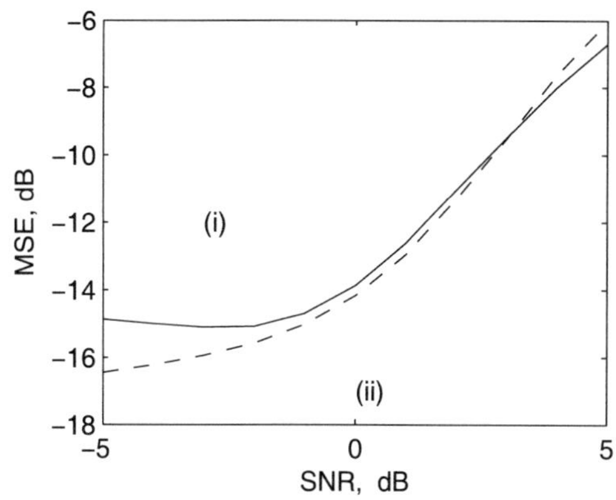

Figure 4. Demodulation performance for Example 2: (i) EKF and (ii) Nonlinear observer.

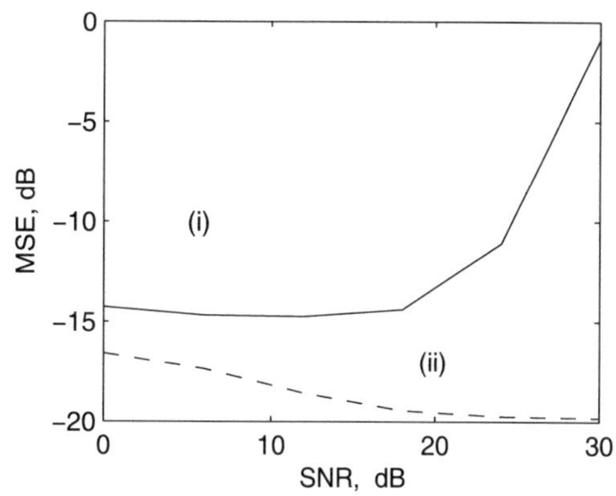

Figure 5. Demodulation performance for Example 3: (i) EKF and (ii) Nonlinear observer.

A speech utterance, namely, the phrase "Matlab is number one", was sampled at 8 kHz and used to synthesize a unity-amplitude FM signal. An EKF demodulator was constructed for the above model with σ_w^2 = 0.02. In a nonlinear observer design it was found that suitable parameter choices were $\Sigma_k = \begin{bmatrix} 0.001 & 0.08 \\ 0.08 & 0.7 \end{bmatrix}$. The nonlinear observer gains were censored at each time k according to the stable gain space of Fig. 3. The results of a simulation study using 100 realisations of Gaussian measurement noise sequences are shown in Fig. 4. The figure demonstrates that enforcing stability can be beneficial at low SNR, at the cost of degraded high-SNR performance.

Example 3 [10]. Suppose that there are two superimposed FM signals present in the same frequency channel. Neglecting observation noise, a suitable approximation of the demodulator error system in the form (36) is given by

$$\begin{bmatrix} \tilde{\omega}_{k+1}^{(1)} \\ \tilde{\phi}_{k+1}^{(1)} \\ \tilde{\omega}_{k+1}^{(2)} \\ \tilde{\phi}_{k+1}^{(2)} \end{bmatrix} = (A - K_k\bar{C}) \begin{bmatrix} \tilde{\omega}_{k}^{(1)} \\ \tilde{\phi}_{k}^{(1)} \\ \tilde{\omega}_{k}^{(2)} \\ \tilde{\phi}_{k}^{(2)} \end{bmatrix} - K_k \begin{bmatrix} \sin(\tilde{\phi}_k^{(1)}) - \tilde{\phi}_k^{(1)} \\ \sin(\tilde{\phi}_k^{(2)}) - \tilde{\phi}_k^{(2)} \end{bmatrix}, \tag{44}$$

where $A = \mathrm{diag}(A^{(1)}, A^{(1)})$, $A^{(1)} = \begin{bmatrix} \mu_\omega & 0 \\ 1 & 1 \end{bmatrix}$, $\bar{C} = \begin{bmatrix} 0 & 1 & 0 & 0 \\ 0 & 0 & 0 & 1 \end{bmatrix}$. The linear part of (44) may be written as $G(z) = \bar{C}(zI - (A - K_k\bar{C}))^{-1}K_k$. Two 8-kHz speech utterances, "Matlab is number one" and "Number one is Matlab", centred at ±0.25 rad/s, were used to synthesize two superimposed unity-amplitude FM signals. Simulations were conducted using 100 realisations of Gaussian measurement noise sequences. The test condition (41) was

---

"To avoid criticism, do nothing, say nothing, be nothing." *Elbert Hubbard*

evaluated at each time k for the above parameter values with β = 1.2, q = 0.001, δ = 0.82 and used to censor the gains. The resulting co-channel demodulation performance is shown in Fig. 5. It can be seen that the nonlinear observer significantly outperforms the EKF at high SNR.

Two mechanisms have been observed for occurrence of outliers or faults within the co-channel demodulators. Firstly errors can occur in the state attribution, that is, there is correct tracking of some component speech message segments but the tracks are inconsistently associated with the individual signals. This is illustrated by the example frequency estimate tracks shown in Figs. 6 and 7. The solid and dashed lines in the figures indicate two sample co-channel frequency tracks. Secondly, the phase unwrapping can be erroneous so that the frequency tracks bear no resemblance to the underlying messages. These faults can occur without any significant deterioration in the error residual.

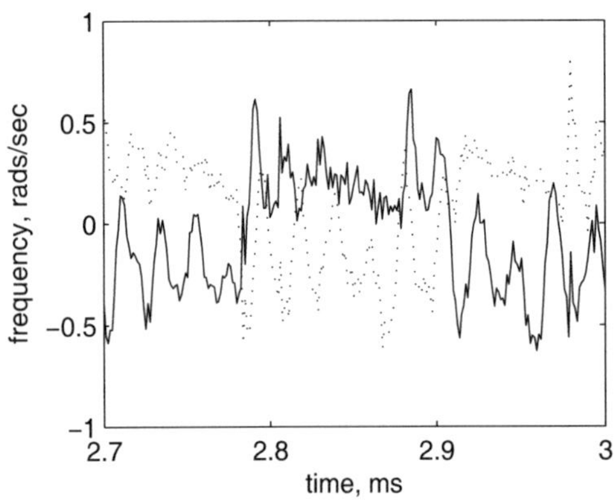

Figure 6. Sample EKF frequency tracks for Example 3.

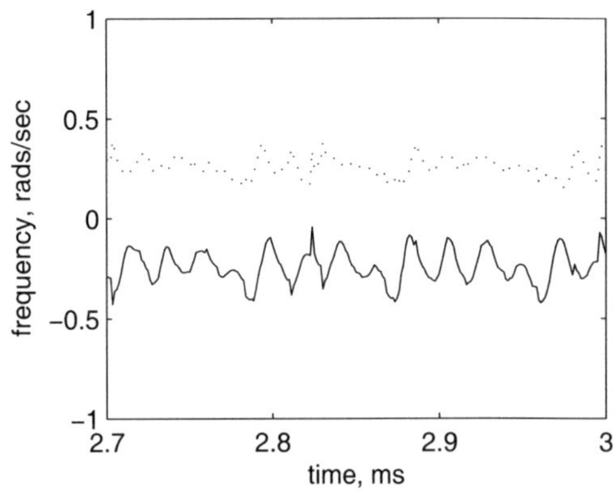

Figure 7. Sample Nonlinear observer frequency tracks for Example 3.

The EKF demodulator is observed to be increasingly fault prone at higher SNR. This arises because lower SNR designs possess narrower bandwidths and so are less sensitive to nearby frequency components. The figures also illustrate the trade-off between stability and optimality. In particular, it can be seen from Fig. 6, that the sample EKF speech estimates exhibit faults in the state attribution. This contrasts with Fig. 7, where the nonlinear observer's estimates exhibit stable state attribution at the cost of degraded speech fidelity.

10.4 Robust Extended Kalman Filtering

10.4.1 Nonlinear Problem Statement

Consider again the nonlinear, discrete-time signal model (2), (7). It is shown below that the H_∞ techniques of Chapter 9 can be used to recast nonlinear filtering problems into a model uncertainty setting. The following discussion attends to state estimation, that is, $C_{1,k} = I$ is assumed within the problem and solution presented in Section 9.3.2.

"You have enemies? Good. That means you've stood up for something, sometime in your life." *Winston Churchill*

The Taylor series expansions of the nonlinear functions $a_k(.)$, $b_k(.)$ and $c_k(.)$ about filtered and predicted estimates $\hat{x}_{k/k}$ and $\hat{x}_{k/k-1}$ may be written as

$$a_k(x_k) = a_k(\hat{x}_{k/k}) + \nabla a_k(\hat{x}_{k/k})(x_k - \hat{x}_{k/k}) + \Delta_1(\tilde{x}_{k/k}), \tag{45}$$

$$b_k(x_k) = b_k(\hat{x}_{k/k}) + \Delta_2(\tilde{x}_{k/k}), \tag{46}$$

$$c_k(x_k) = c_k(\hat{x}_{k/k-1}) + \nabla c_k(\hat{x}_{k/k-1})(x_k - \hat{x}_{k/k-1}) + \Delta_3(\tilde{x}_{k/k-1}), \tag{47}$$

where $\Delta_1(.)$, $\Delta_2(.)$, $\Delta_3(.)$ are uncertainties that account for the higher order terms, $\tilde{x}_{k/k} = x_k - \hat{x}_{k/k}$ and $\tilde{x}_{k/k-1} = x_k - \hat{x}_{k/k-1}$. It is assumed that $\Delta_1(.)$, $\Delta_2(.)$ and $\Delta_3(.)$ are continuous operators mapping $\ell_2 \to \ell_2$, with H_∞ norms bounded by δ_1, δ_2 and δ_3, respectively.

Substituting (45) – (47) into the nonlinear system (2), (7) gives the linearised system

$$x_{k+1} = A_k x_k + B_k w_k + \mu_k + \Delta_1(\tilde{x}_{k/k}) + \Delta_2(\tilde{x}_{k/k})w_k, \tag{48}$$

$$z_k = C_k x_k + \pi_k + \Delta_3(\tilde{x}_{k/k-1}) + v_k, \tag{49}$$

where $A_k = \nabla a_k(x)\big|_{x=\hat{x}_{k/k}}$, $C_k = \nabla c_k(x)\big|_{x=\hat{x}_{k/k-1}}$, $\mu_k = a_k(\hat{x}_{k/k}) - A_k\hat{x}_{k/k}$ and $\pi_k = c_k(\hat{x}_{k/k-1}) - C_k\hat{x}_{k/k-1}$.

Note that the first-order EKF for the above system arises by setting the uncertainties $\Delta_1(.)$, $\Delta_2(.)$ and $\Delta_3(.)$ to zero as

$$\hat{x}_{k/k} = \hat{x}_{k/k-1} + L_k(z_k - c_k(\hat{x}_{k/k-1})), \tag{50}$$

$$\hat{x}_{k+1/k} = a_k(\hat{x}_{k/k}), \tag{51}$$

$$L_k = P_{k/k-1}C_k^T(C_k P_{k/k-1} C_k^T + R_k)^{-1}, \tag{52}$$

$$P_{k/k} = P_{k/k-1} - P_{k/k-1}C_k^T(C_k P_{k/k-1} C_k^T + R_k)^{-1} P_{k/k-1} C_k, \tag{53}$$

$$P_{k+1/k} = A_k P_{k/k-1} A_k^T + B_k Q_k B_k^T . \tag{54}$$

10.4.2 Robust Solution

Following the approach in Chapter 9, instead of addressing the problem (48) – (49) which possesses uncertainties, an auxiliary H_∞ problem is defined as

$$x_{k+1} = A_k x_k + B_k w_k + \mu_k + s_k, \tag{55}$$

$$z_k = C_k x_k + \pi_k + v_k + t_k, \tag{56}$$

"Fight the good fight." *Timothy 4:7*

$$\tilde{x}_{k/k} = x_k - \hat{x}_{k/k}, \tag{57}$$

where $s_k = \Delta_1(\tilde{x}_{k/k}) + \Delta_2(\tilde{x}_{k/k})w_k$ and $t_k = \Delta_3\tilde{x}_{k/k} \approx \Delta_3\tilde{x}_{k/k-1}$ are additional exogenous inputs satisfying

$$\|s_k\|_2^2 \le \delta_1^2 \|\tilde{x}_{k/k}\|_2^2 + \delta_2^2 \|w_k\|_2^2, \tag{58}$$

$$\|t_k\|_2^2 \le \delta_3^2 \|\tilde{x}_{k/k}\|_2^2 \le \delta_3^2 \|\tilde{x}_{k/k-1}\|_2^2. \tag{59}$$

A sufficient solution to the auxiliary H∞ problem (55) – (57) can be obtained by solving another problem in which w_k and v_k are scaled in lieu of the additional inputs s_k and r_k. The scaled H∞ problem is defined by

$$x_{k+1} = A_k x_k + B_k c_w w_k + \mu_k, \tag{60}$$

$$z_k = C_k x_k + c_v v_k + \pi_k, \tag{61}$$

$$\tilde{x}_{k/k} = x_k - \hat{x}_{k/k}, \tag{62}$$

where c_w, $c_v \in \mathbb{R}$ are to be found.

Lemma 2 [12]: *The solution of the H∞ problem (60) – (62), where v_k is scaled by*

$$c_v^2 = 1 - \gamma^2\delta_1^2 - \gamma^2\delta_3^2, \tag{63}$$

and w_k is scaled by

$$c_w^2 = c_v^2(1 + \delta_2^2)^{-1}, \tag{64}$$

is sufficient for the solution of the auxiliary H∞ problem (55) – (57).

Proof: *If the H∞ problem (50) – (52) has been solved then there exists a $\gamma \ne 0$ such that*

$$\|\tilde{x}_{k/k}\|_2^2 \le \gamma^2(\|w_k\|_2^2 + \|s_k\|_2^2 + \|t_k\|_2^2 + \|v_k\|_2^2)$$

$$\le \gamma^2(\|w_k\|_2^2 + \delta_1^2\|\tilde{x}_{k/k}\|_2^2 + \delta_2^2\|w_k\|_2^2 + \delta_3^2\|\tilde{x}_{k/k}\|_2^2 + \|v_k\|_2^2),$$

which implies

$$(1 - \gamma^2\delta_1^2 - \gamma^2\delta_3^2)\|\tilde{x}_{k/k}\|_2^2 \le \gamma^2((1 + \delta_2^2)\|w_k\|_2^2 + \|v_k\|_2^2)$$

"You can't wait for inspiration. You have to go after it with a club." *Jack London*

and

$$\left\|\tilde{x}_{k/k}\right\|_2^2 \le \gamma^2 (c_w^{-2}\left\|w_k\right\|_2^2 + c_v^{-2}\left\|v_k\right\|_2^2) .$$ □

The robust first-order extended Kalman filter for state estimation is given by (50) - (52),

$$P_{k/k} = P_{k/k-1} - P_{k/k-1}\begin{bmatrix} I & C_k^T \end{bmatrix}\begin{bmatrix} P_{k/k-1} - \gamma^2 I & P_{k/k-1}C_k^T \\ C_k P_{k/k-1} & R_k + C_k P_{k/k-1} C_k^T \end{bmatrix}^{-1}\begin{bmatrix} I \\ C_k \end{bmatrix} P_{k/k-1}$$

and (54). As discussed in Chapter 9, a search is required for a minimum γ such that $\begin{bmatrix} P_{k/k-1} - \gamma^2 I & P_{k/k-1}C_k^T \\ C_k P_{k/k-1} & R_k + C_k P_{k/k-1} C_k^T \end{bmatrix} > 0$ and $P_{k/k-1} > 0$ over $k \in [1, N]$. An illustration is provided below.

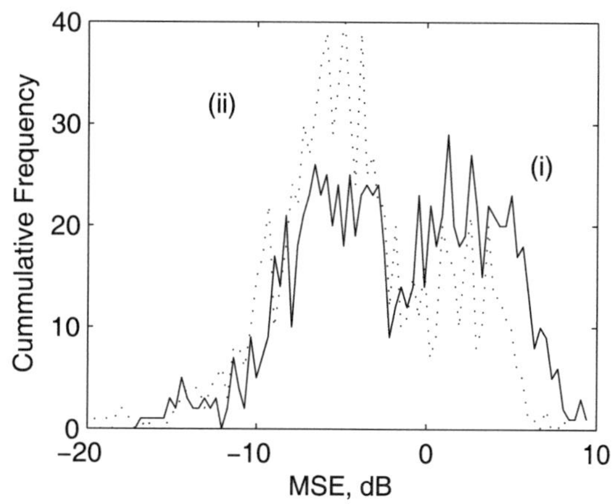

Figure 8. Histogram of demodulator mean-square-error for Example 4: (i) first-order EKF (solid line) and first-order robust EKF (dotted line).

Example 4 [12]. Suppose that an FM signal is generated by[17]

$$\omega_{k+1} = \mu_\omega \omega_k + w_k , \tag{65}$$

$$\phi_{k+1} = \arctan(\mu_\phi \phi_k + \omega_k) , \tag{66}$$

$$z_k^{(1)} = \cos(\phi_k) + v_k^{(1)} , \tag{67}$$

$$z_k^{(2)} = \sin(\phi_k) + v_k^{(2)} . \tag{68}$$

The objective is to construct an FM demodulator that produces estimates of the frequency message ω_k from the noisy in-phase and quadrature measurements $z_k^{(1)}$ and $z_k^{(2)}$, respectively. Simulations were conducted with $\mu_\omega = 0.9$, $\mu_\phi = 0.99$ and $\sigma^2_{v^{(1)}} = \sigma^2_{v^{(2)}} = 0.001$. It was found for $\sigma^2_w < 0.1$, where the state behaviour is almost linear, a robust EKF does not

---

"Happy is he who gets to know the reasons for things." *Virgil*

improve on the EKF. However, when σ_w^2 = 1, the problem is substantially nonlinear and a performance benefit can be observed. A robust EKF demodulator was designed with

$$x_k = \begin{bmatrix} \phi_k \\ \omega_k \end{bmatrix},\ A_k = \begin{bmatrix} \frac{\mu_\phi}{(\mu_\phi \hat{\phi}_{k/k} + \hat{\omega}_{k/k})^2 + 1} & \frac{\mu_\phi}{(\mu_\phi \hat{\phi}_{k/k} + \hat{\omega}_{k/k})^2 + 1} \\ 0 & \mu_\omega \end{bmatrix},\ C_k = \begin{bmatrix} -\sin(\hat{\phi}_{k/k-1}) & 0 \\ \cos(\hat{\phi}_{k/k-1}) & 0 \end{bmatrix},$$

$\delta_1 = 0.1$, $\delta_2 = 4.5$ and $\delta_3 = 0.001$. It was found that $\gamma = 1.38$ was sufficient for $P_{k/k-1}$ of the above Riccati difference equation to always be positive definite. A histogram of the observed frequency estimation error is shown in Fig. 8, which demonstrates that the robust demodulator provides improved mean-square-error performance. For sufficiently large σ_w^2, the output of the above model will resemble a digital signal, in which case a detector may outperform a demodulator.

10.5 Nonlinear Smoothing

10.5.1 Approximate Minimum-Variance Smoother

Consider again a nonlinear estimation problem where $x_{k+1} = a_k(x_k) + B_k w_k$, $z_k = c_k(x_k) + v_k$, with $x_k \in \mathbb{R}$, in which the nonlinearities $a_k(.)$, $c_k(.)$ are assumed to be smooth, differentiable functions of appropriate dimension. The linearisations akin to Extended Kalman filtering may be applied within the smoothers described in Chapter 7 in the pursuit of performance improvement. The fixed-lag, Fraser-Potter and Rauch-Tung-Striebel smoother recursions are easier to apply as they are less complex. The application of the minimum-variance smoother can yield approximately optimal estimates when the problem becomes linear, provided that the underlying assumptions are correct.

Procedure 1. An approximate minimum-variance smoother for output estimation can be implemented via the following three-step procedure.

Step 1. Operate

$$\alpha_k = -\Omega_k^{1/2}(z_k - c_k(\hat{x}_{k/k-1})), \tag{69}$$

$$\hat{x}_{k/k} = \hat{x}_{k/k-1} + L_k(z_k - c_k(\hat{x}_{k/k-1})), \tag{70}$$

$$\hat{x}_{k+1/k} = a_k(\hat{x}_{k/k}), \tag{71}$$

on the measurement z_k, where $L_k = P_{k/k-1}C_k^T\Omega_k^{-1}$,

$$\Omega_k = C_k P_{k/k-1} C_k^T + R_k,$$

$$P_{k/k} = P_{k/k-1} - P_{k/k-1}C_k^T\Omega_k^{-1}C_k P_{k/k-1},$$

$$P_{k+1/k} = A_k P_{k/k} A_k^T + B_k Q_k B_k^T, \tag{72}$$

$$A_k = \left.\frac{\partial a_k}{\partial x}\right|_{x=\hat{x}_{k/k}} \text{ and } C_k = \left.\frac{\partial c_k}{\partial x}\right|_{x=\hat{x}_{k/k-1}}.$$

"You can recognize a pioneer by the arrows in his back" *Beverly Rubik*

Step 2. Operate (69) – (71) on the time-reversed transpose of α_k. Then take the time-reversed transpose of the result to obtain β_k.

Step 3. Calculate the smoothed output estimate from

$$\hat{y}_{k/N} = z_k - R_k\beta_k . \tag{73}$$

10.5.2 Robust Smoother

From the arguments within Chapter 9, a smoother that is robust to uncertain w_k and v_k can be realised by replacing the error covariance correction (72) by

$$P_{k/k} = P_{k/k-1} - P_{k/k-1}\begin{bmatrix} C_k^T & C_k^T \end{bmatrix}\begin{bmatrix} C_kP_{k/k-1}C_k^T - \gamma^2 I & C_kP_{k/k-1}C_k^T \\ C_kP_{k/k-1}C_k^T & R_k + C_kP_{k/k-1}C_k^T \end{bmatrix}^{-1}\begin{bmatrix} C_k \\ C_k \end{bmatrix}P_{k/k-1}$$

within Procedure 1. As discussed in Chapter 9, a search for a minimum γ such that $\begin{bmatrix} C_kP_{k/k-1}C_k^T - \gamma^2 I & C_kP_{k/k-1}C_k^T \\ C_kP_{k/k-1}C_k^T & R_k + C_kP_{k/k-1}C_k^T \end{bmatrix} > 0$ and $P_{k/k-1} > 0$ over $k \in [1, N]$ is desired.

10.5.3 Application

Returning to the problem of demodulating a unity-amplitude FM signal, let $x_k = \begin{bmatrix} \omega_k \\ \phi_k \end{bmatrix}$, $A = \begin{bmatrix} \mu_w & 0 \\ 1 & \mu_\phi \end{bmatrix}$, $B = \begin{bmatrix} 1 & 0 \end{bmatrix}$, $z_k^{(1)} = \cos(\phi_k) + v_k^{(1)}$, $z_k^{(2)} = \sin(\phi_k) + v_k^{(2)}$, where ω_k, ϕ_k, z_k and v_k denote the instantaneous frequency message, instantaneous phase, complex observations and measurement noise respectively. A zero-mean voiced speech utterance "a e i o u" was sampled at 8 kHz, for which estimates $\hat{\mu}_\omega$ = 0.97 and $\hat{\sigma}_w^2$ = 0.053 were obtained using an expectation maximization algorithm. An FM discriminator output [13],

$$z_k^{(3)} = \left(z_k^{(1)} \frac{dz_k^{(2)}}{dt} - z_k^{(2)} \frac{dz_k^{(1)}}{dt} \right)\left((z_k^{(1)})^2 + (z_k^{(1)})^2 \right)^{-1}, \tag{74}$$

serves as a benchmark and as an auxiliary frequency measurement for the above smoother. The innovations within Steps 1 and 2 are given by $\begin{bmatrix} z_k^{(1)} \\ z_k^{(2)} \\ z_k^{(3)} \end{bmatrix} - \begin{bmatrix} \cos(\hat{x}_k^{(2)}) \\ \sin(\hat{x}_k^{(2)}) \\ \hat{x}_k^{(1)} \end{bmatrix}$ and $\begin{bmatrix} \alpha_k^{(1)} \\ \alpha_k^{(2)} \\ \alpha_k^{(3)} \end{bmatrix} - \begin{bmatrix} \cos(\hat{x}_k^{(2)}) \\ \sin(\hat{x}_k^{(2)}) \\ \hat{x}_k^{(1)} \end{bmatrix}$ respectively. A unity-amplitude FM signal was synthesized using μ_ϕ = 0.99 and the SNR was varied in 1.5 dB steps from 3 dB to 15 dB. The mean-square errors were calculated over 200 realisations of Gaussian measurement noise and are shown in Fig. 9. It can be seen from the figure, that at 7.5 dB SNR, the first-order EKF improves on the FM discriminator MSE by about 12 dB. The improvement arises because the EKF

"The farther the experiment is from theory, the closer it is to the Nobel Prize." *Irène Joliot-Curie*

demodulator exploits the signal model whereas the FM discriminator does not. The figure shows that the approximate minimum-variance smoother further reduces the MSE by about 2 dB, which illustrates the advantage of exploiting all the data in the time interval. In the robust designs, searches for minimum values of γ were conducted such that the corresponding Riccati difference equation solutions were positive definite over each noise realisation. It can be seen from the figure at 7.5 dB SNR that the robust EKF provides about a 1 dB performance improvement compared to the EKF, whereas the approximate minimum-variance smoother and the robust smoother performance are indistinguishable.

This nonlinear example illustrates once again that smoothers can outperform filters. Since a first-order speech model is used and the Taylor series are truncated after the first-order terms, some model uncertainty is present, and so the robust designs demonstrate a marginal improvement over the EKF.

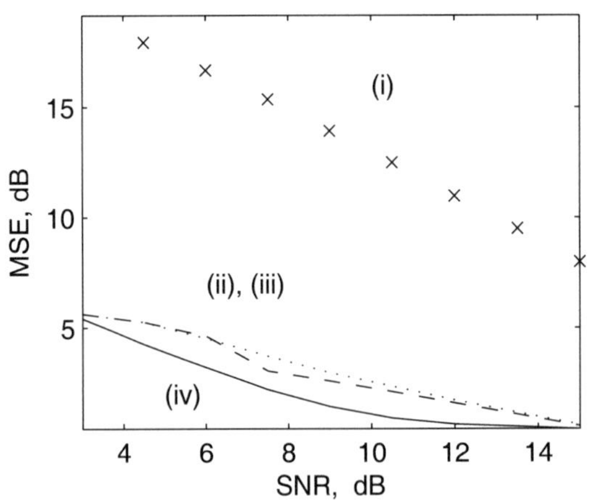

Figure 9. FM demodulation performance comparison: (i) FM discriminator (crosses), (ii) first-order EKF (dotted line), (iii) Robust EKF (dashed line), (iv) approximate minimum-variance smoother and robust smoother (solid line).

10.6 Constrained Filtering and Smoothing

10.6.1 Background

Constraints often appear within navigation problems. For example, vehicle trajectories are typically constrained by road, tunnel and bridge boundaries. Similarly, indoor pedestrian trajectories are constrained by walls and doors. However, as constraints are not easily described within state-space frameworks, many techniques for constrained filtering and smoothing are reported in the literature. An early technique for constrained filtering involves augmenting the measurement vector with perfect observations [14]. The application of the perfect-measurement approach to filtering and fixed-interval smoothing is described in [15].

"They thought I was crazy, absolutely mad." *Barbara McClintock*

Constraints can be applied to state estimates, see [16], where a positivity constraint is used within a Kalman filter and a fixed-lag smoother. Three different state equality constraint approaches, namely, maximum-probability, mean-square and projection methods are described in [17]. Under prescribed conditions, the perfect-measurement and projection approaches are equivalent [5], [18], which is identical to applying linear constraints within a form of recursive least squares.

In the state equality constrained methods [5], [16] - [18], a constrained estimate can be calculated from a Kalman filter's unconstrained estimate at each time step. Constraint information could also be embedded within nonlinear models for use with EKFs. A simpler, low-computation-cost technique that avoids EKF stablity problems and suits real-time implementation is described in [19]. In particular, an on-line procedure is proposed that involves using nonlinear functions to censor the measurements and subsequently applying the minimum-variance filter recursions. An off-line procedure for retrospective analyses is also described, where the minimum-variance fixed-interval smoother recursions are applied to the censored measurements. In contrast to the afore-mentioned techniques, which employ constraint matrices and vectors, here constraint information is represented by an exogenous input process. This approach uses the Bounded Real Lemma which enables the nonlinearities to be designed so that the filtered and smoothed estimates satisfy a performance criterion.

10.6.2 Problem Statement

The ensuing discussion concerns odd and even functions which are defined as follows. A function g_o of X is said to be odd if $g_o(-X) = -g_o(X)$. A function f_e of X is said to be even if $f_e(-X) = f_e(X)$. The product of g_o and f_e is an odd function since $g_o(-X)f_e(-X) = -g_o(X)f_e(X)$.

Problems are considered where stochastic random variables are subjected to inequality constraints. Therefore, nonlinear censoring functions are introduced whose outputs are constrained to lie within prescribed bounds. Let $\beta \in \mathbb{R}^p$ and $g_o : \mathbb{R}^p \to \mathbb{R}^p$ denote a constraint vector and an odd function of a random variable $X \in \mathbb{R}^p$ about its expected value $E\{X\}$, respectively. Define the censoring function

$$g(X) = E\{X\} + g_o(X,\beta), \tag{75}$$

where

$$g_o(X,\beta) = \begin{cases} \beta & \text{if } \beta \le X - E\{X\} \\ X - E\{X\} & \text{if } -\beta < X - E\{X\} < \beta \\ -\beta & \text{if } X - E\{X\} \le -\beta \end{cases}. \tag{76}$$

"If at first, the idea is not absurd, then there is no hope for it." *Albert Einstein*

By inspection of (75) – (76), $g(X)$ is constrained within $E\{X\} \pm \beta$. Suppose that the probability density function of X about $E\{X\}$ is even, that is, is symmetric about $E\{X\}$. Under these conditions, the expected value of $g(X)$ is given by

$$\begin{aligned} E\{g(X)\} &= \int_{-\infty}^{\infty} g(x) f_e(x) dx \\ &= E\{X\} \int_{-\infty}^{\infty} f_e(x) dx + \int_{-\infty}^{\infty} g_o(x, \beta) f_e(x) dx \\ &= E\{X\} . \end{aligned} \tag{77}$$

since $\int_{-\infty}^{\infty} f_e(x) dx = 1$ and the product $g_o(x, \beta) f_e(x)$ is odd.

Thus, a constraining process can be modelled by a nonlinear function. Equation (77) states that $g(X)$ is unbiased, provided that $g_o(X,\beta)$ and $f_X(X)$ are odd and even functions about $E\{X\}$, respectively. In the analysis and examples that follow, attention is confined to systems having zero-mean inputs, states and outputs, in which case the censoring functions are also centred on zero, that is, $E\{X\} = 0$.

Let $w_k = \begin{bmatrix} w_{1,k} & \dots & w_{m,k} \end{bmatrix}^T \in \mathbb{R}^m$ represent a stochastic white input process having an even probability density function, with $E\{w_k\} = 0$, $E\{w_j w_k^T\} = Q_k \delta_{jk}$, in which δ_{jk} denotes the Kronecker delta function. Suppose that the states of a system $\mathcal{G}: \mathbb{R}^m \to \mathbb{R}^p$ are realised by

$$x_{k+1} = A_k x_k + B_k w_k , \tag{78}$$

where $A_k \in \mathbb{R}^{n \times n}$ and $B_k \in \mathbb{R}^{n \times m}$. Since w_k is zero-mean, it follows that linear combinations of the states are also zero-mean. Suppose also that the system outputs, y_k, are generated by

$$y_k = \begin{bmatrix} y_{1,k} \\ \vdots \\ y_{p,k} \end{bmatrix} = \begin{bmatrix} g_o(C_{1,k} x_k, \theta_{1,k}) \\ \vdots \\ g_o(C_{p,k} x_k, \theta_{p,k}) \end{bmatrix} , \tag{79}$$

where $C_{j,k}$ is the jth row of $C_k \in \mathbb{R}^{p \times m}$, $\theta_k = [\theta_{1,k} \; \dots \; \theta_{p,k}]^T \in \mathbb{R}^p$ is an input constraint process and $g_o(C_{j,k} x_k, \theta_{j,k})$, $j = 1, \dots p$, is an odd censoring function centred on zero. The outputs $y_{j,k}$ are constrained to lie within $\pm\theta_{j,k}$, that is,

$$-\theta_{j,k} \le y_{j,k} \le \theta_{j,k} . \tag{80}$$

For example, if the system outputs represent the trajectories of pedestrians within a building then the constraint process could include knowledge about wall, floor and ceiling positions.

"It was not easy for a person brought up in the ways of classical thermodynamics to come around to the idea that gain of entropy eventually is nothing more nor less than loss of information." *Gilbert Newton Lewis*

Similarly, a vehicle trajectory constraint process could include information about building and road boundaries.

Assume that observations $z_k = y_k + v_k$ are available, where $v_k \in \mathbb{R}^p$ is a stochastic, white measurement noise process having an even probability density function, with $E\{v_k\} = 0$, $E\{v_k\} = 0$, $E\{v_j v_k^T\} = R_k \delta_{j,k}$ and $E\{w_j v_k^T\} = 0$. It is convenient to define the stacked vectors $y = [y_1^T \; \ldots \; y_N^T]^T$ and $\theta = [\theta_1^T \; \ldots \; \theta_N^T]^T$. It follows that

$$\|y\|_2^2 \le \|\theta\|_2^2 . \tag{81}$$

Thus, the energy of the system's output is bounded from above by the energy of the constraint process.

The minimum-variance filter and smoother which produce estimates of a linear system's output, minimise the mean square error. Here, it is desired to calculate estimates that trade off minimum mean-square-error performance and achieve

$$\|\hat{y}\|_2^2 \le \|\theta\|_2^2 . \tag{82}$$

Note that (80) implies (81) but the converse is not true. Although estimates $\hat{y}_{j,k}$ of $y_{j,k}$ satisfying $-\theta_{j,k} \le \hat{y}_{j,k} \le \theta_{j,k}$ are desirable, the procedures described below only ensure that (82) is satisfied.

10.6.3 Constrained Filtering

A procedure is proposed in which a linear filter $\mathcal{H}: \mathbb{R}^p \to \mathbb{R}^p$ is used to calculate estimates $\hat{y}$ from zero-mean measurements z_k that are constrained using an odd censoring function to obtain

$$\underline{z}_k = \begin{bmatrix} \underline{z}_{1,k} \\ \vdots \\ \underline{z}_{p,k} \end{bmatrix} = \begin{bmatrix} g_o(z_{1,k}, \gamma^{-1}\theta_{1,k}) \\ \vdots \\ g_o(z_{p,k}, \gamma^{-1}\theta_{p,k}) \end{bmatrix}, \tag{83}$$

which satisfy

$$\|\underline{z}\|_2^2 \le \gamma^{-2} \|\theta\|_2^2 . \tag{84}$$

where $\underline{z} = [\underline{z}_1^T \; \ldots \; \underline{z}_N^T]^T$, for a positive $\gamma \in \mathbb{R}$ to be designed. This design problem is depicted in Fig. 10.

"Man's greatest asset is the unsettled mind." *Isaac Asimov*

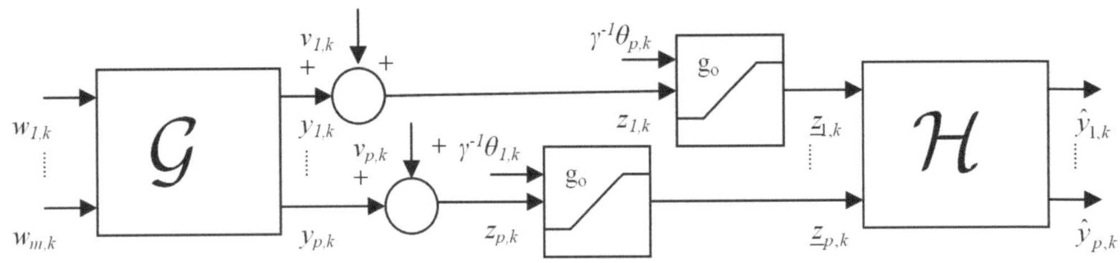

Figure 10. The constrained filtering design problem. The task is to design a scalar γ so that the outputs of a filter $\mathcal{H}$ operating on the censored zero-mean measurements $[\underline{z}_{1,k}^T \; \cdots \; \underline{z}_{p,k}^T]^T$ produce output estimates $[\hat{y}_{1,k}^T \; \cdots \; \hat{y}_{p,k}^T]^T$, which trade off mean square error performance and achieve $\|\hat{y}\|_2^2 \le \|\theta\|_2^2$.

Censoring the measurements is suggested as a low-implementation-cost approach to constrained filtering. Design constraints are sought for the measurement censoring functions so that the outputs of a subsequent filter satisfy the performance objective (82). The recursions akin to the minimum-variance filter are applied to calculate predicted and filtered state estimates from the constrained measurements $\underline{z}_k$ at time k. That is, the output mapping C_k is retained within the linear filter design even though nonlinearities are present with (83). The predicted states, filtered states and output estimates are respectively obtained as

$$\hat{x}_{k+1/k} = (A_k - K_k C_k)\hat{x}_{k/k-1} + K_k \underline{z}_k , \tag{85}$$

$$\hat{x}_{k/k} = (I - L_k C_k)\hat{x}_{k/k-1} + L_k \underline{z}_k , \tag{86}$$

$$\hat{y}_{k/k} = C_k \hat{x}_{k/k} , \tag{87}$$

where $L_k = P_{k/k-1}C_k^T(C_k P_{k/k-1} C_k^T + R_k)^{-1}$, $K_k = A_k L_k$, and $P_{k/k-1} = P_{k/k-1}^T > 0$ is obtained from $P_{k/k} = P_{k/k-1} - P_{k/k-1}C_k^T(C_k P_{k/k-1} C_k^T + R_k)^{-1} C_k P_{k/k-1}$, $P_{k+1/k} = A_k P_{k/k} A_k^T + B_k Q_k B_k^T$. Nonzero-mean sequences can be accommodated using deterministic inputs as described in Chapter 4. Since a nonlinear system output (79) and a nonlinear measurement (83) are assumed, the estimates calculated from (85) – (87) are not optimal. Some properties that are exhibited by these estimates are described below.

Lemma 3 [19]: *In respect of the filter (85) – (87) which operates on the constrained measurements (83), suppose the following:*

- *(i) the probability density functions associated with w_k and v_k are even;*
- *(ii) the nonlinear functions within (79) and (83) are odd; and*
- *(iii) the filter is initialized with $\hat{x}_{0/0} = E\{x_0\}$.*

Then the following applies:

- *(i) the predicted state estimates, $\hat{x}_{k+1/k}$, are unbiased;*
- *(ii) the corrected state estimates, $\hat{x}_{k/k}$, are unbiased; and*
- *(iii) the output estimates, $\hat{y}_{k/k}$, are unbiased.*

"A mind that is stretched by a new idea can never go back to its original dimensions." *Oliver Wendell Holmes*

Proof: *(i) Condition (iii) implies* $E\{\tilde{x}_{1/0}\}$ = *0, which is the initialization step of an induction argument. It follows from (85) that*

$$\hat{x}_{k+1/k} = (A_k - K_k C_k)\hat{x}_{k/k-1} + K_k(C_k x_k + v_k) + K_k(\underline{z}_k - C_k x_k - v_k). \quad (88)$$

Subtracting (88) from (78) gives $\tilde{x}_{k+1/k}$ = $(A_k - K_k C_k)\tilde{x}_{k/k-1} - B_k w_k - K_k v_k - K_k(\underline{z}_k - C_k x_k - v_k)$ *and therefore*

$$E\{\tilde{x}_{k+1/k}\} = (A_k - K_k C_k)E\{\tilde{x}_{k/k-1}\} + B_k E\{w_k\} - K_k E\{v_k\} - K_k E\{\underline{z}_k - C_k x_k - v_k\}. \quad (89)$$

From above assumptions, the second and third terms on the right-hand-side of (89) are zero. The property (77) implies $E\{\underline{z}_k\}$ = $E\{z_k\}$ = $E\{C_k x_k + v_k\}$ *and so* $E\{\underline{z}_k - C_k x_k - v_k\}$ *is zero. The first term on the right-hand-side of (89) pertains to the unconstrained Kalman filter and is zero by induction. Thus,* $E\{\tilde{x}_{k+1/k}\}$ = *0.*

(ii) Condition (iii) again serves as an induction assumption. It follows from (86) that

$$\hat{x}_{k/k} = \hat{x}_{k/k-1} + L_k(C_k x_k + v_k - C_k\hat{x}_{k/k-1}) + L_k(\underline{z}_k - C_k x_k - v_k). \quad (90)$$

Substituting $x_k = A_{k-1}x_{k-1} + B_{k-1}w_{k-1}$ *into (90) yields* $\tilde{x}_{k/k} = (I - L_k C_k)A_{k-1}\tilde{x}_{k-1/k-1} + (I - L_k C_k)B_{k-1}w_{k-1} - L_k v_k - L_k(\underline{z}_k - C_k x_k - v_k)$ *and* $E\{\tilde{x}_{k/k}\} = (I - L_k C_k)A_{k-1}E\{\tilde{x}_{k-1/k-1}\} = (I - L_k C_k)A_{k-1} \ldots (I - L_1 C_1)A_0 E\{\tilde{x}_{0/0}\}$. *Hence,* $E\{\tilde{x}_{k/k}\}$ = *0 by induction.*

(iii) Defining $\tilde{y}_{k/k} = y_k - \hat{y}_{k/k} = y_k + C_k(x_k - \hat{x}_{k/k}) - C_k x_k = C_k\tilde{x}_{k/k} + y_k - C_k x_k$ *and using (77) leads to* $E\{\tilde{y}_{k/k}\} = C_k E\{\tilde{x}_{k/k}\} + E\{y_k - C_k x_k\} = C_k E\{\tilde{x}_{k/k}\}$ = *0 under condition (iii).* □

Recall that the Bounded Real Lemma (see Lemma 7 of Chapter 9) specifies a bound for a ratio of a system's output and input energies. This lemma is used to find a design for γ within (83) as described below.

Lemma 4 [19]: *Consider the filter (85) – (87) which operates on the constrained measurements (83). Let* $\underline{A}_k = A_k - K_k C_k$, $\underline{B}_k = K_k$, $\underline{C}_k = C_k(I - L_k C_k)$ *and* $\underline{D}_k = C_k L_k$ *denote the state-space parameters of the filter. Suppose for a given* $\gamma_2 > 0$, *that a solution* $M_k = M_k^T > 0$ *exists over k* ∈ *[1, N] for the Riccati Difference equation resulting from the application of the Bounded Real Lemma to the system* $\begin{bmatrix} \underline{A}_k & \underline{B}_k \\ \underline{C}_k & \underline{D}_k \end{bmatrix}$. *Then the design* $\gamma = \gamma_2$ *within (83) results in the performance objective (82) being satisfied.*

Proof: *For the application of the Bounded Real Lemma to the filter (85) – (87), the existence of a solution* $M_k = M_k^T > 0$ *for the associated Riccati difference equation ensures that* $\|\hat{y}\|_2^2 \le \gamma_2^2\|\underline{z}\|_2^2 - x_0^T M_0 x_0 \le \gamma_2^2\|\underline{z}\|_2^2$, *which together with (84) leads to (82).* □

It is argued below that the proposed filtering procedure is asymptotically stable.

"All truth passes through three stages: First, it is ridiculed; Second, it is violently opposed; and Third, it is accepted as self-evident." *Arthur Schopenhauer*

Lemma 5 [19]: *Define the filter output estimation error as* $\tilde{y} = y - \hat{y}$. *Under the conditions of Lemma 4,* $\tilde{y} \in \ell_2$.

Proof: *It follows from* $\tilde{y} = y - \hat{y}$ *that* $\|\tilde{y}\|_2 \le \|y\|_2 + \|\hat{y}\|_2$, *which together with (10) and the result of Lemma 4 yields* $\|\tilde{y}\|_2 \le 2\|\theta\|_2$, *thus the claim follows.* □

10.6.4 Constrained Smoothing

In the sequel, it is proposed that the minimum-variance fixed-interval smoother recursions operate on the censored measurements $\underline{z}_k$ to produce output estimates $\hat{y}_{k/N}$ of y_k.

Lemma 6 [19]: *In respect of the minimum-variance smoother recursions that operate on the censored measurements* $\underline{z}_k$, *under the conditions of Lemma 3, the smoothed estimates,* $\hat{y}_{k/N}$, *are unbiased.*

The proof follows *mutatis mutandis* from the approach within the proofs of Lemma 5 of Chapter 7 and Lemma 3. An analogous result to Lemma 5 is now stated.

Lemma 7 [19]: *Define the smoother output estimation error as* $\tilde{y} = y - \hat{y}$. *Under the conditions of Lemma 3,* $\tilde{y} \in \ell_2$.

The proof follows *mutatis mutandis* from that of Lemma 5. Two illustrative examples are set out below. A GPS and inertial navigation system integration application is detailed in [19].

Example 5 [19]. Consider the saturating nonlinearity

$$g_o(X,\beta) = 2\beta\pi^{-1}\arctan\left(\pi X(2\beta)^{-1}\right). \tag{91}$$

which is a continuous approximation of (76) that satisfies $|g_o(X,\beta)| \le |\beta|$ and $\frac{dg_o(X,\beta)}{dX}$ = $\left(1 + (\pi X)^2(2\beta)^{-2}\right)^{-1} \approx 1$ when $(\pi X)^2(2\beta)^{-2} << 1$. Data was generated from (78), (79), (91), where $A = \begin{bmatrix} 0.9 & 0 \\ 0 & 0.9 \end{bmatrix}$, $B = C = \begin{bmatrix} 1 & 0 \\ 0 & 1 \end{bmatrix}$, Gaussian, white, zero-mean processes with $Q = R = \begin{bmatrix} 0.01 & 0 \\ 0 & 0.01 \end{bmatrix}$. The constraint vector within (80) was chosen to be fixed, namely, $\theta_k = \begin{bmatrix} 0.5 \\ 0.5 \end{bmatrix}$, $k \in [1, 10^5]$. The limits of the observed distribution of estimates, $\hat{y}_{k/k} = \begin{bmatrix} \hat{y}_{1,k/k} \\ \hat{y}_{2,k/k} \end{bmatrix}$, arising by

"Everything we know is only some kind of approximation, because we know that we do not know all the laws yet. Therefore, things must be learned only to be unlearned again or, more likely, to be corrected." *Richard Phillips Feynman*

operating the minimum-variance filter recursions on the raw data $z_k = y_k + v_k$ are indicated by the outer black region of Fig. 11. It can be seen that the filter outputs do not satisfy the performance objective (82), which motivates the pursuit of constrained techniques. A minimum value of $\gamma_2 = 1.24$ was found for the solutions of the Riccati difference equation mentioned specified within Lemma 4 to be positive definite. The filter (85) - (87) was applied to the censored measurements $\underline{z}_k = \begin{bmatrix} \underline{z}_{1,k} \\ \underline{z}_{2,k} \end{bmatrix} = \begin{bmatrix} g_o(z_{1,k}, \gamma^{-1}\theta_{1,k}) \\ g_o(z_{2,k}, \gamma^{-1}\theta_{2,k}) \end{bmatrix}$ using (91). The limits of the observed distribution of the constrained filter estimates are indicated by the inner white region of Fig. 11. The figure shows that the constrained filter estimates satisfy (82), which illustrates Lemma 5.

Example 6 [19]. Measurements were similarly synthesized using the parameters of Example 5 to demonstrate constrained fixed-interval smoother performance. A minimum value of $\gamma_2 = 5.6$ was found for the solutions of the Riccati difference equation mentioned within Lemma 4 to be positive definite. The superimposed distributions of the unconstrained and constrained smoothers are respectively indicated by the inner and outer black regions of Fig. 12. It can be seen by inspection of the figure that the constrained smoother estimates meets (80), where as those produced by the standard smoother do not.

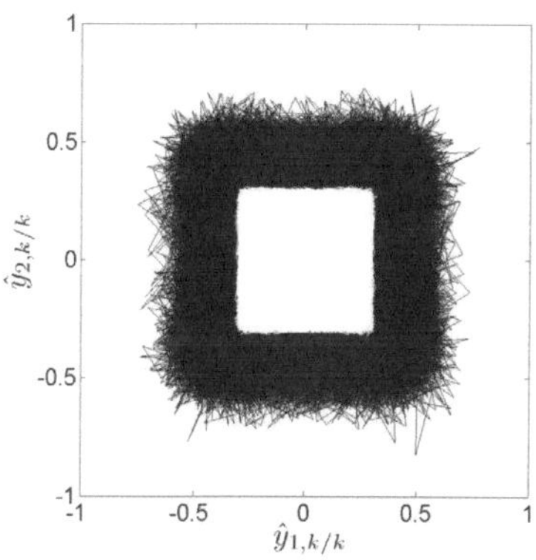

Figure 11. Superimposed distributions of filtered estimates for Example 4: unconstrained filter (outer black); and constrained filter (middle white).

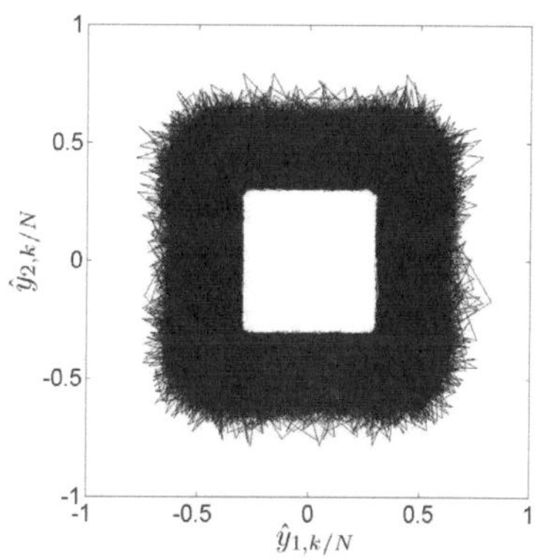

Figure 12. Superimposed distributions of smoothed estimates for Example 5: unconstrained smoother (outer black); and constrained smoother (middle white).

"An expert is a man who has made all the mistakes which can be made in a very narrow field." *Niels Henrik David Bohr*

The above examples involved searching for minimum value of γ_2 for the existence of positive definite solutions for the Riccati equation alluded to within Lemma 4. The need for a search may not be apparent as stability is guaranteed whenever a positive definite solution for the associated Riccati equation exists. Searching for a minimum γ_2 is advocated because the use of an excessively large value can lead to a nonlinearity design that is conservative and exhibits poor mean-square-error performance. If a design is still too conservative then an empirical value, namely, $\gamma_2 = \left\|\hat{y}\right\|_2 \left\|\underline{z}\right\|_2^{-1}$, may need to be considered instead.

10.7 Conclusion

In this chapter it is assumed that nonlinear systems are of the form $x_{k+1} = a_k(x_k) + b_k(w_k)$, $y_k = c_k(x_k)$, where $a_k(.)$, $b_k(.)$ and $c_k(.)$ are continuous differentiable functions. The EKF arises by linearising the model about conditional mean estimates and applying the standard filter recursions. The first, second and third-order EKFs simplified for the case of $x_k \in \mathbb{R}$ are summarised in Table 1.

The EKF attempts to produce locally optimal estimates. However, it is not necessarily stable because the solutions of the underlying Riccati equations are not guaranteed to be positive definite. The faux algebraic Riccati technique trades off approximate optimality for stability. The familiar structure of the EKF is retained but stability is achieved by selecting a positive definite solution to a faux Riccati equation for the gain design.

H_∞ techniques can be used to recast nonlinear filtering applications into a model uncertainty problem. It is demonstrated with the aid of an example that a robust EKF can reduce the mean square error when the problem is sufficiently nonlinear.

Linearised models may be applied within the previously-described smoothers in the pursuit of performance improvement. Nonlinear versions of the fixed-lag, Fraser-Potter and Rauch-Tung-Striebel smoothers are easier to implement as they are less complex. However, the application of the minimum-variance smoother can yield approximately optimal estimates when the problem becomes linear, provided that the underlying assumptions are correct. A smoother that is robust to input uncertainty is obtained by replacing the approximate error covariance correction with an H_∞ version. The resulting robust nonlinear smoother can exhibit performance benefits when uncertainty is present.

In some applications, it may be possible to censor a system's inputs, states or outputs, rather than proceed with an EKF design. It has been shown that the use of a nonlinear censoring function to constrain input measurements leads to bounded filter and smoother estimation errors.

"Most of what I learned as an entrepreneur was by trial and error." *Gordon Earl Moore*

	Linearisation	Predictor-Corrector Form
1st-order EKF	$A_k = \left.\frac{\partial a_k(x)}{\partial x}\right\rvert_{x=\hat{x}_{k/k}}$ $C_k = \left.\frac{\partial c_k(x)}{\partial x}\right\rvert_{x=\hat{x}_{k/k-1}}$ $B_k = b_k(\hat{x}_{k/k})$	$\hat{x}_{k/k} = \hat{x}_{k/k-1} + L_k(z_k - c_k(\hat{x}_{k/k-1}))$ $\hat{x}_{k+1/k} = a_k(\hat{x}_{k/k})$
2nd-order EKF	$A_k = \left.\frac{\partial a_k(x)}{\partial x}\right\rvert_{x=\hat{x}_{k/k}}$ $C_k = \left.\frac{\partial c_k(x)}{\partial x}\right\rvert_{x=\hat{x}_{k/k-1}}$ $B_k = b_k(\hat{x}_{k/k})$	$\hat{x}_{k/k} = \hat{x}_{k/k-1} + L_k\left(z_k - c_k(\hat{x}_{k/k-1}) - \frac{1}{2}\left.\frac{\partial^2 c_k}{\partial x^2}\right\rvert_{x=\hat{x}_{k/k-1}}\right)$ $\hat{x}_{k+1/k} = a_k(\hat{x}_{k/k}) + \frac{1}{2}P_{k/k}\left.\frac{\partial^2 a_k}{\partial x^2}\right\rvert_{x=\hat{x}_{k/k}}$
3rd-order EKF	$A_k = \left.\frac{\partial a_k(x)}{\partial x}\right\rvert_{x=\hat{x}_{k/k}} + \frac{1}{6}P_{k/k}\left.\frac{\partial^2 a_k}{\partial x^2}\right\rvert_{x=\hat{x}_{k/k}}$ $C_k = \left.\frac{\partial c_k(x)}{\partial x}\right\rvert_{x=\hat{x}_{k/k-1}} + \frac{1}{6}P_{k/k-1}\left.\frac{\partial^2 c_k}{\partial x^2}\right\rvert_{x=\hat{x}_{k/k-1}}$ $B_k = b_k(\hat{x}_{k/k})$	$\hat{x}_{k/k} = \hat{x}_{k/k-1} + L_k\left(z_k - c_k(\hat{x}_{k/k-1}) - \frac{1}{2}\left.\frac{\partial^2 c_k}{\partial x^2}\right\rvert_{x=\hat{x}_{k/k-1}}\right)$ $\hat{x}_{k+1/k} = a_k(\hat{x}_{k/k}) + \frac{1}{2}P_{k/k}\left.\frac{\partial^2 a_k}{\partial x^2}\right\rvert_{x=\hat{x}_{k/k}}$

Table 1. Summary of first, second and third-order EKFs for the case of $x_k \in \mathbb{R}$.

10.8 Problems

Problem 1. Use the following Taylor series expansion of $f(x)$

$$f(x) = f(x_0) + \frac{1}{1!}(x - x_0)^T \nabla f(x_0) + \frac{1}{2!}(x - x_0)^T \nabla^T \nabla f(x_0)(x - x_0)$$

$$+\frac{1}{3!}(x - x_0)^T \nabla^T \nabla (x - x_0) \nabla f(x_0)(x - x_0)$$

$$+\frac{1}{4!}(x - x_0)^T \nabla^T \nabla (x - x_0) \nabla (x - x_0) \nabla f(x_0)(x - x_0) + \ldots,$$

"The capacity to blunder slightly is the real marvel of DNA. Without this special attribute, we would still be anaerobic bacteria and there would be no music." *Lewis Thomas*

to find expressions for the coefficients α_i within the functions below.

(i) $f(x) = \alpha_0 + \alpha_1(x - x_0) + \alpha_2(x - x_0)^2$.

(ii) $f(x) = \alpha_0 + \alpha_1(x - x_0) + \alpha_2(x - x_0)^2 + \alpha_3(x - x_0)^3$.

(iii) $f(x,y) = \alpha_0 + \alpha_1(x - x_0) + \alpha_2(x - x_0)^2$.

$$+\alpha_3(y - y_0) + \alpha_4(y - y_0)^2 + \alpha_5(x - x_0)(y - y_0)$$

(iv) $f(x,y) = \alpha_0 + \alpha_1(x - x_0) + \alpha_2(x - x_0)^2 + \alpha_3(x - x_0)^3$

$$+\alpha_4(y - y_0) + \alpha_5(y - y_0)^2 + \alpha_6(y - y_0)^3$$

$$+\alpha_7(x - x_0)(y - y_0) + \alpha_8(x - x_0)^2(y - y_0)$$

$$+\alpha_9(x - x_0)(y - y_0)^2.$$

(v) $f(x,y) = \alpha_0 + \alpha_1(x - x_0) + \alpha_2(x - x_0)^2 + \alpha_3(x - x_0)^3 + \alpha_4(x - x_0)^4$

$$+\alpha_5(y - y_0) + \alpha_6(y - y_0)^2 + \alpha_7(y - y_0)^3 + \alpha_8(y - y_0)^4$$

$$+\alpha_9(x - x_0)(y - y_0) + \alpha_{10}(x - x_0)^2(y - y_0)$$

$$+\alpha_{11}(x - x_0)(y - y_0)^2 + \alpha_{12}(x - x_0)^3(y - y_0)$$

$$+\alpha_{13}(x - x_0)(y - y_0)^3 + \alpha_{14}(x - x_0)^2(y - y_0)^2.$$

Problem 2. Consider a state estimation problem, where $x_{k+1} = a_k(x_k) + B_k w_k$, $y_k = c_k(x_k)$, $z_k = y_k + v_k$, in which w_k, x_k, y_k, v_k, $a_k(.)$, B_k, $c_k(.) \in \mathbb{R}$. Derive the

(i) first-order,

(ii) second-order,

(iii) third-order and

(iv) fourth-order EKFs,

assuming the required derivatives exist.

Problem 3. Suppose that an FM signal is generated by $a_{k+1} = \mu_a a_k + w_k^{(1)}$, $\omega_{k+1} = \mu_\omega \omega_k + w_k^{(2)}$, $\phi_{k+1} = \phi_k + \omega_k$, $z_k^{(1)} = a_k \cos(\phi_k) + v_k^{(1)}$ and $z_k^{(2)} = a_k \sin(\phi_k) + v_k^{(2)}$. Write down the recursions for

(i) first-order and

(ii) second-order

EKF demodulators.

"I am quite conscious that my speculations run quite beyond the bounds of true science." *Charles Robert Darwin*

Problem 4. (Continuous-time EKF) Assume that continuous-time signals may be modelled as $\dot{x}(t)$ = a(x(t)) + w(t), y(t) = c(x(t)), z(t) = y(t) + v(t), where $E\{w(t)w^T(t)\} = Q(t)$ and $E\{v(t)v^T(t)\} = R(t)$.

(i) Show that approximate state estimates can be obtained from $\dot{\hat{x}}(t) = a(\hat{x}(t)) + K(t)\big(z(t) - c(\hat{x}(t))\big)$, where $K(t) = P(t)C^T(t)R^{-1}(t)$, $\dot{P}(t) = A(t)P(t) + P(t)A^T(t) - K(t)C(t)P(t) + Q(t)$, $A(t) = \left.\frac{\partial a(x)}{\partial x}\right|_{x=x(t)}$ and $C(t) = \left.\frac{\partial c(x)}{\partial x}\right|_{x=x(t)}$.

(ii) Often signal models are described in the above continuous-time setting but sampled measurements z_k of $z(t)$ are available. Write down a hybrid continuous-discrete version of the EKF in corrector-predictor form.

Problem 5. Consider a pendulum of length ℓ that subtends an angle $\theta(t)$ with a vertical line through its pivot. The pendulum's angular acceleration and measurements of its instantaneous horizontal position (from the vertical) may be modelled as $\frac{d^2\theta(t)}{d\theta^2(t)} = -\frac{g}{\ell}\sin(\theta(t)) + w(t)$ and $z(t) = \ell\sin(\theta(t)) + v(t)$, respectively, where g is the gravitational constant, $w(t)$ and $v(t)$ are stochastic inputs.

(i) Set out the pendulum's equations of motion in a state-space form and write down the continuous-time EKF for estimating $\theta(t)$ from $v(t)$.

(ii) Use Euler's first-order integration formula to discretise the above model and then detail the corresponding discrete-time EKF.

10.9 Glossary

∇f	The gradient of a function f, which is a row-vector of partial derivatives.
$\nabla^T\nabla f$	The Hessian of a function f, which is a matrix of partial derivatives.
$tr(P_k)$	The trace of a matrix P_k, which is the sum of its diagonal terms.
FM	Frequency modulation.
Δ_f	The forward difference operator with $\Delta_f e_k = e_k^{(i)} - e_{k-1}^{(i)}$.

10.10 References

[1] A. P. Sage and J. L. Melsa, *Estimation Theory with Applications to Communications and Control*, McGraw-Hill Book Company, New York, 1971.
[2] A. Gelb, *Applied Optimal Estimation*, The Analytic Sciences Corporation, USA, 1974.
[3] B. D. O. Anderson and J. B. Moore, *Optimal Filtering*, Prentice-Hall Inc, Englewood Cliffs, New Jersey, 1979.

"What we observe is not nature itself, but nature exposed to our mode of questioning." *Werner Heisenberg*

[4] T. Söderström, *Discrete-time Stochastic Systems: Estimation and Control*, Springer-Verlag London Ltd., 2002.
[5] D. Simon, *Optimal State Estimation, Kalman H_∞ and Nonlinear Approaches*, John Wiley & Sons, Inc., Hoboken, New Jersey, 2006.
[6] R. R. Bitmead, A.-C. Tsoi and P. J. Parker, "Kalman filtering approach to short time Fourier analysis", *IEEE Transactions on Acoustics, Speech and Signal Processing*, vol. 34, no. 6, pp. 1493 - 1501, Jun. 1986.
[7] M.-A. Poubelle, R. R. Bitmead and M. Gevers, "Fake Algebraic Riccati Techniques and Stability", *IEEE Transactions on Automatic Control*, vol. 33, no. 4, pp. 379 - 381, Apr. 1988.
[8] R. R. Bitmead, M. Gevers and V. Wertz, *Adaptive Optimal Control. The thinking Man's GPC*, Prentice Hall, New York, 1990.
[9] R. R. Bitmead and Michel Gevers, "Riccati Difference and Differential Equations: Convergence, Monotonicity and Stability", In S. Bittanti, A. J. Laub and J. C. Willems (Eds.), *The Riccati Equation*, Springer Verlag, 1991.
[10] G. A. Einicke, L. B. White and R. R. Bitmead, "The Use of Fake Algebraic Riccati Equations for Co-channel Demodulation", *IEEE Transactions on Signal Processing*, vol. 51, no. 9, pp. 2288 - 2293, Sep., 2003.
[11] C. A. Desoer and M. Vidyasagar, *Feedback Systems : Input Output Properties*, Academic Press, NewYork, 1975.
[12] G. A. Einicke and L. B. White, "Robust Extended Kalman Filtering", *IEEE Transactions on Signal Processing*, vol. 47, no. 9, pp. 2596 - 2599, Sep., 1999.
[13] J. Aisbett, "Automatic Modulation Recognition Using Time Domain Parameters", *Signal Processing*, vol. 13, pp. 311-323, 1987.
[14] P. S. Maybeck, *Stochastic models, estimation, and control*, Academic Press, New York, vol. 1, 1979.
[15] H. E. Doran, "Constraining Kalman filter and smoothing estimates to satisfy time-varying restrictions", *Review of Economics and Statistics*, vol. 74, no. 3, pp. 568 - 572, 1992.
[16] D. Massicotte, R. Z. Morawski and A. Barwicz, "Incorporation of a Positivity Constraint Into A Kalman-Filter-Based Algorithm for Correction of Spectrometric Data", *IEEE Transactions on Instrumentation and Measurement*, vol. 44, no. 1, pp. 2 - 7, 1995.
[17] D. Simon and T. L. Chia, "Kalman Filtering with State Equality Constraints", *IEEE Transactions on Aerospace and Electronic Systems*, vol. 38, no. 1, pp. 128 - 136, 2002.
[18] S. J. Julier and J. J. LaViola, "On Kalman Filtering Within Nonlinear Equality Constraints", *IEEE Transactions on Signal Processing*, vol. 55, no. 6, pp. 2774 - 2784, Jun. 2007.
[19] G. A. Einicke, G. Falco and J. T. Malos, "Bounded Constrained Filtering for GPS/INS Integration", *IEEE Transactions on Automated Control*, 2012 (to appear).

"We know nothing in reality; for truth lies in an abyss." *Democritus*